MW01503232

# CANON LAW SOCIETY
# OF AMERICA

# PROCEEDINGS
# OF
# THE SIXTY-FOURTH
# ANNUAL CONVENTION

## CINCINNATI, OHIO
## OCTOBER 7 – 10, 2002

CANON LAW SOCIETY OF AMERICA
THE CATHOLIC UNIVERSITY OF AMERICA
WASHINGTON, DC 20064

© Copyright 2002 by Canon Law Society of America

ISBN: 0-943616-99-9
SAN: 237-6296

The Canon Law Society of America's programs and publications are designed solely to help canonists maintain their professional competence. In dealing with specific canonical matters, the canonist using Canon Law Society of America publications or orally conveyed information should also research original sources of authority.

The views and opinions expressed in this publication are those of the individual authors and do not represent the views of the Canon Law Society of America (CLSA), its Board of Governors, Staff or members. The CLSA does not endorses the views or opinions expressed by the individual authors. The publisher and authors specifically disclaim any liability, loss or risk, personal or otherwise, which is incurred as a consequence, directly or indirectly, of the use, reliance, or application of any of the contents of this publication.

Printed in the United States of America

Canon Law Society of America
The Catholic University of America
Caldwell Hall 431
Washington, DC 20064

# TABLE OF CONTENTS

## OFFICERS' REPORTS

## COMMITTEE REPORTS

# FORWARD

I am pleased to present the *Proceedings* of the sixty-fourth annual convention held in Cincinnati, Ohio, October 7 to 10, 2002. The Canon Law Society of America annually publishes to our members and to others in the canonical community the major address and seminars presented at the annual meeting. Each year an attempt is made to produce the *CLSA Proceedings* as soon as possible after the convention.

In the collection of materials for this manuscript, I wish to express my gratitude to the presenters who provided their final texts in a most timely fashion. Preparation of the texts for publication was facilitated this year by the submission of electronic versions of the presentations. In the preparation of the texts, every attempt was made to maintain consistency by relying on both The Chicago Manual of Style and the style of previous issues of *CLSA Proceedings*.

In this year's edition of *CLSA Proceedings*, readers will find the final report of the task force studying the selection of bishops in the United States. Established by convention resolution in 1996, the committee fulfilled its mandate and reports back to members on this particular topic in *CLSA Proceedings*. Readers will also find in this volume a slight alteration to reporting of tribunal statistics. The traditional divisions of first and second instance tribunals was retained. The slight innovation is to sub-divide the material by sections. All statistical material available for a particular diocese or archdiocese will be contained in one particular section.

The Canon Law Society of America, established on November 12, 1939 as a professional association dedicated to the promotion of both the study and the application of canon law in the Catholic Church today numbers over 1500 members who reside in the United States and forty other countries. *CLSA Proceedings* 64 (2002) should take its place among previous volumes as a professional resource. The text contains a high degree of consistency and accuracy which should further scholarly research. Additional copies of this volume may be found at CLSA Publications, P.O. Box 463, Annapolis Junction, MD 20701-0463 or at the CLSA website: www.clsa.org.

For membership information on the Canon Law Society of America, contact the office of the Executive Coordinator or our website.

Arthur J. Espelage, O.F.M.
Executive Coordinator
Canon Law Society of America
431 Caldwell Hall
Washington, DC 20064

CLSA PROCEEDINGS 64 (2002) 1-13

# COMPLEMENTARITY AND THE CLERGY

VERY REVEREND LAWRENCE A. DINARDO, JCL

## *Introduction*

First, may I take a moment to express my appreciation to the Board of Governors and the Convention Planning Committee for offering me the opportunity to present this refection on "Complementarity and the Clergy" at this assembly of the Canon Law Society of America. This topic is significant since it touches both our spiritual and canonical lives in the Church. The spiritual dimension of the topic is rooted in the service that affects our lives as members of the Christian Faithful from those in ministry and the service that we offer in our various ministries as we serve the faithful entrusted to our care. The canonical dimension of the topic is rooted in the fact that we are the people who have been called and to whom has been entrusted the care of the law, seeing that it is properly understood and implemented in our particular churches and religious institutes. These two important and intertwined dimensions make the topic of "complementarity" or "collaboration" an important discussion as we gather at this Convention. Additionally, the topic is one side of a two-sided coin. One side frames the question as the collaboration between the laity and the clergy. Our earlier presentation, by Doctor Myriam Wijlens and John J. Grogan, focused on an identification of the specific canonical position of the clergy, laity and those who hold office in the Church and examined some concrete examples of complementarity of professional laity and other members of the People of God. This topic focuses primarily on the clergy and the complementarity between the clergy and the laity. The emphasis has been placed on the clergy and their need to collaborate with the laity rather than the reverse. It is this general perspective that is the basis for this paper.

When I was first ask to offer these reflections, I wondered why me! I am not a professor of canon law, I have not written extensively on this area of law, and I am by no means a scholar. I am, however, a continual student of the law, a practitioner of canon law for almost twenty-five years in diocesan administration and additionally, for the last fifteen years a pastor in several parishes. It is with this background that I believe that the Convention Planning Committee asked that I offer some reflections on this topic that is so important in both diocesan and parish ministry.

Like any good canonist I began my research into this ever-emerging topic by surveying the current, as well as past literature, on the topic of collaboration between the clergy and the laity. There are many noteworthy articles in canonical literature on this topic. Some of the notable literature includes two articles by Lynda Robitaille entitled *Collaboration and Cooperation Between the Clergy and Laity in the Parish, Tribunal and Chancery*,[1] found in an edition of *Periodica* and *A Subtext in the Canonical Discussion of Clergy/Laity Issues: Gender*,[2] found in *Studia Canonica*. Another article can be found in the *Canon Law Society of America Proceedings* by Joseph Koury entitled *The Code and Collaboration: Recent Literature*.[3] An article by Rosemary Smith entitled *Lay Persons in the Diocesan Curia: Legal Structures and Practical Issues*,[4] is also in the *Canon Law Society of America Proceedings*. Finally, an article by John Beal entitled, *The Exercise of the Power of Governance by Lay People: the State of the Question*.[5] In addition to these scholarly articles, the Apostolic See has issued at least two, among others, documents for our consideration as we discuss this topic. The first is the Circular Letter of the Congregation for the Clergy entitled, *The Priest: Teacher of the Word, Minister of the Sacraments, Leader of the Community*.[6] The second is from Congregation of the Clergy (Interdicasterial Instruction) entitled, *Some Questions Regarding Collaboration of Non-ordained Faithful in Priests' Sacred Ministry*.[7] In addition to Vatican and other canonical literature, the United States Conference of Catholic Bishops has issued several documents related to the point of discussion. First, the Lay Ministry Subcommittee issued a report entitled, *Lay Ecclesial Ministry: State of the Question*[8] and the Bishop's Committee on Priestly Life and Ministry authored a monograph entitled, *A Sherpherd's Care:*

---

[1] Lynda Robitaille, "Collaboration and Cooperation Between the Clergy and the Laity in the Parish, Tribunal and Chancery," *Periodica* 89 (2000): 593-633.

[2] Lynda Robitaille, "A Subtext in the Canonical Discussion of Clergy/Laity Issues: Gender," *Studia Canonica* 34 (2000): 467-488.

[3] Joseph J. Koury, S.J., "The Code and Collaboration: Recent Literature," *Canon Law Society of America Proceedings* 54 (1992): 162-184.

[4] Rosemary Smith, SC, "Lay Persons in the Diocesan Curia: Legal Structures and Practical Issues," *Canon Law Society of America Proceedings* 49 (1987): 67-76.

[5] John P. Beal, "The Exercise of the Power of Governance by Lay People: the State of the Question," *The Jurist* 55 (1995): 1-92.

[6] Congregation for the Clergy (Circular Letter), "The Priest: Teacher of the Word, Minister of the Sacraments, Leader of the Community," in English in *Origins* 29 (1999): 197-211.

[7] Congregation for the Clergy (Interdicasterial Instruction), "Some Questions Regarding Collaboration of Non-ordained Faithful in Priests' Sacred Ministry," in English in *Origins* 27 (1997): 397-409.

[8] United States Conference of Catholic Bishops, "Lay Ecclesial Ministry: State of the Question," in *Origins* 29 (2000): 497-512.

*Reflections on the Changing Role of the Pastor.*[9] All of these articles, documents and reflections focus on very important questions that surround this discussion. These questions range from:

- Whether or not ministry flows from our baptism or from ordination or from both?
- How does one view the notion of jurisdiction in the church, that is; whether one ascribes to the Roman, German or some other school of thought?
- What are the proper liturgical roles for the laity/clergy both in law and in practice?
- Whether or not lay ministry has only become necessary due to the lack of clergy?
- What is meant by collaboration or complementarity?

While all of these questions are important to the overall discussion of the topic, I was surprised that just as I was reviewing the available literature in remote preparation for this paper, an article appeared in the May 15, 2002 issued of *L'Osservatore Romano* entitled *Remember you are First and Foremost Priests: Not Corporate Executives.*[10] This was an allocution given by Our Holy Father to the Bishops' Conference of the Antilles during their visit *Ad limina Apostolorum.* What perked my interest was the earlier version found in the daily Vatican Information Service of (May 7, 2002). In that daily report, the same allocution was entitled: *Complementarity, Not Equality, Between Priests and Laity.*[11]

In his allocution the Holy Father said: "It is sometimes true that the awakening of the lay faithful in the Church has coincided with some problems about the vocation to the priesthood, and also the reduction of numbers of those entering the seminary in the Churches entrusted to your care. As pastors, you are deeply concerned since the Catholic Church cannot exist without priestly ministry which Christ himself desires for her."[12]

The Holy Father continues: "Some people affirm that the decreased number of priests is the work of the Holy Spirit and that God himself will guide his Church and will bring about the replacing of priests in the government of the Church with the lay faithful. Such an affirmation certainly fails to take into account what the

[9] United States Conference of Catholic Bishops, "A Shepherd's Care: Reflections on the Changing Role of Pastor," (Washington, United States Catholic Conference of Bishops, 1987).

[10] Pope John Paul II, "Remember You are First and Foremost Priests: Not Corporate Executives," *L'Osservatore Romano* Weekly English Edition 20 (May 12, 2002): 6.

[11] Pope John Paul II, "Complementarity, Not Equality, Between Priests and Laity," *Vatican Information Service* 83 (May 7, 2002): 1-2.

[12] Pope John Paul II, "Remember You are First and Foremost Priests: Not Corporate Executives" 6.

Council Fathers said when they sought to promote greater lay involvement in the Church. In their teaching, the Council Fathers wanted to highlight the deep complementarity between the priests and the lay people that is implicit in the nature of the Church as communion. An erroneous understanding of this complementarity has at times led to a crisis of identity and confidence among priests, and also to forms of lay involvement that are too clerical or too politicized."[13]

The articles notes, "The involvement of the laity becomes a form of clericalism when the sacramental or liturgical roles that belong to the priest are taken over by the faithful or when the laity start to perform tasks of pastoral governance proper to the priest. In such situations, what the Council taught on the essential secular character of the lay vocation is often disregarded (*Lumen Gentium* # 31). It is the priest who, as an ordained minister and in the name of Christ, presides over the Christian community in the sphere of her liturgical and pastoral activity. The laity assists him in many ways in this work. The primary place for the exercise of the lay vocation is the economic, social, political and cultural world. It is in this world that lay people are primarily but not exclusively invited to live their baptismal vocation not as passive consumers but as active members of the great work that expresses what is distinctively Christian. It belongs to the office of the priest to preside over the Christian community so that lay people can carry out their own ecclesial and missionary task."[14]

The Holy Father concludes: "the involvement of lay people is politicized when the laity become absorbed by the exercise of 'authority' within the Church. This happens when the Church is no longer seen in terms of the 'mystery' of grace that characterizes her, but in sociological or political terms, often on the basis of a misunderstanding of the notion of the 'People of God,' a notion that has deep roots and was so opportunely put to use by the Second Vatican Council. When it is not service but power that shapes every form of government in the Church, whether exercised by the clergy or by the laity, opposing interests begin to make themselves felt.

"Clericalism for priests is the kind of governance that comes more from the use of power rather that from the spirit of service; it always gives rise to all sorts of antagonism between the priests and the people. Such clericalism can also be found in certain forms of lay leadership that does not reasonable respect the transcendental and sacramental nature of the Church. Both of these attitudes are harmful. What the Church needs is a deeper and more creative sense of complementarity between the vocation of the priest and the vocation of the lay people."[15]

As one carefully examines the allocution of the Holy Father it is evident that four important points are made. First, that the essential differences between the

[13] Ibid.

[14] Ibid.

[15] Ibid.

common priesthood of the faithful and the ministerial priesthood must be clearly understood and accepted. Second, clericalism can become and is an obstacle to complementarity between the clergy and the laity. Third, the practical applications of complementarity are found in the three-fold *munera*, to teach, to shepherd and to sanctify. Fourth, there is an absolute need for complementarity in the "mystery" of the Church. It is these four points that will be briefly explored.

### Common Priesthood and Ministerial Priesthood

The common priesthood of the faithful and the ministerial priesthood, though they differ essentially, are nonetheless ordered one to another since each in its proper way shares in the one priesthood of Jesus Christ.

The essential difference between the common priesthood of the faithful and the ministerial priesthood, as indicated in the Instruction on *Some Questions Regarding Collaboration of Non-ordained Faithful in Priests' Sacred Ministry*, is not found in the priesthood of Jesus, which remains forever one and indivisible, nor in the sanctity to which all the faithful are called: Indeed the ministerial priesthood does not signify a greater degree of holiness with regard to the common priesthood of the faithful.[16]

The characteristics which differentiate the ministerial priesthood from the common priesthood of the faithful can be summarized as follows:

- The ministerial priesthood is rooted in the apostolic succession and vested with *potestas sacra*, consisting of the faculty and responsibility of acting *in persona christi* the head and shepherd.
- It is the ministerial priesthood that renders its sacred ministers servants of Christ and of the Church by means of authoritative proclamation of the Word of God, the administration of the sacraments and the pastoral directions of the faithful.
- To the common priesthood of the faithful can be entrusted, first, those functions that flow from the call of baptism and second, certain offices and functions that are part of pastoral ministry but do not require the character of orders. In this way it is not merely assistance but a mutual enrichment of the common Christian vocation.[17]

It is clear in the Holy Father's reflections that the sacred ministry of priesthood is critical to the life of the Church. Without the ministerial priesthood there can be no sacramental nature of the Church. Without priests, the Church as established

---

[16] Congregation for the Clergy, "Some Questions Regarding Collaboration of the Non-ordained Faithful in Priests Sacred Ministry," 400.

[17] Ibid. 401.

and intended by Christ cannot truly exist. Thus, the role and nature of the ministerial priesthood must be clear and unambiguous so that people do not confuse the proper roles of the priest and people. One of the strong recommendations of the Lay Ministry Report published by the United States Conference of Catholic Bishops was that "it is essential to maintain distinctions between those ecclesial ministries that are entrusted to the laity appropriately because of their baptismal call and those ministries, ordinarily reserved to the ordained, which are delegated to the laity by exception in case of need."[18] Thus, a clear understanding of both the common and ministerial priesthood will work to make complementarity a reality.

## Clericalism as an Obstacle

What is of interest in the entire allocution is the fact that the Holy Father is concerned about clericalism that can become an obstacle to the complementarity that is desired. This clericalism is evident when it is power and not service that shapes the life of the priest and his work in the Church. It is important to note that ordination brings about a sacred character necessary for the Church. It allows the Church to continue the sacramental ministry of Jesus. However, the laying on of hands and the words of ordination do not infuse the person with additional wisdom, gifts or talents. It gives the ordained sacramental grace by which one hopefully understands their personal limitation and the need that exists to work together in collaboration with the lay members of the Christian Faithful in order to establish God's kingdom here on earth. A false sense of clericalism can not only, as the Holy Father says, bring antagonism between the priest and people but can inhibit the proclamation of the Gospel, the spreading of the faith and in fact destroy the heart and soul of the people entrusted to the care of the priest. Additionally, it is the recognition that complementarity is not just a word that we speak or a necessity growing out of a dearth of clergy but a reality that has been given to the Church so that the Church can grow and spread to the ends of the earth.

While the primary focus of the allocution is on the clericalism that can infect the clergy, the document does speak of a "clericalism" that can also affect the role of the laity. This occurs when individuals attempt to exercise the same "authority" not service over other members of the Christian Faithful. The reality of the situation is one in which clericalism of any kind, whether within the clergy or laity, prohibits the person from being a true servant and thus fulfilling the baptismal call to holiness. Clericalism becomes an obstacle to performing those tasks and responsibilities that have been entrusted to a person either by their call at baptism or by ordination or their deputation to act. It is clericalism that blocks full complementarity between the clergy and laity, a clericalism that refuses to accept

---

[18] United States Conference of Catholic Bishops, "Lay Ministry: State of the Question," 508.

the gifts and talents of people, given by the Lord, "who knows us by name."[19]

## Practical Applications

Within the *Code of Canon Law* and the practical experience of ministry in the Church, there are many ways in which complementarity exists and are mutually accepted for the growth of the Church. Some specific areas of mutual collaboration can be found in the teaching, governing or shepherding and sanctifying work of the Church.

### A. Teaching Office of the Church

In the office of teaching the documents of the Church have focused primarily on the Ministry of the Word (preaching) and the Ministry of the Eucharist (Extraordinary Ministers of the Eucharistic). While various documents, including the complementary norms of the United States Conference of Catholic Bishops, already offer instruction in the proper role of the laity in the area of preaching[20] and the Vatican Instruction outlines the role of the laity in the area of Eucharistic Ministers,[21] we might want to focus on some other aspects that have been part and parcel of the role of the laity in this country as well as other parts of the world. The role of the catechist to young people and adults has been almost exclusively the domain of the laity in this country. With the continual development of the Rite of Christian Initiation of Adults and of Children along with a growing concern for evangelization of the unchurched and unbelievers, the role of the Catechist, professional Director of Religious Education, Pastoral Minister, Youth Minister and Social Minister, to name just a few, the lay faithful has become increasingly more important for the continuation of the Church and the spreading of the Gospel.

Additionally, the role of the laity, particularly the religious, has been the rock on which the Catholic School System has existed in the United States. Although today, while most of our catholic schools are staffed by lay people, they remain an every increasing important part of the ministry to teach the Word of God.

These two aspects of the teaching ministry are examples in which without the recognition of the special gifts and talents that have been given to the lay person for the ministry of Church much of the important work would not have been accomplished. It is imperative that those who are clergy recognize this enormous contribution to the Church, an example of the baptismal call being employed in the

---

[19] Cf. Jeremiah 1:4-9, Paraphrase from the Reading from the Old Testament for the Conferral of Holy Orders.

[20] United States Conference of Catholic Bishops, "Complementary Norms on Lay Preaching," (Washington, United States Conference of Catholic Bishops 2001).

[21] Congregation for the Clergy (Interdicasterial Instruction) 405-406.

Church, and the lay members see these as ministries that are critical for the future of the Church.

## B. Shepherding or Governing Office of the Church

In the office of governing, the canons make a variety of statements regarding the participation of the laity in the Church. Lynda Robitalle lists a number of the ways in which the laity participate in the power of governance:

- Consultative bodies (c. 228, §2), diocesan synods (c. 463), diocesan pastoral council (c. 512), parish councils (c. 536), finance councils of the diocese (c. 492) and of the parish (c. 537).
- Holding various administrative offices, diocesan chancellor (c. 483, §2), notary (c. 483, §2), fiscal officer of the diocese (c. 494, §1).
- Judicial Offices such as judge (c. 1421, §2), *ponens* (c. 1429), auditor (c. 1428), assessor (c. 1424), promoter of justice (c. 1435) and defender of the bond (c. 1435).[22]

Within the context of the office of governance or shepherding, two examples, on the diocesan level, give us an insight into the complementarity between the clergy and the laity. These areas are the judicial and consultative arenas of the Church. In these areas I would like to highlight two activities in which complementarity is important. The first is the ministry of the Tribunal. While the literature often speaks of the roles that can be performed by the laity (judge, *ponens*, assessors, defender of the bond, promoter of justice, [excluding penal cases that involve clergy], the code does not indicate the role of the laity in the overall effective and efficient operation of the Tribunal. While the code defines the role of the judicial vicar (c. 1420) in terms of his responsibility to judge,[23] the code does not speak of the role of the Tribunal Administrator/Tribunal Director or Tribunal Coordinator. All of us who have worked in Tribunal ministry know, the individuals who exercises this role plays a significant, if not essential, role in the operation of the Tribunal and in fact is its very life blood. Where would most of

---

[22] Robitalle, "Collaboration and Cooperation Between the Clergy and Laity," 622.

[23] *Codex Iuris Canonici auctoritate Ioannes Paulii PP. II promulgatus* (Vatican City: Libreria Editrice Vaticana, 1983) c. 1420, §1: "Quilibet Episcopus dioecesanus tenetur Vicarium iudicialem seu Officialem constituere cum potestate ordinaria iudicandi, a Vicario generali distinctum, nisi parvitas dioecesis autr paucitas causarum aliud suadeat." English translation from *Code of Canon Law, Latin-English Edition* (Washington, Canon Law Society of America, 1999) c. 1420, §1: "Each diocesan bishop is bound to appoint a judicial vicar, or officialis, with ordinary power to judge, distinct from the vicar general unless the small size of the diocese or the small number of cases suggests otherwise." All subsequent English translations of canons from the code will be taken from this source unless otherwise indicated.

Tribunals be if the coordinators/administrators or directors did not exist? While we can all speak to their essential importance to the work of the Tribunal and thus the Church, we also must admit that conflict can and does arise between the lay person, who holds this responsible position and the priest who is the judicial vicar and other clergy who work in the office. Although may of the problems that might exist are based on mere personalities, it is my belief that much of it can arise from a struggle between the clergy and laity over "who is really in charge." The struggle really is between those in sacred orders and those deputed to act on behalf of the Church. It is precisely in this area that complementarity can and should become a reality. Mutual respect not "power" or "authority" should be our goal. Our common purpose is the *salus animarum* and our mutual desire to serve the Christian Faithful. Sometimes we attempt to resolve our differences with additional "flow" charts or enhanced "job descriptions" but in reality the resolution exists in the understanding and acceptance of the gifts that we have received and the use of those gifts for the Church and in particular for the people whom we serve.

A second area of complementarity exists is the various consultative groups on the diocesan level. I would like to highlight one extraordinary consultative group for our consideration. The diocesan synod is an institution called for by the code but infrequently used by the particular churches. Canon 460 states: "a diocesan synod is a group of selected priests and other Christian Faithful of a particular church which offer assistance to the diocesan bishop for the good of the entire diocesan community according to the norms of the following canons."[24]

In my experience as one of the Chairpersons of the Diocesan Synod held in my diocese in 1997-2000 there are very few moments in the Church in which the clergy, religious and laity are brought together to offer the local church a vision for the future and in which complementarity between the clergy and laity can be found. The diocesan synod is one such event. The relationship existed in three areas. First, the area of a broad consultation on both the parish and diocesan levels; second, the interfacing between the clergy and laity at the synod itself about the topics of importance and third, the consensus for the future direction of the Church established by the synod delegates.

In our experience the most important part of the synodal process was the broad consultation in preparation for the synod. Position papers (*lineamenta*) were presented to the faithful in both print and electronic form for discussion. Town Hall meetings were held to discuss these position papers and recommendations came from all segments of the diocese. As a personal note, the consultation process enlivened the diocese and assisted in revitalization, while the recommenda-

---

[24] Canon 460: "Synodus dioecesana est coetus delectorum sacerdotum aliorumque christifidelium Ecclesiae particularis, qui in bonum totius communitatis dioecesanae Episcopo dioecesano adiutricem operam praestant, ad normam canonum qui sequuntur."

tions from the consultation served as the based for much of the final goals and objectives adopted by the Synod.

The interfacing of the clergy and laity at the sessions of the synod was a true form of complementarity. While the clergy and laity understood their distinction roles in the Church, they also realized that all must work together in order to continue the work of the Church.

What was evident throughout this process was that the laity of the present moment are certainly different than the laity of past. The oral presentations by the laity were inspiring and the depth of their devotion and knowledge certainly bought about a mutual respect that is essential if clergy and laity are to work together. While the respect for laity and their desire to participate in the Church has been evident in the Church since the Second Vatican Council, the presentations by the lay members of the synod (who were the majority) confirmed the importance in the Church for a mutuality between the clergy and the lay members of the one Church.

Finally, the ability of both clergy and laity to come to consensus on important issues for the future of the local church brought to bear how important the relationship is between the clergy and laity. Peter Drucker once said that "process is more important that product."[25] In the case of the Church, the product, which is the furtherance of the mission of the Church, can only come about by a process that brings together clergy and laity. The synodal process is, in my mind, a shining example of this process that leads to a greater mutual respect and desire to work together in the Church, which in fact is complementarity.

On the parish level, we have all experienced the role of the parish pastoral council. Canon 536 indicates that:

- It is not required by law (only if the bishop judges it opportune);
- It is presided over by the pastor;
- Its membership is the Christian Faithful and other who share in pastoral ministry give help in fostering pastoral activity.[26]

We have all experienced the role of "parish councils." In many places this experience is with "elected" members, usually a popularity contest, who see their primary mission as dealing with finances and/or buildings and grounds. It is sometimes difficult to move beyond these limitations to the pastoral aspects of a parish such as liturgy, education, and apostolic work. Many times this is the desire

---

[25] Peter F. Drucker, "Management: Tasks, Responsibilities, Practices." (New York, Harper & Row 1974): 89.

[26] Canon 536, §1: "If the diocesan bishop judges it opportune after he has heard the presbyteral council, a pastoral council is to be established in each parish, over which the pastor presides and in which the Christian Faithful, together with those who share in pastoral care by virtue of their office in the parish, assist in fostering pastoral activity." Canon 536, §2: "A pastoral council possess a consultative vote only and is governed by the norms established by the diocesan bishop."

of the pastor who seeks to keep himself insulated from the parishioners or keeps all the "pastoral" roles to himself so as to avoid any need for a possible personal transformation. On the other hand, we all recognize that the parish and its mission cannot exist in such a fashion. The laity are already involved in many aspects of parish life from education to social ministry. The parish pastoral council can be a source of greater collaboration. Maybe we should think outside the ordinary way of forming a council from "election," the most common form to a " discernment" process. Religious women have given us great models for this type of process. Now don't think "does this guy know what he is asking" or this is "to sophisticated for my people." To the contrary, it enlivens the desire of the people to participate. In my small parish in Pittsburgh (1000 people, average age 60+) we employed this process by asking people to speak at Town Hall meetings to as to what they had to offer the parish around the areas of liturgy, education, and apostolic ministry. The witness presentations, given as part of the Pentecost Triduum, especially from the more senior parishioners, were awe-inspiring. The selection of the members of the Council occurred after all those who desired to be on the Parish Pastoral Council had given their brief presentation. What does this have to do with complementarity? A great deal since it speaks to the primary issue at hand which is a need for clergy and laity to respect the gifts and talents of each other, to recognize that we are all in the same struggle and to realize that we all the same common goal which is the building of the Church here on earth and preparing for the life yet to come.

## C. Sanctifying Office of the Church

In the office of sanctification, the *Code of Canon Law* point out opportunities for expanded ministries. Some of the possibilities are:

- Minister of baptism (cc. 230, §3; 861, §2)
- Eucharistic minister (cc. 230, §3; 910, §2; 911, §2)
- Official witness of weddings (c. 1112)
- Presider of funerals
- Presider of liturgy of the Word in the absence of the priest (c. 517)
- Minister of sacramentals (c. 1168)
- Minister of the word (cc. 758-759; 766)[27]

While all of these areas speak to complementarity, one of the more interesting

---

[27] Robitalle, "Collaboration and Cooperation Between the Clergy and Laity," 621.

aspects is what is envisioned in canon 517, §2.[28] It is clear that the intent of the canon is meant as an extraordinary measure "where a dearth of priests exists." However, as Lynn Robitaille so notes: "the ultimate example of clergy-laity collaboration is the situation envisioned in canon 517, §2 of pastoral collaborator, parochial minister, lay administrator, parish leader, parish life coordinator etc."[29] The question that she asks is "whether or not, if there were enough priests, would this kind of collaborative ministry die?" While some may argue that the intention of the law is extraordinary, when the circumstances no longer exist, the need for the extraordinary measures no longer exist, it is clear that there is more to the understanding of this canon than mere "replacement." The intent is the recognition of the talents and gifts of people in order to bring about a vibrant Church.

While all the above references are not a taxative listing of the various ministries that are open to the laity, the list does give examples in which the *Code of Canon Law* recognizes the role of the laity in performing roles in the Church. What is critical is not what the law indicates but the acceptance, on the part of the clergy, the roles that the Church allows for members of the common priesthood of the faithful. It is in this area that clericalism often becomes the greatest obstacle in building the kingdom of God. The reasons for this clericalism might come from a self pride that exists in the clergy or a sense of a loss of identity regarding the ministerial priesthood, but the reality of the matter is that if the ordained and non-ordained perform those functions which are proper to them either by the call of their baptism or by sacred orders or by deputation, no loss of identity should exist. It is when either the clergy or laity enters into those areas of ministry that are proper to the other does confusion and possible loss of identity exists.

*Conclusion*

Given these dimensions, how can we be truly complementary in the mutual ministry to build the kingdom of God? I would offer four conclusions to this presentation. First, we must all recognize the distinctions between the common priesthood of the lay faithful and ministerial priesthood. This understanding must begin with the knowledge that all the baptized (lay and clergy) are all part of the common priesthood. That priesthood calls us to a life seeking personal holiness and proclaiming the message of Jesus in both our word and deed.

Secondly, ordination brings about a special character to act *in persona Christi*. While Ordination forms a special relationship it does not change the personal

---

[28] Canon 517, §2: "If, because of a lack of priests, the diocesan bishop has decided that participation in the exercise of the pastoral care of a parish is to be entrusted to a deacon, to another person who is not a priest, or to a community of persons, he is to appoint some priest who, provided with the power and faculties of a pastor, is to direct the pastoral care."

[29] Robitalle, "Collaboration and Cooperation Between the Clergy and Laity," 623-624.

talents and abilities of the one ordained. The recognition of ones abilities or inability is critical to any discussion on complementarity.

Third, one should not simply believe that the laity "fills in" for clerical inadequacy or diminished numbers since this is a rather egocentric approach. Clergy must recognize the gifts and talents that God has given to lay people.

Fourth, the acceptance of these talents and gifts as essential for the Church and the proclamation of the Gospel are imperative if we are to begin to work collaboratively. On the part of the laity, the recognition of the distinction of roles and the acceptance of the ministerial priesthood as essential for the life of the Church is important is complementarity is to be truly achieved.

Finally, as the allocution the Holy Father notes; "communion of priesthood and laity is the very heart of the Church."[30] It is communion that we seek so that the Church of Christ may flourish in our lifetime and that we may be *Colleagues in Service: Clergy and Laity in the Church.*[31]

---

[30] Pope John Paul II, "Remember You are First and Foremost Priests: Not Corporate Executives," 6.

[31] This is the theme of the 2002 Convention of the Canon Law Society of America held in Cincinnati, Ohio.

# COMPLEMENTARITY IN AN ERA OF
# HEIGHTENED ACCOUNTABILITY[1]

## JOHN J. GROGAN, ESQ.[2]

I want to thank the Canon Law Society of America for inviting me here this morning. Today's proceeding is a welcome opportunity to think, constructively, I hope, about issues that are vitally important to me personally and to the future of our Church.

My title is Complementarity in an Era of Heightened Accountability. I chose that title before the recent crisis. I was thinking not of sexual scandal but rather of the growing, albeit belated, social consensus[3] that religious institutions are and should be encouraged to remain a vital component of the social service and civil society infrastructure in the United States. I intended to reflect on the role that the laity must play in helping the Church maintain its position as a force for justice in the American culture. That is still my goal, but, as we have seen, the story line has changed and accountability today means something a little more basic.

My competence (such as it is) to speak to today's topic is that I co-founded and for six years directed a "collaborative ministry," i.e., a work of the Church conducted by lay people and religious.[4] Although much of my time this morning

---

[1] This address is, for the most part, published as given. Footnotes are included to direct the reader to source material and/or to elaborate on information not given in the address.

[2] B.A. Fordham University (1988), J.D. University of Pennsylvania Law School (1993). The opinions expressed in this address are solely those of the author. The author wishes to express his thanks to the CLSA and in particular to the Rev. James J. Conn, S.J.

[3] The recently emphasis on the value of "faith-based" socials service and community building enterprises is exemplified by the United States Supreme Court's decision in *Zelman, et. al. v. Simmons Harris et. al.*, 122 S.Ct 2460 (2002) establishing the constitutionality of school vouchers used by parents in parochial schools and also the Bush Administration's "faith based" initiatives that received considerable media attention prior to September 11, 2001 and which resulted in the House's passage of the Charitable Choice Act, 147 Cong. Rec. H4281 (daily ed. July 19, 2001). The CCA is part of a larger bill, the Community Solutions Act of 2001, H.R. 7, 107th Cong. § 201 (2001). The CCA subsequently stalled in the Senate.

[4] From 1994 through 2001, Mr. Grogan was associated with the Camden Center for Law and Social Justice, a non-profit law firm working on behalf of the working poor in Camden New Jersey. Mr. Grogan co-founded the Center in 1994 in partnership with David R. Brooks, a Jesuit priest and lawyer. From its inception, the Center has been very much a work of the Church. The Center serves the needs of the poor of Camden and Southern New Jersey and operates in fidelity to Catholic social teaching.

will be spent discussing the difficulties of that work, it is the most important work of my life so far and I hold it dear. It is because of that work that I am here today.

Which brings me to a point about our current troubles.

I am not a representative of any lay association or group. I take no position on any movement that has sprung up as result of the current crisis. My guess, and it is only a guess at this point, is that there is much good that can come from a newly energized laity. There is also some potential for harm which I think is worth putting to you, for it bears on the broader thrust of my presentation.

To the extent recent "lay movements" are focused myopically and, in my view, naively, on "power," they are misconceived.

The American Church has been seduced by the rhetoric of power. So much of our churchly politics, from right, left, and center, is based on an analysis of power: who supposedly has it and who supposedly wants it. We consistently impose ill-fitting political templates on the dynamic mass of our Church-life and we consistently get it wrong. And our errors become our reality and make dialogue and cooperation, indeed make being a Church, increasingly difficult. We have a widespread, and, frankly, dangerous penchant for misunderstanding power: what it is, where it comes from, who should wield it, and in what situations.

It would be funny if it were not so tragic. Some of the laity complain that the clergy will not share their power. And yet among priests, the talk I hear is not of power but powerlessness. Collectively, we have forgotten that the issue is not who will have power, but rather who will serve.

That is the question I want to discuss with you this morning: Who shall serve?

My remarks today are focused specifically on the role of the laity in the Church's mission to promote social justice. By social justice, I mean the hospitals, social agencies, community organizing efforts, legislative advocacy work, medical clinics, soup kitchens, law offices and most importantly, schools that the Church has sponsored and maintained to the great benefit of American civilization. This

---

It has practice areas in civil rights law, consumer law, family law, the representation of non-profit organizations and immigration law. Currently, immigration related cases make up well over 80 percent of the Center's case load. The Center receives funding from the local Diocese, from the Maryland Province of the Society of Jesus, from independent foundations and from modest, self-generated revenues. In many ways the Center is typical of Catholic social ministry. It is parish based, linked both locally and nationally, indeed internationally to a host of Church related social initiatives and networks. The Center works closely with the New Jersey Catholic Conference and the Catholic Legal Immigration Network, Inc. The Center is an independent 501(c)(3) non-profit corporation. Its board of directors is composed of members appointed by the Bishop of Camden and by the Provincial of the Maryland Province. The Center is also a participant in the Holy Name of Camden/Jesuit Urban Service Team, Inc., (HNC-JUST) a collaborative, social-change intiative made up of the Center, Guadelupe Family Services, Inc., St. Luke's Catholic Medical Services, the Holy Name School and the Holy Name Parish. HNC-JUST pursues cooperative ministry on behalf of the poor and marginalized in the City of Camden. In 2001, Mr. Grogan resigned as director of the Camden Center and entered private practice. Today, the Center is directed by Vincent G. Guest, Esq. More information about the Center and about HNC-JUST can be most readily obtained though the Internet at **www.hnc-just.org**.

16

is the aspect of the Church's mission in which I have the most experience. It is an area of the Church's mission where a fair amount of lay collaboration has already come about. It is also the area that is, we are taught, the special province of the laity.[5] It is because the mission of social justice is to be entrusted primarily to the laity that it makes, I hope, an interesting area of churchly endeavor to examine questions of lay complementarity and collaboration. It also, frankly, allows me to avoid very vexing questions about lay collaboration in explicitly pastoral ministry. It is, all things considered, an easier place to begin the conversation.

*   *   *  *

Who shall serve?

In answering that question, we confront a host of difficult, sometimes painful truths about the current state of the Church.

We are unprepared to be the Church that the Holy Spirit, speaking eloquently through the Second Vatican Council, calls us to be. Our unpreparedness prevents us from being, in the words of John Paul II, about that "great Venture, both challenging and wonderful [. . .] the re-evangelization so much needed by the present world."[6]

---

[5] The documentary sources for this proposition are numerous; the highlights include the following:

(1) *Catechism of the Catholic Church*, Liberia Editrice Vaticana, Ignatius Press 1994, § 898 provides as follows:

> It pertains to them in a special way so to illuminate and order all temporal things with which they are closely associated that these may always be effected and grow according to Christ and may be to the glory of the Creator and the Redeemer, quoting *Lumen Gentium*, 31 § 2 (November 21, 1964).

(2) *Catechism of the Catholic Church, supra*, § 899 states in relevant part:

> The initiative of lay Christians is necessary especially when the matter involves discovering or inventing the means for permeating social, political and economic with the demands of Christian doctrine and life.

(3) Encyclical Letter, *Sollicitudo Rei Socialis*, (December 30, 1987), § V, ¶ 47:

> It is appropriate to emphasize the preeminent role that belongs to the laity both men and women, as was reaffirmed in the recent Assembly of the Synod. It is their task to animate temporal realities with Christian commitment, by which they show that they are witness and agents of peace and justice (emphasis in the original).

(4) Encyclical Letter, *Centesimus Annus*, Chapter 3, ¶ 25. (May 1, 1991):

> In union with all people of good will, Christians, especially the laity, are called to this task of imbuing human realities with the Gospel.

[6] Post-Synodal Apostolic Exhortation, *Christifideles Laici*, ¶64 (December 30, 1988).

17

Changes are afoot within the Catholic Church in America; we are emerging from a clerically dominated model of the institutional church, on our way to a Church, which John Paul II teaches, is characterized by "a diversity and a complementarity of vocations and states of life, of ministries, of charisms and responsibilities."[7] That is our destiny and our aspiration. On that I trust we can agree. A new Church is being born, but it is not yet here and this period of "transition" is disorienting.

To say that we are moving away from a clerically dominated model of Church is *not* to celebrate a liberation from tyranny. I want to be clear that when I use the words clergy or clerical, I am not speaking of a sin or a disease. I do not read the promise that Vatican II holds for the laity to be an apology for the older model now passing.

The roots of our unpreparedness run deep. Some are cultural: for as much as our Church has helped to transform the American culture, we have been shaped by it as well. Our Americanism, God bless it, often gets in the way of understanding the nature of the Church we are called to be and impedes our development of an appropriate "ecclesial consciousness."[8]

Some of our unpreparedness is sociological. The American Church came of age in a priest – and nun-rich era – an era that may have been as much of a sociological anomaly as the current dearth of vocations. With so much surplus free labor available, we, religious, clergy and laity, learned bad habits – habits of thought about who should perform certain roles within the Church's broader ministry to the world – habits that are hard to break.

Some of it is psychological, or perhaps I should say, generational. With so much important work to do, so much at stake, too many in our Church seem to be going through a collective mid-life crisis; a peculiar, and a maddening loss of confidence.

Nor is this unpreparedness one-sided, all the fault of inflexible, power mad priests. The truth of our situation today, I believe, is that while I believe there are many thousands of lay people willing to give a significant portion of their lives to the Church's ministry in the world, there are far too few who are able or willing to seek that service on terms that respect the fundamentally different competencies within an authentically hierarchical community.[9] That a hierarchical community can be both just and life giving is a very hard lesson to learn, and even harder to teach. We will have to resolve our collective misapprehensions about power, before this log jam can be broken and before the laity can embrace their unique role in the work of the Church. I do know this: the more lay collaboration there is, the

[7] *Christifideles Laici*, supra, ¶ 20.

[8] *Christifideles Laici*, supra, ¶ 60.

[9] For a helpful summary overview of those "states of life" within the Church, *see* the address of my co-presenter, Dr. Miriam Wijlens, also published in these proceedings.

more clergy/religious and lay people work side by side in meaningful well-managed ministries, the closer we all come to internalizing the very difficult truths about being a Church.

For now, however, this is a disorienting time and we are at sea.

And while we are at sea, bad things are happening to the people we are called to protect and nurture. While we wring our hands in anxiety over the future of the Church, we are closing schools and parishes and scaling back our social institutions and thereby failing the people who need us most – the poor, the immigrant, the young and the female. I am concerned that in this time of transition, we will be tempted to re-negotiate the Church's historic commitments to the culture.

Some view this as a long overdue return to "first things" where the Church finally gets out of the business of bingo and basketball leagues and returns to a focus on piety. Others view it as a clear-eyed embrace of the future, i.e., that the Church of the future will simply not maintain the same social institutions as the Church of the past. I view it as a short-sighted capitulation to difficult circumstances, circumstances that are very much of our own making.[10]

Suffice it to say, our unpreparedness is not without consequences which are, as usual, foisted on those least able to bear them. And that should give us a sense of urgency.

There are three areas or themes that, in my view, capture the dimensions of our difficulty: Invitation, Formation and Organization. If we want to advance the conversation about complementarity and collaboration, we must assess how it is that lay people are *invited* into the work of the Church (Invitation). Likewise we must take stock of the resources available to *prepare* the laity for this work (Formation). Lastly, we need to make a hard study of how the work of justice is organized and come to understand how organizational and accountability structures either promote or inhibit lay collaboration (Organization).

As we assess these three areas, we see not only the obstacles that hold us back, but also, I hope, get a glimpse of what might speed our progress forward.

*Invitation*

Lay collaboration begins much as any vocation begins – with an invitation – a personal invitation.

It is, of course, ultimately God who invites; but for reasons unknown to us, God's call is usually couched in an all too human voice – like ours. And that is the first step, understanding that those in ministry, lay, clergy and religious, but

---

[10] We content ourselves with standing in judgment on our age as if its problems were not our problems, as if its failures were not our own, as if the challenges confronting it were not confronting us." John Cogley, "The Catholic and the Liberal Society," *America*, 101 (4 July 1959): 495 *quoted in* David J. O'Brien, *Public Catholicism*, p. 212, MacMillan: New York 1989.

particularly clergy and religious, have an obligation to invite the laity into ministry. In this day and age, such an invitation requires courage.

Consider the courage of David Brooks, the Jesuit priest who invited me to start the Camden Center for Law and Social Justice. I did not know him well. Nevertheless, he asked if I would set aside whatever career plans I had and come to work in Camden New Jersey to help him start the Center.

Consider what he was placing at risk in such an invitation: He was asking me to join him, to value what he valued, that is, and in no small way, to value him and the choices he had made in his life.

What he could not know, perhaps because I did not know it myself until that very moment, was that I was waiting for someone to ask me to do something just like that. I was looking for someone to challenge me to live out my convictions, not in an abstract or intellectual way, but with an idea, a project, that was for all its hardships, essentially doable. In sum, his invitation to me was not a general "Why don't you do something for Christ" admonition. Is was, "Why don't you do this very specific, albeit difficult, thing, which you are qualified to do, with me, for Christ?" There is all the difference in the world is those two types of invitations: one is preachy blandishment the other is genuine invitation.

Personal invitation works. But like any relationship based on love, invitation risks rejection and hurt. I honestly believe that many religious and clergy are shy about inviting laity into more mature and encompassing forms of ministry because they fear they will be rejected – personally rejected. I mean this with all sincerity. I think, today especially, so many religious and clergy feel that the life's choices they have made are so little understood by the laity as to make them appear freakish. And here of course is one more of the negative consequences of the current crisis, as if priests did not need one more reason to feel alienated and alone. As a result, for too many religious and clergy there is a general avoidance of the laity on a social level, too few genuine friendships with the laity. Again I do not think this is out of a sense of elite clericalism but from a fear that they are ever misunderstood, ever watched. And this inhibits invitation.

Another obstacle to invitation is the well-meaning sense many religious and clergy have that to invite the laity into serious ministry is to ask them to make financial sacrifices that are simply imprudent or impossible particularly if the lay person has a family to support. Two things are amiss here: (1) many laity are willing to make financial sacrifices in any case, and (2) implicit within the hesitation to invite is the assumption that the forms of ministry which exist today are set in stone. Such assumptions excuse us from the very hard work of reorganizing the ministry of social justice to make lay collaboration more likely.

In the face of all of that, it takes a certain faith and courage to make an invitation to ministry: faith that you are speaking not your own desire but the Church's. I have harped on the duty of religious to do the inviting. Surely we all have an obligation to invite, but lay ministry is in such an embryonic stage; there are so few models of lay ministry; invitation will not happen simply through example. A sign up-sheet in the back of the church will not do. The fact of the matter is that although the model of the Church is changing, religious and clergy remain in a privileged position where more often than not they have the authority and credibility to invite lay people into specific ministries. And in these changing times they must see invitation as a vital aspect of their own ministry.

*Formation*

Perhaps another reason some are reluctant to invite is because of a legitimate concern about competence. Again, I do not think that such a concern comes from a denigration of the capacity of lay people but rather from a well-founded fear that we do not have the training and on-going formation necessary to give lay people the depth of knowledge and spiritual resources true ministry requires.

Sound lay formation must consist of spiritual, doctrinal and professional development. At the risk of crass over-simplification, lay formation for ministry must provide the resources to answer three basic questions: (1) Am I called to serve? (spirituality); (2) How is my service authentically part of the Church's salvific mission? (doctrine); and (3) having decided to serve, what must be done and how? (professional competence). The last kind of formation, professional competence, is perhaps the easiest to define and obtain.

Spiritual and doctrinal formation, however, are less easily defined and less easily obtained. To be sure, lay people go to seminaries; they frequent retreat houses, some undergo regular spiritual direction. However, if a lay "vocation" is not rooted in a "living community" of faith – a truly Eucharistic community, I believe, and these are strong words, but I know from my own experience that such a vocation is less than it should be.

Currently, too much of what passes for "lay formation" is merely allowing the laity to approximate the formation experiences of religious. Authentic lay formation must begin by drawing the fundamental and necessary distinctions about states of life within the Church. Lay people must come to understand that they have a critical role to play in the mission of the Church, a role they are uniquely and preeminently qualified to carry out. The singular and distinctive characteristic of that lay vocation is its roots in community – the lay persons' immersion in the real flesh and blood of the temporal order.

Ideally it would be the local faith community that would call a lay vocation into actuality by voicing the invitation that we have just discussed. The community would then facilitate the formal training and education such a vocation required. And the community would sustain the lay vocation as a day in day out source of spiritual nourishment.

If we are serious about effective lay formation it is not enough to talk about seminary extension programs, or third order movements, although these are very good things. To talk meaningfully about the state of lay formation we have to talk about something quite troubling, the state of our local faith communities, and for most of us in the work-a-day Church that means talking about the parish.

Few of us are experts in pastoral theology, though some of you may be fine pastors. All *I* can do, is raise the question: Do we really believe that our parishes are such "living communities" capable of birthing and nurturing authentic lay vocations? If not, how do we make them so? These are difficult questions that I hope are occupying creative minds. Because if we do not find a way to situate lay vocations within specific, local communities of faith, we will never fully actualize the potential of the laity.

In various corners of the Church, we do find people and institutions – some of them parishes – that are striving to be these "living communities" that can truly form the laity.

Many religious orders are taking a lead in this area. Many are making efforts to develop lay formation programs. I know the Jesuits best and I can tell you that at a recent General Congregation, Father Klovenbach made it absolutely clear that the Society was to re-conceive its commitment to social justice to focus not so much on the individual work of Jesuits on behalf of justice, but rather what Jesuits can do to prepare the laity to carry out *their* mission.[11] It is a remarkably courageous and clear-headed vision.

Other religious communities are also developing programs to provide the laity opportunities for service and to share the spirituality of their founders and foundresses. Many have created formal service programs for young people: JVC, La Sallian Volunteers, Mercy Corp etc. The Jesuits have extended the concept to include older retired people with their Ignatian Lay Volunteer Corp. The Jesuits and Christian Brothers, again two groups I know relatively well, have inaugurated programs to help form the ministerial identities of the lay people teaching in their schools. The Jesuits of the Maryland Province regularly convene a working group of laity who are in leadership roles in various Jesuit ministries.

These are all sound beginnings but they remain somewhat at the margin of our

---

[11] For example, *see* 34th General Congregation of the Society of Jesus, Decree 13, ¶ 354:

> The emerging " Church of the Laity" will also have an impact on our own Jesuit apostolic works. This transformation can enrich these works and expand their Ignatian character if we know how to cooperate with the grace of the emergence of the laity. When we speak of "our apostolates," we will mean something different by "our." It will signify a genuine Ignatian partnership of laity and Jesuits, each of us acting according to our proper vocation. Lay persons will rightly take on a greater role of responsibility and leadership within these works. Jesuits will be called on to support them in their initiative by Ignatian formation, the witness of our priestly and religious lives, and promotion of Jesuit apostolic values. If our service will be more humble, it will also be more challenging and creative, more in accord with the graces we have received. This actualization of the lay vocation can show more clearly the grace of our vocation.

Churchly life. They must be brought into the mainstream – into the parish.

The essentials of formation for the laity are familiar. The most effective lay formation programs for social ministry will stress service, responsiveness to suffering and simplicity.[12] Being clear about these elements is essential. Formation for ministry is not a twelve-step, self help program. It is conducted for some articulated purpose – some particular *service* that needs to be carried out. In the area of social ministry that service should be directed to the poor and vulnerable. No matter how remote the actual service may be from the day to day lives of the poor; effective formation must bring the minister into contact with the suffering Christ for while formation for ministry is not "self-help" it is fundamentally redemptive and there is no redemption without *suffering*. Finally, authentic formation for ministry should stress *simplicity*; simplicity in manner (well-developed teaching methods), simplicity in aspiration (clear attainable goals) and simplicity of spirit (humility).

These elements in addition to rigorous standards of professional competence will ensure effective, life-giving lay formation.

If we want the laity to engage in social ministry, we must also demand, for their sake and for the sake of those they will serve, that they pursue their ministry with professional excellence. We cannot afford to allow our lay formation to be "dumbed down." And we do not need to. It is a peculiar thing, but people who commit themselves to service, no matter what it is, want that service to tax them, to challenge them and make them grow. We cannot forget that.

*Organization*

Developing an ethic of excellence within a ministry demands careful attention to organizational dynamics and organizational structure. Once again, issues of power – cast as authority and accountability – rear their head.

And here we come to a fundamental clash of cultures between the laity and the clergy and religious. Church organizations, to a large degree, by design or default, rely on personalist management and accountability structures. Authority in this model is exercised though personal ties – a priest is accountable to his bishop for example. It is even more so in religious orders where the "superior" acting locally or on a provincial level has a direct relationship with the individual member of the order.

Whatever the benefits of this kind of personalist management ethic (and I do not mean to suggest that they are not real or that they should necessarily change within their proper context), that kind of management and accountability structure is very foreign to most lay people.

---

[12] As the United States Bishop's point out, service, suffering and simplicity are the constituent elements of holiness. USCCB, *Called and Gifted for the Third Millennium* at 4 (1995).

23

Lay people work in a very different world. For most, lines of accountability are excruciatingly clear. For many, success or failure is all too easily measured. We live in a world of sales quotas, frequent evaluations and over all, bottom line objectives.

Lay people are also used to a great deal more transparency in decision making. Most of us, even if we are not allowed to participate in the decisions that shape our work lives, at least understand the criteria that shape those decisions. Lay people are used to working in a bureaucratic model in which the rules, roles and responsibilities are clear.

This is less true in most ministries. Decision making within religious and clerical circles, especially as it effects personnel, is incredibly opaque. Moreover, there is a general disinclination to spend the time and energy necessary to discuss responsibility and accountability within ministries. There is a wildly mistaken view that people motivated by the love of God do not need to worry about structure – about lines of authority, job descriptions or any of the other trappings of bureaucracy. And this breeds trouble.

Consider the organization within which I worked in Camden. The combined ministries consisted of five separate entities – a law center, social service agency, medical clinic, parish and school. Three of those entities were formally structured non-profit corporations with boards of directors. All of those ministries also reported to the relevant diocesan vicars. The Jesuit Province had his own Office of Social and Pastoral Ministries with an Assistant Provincial in charge. There were two other women's religious orders involved with their own provincial super-structures. We also formed a joint fundraising corporation which had its own board. There was a local Jesuit superior who had charge of the Jesuits in Camden. Then there were more than forty-five lay people working full-time in the various ministries.

Just figuring out who was in charge was a major challenge. Authority lines were hopelessly crossed.

So far, through good will, prayer and luck, this ministry has avoided serious problems. Yet it remains vulnerable to some crisis, some irregularity in the work place, a personal indiscretion, some unfortunate but inevitable occurrence that will rock that structure and expose what will then appear to the outside world as outrageous conflicts of interests, management gaps, and failures of accountability. We need look no further than the headlines of last spring to see how convoluted and in-bred our organizational structures can seem. Indeed, they can seem that way because, too often, they are that way.

And again I caution – this is not solely a problem created by power happy hierarchs. Many lay and religious who self-identify as forward looking progressives committed to the Church of the future, are themselves complicit in passive-aggressive organizational dynamics where everyone "discerns" what God is calling them to do as part of their own "personal journey." I am reminded of a crusty old

Jesuit pastor who remarked that it was funny how no one ever discerned that God was calling him to clean the parish van. If the choice is between a personalist and a bureaucratic management ethic, too many are quick to view one as inherently just and Gospel centered, the other as alien and wholly inappropriate to ministry.

It is this maddening tendency to refuse to think critically about structure that dooms many social ministries to becoming self-referential phenomena where no real evaluation is done; where ministries are defined in terms of personal preferences; where people can, with straight faces, describe their job as "witnessing for peace" or their ministry as a "ministry of presence."

Lay people, who will need to blend ministry and family, simply need more structure if they are to collaborate. Religious and clergy who are serious about lay collaboration must help create ministries that pay attention to structure, to organizational dynamics, and to accountability. If the Church's social ministry is to survive, then we are going to have to become much more nimble in our use of people and resources. We will have to build ministries where lay people can serve for a time and then leave for a time. We must build ministries that take full advantage of flexible schedules, job sharing and all of the other human resource techniques that we can devise that allow people to work out a sustainable balance between work and family, service and sustenance. In light of recent times, it is a conversation that we can no longer postpone.

If we are to become the Church that Vatican II is calling us to be, much will have to change. Much will have to be learned, and more importantly, much will have to be unlearned. We must wean ourselves from old habits. I am afraid, that religious must once again take the lead in this transformation and they must do it with a laity that too often will lack the formation necessary to seek collaboration on just or prudent terms. Much patience will be required. But great things can be accomplished.

Our task is to get about the work of justice, a work that we know is given to us as a sacred trust, and which we know can only be effectively pursued through increased collaboration born not of a will to power but from a genuine call to service.

CLSA PROCEEDINGS 64 (2002) 27-47

# ECCLESIAL LAY MINISTRY, CLERGY AND COMPLEMENTARITY

## Myriam Wijlens

Thank your for the invitation to speak to you, a group of distinguished canon lawyers. It is always a pleasure for me "to return" to the USA, as I recently spontaneously described my traveling between Europe and the USA. The openness and friendliness I experience in this continent gives me a sense of coming home. Maybe it is the particular subject that we are to treat this morning on the complementarity of laity and clergy that I enjoy my return to the States because the complementarity and the actual cooperation between myself, as a lay woman, and clergy is at times quite different both in its understanding and its actualization depending on the different places and countries in which I work (The Netherlands, Germany, Rome and the USA). It has always been a privilege to enjoy positive experiences in your country.

When earlier this year Father James Conn S.J. invited me on behalf of the Convention Planning Committee to speak, he proposed that in his lecture Mr. John Grogan would focus on the laity in the world whereas I would focus more on the professional laity in the Church. We were asked to reflect on the support of clergy to the work of the laity. We were informed that a priest would speak about the complementarity of laity to clergy. The invitation expressed that taking into account ones personal experiences and expectations would be welcomed.

In discussing the invitation and the content of what we thought we could say, John Grogan and I decided that I would lay out some of the foundational issues and that, therefore, I would speak first.

The time granted to me is rather limited. So after a short introduction in which I will clarify who we are talking about and what the underlying premises are under the question as the planning committee presented it to us, I will outline the issue that I believe a deeper study on professional laity will have to address. Such a study will have to focus on a fundamental question: are we considering the issue of lay (ecclesial) ministry from the right perspective?

### 1. Who are we talking about?

It seems that in the requests we received from the planning committee they are operating on the following divisions we have in our Church:

27

1. There are persons who are baptized and confirmed. With baptism they share in the threefold ministry of Christ. They are called to live their faith. In this group we find people who never actively live their faith as well as those who are very much engaged in the life of the Church or in the world. They would, however, not be commissioned by church authority to do so, but would respond exclusively to their baptismal gifts.

2. There are persons who are baptized, confirmed and who are mandated by ecclesiastical authority to take on a specific task either within the community of faithful or within the world. At times they might have been granted an ecclesiastical office. In this group we may find persons who are mandated to represent the Catholic Church or the Holy See in international meetings, such as the World Conference on Women. This is a clear task set for a specified time, and it is clearly a task in the world. Other persons in this group are, for example, directors of religious education, lay judges, lay chancellors, professors of theology or of canon law, hospital chaplains, those who are appointed in virtue of canon 517, §2, etc. This latter group is active within the faith community. In the United States, I believe this latter group is referred to as "lay ecclesial ministers." They are lay persons, who not only respond to their baptismal call, but who have also a place in the communion of the Church which is "submitted to the judgment and supervision of the hierarchy."[1] That is what the word "ecclesial" in lay ecclesial ministry refers to. Thus, it is not simply an activity undertaken on personal initiative.

Other characteristics of these persons are that they have obtained some education and are thus qualified and equipped for the tasks granted to them; the "mandate" they hold has been granted by the diocesan bishop or his representative. The tasks or office might have been conferred within a public ritual or liturgy, but this is not necessarily so. (An interesting example might be the liturgical celebration in some German dioceses. Upon having completed a successful education as "pastoral workers," the diocesan bishop receives them within the context of a celebration of the Eucharist, into the "service of the diocese." In this ceremony, they promise obedience to the bishop and his successors and obtain a [civilly valid] contract for an indefinite time with the diocese. They also receive a mandate for their first concrete assignment to, for example, a parish or a hospital.)[2]

---

[1] Committee on the Laity, United States Conference of Catholic Bishops, *Lay Ecclesial Ministry: The State of the Questions. A Report of the Subcommittee on Lay Ministry,* (Washington DC: USCCB, 1999): 7.

[2] See in an attachment the text of the pertinent sections from the liturgical celebration in the diocese of Münster – as celebrated on September 29, 2002 – and of a ceremony held in the diocese of Basel (Switzerland) on June 12, 1993. The latter text shows great similarities to a kind of "incardination": the diocesan bishop and the lay person enter into a mutual commitment: the bishop promises to provide for a fitting position in the diocese, the lay person promises obedience to the diocesan bishop and his

3. There are persons (men) who are baptized, confirmed and ordained. They can perform certain actions allowed by canon law. They can be deacons, priests, or bishops who although incardinated into a certain diocese do not hold a concrete office. In the terms of Vatican II, we would speak about bishops who are members of the college of bishops; but who have not yet obtained an office or do not any longer hold an office. It is the same for priests and (permanent) deacons: they are ordained and only subsequently they are assigned to a specific (pastoral) ministry.

4. There are men who are baptized, confirmed, ordained and who in the pre-Vatican II and 1917 code terminology have been granted jurisdiction. Often the power held is attached to an ecclesiastical office. Here we can think of the functions such as permanent deacons, of parish priests, diocesan bishops, etc.

In the following sections I would like to make some remarks to this division.

## 2. The Ecumenical Dimension of Being Baptized

The four different sections give the impression that there is a clear distinction in the Catholic Church. But is this picture so clear? It seems that the division is based on the former ecclesiology which held that the Church of Christ is to be equated exclusively with the Roman Catholic Church. After all, it seems that we say that laity are those who are baptized and are confirmed. What does this say about those who are baptized outside the Catholic Church? They too are incorporated into Christ through their baptism and possibly received confirmation. They thus participate in the threefold ministry of Christ and, therefore, participate in the mission of the Church of Christ which is to proclaim the good news and to see to salvation. To be aware of the role of these Christians is not irrelevant, because there are offices in the Catholic Church that can be and are de facto exercised by non-Catholics.[3] Such offices might be the finance officer or the notary. These baptized non-Catholics might feel called to work for the Catholic Church or to take part in the mission that the laity exercise in the world. I was recently asked whether a bishop could appoint an Orthodox priest to the office of judge for a marriage tribunal. The intention was to have this priest participate in a collegiate tribunal in which the validity of marriages entered into by one Roman Catholic party and by an Orthodox would be adjudicated. If this would not be

---

successors. Moreover, the spouses promise to assist their partners. Questions should be raised about the theological nature and theological and canonical implications of the content of these celebrations.

[3] Several tribunals around the world have baptized non-Catholic notaries. At times they are not even baptized. Some judicial vicars in India informed me that sometimes they cannot find adequate Catholics to fill this position. They argue that since the law concerning this office does not require (full) communion with the Catholic Church, and since the office requires skills of reading, writing, typing and honesty, the office can be filled with a non-Catholic person when a Catholic cannot be found.

possible, could he be appointed as assessor (c. 1425, §4)?[4] I believe these are areas where we have not thought about the canonical and practical implications of the new understanding of Church, namely that the Church of Christ subsists in the Catholic Church. Thus, the discussion about laity and clergy cannot forget to attend to the notion of the church as well.

### 3. Cooperation or Complementarity?

When canonists hear the title of a presentation is "Professional Laity, Clergy and Complementarity," many think almost automatically about canon 129, §2. They then might sigh quietly, because they know too well that at this point they might find themselves in that long and as it seems never ending discussion about the meaning of *cooperare* and *participare*. Some probably wish that *cooperare* really means *participare* because they want the laity to "move forward" and others might argue that the time has come to put a halt to the clericalization of the laity and thus *cooperare* really means that they cannot participate in the power of governance. The well documented study by John Beal on the laity and the power of governance[5] reveals that the discussion on the subject seems to be stagnating. It appears that the different schools of thought are fixed in their positions and that once you are familiar with a specific position it is relatively easy to predict what the answer to certain questions such as the dispensing power of the laity, or the capacity of a lay person to hold a position as that mentioned in canon 517, §2 will be. Thus, you might say what else can we say about this topic?

After having studied the different arguments put forward by the different schools of thought, I started to wonder whether we have been asking the right question. What has been the question so far? I can see two issues: first, they all center not on the question of complementarity but on the question of cooperation of clergy and laity; secondly, in the context of that cooperation they focus around the question of ordination. Some scholars see ordination as an indispensable prerequisite to be able to exercise jurisdiction. They take recourse to the affirmation by Vatican II that there is a unity of the power of orders and of jurisdiction for the bishop and apply this therefore to all. Other scholars invoke historical arguments to state that the power of orders is not always necessary in order to be able to exercise jurisdiction. We should note that no matter from whatever side the arguments are put forward, "ordination" is a central point of departure. Thus, whoever reflects on the issue responds to the question: Can those

---

[4] The question is interesting because the Catholic Church does recognize the power of priests belonging to an orthodox church "to bind and loose" in respect to the sacrament of penance (cf. c. 844, §2): these priests are validly ordained, but they are not in full communion.

[5] John Beal, "The Exercise of the Power of Governance by Lay People: State of the Question," *The Jurist* 55 (1995): 1-92.

who have not received ordination exercise power of governance? Note, also that when speaking about the laity, they are still very much seen as non-ordained. Therefore, the question is not: is baptism and confirmation necessary in order to exercise power of governance? Or is being in full communion necessary to exercise power of governance?

I have the strong impression that discussions about holding an ecclesiastical office focus as well on ordination or its absence. This focusing on ordination in relation to powers and offices is also central in the 1997 instruction on the cooperation of laity and clergy.[6] The main question of this instruction seems to be: How can we do justice to the ministerial priesthood in light of the increased activities of laity within the church?

Is it surprising that these discussions focus on ordination? In light of history the answer must be "no." Since the middle ages, the understanding that the community is subject of the liturgy and that the proclamation of the Word enjoys an imminent importance in the community, was replaced by an understanding that there were two separate classes. There were clerics and there were lay persons. Gratian affirmed the existence of two differing classes (*genera*) of Christians. There were those who are set free for the divine service and who are devoted to contemplation and prayer. They are to stay away from worldly issues. These are the clerics and those who are religious. The other Christians are laity. The Greek word *laos* means in Latin *populus* (people). They are allowed to possess temporal goods, but only to use them; they are allowed to marry, develop the earth, go to court, bring their gifts to the altar, etc.[7] This differentiation is not just a moral one nor is it just a determination of competency. There is more to it; the true faithful are the clerics and the religious. The others are permitted to occupy themselves with worldly issues or temporal goods. The consequences of this division were that the laity were juridically excluded from true ecclesial affairs. Even though we should know that the juridical implications are to be seen in a specific historical context, namely the freedom and independence of the church vis-à-vis the powers exercised by sovereigns, and that it thus does not refer to the contemporary meaning of the word "laity", it nevertheless went into history as such.[8] The division, according to Hervé Legrand, implies the approval of the identity and

[6] Congretatio pro Clericis et aliae, Instructio "De quibusdam quaestionibus circa fidelium laicorum cooperationem sacerdotum ministerium spectantem," *AAS* 89 (1997): 852-877. The English translation on the Webiste of the Vatican renders this as "Instruction on Certain Questions Regarding the Collaboration of the Non-ordained Faithful in the Sacred Ministry of Priests." This translation sets different accents: "fidelium laicorum" is translated with "non-ordained" and not with "lay faithful"; "cooperare" is translated with "collaboration." The French translation provided on the Website is correct as is the German and the Italian.

[7] Decretum Gratiani, C.12, q. 1, c.7.

[8] Ruud G.W. Huysmans, *Het Recht van de Leek in de Rooms-katholieke kerk van Nederland,* (Hilversum: Gooi en Sticht, 1986): 11-13.

autonomy of the clergy vis-à-vis (the rest) of the community which is declared incapable and incompetent with respect to matters of faith.[9] Whereas initially, the word clergy (klèros) referred to the whole community as God's heirs (Rom 8:17; Col 1:12), the word became thus reserved for a group in the church. Due to criticism by the Reformation against this twofold division, the Counter Reformation reacted with a theology which would remain until Vatican II and which holds, according to Ton van Eijk, four characteristics. First, ordained ministry is understood as a faculty, or as a power, which in particular manifests itself in speaking the words of consecration (de verba Christi) in the Eucharist and in giving absolution in the sacrament of penance (potestas consecrandi et absolvendi). This power is conferred at ordination by consecrating bishops to the person who is to be consecrated a bishop and by a bishop to a priest (presbyter) or deacon. Second, the person exercises this received power in persona Christi. This terminology, which finds its origin in scholastic thinking, did not mean even in that theology that the ordained minister acts as if he replaces Christ. It did, however, obscure that he also acts in persona ecclesiae, and there is a danger that this terminology isolates it from this.[10] The christological foundation that is applied here appears also in that the ordained minister is spoken of as an alter Christus. It is not difficult to see how such a strong christological foundation for ordained ministry could easily underrate a spirituality for all Christians based on baptism. In this one sided christologically oriented theology of ministry, Christ, to whom all power (exousia) has been given, granted it to Peter and the other apostles. They in turn handed it over to the bishop of Rome and the other bishops. The latter granted it partially to the presbyters (not to the deacons though because they were not always destined for the priesthood). As a consequence of this the Church came to be understood as a pyramid of which the laity formed the large base. They are the ones who receive, who as church are being taught (ecclesia discens) and are to be differentiated from the church that teaches (ecclesia docens).

Thirdly, van Eijk writes, this sharp differentiation between clergy and religious

[9] Hervé M. Legrand, "La réalisation de l'église en un lieu," in Bernard Lauret / François Refoulé (éd.), Initiation à la pratique de la théologie, III. II (Paris, Cerf, 1983): 184 (la tendance à disqualifier religieusement les laïcs) en 186 (l'autonomisation des clercs et leur scission d'avec l'ecclesia). In his reflections Legrand points out that the theology preceding Vatican II saw ministry (and ordination) too much irrespective of the connection to the local church (180-182) and to the working of the Holy Spirit. Vatican II did pay attention to the Holy Spirit and its working in the Church (LG 4), but its place remains modest according to Legrand (159-161). He writes that this has consequences for understanding ministry as well. He, therefore, proposes that ministry is reconsidered not only from a christological perspective, but also in the context of a communio ecclesiology.

[10] See also Bernard-Dominique Marliangeas, Clés pour une théologie du ministère. In persona Christi – In persona Ecclesiae. Théologie historique, vol. 51 (Paris, Beauchesne, 1978). In this book Marlianges investigates the history of the terms in persona Christi and in (ex) persona ecclesiae as the great scholastics used them. He shows that in juridic terms this is equivalent to the term nomine Ecclesiae (p. 235).

on the one hand and laity on the other hand did not just come about around the beginning of the second millennium. The development of a clergy and with it of a clericalization and consideration of offices in an hierarchical order started already around the 4th and 5th century. From this time, the offices and functions within the community are entrusted to a specific group in the sense that those are in a specific state of life (clergy) are placed into a specific order in relation to each other. This order is to be followed step by step and is seen as a career till one arrives at the final step, which is the office of bishop. Thus, there is a hierarchy of competencies and duties.[11]

Fourthly, already very early in history – between the years 180 and 260 – the power of the group of ordained ministers is typified as "priestly" and is thus considered in particular in relation to sacramental celebrations. The term "priesthood" refers to this, for the two other functions, namely to proclaim and to govern, disappear behind this terminology. Thus what in 1 Peter 2:5, 9 is called the "people of priests" becomes the "people of the priests."[12]

Van Eijk concludes that what we see in this pre-conciliar theology of ministry is legitimate when taken each point on its own, but seen together they display some limitations. There is a rather limited foundation of ordained ministry in the (local) community of faithful, and it is being restricted to its priestly function.[13] Theologians call it a theology of an isolated Christ – representation, in as far as it has become isolated from the Church which is the whole body of Christ. Thus, there appeared an imbalance in the Church: the clergy were the actors, the laity the recipients of pastoral care. A lay person came to be understood as someone who is not a cleric. It was someone who belongs to the ordinary people and who did not belong to those who hold power and offices.[14]

---

[11] Van Eijk (*Teken van aanwezigheid*, 274) follows here A. Faivre, *Naissance d'une hiérarchie*. Théologie historique, vol. 40 (Paris, Beauchesne, 1977).

[12] As Antoine Faivre formulates it on p. 83 of *Ordonner la fraternité. Pouvoir d'innover et retour à l'ordre dans l'Église ancienne* (Histoire), Paris 1992: "Du peuple du prêtre au peuple des prêtres." (Cited by van Eijk, *Teken van Aanwezigheid*, 274).

[13] Hervé Legrand describes this forcefully in his contribution "La réalisation de l'église en un lieu," in Bernard Lauret / François Refoulé (éd.), *Initiation à la pratique de la théologie*, III/II (Paris: Cerf, 1983): 181-193.

[14] There is thus a monarchical or pyramidal model of the church. Edward Schillebeeckx writes that the monarchical model for the church is theologically founded in 1) the predominance of a Christology which forgets the influence of the Holy Spirit on the lowest level of the church and 2) in the social significance of papal infallibility. In this understanding the pope becomes the representative of Christ in this world not unlike the governors were the representatives of the Roman emperor in distant places. The gift of the Holy Spirit for the lower level is changed into a faithful obedience to what the top of the hierarchy has decided and proclaimed. In this understanding laity are not subjects, that is carriers and makers of what the church is, but they become objects of hierarchical decisions, preaching and pastoral care. This perspective moreover takes away from the other authorities (e.g., bishops and the community of faithful) their original Christian authority. Edward Schillebeeckx, *Mensen als verhaal van God* (Baarn: Nelissen,1990): 216-217; English translation: *Church: The Human Story of God* (New York:

This differentiation between laity and clergy based on the reception of orders is not in agreement with the Old Testament's meaning of the word *laos*. There it was used in opposition to the *ethnè*, the pagans. Thus "laity" is an honorary title for those who have been chosen. In the First Letter of St. Peter we read: "But you are a chosen generation, a royal priesthood, an holy nation, a peculiar people" (1 Petr. 2:9). Thus, due to this commonly being chosen, all baptized belong to the people of God; and the division line is not between clergy, religious and laity, but between Christians and non-Christians.

Considering all of this, it is not really a surprise that when theologians and canonists hear the title of the lecture "Laity and Clergy in Complementarity," they almost instinctively reflect about cooperation – and not about complementarity – and that within this theological framework they indeed cannot state that laity can participate in the power, because of the theological premises. They focus on the question: How can lay persons cooperate in the work of the priests? A response is difficult to that because of the theological context or point of departure.

Is the question about complementarity correct? Vatican II and several theologians after the Council assist us to understand that the question is correct, because of the change in understanding about the Church itself.

### 4. Vatican II and the Notion of Complementarity

Vatican II made major changes in understanding the Church. In particular the history of the dogmatic constitution on the Church, *Lumen gentium* reveals that the Council was aware that only one image for understanding the Church would be insufficient to explain its nature. Moreover, the Fathers decided that there is a need first to reflect on all the faithful as such, and subsequently to address the particular ecclesiological issues concerning the different groups in the Church. The Council affirmed a fundamental equality of all baptized, of all Christians, which precedes the subsequent important distinctions and transcends these distinctions. As we all know, Vatican II has clearly underlined these thoughts as it decided that the chapters on the hierarchy, the laity and the religious must be preceded by a chapter on the people of God. We should take notice of this, because the Council did not just recognize the position of the laity in virtue of baptism. It did do that, but it went even one step further. It positioned all the baptized together before making the distinctions among them. Thus, every Christian is an active responsible member of the Church. All baptized participate in the mission of the Church, which is "the coming of God's Kingdom and the accomplishment of salvation for the whole human race" (*GS* 45).

Why was the Council able to do this? Well, the council accentuated that the Church which met and was built up after Easter should not only be seen as the

Crossroad, 1990): 198-199.

Body of Christ, but also as the temple or community (*koinonia*) of the Holy Spirit. In the post paschal texts which narrate how people were commissioned, we see that Christ is still sending people, but this sending cannot be seen without considering the Holy Spirit and the local church for and in which people are sent. Thus, in agreement with this approach, Vatican II made a turn from an almost exclusively christomonistic[15] approach to a perspective where the christological and the pneumatological line are kept together. This approach is important because in it the local church holds a relevant position. Ministry is exercised with other ministers and it is done both for and within the whole community. Ministry is, therefore, seen in relation to a concrete community.

Vatican II situated ministry within the local church (diocese) and within the parish. The Decree on the Bishops reveals this when it describes the diocese /particular church. "A diocese is a section (*portio*) of the people of God whose pastoral care is entrusted to a bishop in cooperation with his priests. Thus, in conjunction with their pastor and gathered by him into one flock in the Holy Spirit through the gospel and the Eucharist, they constitute a particular church."[16] The different elements listed here are not all of the same rank: the Church is gathered in the Holy Spirit who is the first "builder" of the community. There is the gospel and there are the sacraments (the Eucharist is mentioned as the main sacrament, but it may not be dissociated from the other sacraments, in particular baptism). The pastor (bishop) stands in service of this all.[17] We see a "testimony" of this emphasis on the community in the *Code of Canon Law* where we find titles such as: "Particular Churches and the Authority Established in them" and "Parishes, Pastors and Parochial Vicars." These titles express that there is first the community and that in that community there is ministry. The canons describing a diocese and a parish do the same: "A diocese is a portion of the people of God which is entrusted for pastoral care to a bishop with the cooperation of the presbyterate [...]"[18] (c. 369) and "The parish is a definite community of the Christian faithful [...]; the pastoral care is entrusted to a pastor as its own shepherd under the authority of the bishop." Thus ministry is to be understood from within the

---

[15] "A Christomonistic model of the Church is one that identifies the Church exclusively with Christ without accounting for the presence and action of the Holy Spirit," Susan Wood, *Sacramental Orders, Lex Orandi* Series (Collegeville: Liturgical Press, 2000): 25.

[16] CD 11. English translation from Norman P. Tanner, *Decrees of the Ecumenical Councils* (London: Sheed & Ward, 1990).

[17] Hervé Legrand provides a detailed theological commentary to the different aspects and can show how the local dimension of the church is of relevance as well as the working of the Holy Spirit and how (ordained) ministry is to be understood in this context. Legrand, "L'église se réalise en un lieu," 159-171

[18] English translations are taken from *Code of Canon Law: Latin English Edition, New English Translation* (Washington DC: Canon Law Society of America, 1999).

community.[19]

It should be noted that whereas there is an increasing debate on the ministry of the bishop within the local church,[20] the question may be raised whether the discussions about lay ministry, also by canonists, is carried out within this new ecclesiology where not just baptism and confirmation are decisive – for that would again focus on the individual and his relationship with God – but where the community as such is the receiver of the different ministries.

As a model for such an understanding of ministries, the Church of Corinth (1 Cor 12:14) could function. It saw the diversity of *charismas* in relation to the same Spirit, the many forms of *diakonia* in relation to the same Lord Jesus Christ, and the many forms of activities (*energèta*) in relation to the same God. Essential in the letter of St. Paul is that there are many *charismas*, but one Spirit (12:4) and that this is all the work of the one and same Spirit who divides as he pleases (12:11). Unity and diversity are co-existing and the Spirit is the source of both. When unity and diversity coexist, unity cannot be uniformity; and thus, there must be diversity. The Holy Spirit grants a diversity of gifts that cannot be derived from each other. Yet, he connects them in that the individual gifts and its carriers are not left in isolation, but are related to each other in a community. As source of community, the Spirit is not a source of chaos, of anarchy; but is one of order, of structure and communication. Or to say it with the words of St. Paul, as he concludes this section in the letter to the Corinthians, "God is not the author of confusion, but of peace" (1 Cor 14:33).

Thus with the model of the Church of Corinth, we see that St. Paul emphasizes that there is a great diversity of *charismas* and that these *charismas* serve the community. It is also clear that there is, therefore, a true equality of all baptized which precedes the divisions.

The theologian Walter Kasper sees the different *charismas*, ministries and offices as complementary to each other. He takes recourse to the concept of *communio* to explain that there is a diversity in unity in them.[21] Thus the laity, he says, actively take part in the threefold mission of the Church. This should find expression in counsels and synods. However, Kasper emphasizes, Vatican II pointed out that the *communio* ecclesiology also requires that the biblically founded

---

[19] Such a perspective has far reaching consequences for example for the exercise of the office of diocesan bishop. I have attempted to outline them with respect to the legislative task of the bishop in my article: "'For You I am a Bishop, With you I am a Christian': The Bishop as Legislator," *The Jurist* 56 (1996): 68-91.

[20] Discussions about the theological and juridical status of Episcopal conferences are also expressions of this as is the recent active debate about the local and universal church.

[21] Walter Kasper, "Berufung und Sendung des Laien in Kirche und Welt," *Stimmen der Zeit* 205 (1987): 579-593.

differentiation between clerics and laity obtains a new understanding.[22]  The Council stressed the essential difference and not just a gradual difference between the common priesthood of all baptized and the ministerial priesthood. This does not mean that the ministerial priesthood is more intense or higher than the common priesthood.  If that would be true, says Kasper, then clerics would be better Christians, and that is not the case. The common and ministerial priesthood differ not on the level of being Christian, but they refer to different vocations and missions within the communion of all Christians.[23]

Kasper points out that Vatican II intentionally omitted a theological definition of the laity and just provided a typological description. It said that the laity have not received orders, but to his negative qualification the Council added a positive element: they have a special task in the world. This task is now to be seen no longer in the context of a dualistic vision on the world and the sacred, but in the context of the explicit statement that the Church is *in* the world. Thus the world and the church are closely connected.  As the opening lines of *Gaudium et Spes* state: "The joys and the hopes and the sorrows and anxieties of people today, especially of those who are poor and afflicted, are also the joys and hopes, sorrows and anxieties of the disciples of Christ, and there is nothing truly human which does not also affect them."[24]  This implies that the service of the laity in the world is not just a worldly matter, but it also carries an ecclesial dimension.  The laity see to it that the questions and the experiences of the world are present in the Church

---

[22] After I gave the above lecture at the CLSA conference, the acts of a conference on ministry entitled "In Service of the Community" and held in the Spring of 2002 in Germany were published.  In order to remain faithful to what I said at the CLSA conference I can only take these German acts into consideration in my footnotes.

At that conference Cardinal Karl Lehmann emphasized the need for unity in diversity and diversity in unity within a communion ecclesiology.  There is a unity in mission and a diversity in ministry.  He admits that at times it might be quite a challenge to find the balance between the legitimate diversity and the necessary unity.  He sees this confirms in the decree on the Apostolate of the Laity: "In the Church there is a diversity in ministry (*diversitas ministerii*) but unity in mission (*unitas missionis*)" (AA 2).  Thus, he writes, all should be aware that they are working for the same cause and that they obtain their competence and acknowledgement through their specific contribution.  Hence, no one is competent for everything nor is anyone the sole competent person.  Karl Lehmann, "Kirchliche Dienste, Aufgaben und Ämter im deutschsprachigen Raum: Chancen und Gefahren," in Sabine Demel, e.a. (eds.) *Im Dienst der Gemeinde: Wirklichkeit und Zukunftsgestalt der kirchlichen Ämter*, Kirchenrechtliche Bibliothek, vol. 5 (Münster: Lit, 2002): 16. It should be noted that when Lehmann uses the word *Ämter* he does not use it in the sense of *officium* but refers to ordained ministers.  In German the word *officium* is translated with *Amt* as well.  This may contribute to the confusion, because with *Amtsträger* common German parlour refers to ordained ministers exclusively.

[23] Lehmann states that the Latin text of *LG* 10 about the common and ministerial priesthood makes very clear that there is first a communality and only subsequently a differentiation.  He emphasis that ordained ministry cannot be deducted from the common priesthood.  The one who holds an office (*Amtsträger*) does not just stand vis-à-vis the community, but also lives in it.  Lehmann, "Kirchliche Dienste," p. 17-18.

[24] *GS* n.

and are made fruitful for the Church. Thus they bring some fresh air in the Church. At the same time, they should proclaim the faith in the world. Thus, the presence of the laity in the world implies that they participate in the sacramental character of the Church. Therefore, the pastors should provide the laity with "light and strength," should not patronize them and respect their Christian freedom and listen to the laity. The complementarity can thus be found in that the ministerial priesthood is to be of service to the common priesthood. Thus, Vatican II called for a partnership between priests and laity and spoke of a fraternal relationship between the shepherds and the faithful who are entrusted to their care. The priests are called to listen to the specific interests of the laity.[25]

What about the laity who work within the Church, for example the lay ecclesial ministers? Kasper points out that these ministries must be understood as founded in baptism and confirmation and not as derived from orders. These new ministries are neither a supply for nor are they in opposition to the priesthood. Thus, says Kasper, they may not be seen and dealt with as fulfilling a need for the time there is a shortage of priests. They make a positive contribution and are enriching to the ecclesiastical office; they are a sign that the ministry to the world and the ministry to salvation are not two separate entities.[26] Due to the new offices that laity hold, the pastoral activity of the Church will become more "worldly" in the positive sense of the word. The Church, says Kasper, needs this to be able to evangelize more effectively. On the other hand, the laity need priests who are familiar with the world because they are personally engaged in it.

If we now return to the main point of this presentation, namely, whether we are asking the right question we might have to admit that canonists might have to rethink some of the issues. In light of the above outlined considerations, it seems

---

[25] The original is worth citing in full: "Es gibt also innerhalb der gemeinsamen Anteilhabe aller Christgläubigen an allen drei Ämtern Christi unterschiedliche Berufungen und Sendungen. Darin ist die *Differentia specifica* des Laien begründet. In ihrer spezifischen Berufung und Sendung ist ihnen das Amt nicht übergeordnet, sondern dienend zugeordnet. Anders ausgedrückt: Das Konzil hat zu einer partnerschaftlichen Verhältnisbestimmung zwischen Priestern und Laien gefunden. Deshalb hat es ausdrücklich von einem brüderlichen Verhältnis der Hirten zu den ihnen anvertrauten Gläubigen gesprochen und die Hirten ermahnt, auf die berechtigten Anliegen der Laien zu hören. Das ist ein Leitbild von Communio-Ekklesiologie und Mitverantwortung, das noch längst nicht überall der Wirklichkeit entspricht." Kasper, "Berufung und Sendung," 586.

[26] "Von grundsätzlicher Bedeutung ist, dass es sich bei diesen neuen Ämtern um Ämter von Laien handelt, welche ihre sakramentale Grundlage in Taufe und Firmung haben und welche darum nicht als Ausgliederung aus dem Sakrament des Ordo verstanden werden dürfen. Die neuen Ämter der Laien sind weder ein Ersatz noch eine Konkurrenz für die Priester. Sie sind auch kein notwendiges Übel wegen der zu geringen Zahl von Priestern. Sie sind ein positiver Beitrag und Zuwachs für das kirchliche Amt und ein Zeichen dafür, dass Weltdienst und Heilsdienst nicht zwei hermetisch voneinander geschiedene Bereiche sind." Kasper, "Berufung und Sendung," 588.

insufficient to take recourse only to a christological understanding of ministry.[27] We might well have to enter into a framework or model or paradigm in which we take both the christological *and* the pneumatological model. Kasper would call for a use of the *communio* model. In that we might also be able to understand the position of the baptized non Catholics and their gifts to the church.

Let me summarize what we can take as some results from our reflections:

- There are different ecclesiological models for understanding ministry in the Church. We must be attentive to the underlying models we select.[28]
- Vatican II understood ministry to be located within the community. The laity and the ordained have complimentary gifts; they do not stand in opposition.[29]
- The ministry exercised in the world is also an ecclesial ministry because the Church does not stand in opposition to the world, but lives in the world.
- The gifts that ecclesial lay ministers bring to the Church are to be seen neither as a supplying for nor as standing in competition with the gifts that the ordained ministers bring, but they are to be considered and examined on their own merits.
- The current law, in particular the issues expressed in canon 129, deals with questions concerning cooperation or participation. However, understanding lay and ordained ministry as being complementary to each other might lead to a new and fresh approach of understanding the cooperation between them.

---

[27] Lehmann warns to attempt to consider offices (*Ämter*) and ministries (*Dienste*) theologically primarily within an ecclesiological context. He states that the connection with the Church is important and might have been considered insufficiently in the past. However, ecclesiology cannot provide exclusively a foundation of office (*Amt*) and ministry. Christology should hold its primacy position here before ecclesiology. An office holder, he writes, is a "vicar" never a "boss": officeholders (*Amtsträger*) are to make themselves free for Christ (p. 18). In the cooperation of the different charismas, offices and ministries, Lehmann also takes recourse to the Pauline model as presented in 1 Cor 12-14. (Lehmann, "Kirchliche Dienste," 20-27).

[28] Susan Wood identifies four conceptualizations of the Church influencing the relationship between ordained ministry and the Church: a monarchical and hierarchical conceptualization; a eucharistic, collegial model representing the communion of particular churches; the priest, prophet, and king motif that structures the concept of the Church as the people of God; and a theology of the Church as a sacrament of Christ and ordained ministry as a sacrament to the Church. She investigates the 1990 ordination rites and the theology they display. Susan Wood, *Sacramental Orders.*

[29] In a *nota* implementing the *Instructio* on the cooperation of the lay faithful with the ordained the Conference of Bishops of The Netherlands state that initially they as much as the faithful believed that laity were substituting for the diminishing number of clergy. However, they state, over the past 20 to 30 years they have discovered that many professional lay persons do not feel a vocation to the priesthood and are not working from an awareness that they are not priests. On the contrary, the bishops write, the ecclesial lay ministers have discovered for themselves and revealed to the community that they have their own specific call. The bishops evaluate this positively. Conference of Bishops of the Netherlands, "Meewerken in het pastoraat: Beleidsnota bij de 'Instructie over enige vragen betreffende de medewerking van lekengelovigen aan het dienstwerk van de priesters'," *Een-Twee-Een, Kerkelijke Documentatie* 27 (1999) no. 8, 3-37.

*Conclusion*

This presentation focused around the question: are we raising the right issues in relation to professional laity, clergy and complementarity? Must we reconsider or reformulate the issues? With Vatican II, the Church has entered into a new phase. The Fathers were able to look at the old in a new way because with the help of theologians they were able to raise new questions. An attentive reading of the conciliar texts and even more so of the discussions of these texts, reveal that the Fathers set a train in motion. They believed that the Holy Spirit guided them in doing so, but they were also aware that they could not see all the implications of their teaching. We, the Church, are invited to enter into that same dynamics. Pope Paul VI called for this when speaking to students and professors of canon law about a "*novus habitus mentis.*" In relation to the Church and to ministry – and I do not want to limit it here just to lay ministry – we are invited to reflect and be open to what the Holy Spirit might grant us.

*Appendix*

Two examples of a Liturgy in which Lay Pastoral Workers are Mandated.

1. Diocese of Münster (Germany), September 29, 2002

The text below is that section that follows the homily and precedes the prayers of the faithful. There are three parts in it: the presentation of the candidates, the promises by the candidates, the granting of the mandate by the bishop. After the ceremony the pastoral workers enjoy a permanent contract with the diocese for pastoral work, they are assigned to a specific parish or pastoral work (e.g., hospital).

| **1. Presentation of the Candidates** | **1. *Vorstellung der Kandidatinnen und Kandidaten*** |
|---|---|
| *Person mandated by the bishop:* Dear Bishop: [number] women and men declared themselves willing to cooperate in the pastoral ministry of the diocese of Münster as pastoral workers. As lay persons they exercise a ministry among the people of God in unity with you, their bishop, and with the priests and deacons. Now that they have successfully completed | Bischöflicher Beauftragter: *Lieber Herr Bischof, [anzahl] Frauen und Männer haben sich bereit erklärt, als Pastoralreferentinnen und Pastoralreferenten im pastoralen Dienst des Bistums Münster mitzuarbeiten. Als Laien üben sie ihren Dienst inmitten des Volkes Gottes in Einheit mit Ihnen, ihrem Bischof, und den Priestern und* |

their formation I petition that you grant them an ecclesiastical mandate.

They are:
*The candidates are individually called and they come forward into the apsis of the church and form a semi-circle in front of the bishop.*

## 2. Declaration of Willingness by the Candidates
*Bishop:*
Dear pastoral workers,

You would like to work in the pastoral ministry of the diocese of Münster. Through your ministry you are to co-operate in the growth of lively communities. It is for this that you petition a mandate and mission from the church. Before I shall mandate you, I ask you:

Are you willing to engage yourself with all your strength in to the service of the Gospel and the Church?

*Pastoral workers:*

Yes, I am willing!

*Bishop:* Are you willing to live in agreement with the Gospel and the Church so as to give witness to your faith?

*Pastoral workers:*

Yes, I am willing!

*Diakonen aus. Ich bitte Sie, ihnen nach erfolgreich abgeschlossener Ausbildung die Kirchliche Beauftragung zu erteilen.*

Es sind:
*Die Kandidatinnen und Kandidaten werden einzeln namentlich aufgerufen und bilden im Chorraum vor dem Bischof einen Halbkreis.*

## 2. Bereitschaftserklärung der Kandidatinnen und Kandidaten
Bischof:
*Liebe Pastoralreferentinnen und Pastoralreferenten,*
*Sie wollen mitarbeiten im pastoralen Dienst des Bistums Münster. Durch Ihren Dienst sollen Sie mitwirken am Wachstum lebendiger Gemeinden. Dafür erbitten Sie die Beauftragung und Sendung durch die Kirche. Bevor ich Sie nun beauftrage, frage ich Sie:*

*Sind Sie bereit, sich mit ganzer Kraft im Dienst des Evangeliums und der Kirche einzusetzen?*

Pastoralreferentinnen und Pastoralreferenten:
*Ich bin bereit!*

Bischof: *Sind Sie bereit, gemäß dem Auftrag des Evangeliums und der Kirche zu leben, um so Zeugnis Ihres Glaubens abzulegen?*

Pastoralreferentinnen und Pastoralreferenten:
*Ich bin bereit!*

**Bishop:** Are you willing to exercise this ministry with reference and in obedience to the bishop and to do so together with the priests, deacons and laity in service of the salvation of all?

*Pastoral workers:*

Yes, I am willing and I promise!

**Bishop:** As a sign of your willingness then profess the apostolic creed!

*Pastoral workers:*

I believe in God, the Father almighty …

### 3. Granting of the Mandate
**Bishop:** I mandate you to the ministry in the Church of Münster. Serve the people through the witness of faith, hope and love, and help in building the community of the Lord.

Let us pray:
God, in your love you guide the Church and grant her persons with different charisms. Bless + these women and men. Let them grow in faith and in love, so that they can bear rich fruit. Open their hearts for the joy and hope, the sadness and fear of the people with whom they live. Help them, to give witness to you and to let the people experience your love. We ask you this through Christ our Lord.

Bischof: *Sind Sie bereit, in Ehrfurcht und Gehorsam gegenüber dem Bischof Ihren Dienst zu tun und mit den Priestern, Diakonen und Laien zusammenzuarbeiten zum Heil aller?*

Pastoralreferentinnen und Pastoralreferenten:
*Ich bin bereit und verspreche es!*

Bischof: *So sprechen Sie nun als Zeichen Ihrer Bereitschaft das Apostolische Glaubensbekenntnis!*

Pastoralreferentinnen und Pastoralreferenten:
*Ich glaube an Gott, den Vater, den Allmächtigen, ...*

### 3. Beauftragung
Bischof: *Ich beauftrage Sie zum Dienst in der Kirche von Münster. Dienen Sie den Menschen mit dem Zeugnis des Glaubens, der Hoffnung und der Liebe und helfen Sie mit beim Aufbau der Gemeinde des Herrn.*

Lasset uns beten:
*Gott, in deiner Liebe führst du die Kirche und schenkst ihr Menschen mit verschiedenen Gnadengaben. Segne + diese Frauen und Männer. Lass sie im Glauben und in der Liebe wachsen, damit sie reiche Frucht bringen. Öffne ihre Herzen für die Freude und die Hoffnung, die Trauer und die Angst der Menschen, mit denen sie leben. Hilf ihnen, dich zu bezeugen und deine Liebe den Menschen erfahrbar zu machen. Darum bitten wir dich durch Christus, unseren Herrn.*

| | |
|---|---|
| *All*: Amen | Alle: *Amen.* |
| *Bishop:* The center of your ministry and your life is the Gospel and the faith of the Church. As a symbol of it I give you Holy Scriptures. | Bischof: *Mitte Ihres Dienstes und Ihres ganzen Lebens ist das Evangelium und der Glaube der Kirche. Zum Zeichen dafür überreiche ich Ihnen die Heilige Schrift.* |
| *The bishop gives the mandated person a Bible.* | Der Bischof überreicht den Beauftragten eine Bibel. |

## 2. Diocese of Basel (Switzerland)

For the diocese of Basel I refer to a celebration of June 12, 1993. The presider was an auxiliary bishop of the diocese. The celebration has two parts: one concerns those who enter a so-called *institutio* the others receive a *missio canonica*. The *institutio* has many similarities with an incardination because there is a lifelong commitment between the diocese and the pastoral worker. Noteworthy is that the marriage partners also make promises.

The celebration has the following order:

Introduction and greeting
Presentation of the candidates by the vice rector (who is the vice rector of the seminary)
Recommendation of the candidates by the vice-rector to the bishop
Litany of all Saints
Celebration of the Word
Homily
*Institutio*
Apostolic Creed
Celebration of the Eucharist
*Missio canonica* for those who did not obtain the *institutio*.

Below follows the text of the *institutio*.

| Questioning of the Candidates | Befragung der Kandidaten/in |
|---|---|
| I ask you: | Ich frage Sie: |
| 1. Are you willing to follow Jesus and to continue in hope what started with him in faith and salvation? | 1. *Sind Sie bereit, Jesus nach zufolgen, und das hoffnungsvoll weiterzutragen, was mit ihm an Glaube und heil aufgebrochen ist?* |
| *Cand.:* I am willing. | Kand.: *Ich bin bereit.* |
| 2. Are you willing to listen to the Word of God, to receive it more intensely in order to cooperate in solidarity with the bishop, the priests, the deacons, the pastoral workers, with all women and men for the building of the church? | 2. *Sind Sie bereit, auf das Wort Gottes zu hören und es immer tiefer aufzunehmen um in Solidarität mit dem Bischof, mit den Priestern, Diakonen, Pastoralassistentinnen und Pastoralassistenten, mit allen Frauen und Männern am Aufbau der Kirche mitzuwirken?* |
| *Cand.:* I am willing. | Kand.: *Ich bin bereit.* |
| 3. Proclaiming belongs to your tasks. Are you willing to proclaim the Good News of Jesus while trusting in the Holy Spirit? | 3. *Zu Ihrem Auftrag gehört die Verkündigung: Sind Sie bereit, in hoffendem Vertrauen auf den Heiligen Geist die Frohe Botschaft Jesu zu verkünden?* |
| *Cand.:* I am willing. | Kand.: *Ich bin bereit.* |
| 4. Diaconia belongs to your tasks. Are you willing to engage yourself fully in particular in your care for the sick, the lonely, the outcasts, the suffering and the poor? | 4. *Zu Ihrem Auftrag gehört die Diakonie. Sind Sie bereit, sich mit Ihrer ganzen Person für die Kranken, einsamen, Verstoßenen, Leidenden und Armen in besonderem Maß einzusetzen?* |
| *Cand.:* I am willing. | Kand.: *Ich bin bereit.* |
| 5. Liturgy belongs to your tasks. Are you willing to celebrate, prepare and lead liturgical services of the | 5. *Zu Ihrem Auftrag gehört die Liturgie. Sind Sie bereit, Gottesdienste der Gemeinde zur Ehre Gottes und* |

44

community in order to honor God and for the salvation of the people?

*Cand.*: I am willing.

6. You shall fulfill your mandate in our diocesan Church under the leadership of the diocesan bishop. Therefore, I ask you: Do you promise to be in solidarity with the diocesan bishop and his successors in co-responsibility for the Church of Basel and to remain with him and his successors in a true dialogue and a loyal obedience?

*Cand.*: I promise it.

**Questioning of the Spouses**
I now ask the spouses to come forward (*The three women stand besides their husbands.*)

Ecclesial ministry is always embedded in the community of the faithful. Without this togetherness a living according to the Gospel is impossible in our church. Therefore I ask you as spouses:

Are you willing to live your own Christian vocation and to carry the ecclesial task of your spouse in solidarity?
*Partners:* I am willing

**Questioning of the Community**
Not only the spouses belong to the community of the faithful, but also you all, family members, acquaintances, friends, representatives from the parishes of

*zum heil der Menschen mitzufeiern, mitzugestalten und zu leiten?*

Kand.: *Ich bin bereit.*

6. *Ihren Auftrag in unserer Bistumskirche erfüllen Sie unter der Leitung des Diözesanbischofs. Deshalb frage ich Sie, mit dem Diözesanbischof und seinen Nachfolgern in Mitverantwortung für die Kirche im Bistum Basel solidarisch zu sein und mit ihm und seinen Nachfolgern in echtem Dialog und loyalem Gehorsam verbunden zu bleiben?*
Kand.: *Ich verspreche es.*

**Befragung der Partnerinnen**
*Ich bitte nun die Ehepartnerinnen hervorzutreten* (Die 3 Frauen stellen sich nun neben ihre Ehemänner.)

*Kirchlicher Dienst ist immer eingebettet in die Gemeinschaft der Glaubenden. Ohne dieses Miteinander ist ein Leben nach dem Evangelium in unserer Kirche unmöglich. Darum frage ich Sie als Ehepartnerinnen:*

*Sind Sie bereit, selber Ihre christliche Berufung zu leben und in Solidarität die kirchliche Aufgabe Ihres Lebenspartners mitzutragen?*
Partnerinnen: *Ich bin bereit.*

**Befragung der Gemeinde**
*Zur Gemeinschaft der Glaubenden gehören nicht nur die Ehepartnerinnen, sondern auch Sie alle, Verwandte, Bekannte, freunde und Freundinnen, Vertreter und*

| | |
|---|---|
| the pastoral workers.  Therefore I ask you also: | *Vertreterinnen aus den Pfarreien der Seelsorgerinnen und Seelsorger. Darum frage ich auch Sie:* |
| Are you willing to accompany and support the ecclesial workers whom I may give the mandate and the mission through your own engagement for a lively community? | *Wollen Sie mit Ihrem Einsatz für eine lebendige gemeinde die kirchliche Mitarbeiter und Mitarbeiterinnen, denen ich die Beauftragung und Sendung erteilen darf, begleiten und unterstützen?* |
| If you consent, I ask you to express this by way of giving applause. | *Falls Sie damit einverstanden sind, bitte ich Sie, dies mit einem Applaus zu bestätigen.* |
| *Community: gives an applause* | Gemeinde: applaudiert. |
| **Promise by the Diocesan Bishop** | *Versprechen des Diözesanbischofs* |
| In the name of the diocesan bishop and his successors I promise to accept you into the ministry of the diocese of Basel. Considering the need in pastoral tasks in the diocese, the bishop is willing to search for an appropriate position for you which considers your experiences and capacities. | *Im Namen des Diözesanbischofs und seiner Nachfolger verspreche ich, Sie in dauernden Dienst der Diözese Basel aufzunehmen. Entsprechend den Notwendigkeiten an pastoralen Aufgaben im Bistum ist der Bischof auch bereit, für Sie eine Stelle zu suchen, die Ihre Erfahrungen und Fähigkeiten, berücksichtigt.* |
| **Reception in the Diocese** | *Indienstnahme* |
| Dear pastoral workers, After you have declared your willingness, I receive you in the permanent ministry as pastoral workers in the diocese of Basel. May God bless you in your work: In the name of the Father, the Son and the Holy Spirit. | *Liebe Seelsorgerinnen und Seelsorger, Nachdem Sie Ihre Bereitschaft bezeugt haben, nehme ich Sie aus in den dauernden Dienst als Seelsorgerin und Seelsorger im Bistum Basel. Gott begleite Ihr Wirken mit seinem Segen: Im Namen des Vaters, des Sohnes und des Heiligen Geistes.* |

Priv.-Doz. Dr. Myriam Wijlens was born in Losser, The Netherlands, in 1962. She obtained a STL from Nijmegen (The Netherlands), a JCL and JCD from Saint Paul University in Ottawa (Canada) and a Habilitation in Münster (Germany). She is currently Assistant Professor of Canon Law at the Theological Faculty of the University of Tilburg in The Netherlands and teaches in the Canon Law Institute in Münster (Germany). She is also a staff member of the tribunal of the diocese of Münster. She has been lecturing in Rome, Washington, DC, and Freiburg (Germany) as well.

She is the author of;

*Theology and Canon Law: The Theories of Klaus Mörsdorf and Eugenio Corecco*, (Lanham, MD: University of Press of America, 1992);

*Sharing the Eucharist: A Theological Evaluation of the Post-Conciliar Legislation*, With a Foreword by Cardinal Willebrands (Lanham, MD: University Press of America, 2000)

*The Ordinary Contentious Trial: A Revised Schematic Overview* (Losser: Wijlens, 2001).

She has also published several articles in German and English in particular on ecclesiological-ecumenical-canonical issues.

CLSA PROCEEDINGS 64 (2002) 49-57

# MAGISTERIUM, MINISTRY, MEMBERSHIP

MOST REVEREND DANIEL E. PILARCZYK

I wish to begin my presentation this afternoon with three prefatory remarks.

First prefatory remark: I probably shouldn't be here, at least not here at the speaker's podium. This is a gathering of professionals who share interest and competence in a very crucial element of the Church's life, an element that seeks to provide justice and predictability and order so that the people of God can carry out its vocation in a cohesive and principled way. As a diocesan bishop I am grateful for the canon law of the Church and grateful for those who help me to do my work in accord with what the law permits and demands. But that doesn't make me qualified to give a keynote to an assembly of canonists.

There was a time when I might have been qualified to speak to theologians about the sacramental theology of Praepositinus of Cremona or to classicists about the significance of facial expression in the works of Tacitus, but I suspect that the years have eaten away even those limited competencies. All I can offer now is twenty-eight years of pastoral experience as a bishop and a willingness to talk.

Second prefatory remark: I am not really sure what the program committee members wanted me to talk about. When Sister Ann Rehrauer wrote to me in March of 2001 she said that the convention intended to examine the ecclesial foundations of the complementary roles of laity and clergy in the Church and the positive aspects of the mutuality of ministry. I thought that was rather abstract and when I was invited to offer a title for what I planned to say, I suggested: Magisterium, Ministry, Membership. In the program that was sent out ahead of time, my keynote address was entitled, "Theological/Vatican II Foundations of Roles and Complementarity." I guess I'm willing to settle for that, but it doesn't seem to have much bite to it. I hope the speech has more zest than the title.

Third prefatory remark: as I reflected on what was being asked of me, it became clear that the question to be addressed was the question of calling. To what are the followers of Christ called? Are they all called to the same thing? Does salvation involve one calling or many? To what extent is the Church a community of likeness, to what extent a community of diversity? The answers to these questions are likely to be different if they are being answered in 2002 than they would be if they were being answered in 1950, thanks to the teachings of Vatican II. So I decided that I could respond to this question of calling by doing my own personal overview of part of *Lumen Gentium* in the light of some contemporary questions about calling and ministry.

That brings me to the end of my prefatory remarks. The rest of what I want to share with you will be divided into two main parts. The first main part will be an overview of the various aspects of the calling to salvation and faith that is addressed to followers of Christ. I will deal with five levels of calling, five contexts in which people are invited to respond to God's call to be saved and to carry out the works of faith. If this part of my presentation were to have its own subtitle, it would be "Structures of Salvation."

In my second, and final, main part I will offer you some questions and some provisional answers that arise from what will have been said about the structures of salvation. The subtitle for this section might be: "What are the issues and whose issues are they?"

Now let's turn to the structures of salvation, to a survey of the contexts in which people are called to salvation. In order to be clear about what we are discussing, I think it will be useful first to say a little bit about what salvation is.

Salvation consists in participation in the life of the risen Christ. We are saved *from* meaninglessness and self-destruction and saved *for* eternal happiness and fulfillment by sharing in the life of Christ, a sharing that comes to us through God's initiative and to which we respond by our acceptance in faith. Other terms, each with its own more refined meaning, are roughly synonymous with salvation. These terms include: justification, righteousness, redemption, sanctification, grace, holiness, eternal life. It is clear that, thus defined, i.e., as the gift of sharing Christ's risen life, salvation can only come in and through Christ.

Now let's look at the most inclusive context of salvation, the context that includes all the others, the context that will persist throughout all eternity: the kingdom of God.

If we were asked to sum up the teaching of Jesus in as few words as possible, in one sentence, that sentence would be, "The kingdom of God is here." The kingdom is what Jesus talked about most of the time. It was the subject of many, perhaps most of His parables. The presence of the kingdom was what Jesus wanted to highlight by His miracles. The terms "kingdom of God" and "kingdom of heaven" occur about a hundred times in the synoptic gospels. Vatican II (*LG* 5) tells us that Christ's word, Christ's works, Christ's presence all served to reveal the kingdom.

The kingdom, of course, is not a political entity. It is, rather, the assumption and manifestation by God of full and final lordship over heaven and earth. It involves a process of growth and development. It is here now, but not in its ultimate completeness. It is already but not yet. It implies the final fulfillment of the will of God for this world and its human creatures, and thus involves righteousness or holiness.

After the death, resurrection, and ascension of Jesus, it became gradually clearer to His disciples that Jesus Himself was the kingdom and that membership in the kingdom meant sharing in the life of the risen Christ. To be in the kingdom meant to be in Christ. And to be in Christ, to share His life is what constitutes salvation, holiness, justification, righteousness. It is to a sharing in the life of God in Christ that all human beings are called, and the acceptance of what God offers us in Christ is what constitutes membership in the kingdom, membership in Christ, salvation. Obviously all human beings have not yet had their chance to accept or reject salvation, and the kingdom has not yet reached its final stage. It is still in process of development. Nor has the rest of created reality, the world, been yet fully and finally reunited to the loving providence of God. But the criteria for belonging to the kingdom – i.e., accepting the gift of the life of Christ – are the same now as they were on Pentecost and will remain the same when God brings the interim growth of the kingdom to fulfillment, when Christ comes again to take all created reality to Himself forever.

The central reality of our human existence, therefore, the basic element that gives it sense and meaning, is salvation, and salvation, by definition, involves participation in the kingdom. What matters most is being in the kingdom of God, and inclusion in the kingdom of God means accepting the life of Christ, responding affirmatively to God's offer of salvation. Everything else has to be subordinated to that and directed toward that. We exist in order to be part of the kingdom. We exist in order to help bring the kingdom to its final fulfillment in every aspect of creation.

We are now ready to examine the second context of salvation, the Church.

In the first two chapters of *Lumen Gentium*, we have a general overview of Vatican II's ecclesiology. The council teaches us in chapter I that the Church is a mystery, i.e., that it is part of God's hidden, saving plan for salvation, a plan that cannot be fully understood by human effort. The council also teaches us that the Church is a sacrament, a sign and a cause of salvation. *Lumen Gentium* highlights the images of the kingdom that Scripture uses (images from pastoral life, agriculture, architecture, and matrimony) finally giving extended treatment in no. 7 to the image of the Church as Body of Christ, insisting that all the Church's members are to be molded into Christ's image until He is formed in them. All this is to say that the Church is an agent or instrument of salvation. Although the council in *LG* 3 seems to identify the Church with the kingdom, it also points out that it is the kingdom "now present in mystery," and, in no. 5, distinguishes the Church from the kingdom a bit when it says that the Church "receives the mission to proclaim and to establish among all peoples the kingdom of Christ and of God," and that the Church is "the initial budding forth of that kingdom." In other words, the Church and the kingdom are not totally identical, not one and the same thing. Later on *LG* will point out (no. 16) that some persons can attain to everlasting salvation (i.e., be part of the kingdom) who do not know the gospel of Christ or His Church. The Church is an instrument of the kingdom, but is not the kingdom pure and simple. There is also, of course, the reality that, as a sadly human institution, the Church through its leaders and its members has often proved itself capable of sinful attitudes and actions which are not consistent with claiming to be the very kingdom of God. Not everybody in the kingdom is in the Church, and not everybody in the Church is necessarily in the kingdom.

In chapter II, the council fathers deal with the work of the Church under the rubric of "The People of God." They teach that membership in the Church is a gift, not an achievement and that all the members of the Church are called to collaborate in the Church's mission to make people holy, to teach about the saving will of Christ, and to make membership in the Church accessible to everybody. Here the council fathers are setting forth a principle that will be repeated more than once in the Council's teaching, i.e., that every single member has a part to play in the saving work of the Church. (cf. *Apostolicam Actuositatem*, no. 2 and *Presbyterorum Ordinis,* no. 2: "There is no member who does not have a part in the mission of the whole Body.")

There are a couple interim conclusions that we can draw from what we have seen so far. One is that the Church is not an end in itself. It exists as an instrument and means of salvation. What really counts is salvation. Another is that all the members of the Church, and of the kingdom, too, for that matter, are fundamentally the same, essentially equal and alike. Their sameness or equality or likeness is based on the one life in Christ that everybody participates in and on the universal call to responsibility for carrying out the Church's mission of salvation. Granted, every human being is different and the circumstances of each human life are different, and therefore every human being will carry out the vocation to help save the world in a somewhat different way. But the fact remains that the principal calling of each of us is the same. Pope or peasant, plumber or philosopher, we are all called to be involved in the salvation of the world, in bringing about the growth of the kingdom.

I observe in passing that this calling to be involved in the salvation of the world also includes a call to be involved in evangelization, i.e., in the communication of God's call to salvation. Evangelization – accepting it and doing it – is as much a part of being in the kingdom as is salvation itself.

Now lets look at the next two contexts of salvation. We might call this section "Divisions in Sameness." It has to deal with basic tasks of salvation that are assigned to different persons in the Church. There are all kinds of different tasks within the Church's mission, but the most basic differentiation is between clergy and laity. *Lumen Gentium* deals with this distinction in chapters III and IV. Chapter III is about the hierarchy (clergy) and Chapter IV about the laity. One could make a case for reversing the order, but I will finesse that problem by dealing with both groups under the one heading ("Divisions in Sameness"). For the sake of simplicity, in my treatment of clergy I will deal mainly with bishops, since the ministry of priests is an extension of one aspect of the bishop's ministry and the ministry of deacons an extension of another aspect.

We can deal with the ministry of bishops by answering three questions: What are bishops for? What do they do? How do they become bishops?

*Lumen Gentium* 18, par. 1 (trans. Flannery) answers our first question very clearly. What are bishops for? "In order to shepherd the people of God [...] Christ the Lord set up in his Church a variety of offices which aim at the good of the whole body. The holders of office, who are invested with a sacred power, are, in fact, dedicated to promoting the interests of their brethren, so that all who belong to the People of God [...] may, through their free and well-ordered efforts toward a common goal, attain to salvation." Bishops exist so that the members of the Church can work together for the progress of the kingdom, i.e., toward the goal of salvation that we all share.

What do bishops do? Note, first of all, that what bishops do is done for the well-being of the other members of the Church. Bishops sanctify, teach, and govern. By presiding over the celebration of the sacraments, they sanctify the faithful, i.e., they make salvation available and deepen its effects in the people they serve (*LG* 24). The teaching office of bishops makes revelation, i.e., the invitation to salvation, available to new disciples and makes clear to those who are already disciples what they have to believe and do in order to remain consistent with the invitation they have already accepted (*LG* 25). By reason of their governing power, bishops exercise leadership and direction over the structures of the Church "only for the edification of their flock in truth and holiness" (*LG* 27). Everything that bishops do is directed toward the service of that portion of the Church for which they are responsible. It's all directed toward the salvation of their people.

How do they become bishops? This is an important question because of the implications it has for the nature of the Church and for all formal Church ministry. *Lumen Gentium* (no. 21, trans. Flannery) teaches that "by the imposition of hands and the words of consecration, the grace of the Holy Spirit is given, and a sacred character is impressed in such wise that bishops [...] take the place of Christ Himself, teacher, shepherd, and priest, and act as His representative (*in eius persona*)." The Church does not make bishops in and of itself, but through the power of Christ. Just as the only way one can attain salvation is through the personal intervention of the risen Christ, generally through the sacrament of baptism, so also the only way one can attain the office of official sanctifier, teacher, and governor in the Church is through the intervention of Christ in the sacrament of Holy Orders.

Just as Christ calls everyone to salvation, so also Christ calls some to this specialized service within the Church. The purpose of this service is to teach and guide and make holy the general membership of the Church so that those members can carry out appropriately the responsibilities for salvation to which they have been called and for which they have been empowered.

Let's now look at that context of salvation, our fourth, the calling to be a lay person. In the good old days we used to define lay persons as those members of the Church who were not clergy and *LG* starts off by defining laity that way (no. 31). But it goes on to a more positive approach (ibid.): laity are those who "seek the kingdom of God by engaging in temporal affairs and by ordering them to the plan of God. [...] They are called there by God." This constitutes "a participation in the saving mission of the Church" (no. 33). "Thus every lay person [...] is at the same time a witness and a living instrument of the mission of the Church itself" (ibid.).

Lay persons exercise the same general kinds of activity in the world that the ordained exercise in the Church. Through their ongoing association with Christ, especially in the Eucharist, they sanctify, i.e., they bring Christ's holiness into the context of the world in which they live (*LG* 34). In their teaching or prophetic role they give the word of God a chance to manifest itself and its implications in the family and in society and reassure the world in which they exist that it has purpose and meaning (*LG* 35). As agents of moral order in the world, lay believers carry out their mission by striving to improve the moral atmosphere of the world and by cooperating in the development of the world's potential.

By way of another interim summary, we can say that clergy are given to the Church for the sake of the salvation of the vast, vast majority of the Church's members who are lay persons, that lay persons are in the Church for the sake of the salvation of the world. Nobody is without responsibility for salvation, his or her own salvation as well as the salvation of the world. We may have different job descriptions in the context of faith, but we all have the same final goal: to bring about the kingdom, to bring about salvation.

That brings us now to the fifth context of calling. This is a relatively new one, and one which is still under study and discussion in the Church. I am referring to lay ecclesial ministers. These are persons whose primary occupation is assisting other members of the Church toward salvation through teaching, organization, or the cultivation of holiness in the name of the Church. While there have always been lay persons in the Church who engaged in activities such as catechesis and sacramental preparation (e.g., parents), the appearance of a whole new cadre of Church workers, professionally trained and employed full time, is a relatively new phenomenon.

There are lots of aspects of ecclesial lay ministry that are under discussion at present (e.g., formation, recognition, compensation, integration into Church structures), but in this present context I only want to address one aspect: what are these people? Are they clergy or laity? And where does their authorization to minister come from?

Put in its bluntest form, the function that most of these persons exercise is a clerical function, namely the pastoral care of other lay members of the Church so that these members can carry out their responsibility for the salvation of the world. Yet they themselves remain lay persons insofar as they have not received the sacrament of orders. It is clear to me that there has to be some way of identifying

54

these lay ecclesial ministers so that those to whom they minister can discern who represents the Church and who doesn't. I believe that lay ecclesial ministers become so by being delegated to their work by someone who has received the call to serve the vocation of the Church's members through the sacrament of Orders. I would offer the following definition:

> A lay ecclesial minister is a fully initiated member of the Church who, after appropriate preparation, is authorized or commissioned by the bishop or his representative to share in the bishop's responsibility as chief pastor for the sanctifying, teaching, and shepherding of the Church, and thus to serve in building up the Body of Christ for carrying out the salvific mission of the Church.

By definition lay ecclesial ministry is dependent on those who have received a commission to care for the Church through the sacrament of Orders. Likewise, lay ecclesial ministry is essentially temporary, only persisting as long as the authorization or commissioning persists.

We have now looked at five contexts in the calling to salvation: 1) the kingdom, 2) the Church, 3) the clergy, 4) the laity, and 5) lay ecclesial ministers, and here are the conclusions we have reached. 1) The whole world is called to share in the kingdom. 2) The Church is the primary and universal instrument of the salvation offered in the kingdom. 3) The proclamation of salvation is carried out mostly by lay persons since they are by far the largest part of the Church and since they are primarily responsible for making the kingdom present in the world. 4) The primary responsibility of the clergy is to sanctify, teach, and organize the Church's lay members so that they (the lay members) can carry out their calling to bring salvation (i.e., the life of the risen Christ) to the world. 5) The work of the clergy can be complemented by appropriately prepared lay persons when these lay persons have been commissioned or delegated by clergy.

When we look on all this in the light of the realities of the contemporary Church, some questions may arise. Earlier on I suggested that this last section of my presentation might be entitled, "What are the issues and whose issues are they?"

First question: is it really important to determine who is important in the Church? It is not important to try to rank the members of the Church so that everybody knows his or her place and can respond with appropriate obsequiousness to those above and treat those below with appropriate detachment. The Church is an organism, a body, and therefore every part of it is important. If all we had in the Church were bishops, we'd really be in bad shape because there wouldn't be anybody to carry out the Church's basic mission, i.e., the sanctification of the world. If all we had in the Church were lay people, we'd be in equally bad shape because there wouldn't be anybody deputed by Christ to teach and sanctify and organize the members. The issue is not importance in the Church (i.e., power), but rather the value and meaning of the diversity in the Church. The issue is not who gets to drive the bus, but whether the people on the bus know where it's going and whether they want to go there.

I think this is something to be concerned about. On the one hand, there are misperceptions about clergy. There is clericalism ("The only thing that matters is clergy") and there is anti-clericalism ("Everything bad is the clergy's doing"). And there are misperceptions about and among laity. Sometimes one gets the impression that certain lay people think that the only way their faith life can be of any significance is the extent to which they are engaged in activities within the Church, and that the alternative to being active in the parish and in the diocese is graced passivity, receiving what the Church offers and carefully investing it for one's own personal spiritual development. It is possible for both clergy and lay people to be so focused on the life of the Church that they forget what the life of the Church is for.

Second question: what is ministry and what is it for? This is a semantic question, but not for that reason irrelevant. Unless we all know what we mean by what we say, we end up being unable to understand one another. Ministry means service, and it is by definition a relationship. Whenever we use the term we need to be clear about who is giving the service and for whom, and for what purpose the service is being given. It is correct to say that a priest exercises ministry and that a parish DRE exercises ministry and that lay men and women exercise ministry as they bring up their children or work at their jobs or professions. But in each of these three contexts ministry means something slightly different. In the case of the priest, it means representing Christ the head of the Church for the purpose of building up God's main instrument of salvation. Its source is the sacrament of Orders. In the case of the DRE, it means representing bishop or priest in carrying out a specific task which is part of the mission of the Church for which she or he has been delegated by an ordained representative of the Church. Ultimately, therefore, the source of ecclesial lay ministry is in Holy Orders received by the person who provides delegation to ministry. For the parent, the person with a job, the professional, ministry means striving to make the world more receptive of the salvation of Christ, making Christ present in the home and in the workplace. The source of this basic lay ministry is not Holy Orders but baptism. Not all ministry is the same, and we only invite confusion if we do not take account of its different meanings and sources.

Third question: why is there so much ferment about who is important in the Church and what ministry means? The basic reason, in my opinion, is that the Church is developing an educated and articulate laity. While most members of the

Church may still be content to go through the cafeteria line and take what appeals to them, an increasing number are becoming aware that they have been called to something more than receptivity. Some well educated and reflective lay persons work at deepening their faith so that they can share the salvation they have received with the world around them. I think that this trend is just beginning. Other lay persons, educated and articulate, are clamoring for more say and more participation in the interior life of the Church. Many of this group want to be Church ministers. This is not bad per se, but, if this is all that is ever expected from lay people, we run the risk of trying to turn what is perceived as a clericalized Church into a laicized Church, and forgetting about salvation. I think that, in God's providence, we may be coming to a renewed awareness of what the Church was meant to be and of the various contexts of calling that constitute its life. The Church is not primarily about priests and bishops bossing lay people. The Church is primarily about lay people working for the kingdom.

Conclusion: There is a rich variety of services needed to bring about the kingdom, but there is one single common purpose that we all share, a purpose which, as all canonists know, constitutes the supreme law in the Church, the salvation of souls (cf. can. 1752).

CLSA PROCEEDINGS 64 (2002) 59-72

# THE PARISH AS EMPLOYER

MRS. LINDA A. BUDNEY

The priorities and programs of parish communities have changed in response to the needs and expectations of parishioners, and so have the people who provide this pastoral care. Pastors continue to bear responsibility for serving and leading the parish community, but today those who assist the pastor in his ministry are many and varied, and often employed. Since 1992 there has been a 20% increase in the number of persons serving parish communities in ministerial roles, and more than 70% of these are lay persons.[1] At the same time, the bishops of the United States are increasingly interested in the question of lay ministry, both in the underlying theology which grounds the participation of the laity in parish work and in the practical implications of employing lay persons for parish ministry. Since before the Industrial Revolution the Church has addressed issues related to employment in general and recently has specifically applied these teachings to employees of the Church. In the United States, both canon and civil law include provisions which put these teachings into practice and which constrain or restrict the Church's employment policies. Recent studies have identified trends and pointed out areas of concern related to parish employment, and the bishops of the United States have begun to respond to some of the needs and concerns of Church employees.

Canonists involved in setting employment guidelines, policies and procedures might well be in a position to question whether diocesan and parish policies are consistent with Church teachings and law, so that those who dedicate themselves to the mission of the Church are treated justly and with the dignity envisioned in Catholic social teachings.

*A Rich History of Catholic Social Teaching Should*
*Inform Church Employment Practices*

The social teachings of the Catholic Church have addressed the dignity of labor and the necessity of paying a just wage. In *Rerum Novarum* (*On the Condition of*

---

[1] Philip J. Murnion and David DeLambo, *Parishes and Parish Ministers: A Study of Parish Lay Ministry* (New York: National Pastoral Life Center, 1999): 21-22.

*Labor*), issued on May 15, 1891,[2] Pope Leo XIII addressed the situation of those who did not own property, who were often forced to work in terrible conditions by greedy employers. He was particularly concerned that workers would accept socialism as a way to overcome miserable conditions. Leo sought to establish that there was no inherent conflict between the wealthy and the working class – each needed the other. Laborers were to fully and freely perform the work assigned to them, and employers were to provide a wage that is sufficient to support himself and his family. Leo asserted that natural justice demanded that a wage be sufficient to support a frugal worker, even if the worker could be induced to accept a lower wage.[3]

The encyclical *Quadragesimo Anno* (*Reconstruction of the Social Order*)[4] was issued by Pope Pius XI during the great worldwide depression. In this encyclical he affirmed the dignity of work and of the workers, which demanded that wages be sufficient to support a worker as well as his family. Pope Pius XI named three factors which must be considered in establishing a just wage. The first was the sufficiency of the wage to meet the needs of the worker. The second dealt with the situation of the business. The pope held that workers could not demand wages which would put the business at risk, but neither could businesses use mismanagement as an excuse to lower the wages of workers below what is just. For Pius XI, the third factor in establishing a just wage was a consideration of the common good, especially insofar as the setting of a wage may influence overall employment in society.[5] Pope Pius XII affirmed these prior teachings in his encyclical on the 150th anniversary of the establishment of the hierarchy in the United States (*Sertum Laetitiae*),[6] in which he reiterated that to be just, a wage must be sufficient to maintain a worker and his family.

Pope John XXIII continued this interest in social conditions. In *Mater et Magistra*, he grounded the social teachings of the Church on the dignity of the individual.[7] He upheld the right to a just wage, which he believed could not be determined solely by the market or by the most powerful.[8] In his final encyclical *Pacem in Terris*, John XXIII further developed the right to a just wage as one of

---

[2] Leo XIII, encyclical letter *Rerum novarum*, May 15, 1981: *AAS* 23 (1890-1891): 641-670. English translation from David J. O'Brien and Thomas A. Shannon, *Catholic Social Thought: The Documentary Heritage* (Maryknoll, NY: Orbis Books, 2001): 14-39.

[3] RN 45, 46.

[4] Pius XI, encyclical letter *Quadragesimo Anno*, May 15, 1931: *AAS* 23 (1931): 177-228. English translation from *Catholic Social Thought*, 42-79.

[5] QA 71, 72.

[6] Pius XII, encyclical letter *Sertum Laetitiae*, November 1, 1939: *AAS* 31 (1939): 645-56.

[7] John XXIII, encyclical letter *Mater et Magistra*, May 15, 1961: *AAS* 53 (1961): 401-64. English translation from *Catholic Social Thought*, 84-128. See especially MM 219-220.

[8] MM 71.

the many rights and obligations that flow from the dignity of the human person.[9]

The Fathers of the Second Vatican Council continued to speak of the dignity of work and of the need for justice in the workplace. In the Pastoral Constitution on the Church in the Modern World (*Gaudium et Spes*),[10] the fathers of the Second Vatican Council addressed the dignity of labor and the obligation of society to provide opportunities for employment, and reaffirmed past teachings on a just wage.

Finally, remuneration for work should guarantee man the opportunity to provide a dignified livelihood for himself and his family on the material, social, cultural, and spiritual level to correspond to the role and productivity of each, the relevant economic factors in his employment, and the common good.[11]

Pope Paul VI continued to reinforce the teachings of his predecessors on the dignity of the worker and the need for a remuneration capable of providing not only a minimum standard of living but also the potential for human growth. The pope also noted a right "to assistance in case of need arising from sickness or age."[12] In *Laborem Exercens* Pope John Paul II applied the teachings of the past to the contemporay world.[13] He particularly cautioned against 'economism', or "considering human labor solely according to its economic purpose."[14] Echoing the teachings of his predecessors, John Paul wrote: "Just remuneration for the work of an adult who is responsible for a family means remuneration which will suffice for establishing and properly maintaining a family and providing for its future."[15] He also mentioned other benefits he considered necessary, such as assistance for work-related accidents, health care, a pension and social security for old age, the right to rest (at least on Sunday), vacation, and also a healthy work environment.[16]

---

[9] John XXIII, encyclical letter *Pacem in Terris*, April 11, 1963: *AAS* 55 (1963): 257-304. English translation from *Catholic Social Thought*, 131-62. See PT 11-27.

[10] Vatican II, pastoral constitution *Guadium et spes*, December 7, 1965: *AAS* 58 (1966): 1025-115. English translation from *Vatican Council II: The Conciliar and Post Conciliar Documents*, ed. Austen Flannery, revised (Northport, NY: Costello Publishing, 1992) 903-1001.

[11] *GS* 67. *GS* 74 speaks of the common good as "the sum total of all those conditions of social life which enable individuals, families, and organizations to achieve complete and efficacious fulfillment."

[12] Paul VI, apostolic letter *Octogesima Adveniens,* May 14, 1971: *AAS* 63 (1971): 400-41. English translation from *Catholic Social Thought*, 265-286. *OA* 14.

[13] John Paul II, encyclical letter *Laborem Exercens*, September 14, 1981: *AAS* 73 (1981): 577-647. English translation in *Origins* 11 (September 24, 1981): 225, 227-44.

[14] *LE* 13.

[15] *LE* 19.

[16] *LE* 19.

In modern times the teachings on employment have been applied to practices within the Church. For example, the 1917 *Code of Canon Law* obliged administrators of ecclesiastical goods to pay good and fair wages and also addressed general working conditions.[17] Documents of the Second Vatican Council also touch on Church practices. The Decree on the Church's Missionary Activity calls for salaries to catechists in missionary territories sufficient to provide a decent standard of living and social security (*AG* 17).[18] The Decree on the Apostolate of the Laity commends those who devote their professional skill to Church service and exhorts the pastors of the Church to provide proper support for them and their families (*AA* 22).[19] In 1971, the Second General Assembly of the Synod of Bishops issued a document, *Justice in the World*, in which the rights of those who work for the Church were upheld.[20]

Within the Church, rights must be preserved. No one should be deprived of his ordinary rights because he is associated with the Church in one way or another. Those who serve the Church by their labor, including priests and religious, should receive a sufficient livelihood and enjoy that social security which is customary in their region. Lay people should be given fair wages and a system for promotion.[21]

The bishops of the United States have also gone on record concerning the Church's responsibilities as an employer. In their pastoral letter *Economic Justice for All: Pastoral Letter on Catholic Social Teaching and the U.S. Economy,*[22] the bishops asserted that the social teachings of the Church must apply within the Church as well, and that the faithful may need to increase their support to move

[17] C. 1524. *Codex Iuris Canonici Pii X Pontificis Maximi iussu digestus Benedicti Papae XV auctoritate promulgatus* (Rome: Typis PolyglottisVaticanis, 1917). See the *Report on Collective Bargaining in Church Institutions* (Washington D.C.: Canon Law Society of America, 1987): 6-7, for a brief discussion of this canon; see also Frank D. Almade, *Just Wages for Church Employees* (New York: Peter Lang, 1993): 80-96, for a more detailed discussion of the application of Church teachings to Church employment practices.

[18] Vatican II, decree *Ad gentes*, December 7, 1965: *AAS* 58 (1966): 947-90. English translation from Flannery, 813-62.

[19] Vatican II, decree *Apostolicam actuositatem*, November 18, 1965: *AAS* 58 (1966): 837-64. English translation from Flannery, 766-98.

[20] Synod of Bishops, Second General Assembly, *De Iustitia in Mundo*, November 30, 1971: *AAS* 63 (1971): 923-43. English translation from *Catholic Social Thought*, 288-300. Almade, in *Just Wages for Church Employees*, 83, makes the point that although this document not strictly a papal teaching, the document was published in the *Acta* at the direction of Pope Paul VI.

[21] *Justice in the World*, in *Catholic Social Thought*, 295.

[22] National Conference of Catholic Bishops, "Economic Justice for All: Catholic Social Teaching and the U.S. Economy," *Origins* 16 (November 27, 1986): 410-455.

toward adequate wages and benefits for church employees.[23]

In summary, in its teachings on employment practices, the Church has consistently made the following points. First, the just treatment of workers is grounded in dignity of human person. Second, workers have the right to wages and social benefits sufficient to meet the needs of both worker and family. Third, the condition of the business and the common good must be considered in arriving at a just wage. Finally, these principles apply as well to the Church's employment practices. These principles have consistently been upheld even as economic conditions and systems have evolved. For example, scholastic writers addressed the situation of agricultural workers and indentured servants, Leo XIII of factory workers and miners during the Industrial Revolution, and Pope John Paul II of those "at the 'intellectual workbench' for example, scientists, journalists, teachers, physicians, and office workers."[24]

### The 1983 Code of Canon Law *Incorporates These Teachings in the Canons Which Address the Employment Relationship*

The 1983 *Code of Canon Law* includes two canons that directly address the Church as employer.

> Can. 231 §1. Lay persons who permanently or temporarily devote themselves to special service in the Church are obliged to acquire the appropriate formation required to fulfill their function properly and to carry out this function conscientiously, eagerly, and diligently.
>
> §2. Without prejudice to the prescript of can. 230, §1, and with the prescripts of civil law having been observed, lay persons have the right to decent remuneration appropriate to their condition so that they are able to provide decently for their own needs and those of their family. They also have a right for their social provision, social security, and health benefits to be duly provided.
>
> Can. 1286—Administrators of goods:
> 1° in the employment of workers are to observe meticulously also the civil laws concerning labor and social policy, according to the principles handed on by the Church;
> 2° are to pay a just and decent wage to employees so that they

---

[23] Ibid., n. 351.
[24] Almade, 35.

are able to provide fittingly for their own needs and those of their dependents.[25]

These canons look at the relationship between the lay employee and the employer from two different perspectives. Canon 231 has as its focus those lay employees whom we might call 'professional' – those who are employed in positions of ministry, whether permanently or just for a time. This canon lays out the obligation of these workers to their jobs, and their corresponding right to remuneration. The focus of canon 1286, on the other hand, is on the responsibilities of the administrator (at the parish level the pastor or the one who takes his place) toward all Church employees. Taken together, these canons raise three major considerations: just wages, other benefits, and the relationship between canon law and civil law in employment matters.[26]

### *Church Employment Practices Are Also Influenced by Civil Law*

According to canon 1286 the Church is bound by at least some civil laws that address labor and social policy. In general, churches are bound to observe the federal and state employment and tax laws as are all employers. Churches must withhold income, social security and medicare taxes, comply with minimum wage laws, observe child labor laws, immigration laws, and laws which involve a statutory duty to report certain matters (for example, the sexual abuse of minors).[27] There are, however, laws from which churches are exempt and laws that exempt organizations on the basis of staff size.

Churches are exempted from COBRA (continuation of health insurance after termination), ERISA (employee retirement income security act), state-based unemployment insurance laws (although churches may "opt in" in some cases for some or all employees), and religious discrimination under equal employment laws

---

[25] *Codex Iuris Canonici auctoritate Ioannis Paulii PP. II promulgatus* (Vatican City: Libreria Editrice Vaticana, 1983. English translation from *Code of Canon Law, Latin-English Edition: New English Translation* (Washington, DC: CLSA, 1999) All subsequent English translations of canons from this code will be taken from this source unless otherwise indicated.

[26] *Report on Collective Bargaining in Church Institutions* (Washington, DC: CLSA, 1987): 4-8. See also Diane L. Barr, "The Obligations and Rights of the Lay Christian Faithful," in *New Commentary on the Code of Canon Law*, ed. John P. Beal et al. (New York/Mahwah, NJ: Paulist Press, 2000): 301-3, and Robert T. Kennedy, "The Administration of Goods," in Beal, 1488-90. Other canons apply indirectly to the employment relationship, for example, the canons which set forth the rights of the Christian faithful and the laity.

[27] Although there are helpful guides to employment law (for example The American Bar Association (ABA), *Guide to Workplace Law* (New York: Three Rivers Press, 1997) and, for dioceses in Indiana, William J. Wood, *Indiana Pastors' Legal Handbook* 3rd edition (Indianapolis: The Indiana Catholic Conference, 2001), opinions should be sought from knowledgeable civil attorneys before formulating policies or taking actions which appear contrary to or outside existing employment policies.

– even for so-called 'secular work'. Laws from which any organization may be exempt because of staff size include the Family and Medical Leave Act (FMLA) and the Worker Adjustment Retraining Notification Act (WARN).[28]

### Implementation of Church Teachings, Canon and Civil Law at the Diocesan and Parish Levels

It is most frequently at the diocesan or parish level that both canon and civil laws are brought to bear on specific employment policies and procedures. There are two different ways of interpreting the Church's requirements to observe civil legislation in employment policies.[29] The "narrow" interpretation holds that only those provisions intended by the civil government to apply to the Church must be implemented in Church practices. A broader interpretation, however, would hold that all those laws to which Church defers should be observed, even those provisions to which the Church is not bound by civil law.[30] This distinction is particularly relevant when civil laws from which the Church is exempt incorporate values found in magisterial teachings, for example continuation of health benefits coverage for a time after an employee is terminated.

It is also important for those drafting policies to obtain counsel on relevant local legislation. In some cases, for example, states have expanded the number of classes covered in anti-discrimination laws[31] and local jurisdictions often address exceptions to at-will employment policies.[32] There may be additional complexities if a diocese spans multiple civil jurisdictions. For example, the archdiocese of Washington, DC includes parts of the state of Maryland, as does the diocese of Wilmington, Delaware.

### What Is the Employment Situation for Employees of Catholic Parishes and What Are Their Concerns?

To what extent is are the laws of the Church and the social teachings on which they are based implemented in the United States? Some studies suggest that improvements are needed for the Church to be an authentic witness to its own teachings on employment practices. The results of the following four studies provide some insight into the employment situation in the United States.

---

[28] William P. Daly and Ellen Doyle, "Workplace Justice: Guidance for Church Leaders," *Church Personnel Issues* (April 2000): 3.

[29] C. 22: Civil laws to which the law of the Church yields are to observed in canon law with the same effects, insofar as they are not contrary to divine law and unless canon law provides otherwise.

[30] *Report on Collective Bargaining in Church Institutions*, 3.

[31] ABA, 9-13.

[32] Ibid., 82-85.

A survey of employees not serving in ministry-related positions revealed that they were not being paid adequately by several just-wage standards and that benefits were inadequate. The survey was conducted in 1989, and targeted employees who were neither covered by union contracts or diocesan agreements, nor represented by professional organizations. The survey revealed that on average these wages were less than half the minimum standards using two different criteria. The highest paid of these positions – business manager – was thousands of dollars less than the Pennsylvania or national standard figures. Some were not paid overtime above their hourly rate and had not been given guidelines regarding sick leave, vacation and personal days.[33]

Research conducted by the National Pastoral Life Center found that the number of employees in ministry-related positions has increased by 35% since 1992, while the number of parish priests has declined by 12%. Lay ministers can be found in 63% of parishes, up from 54% in 1992.[34] In the 1992 survey 42% were religious; this percentage had dropped to 28.9 in 1997.[35] 66 2/3% of the lay parish members had worked previously in another parish, leaving previous jobs for career enhancement, family or personal reasons, and some because of employment conditions.[36] They were drawn to parish ministry by a sense of call by God, an attraction to the work, and many by an invitation by the pastor or other staff members.[37] Far more important to the pastors than academic preparation is the ability to relate well to others,[38] although 33 1/3% of the lay ministers and more than 75% of the religious have masters' degrees.[39] The trend seems to be toward a lay, feminine, local and ministerial approach to pastoral ministry.[40] These lay ministers report over-all satisfaction with their jobs (including salaries), yet 33 1/3% say salaries are inadequate to meet their needs.[41] It is not surprising that a large percentage express satisfaction – almost 50% of the pastors are looking for persons whose family has another source of income and whose health benefits are covered.[42] Lay ministers also express concerns about job stability, especially with a change in parish leadership.[43]

Focus groups sponsored by the National Association for Lay Ministry provided

---

[33] Almade, 97-113.

[34] Murnion, 21-22.

[35] Ibid., 23.

[36] Ibid., 42.

[37] Ibid., 38-42.

[38] Ibid., 40.

[39] Ibid., 27.

[40] Ibid., 22-24.

[41] Ibid., 60.

[42] Ibid., 42.

[43] Ibid., 43.

anecdotal evidence as to job satisfaction and concerns of lay employees in ministry-related positions. Salary and benefits are cited as inadequate, financial support for education and formation is inadequate and lacking, and the lay ministers often do not experience the credibility and respect that they believe are enjoyed by priests and religious.[44]

A study sponsored by the National Conference of Diocesan Directors found that Church professional employees on the average received compensation below that needed to meet the ordinary rights of a family with a thrifty budget, even when non-cash compensation had been valued and added in.[45] Concerning those social benefits seen as integral to human dignity in Church teachings – for example, provision for old age, this study found that "except where required by law, Church employers do not provide adequate coverage of these basic rights."[46]

### *Eliminating Any Disparity Between What the Church Teaches and Current Employment Practices*

In the 1980 pastoral *Called and Gifted*, the bishops of the United States acknowledged the increasing involvement of lay men and women in the ministerial life of the American parish. The bishops also observed that a number of lay persons were preparing themselves professionally to work in the Church, and that many had been hired into positions of leadership.[47] These the bishops referred to as ecclesial ministers, and as a group they are the subject of the project now undertaken by the Subcommittee on Lay Ministry, Committee on the Laity of the U.S. Conference of Catholic Bishops. In 1995 this subcommittee began the Leadership for Lay Ecclesial Ministry Project. The objectives of this project were 1) to provide the bishops with information so that they could better respond with appropriate policies and pastoral practices, 2) to encourage conversation among interested groups to understand the distinct place of lay ministers in parish ministry, and 3) to propose to the bishops a long range plan for exercising leadership for ecclesial lay ministry.[48] The subcommittee sponsored an update to the 1992 survey on law parish ministers, requested input from bishops, lay ministry organizations, diocesan staff and graduate program administrators to identify areas of interest and concern, and sponsored focus groups of bishops to obtain their interests and

---

[44] Dennis Beeman, Philip Dougherty et al, *No Turning Back: A Lay Perspective on Ministry in the Catholic Church in the United States* (Chicago: National Association for Lay Ministry, 1998): 19-33.

[45] *Just Wages and Benefits for Lay and Religious Church Employees: A Final Report* (Washington, DC: National Conference of Diocesan Directors of Religious Education, 1990): 26-36.

[46] Ibid., 33.

[47] Committee on the Laity, National Conference of Catholic Bishops, *Lay Ecclesial Ministry: The State of the Questions* (Washington, DC: USCC, 1999): 2.

[48] *Lay Ecclesial Ministry: The State of the Questions*, 4.

insights. The following topics emerged as important to all consulted: "the term 'lay minister', a theology of lay ministry, the formation of lay ministers, the relationship between lay ministers and ordained ministers, the financial and human resource issues connected with lay ministry, [and] the multicultural issues connected with lay ministry."[49]

Looking at the results of the work of the subcommittee and of the studies discussed earlier, several issues emerge as being important to both the lay ministers and the bishops. Canonists can contribute to this discussion by asking if proposed and existing personnel policies are consistent with Church teachings and law.

### *Is this Compensation System Just?*

A conclusion of the Subcommittee reads in part: "We encourage dioceses and parishes to address creatively the issue of just compensation, which includes both salaries and benefits for lay ecclesial ministers."[50] The effort required to ensure that Church personnel are compensated justly for their work requires that those responsible for setting salaries understand the criteria for determining that a given wage is "just" for the work performed.

William Daly offers a framework for determining a system of just wages for church employees. He cites three considerations: a just wage must be sufficient to meet the needs of the employee; the wage must reward employees for their contributions to the organization; and the relationship among wage rates in a given organization must be reasonable.[51]

The sufficiency standard is applied to those at the lowest level of the pay scale, and asks if the wages are sufficient to cover the necessities of life. Noting that a salary based on the minimum wage would fall below the federal poverty level for a head of household with even one child,[52] Daly discusses three methods of arriving at a living wage. The first is the living wage movement, which organizes to introduce legislation at the local level to pay government workers and contractors a basic living wage, which is often pegged to the poverty line. A second approach involves determining a wage based on an estimated budget for a low-income family. These estimates draw from a number of sources – the Departments of Agriculture and Labor for example – and can be used to calculate a basic hourly which will provide for a family's basic needs. A final method uses data from the Department of Labor's Consumer Expenditure Survey, which tracks income and expenditures, placing a living wage at that point where income and expenditures

---

[49] Ibid., 5.

[50] Ibid., 48.

[51] William P. Daly, "The Just Wage: A Theoretical Framework and Practical Applications, Part 1," *Church Personnel Issues* (March, 2001): 1-3.

[52] Ibid., 4.

are roughly equal.[53]

Daly cautions that once a wage is established it must be adjusted to provide for increases in the cost of living, and also for geographic differences (since the calculation methods use national data the rate must reflect local income and expenses).[54]

The equity standard addresses the extent to which employees are recognized and paid for their contributions to the organization. The determination of a just wages for the skilled employees of an organization involves a consideration of internal equity (the value of positions within an organization), external equity (how the pay structure compares with those of similar organizations) and individual equity (how a given employee's pay compares with that of others doing the same job, taking length of service and performance into account).[55]

According to Daly, "[i]nternal equity addresses pay equity within the organization at the level of the position. It establishes a set of compensable levels, so that positions requiring more skill and responsibility emerge at higher levels and those requiring less skill and responsibility settle into lower levels."[56] To determine external equity, employers compare their pay programs with those of like organizations. This can be a complicated task in that the employer must select the best job markets to use in the comparison and must decide which specific positions to use as the basis for the comparison.[57] Individual equity takes into account the capabilities and performance of individual employees as they compare with others doing the same type of work.[58]

Finally, the reasonableness standard of the just wage addresses the wages of the most highly paid employees in terms of the relationship between the wages of the most highly and least compensated employees.[59] While salaries must be adequate to attract and keep experienced executives, compensating the highest paid of employees must not prevent paying a just wage to the least paid in the organization.[60]

Regarding benefits, two issues are of special concern. The first is the degree to which the local church follows the spirit of the law in determining whether to comply with legislation from which it might be exempt. Does the church do only

---

[53] Ibid., 4-8.

[54] Ibid., 9-10.

[55] William P. Daly, "The Just Wage: A Theoretical Framework and Practical Applications, Part 2," *Church Personnel Issues* (May, 2001): 1.

[56] Ibid., 2.

[57] Ibid., 4-6.

[58] Ibid., 7-8.

[59] William P. Daly, "The Just Wage: A Theoretical Framework and Practical Applications, Part 3," *Church Personnel Issues* (July, 2001): 1.

[60] Ibid., 8.

what it must under civil law or does it try to achieve the ideals espoused in its teachings? The second is the extent to which Church employers might attempt to avoid paying benefits to employees. For example, if diocesan plans require an employee to work a certain number of hours per week to be eligible for benefits, is there a pattern of hiring persons to work just under that level of effort?

Of course, efforts to establish a just compensation package for Church employees are complicated by the limited financial resources of parishes and dioceses. Church teachings on the just wage require us to consider the financial situation of the employer. The financial situation of many Catholic parishes is far from healthy. By the 1980s the contribution of Catholics had declined by 50% (by percentage of income) from 1963 contributions.[61] The study on lay ministry published in 1999 found that in 28.6% parishes did not have sufficient income to meet expenses. While this can be partially explained by a growth in income of Catholics which outstripped any growth in donations, Catholics still lag behind others. Bishops and pastors must impress on the faithful the need to compensate employees fairly and the financial resources needed to do so, but Church administrators must also review the efficiency and priorities of the employing institution to ensure that a just compensation package has a high priority.

### Does this Personnel System Recognize a Need for Formation and Education of Lay Parish Ministers?

The bishops of the United States have recognized that lay ecclesial ministers need an adequate preparation for their work – which hopefully will result in the personal, academic and professional competencies needed for a given ministry position.[62] However, the different paths by which lay men and women come to ministry in the Church demand some flexibility in how and when this preparation is provided. Are required competencies identified before a position is filled?[63] Are these competencies assessed during the hiring process? Is growth recognized and affirmed (with salary increases for example) after a person is already employed? How is it determined whether a given employee has the skills and education needed? Organists can pass proficiency exams administered by neutral parties, but relational-based competencies are more difficult to judge and require a greater commitment of time and effort on the part of the supervising minister.

---

[61] Almade, 125. See also Andrew M. Greeley and William McManus, *Catholic Contributions: Sociology and Policy* (Chicago: Thomas More Press, 1987): 21-60.

[62] *Lay Ecclesial Ministry: The State of the Questions*, 25-41.

[63] See for example *Competency-Based Certification Standards for Pastoral Ministers, Pastoral Associates, Parish Life Coordinators*, developed by the National Association for Lay Ministry, Inc. in 1994.

The bishops of the United States recognize the need for policies and procedures "that guarantee that policy and not personal biases determine continued employment or termination."[64] Most workers in the Church are employed at well. Indeed, most employees in the United States are employees at will, which means that the employer may terminate an employee with no prior notice for any reason. The employee is free to leave as well.[65] The positions of parish workers are particularly vulnerable in at will employment, given the authority of the pastor to hire and terminate employees. Nancy Stevens has pointed out that although magisterial teaching has upheld the right to employment, the "right to reasonable employment security does not mean the right to a particular job. Rather it refers to an employee's right to expect to remain in his/her present employment unless circumstances dictate otherwise, it is a right to reasonable security against arbitrary dismissal."[66]

There are however, employment relationships which protect the worker from arbitrary dismissal while safeguarding the ability of the employer to be an effective steward of parish or diocesan resources. The first is through provision of an ecclesiastical office. In general an office is not lost with a change in the conferring official (c. 184, §2), and the ways in which an office can be lost is regulated by law (cc. 184-196). This alternative would provide substantial protection for the employee, and the employer could maintain flexibility by establishing terms for these offices.[67] This option seems most suitable for positions with significant ministerial responsibilities where abrupt changes might have an adverse effect on the community.

The second option involves the use of contracts. A contract is a legally binding agreement between two or more persons which effects or prevents some change between them. Its effects are recognized in both civil and canon law.

> Canon 1290: Whatever general and specific regulations on contract and payments are determined in civil law for a given territory are to be observed in canon law with the same effects in a matter which is subject to the governing power of the Church, unless the civil regulations are contrary to divine law or canon law makes some other provision, with due regard for the prescription of can. 1547.

---

[64] *Lay Ecclesial Ministry: The State of the Questions*, 49.

[65] ABA, 78-94.

[66] Nancy S. Stevens, "Reasonable Job Security for the Lay At-Will Employee," *Church Personnel Issues* (December, 1995): 3-4.

[67] Ibid., 4-5.

The use of contracts for parish employees can provide reasonable security for a particular length of time. Contracts also typically establish the responsibilities of the position and the circumstances which could lead to early termination of the agreement.

In the third alternative – a 'for cause' termination policy – employees can only be terminated for those things spelled out in the organization's policies or the employee's contract. To implement such a system, pastors or other employers must establish instruments which set forth the duties of and competencies required for each position, must establish ways of measuring compliance and must evaluate employees on a regular basis. An absence of contrary evidence generally favors the employee.[68]

Given that there are means of protecting both the rights of employees and those of parish employers, it is not clear that 'at will' employment is necessary, even for those positions which involve significant cooperation in fulfilling the obligations of the pastor. Whatever the employment relationship, it seems wise for new pastors to review the responsibilities of each ministry position and make appropriate changes before difficulties and misunderstandings occur.

## Conclusion

It is clear from the decline in the number of priests and religious and the increase in the number of lay persons serving in ministerial roles that the Church is becoming more dependent on its lay parish ministers to provide pastoral care to the faithful. It takes time, effort and a sense of commitment to develop the structures that protect the rights of employees and the discretion of employers. Is it worth it? Perhaps it is easier to ask if Church employers are willing to accept the consequences of *not* ensuring that Church employees are treated justly and in a way consistent with magisterial teachings – a lost opportunity to give witness to those teachings on the dignity of human labor and a failure to retain its moral authority as a voice for the poor and exploited.

---

[68] Christopher G. Ponticello, "'For Cause' and 'At Will' Employment: Legal and Moral Implications for the Church as Employer," *Church Personnel Issues* (September, 1993): 4-6. A discussion of those things needed in a 'for cause' system can be found in William P. Daly, "Key 'For Cause' Personnel Policies," *Church Personnel Issues* (September, 1993): 7-11.

CLSA PROCEEDINGS 64 (2002) 73-96

# THE McGRATH THESIS AND ITS IMPACT
# ON A CANONICAL UNDERSTANDING OF
# THE OWNERSHIP OF ECCLESIASTICAL GOODS

REVEREND DANIEL C. CONLIN

My presentation today is about the McGrath thesis, a civil and canonical theory that was quite influential from the mid-1960s until the mid-1970s, and whose lingering effects are still with us today in the canonical domain of ecclesiastical goods. This talk will not go into detail about the canonical counterpoint argument as found in the early 1970s writings of the then Father Adam Maida (now Cardinal Archbishop of Detroit). For a discussion on that I would suggest reading Father Robert Kennedy's excellent summation, "McGrath, Maida, Michiels: Introduction to a Study of the Canonical and Civil Law Status of Church-Related Institutions in the United States," found in *The Jurist*, 50 (1990): 351-401, especially pages 367 and following, or looking at my doctoral dissertation,[1] especially pages 106 to 123.

My talk will be in four parts. First, I will take an extended look at McGrath's life and *curricular vitae*. Second, will be a look at the influentially wide swath of his legal advice and scholarship. Third, I will delve into his legal theory and its canonical consequences. Fourth, I will look at the difference in McGrath's view between legal and equitable title in regard to ownership of property. Should anyone still be awake at the end of my talk I will be happy to take them to lunch.

## Biographical Background[2]

John J. McGrath was born December 12, 1922 in Pittsburgh, Pennsylvania. His father was an attorney as were several other members of his family. When he was 18, John McGrath's mother and brother tragically perished in a house fire. McGrath attended Duquesne University for his undergraduate and law degrees, the former he received in 1943, the latter in 1947. He served in the army during World

---

[1] Conlin, Daniel C., *Canonical and Civil Legal Issues Surrounding The Alienation of Catholic Health Care Facilities In The United States*, 2000, University of Saint Thomas Aquinas, Rome.

[2] My thanks to Mr. John Kovach, archivist for Saint Mary's College, Notre Dame, Indiana, who made the following information available to me from the Saint Mary's archives in a March 11, 2002 letter with enclosures.

73

War II and practiced law in his native city of Pittsburgh from 1947-1950 before entering Mount Saint Mary's of the West seminary. He was ordained a priest at age 31 on May 29, 1954 for the Diocese of Steubenville in Ohio and served briefly there as assistant pastor, assistant chancellor, assistant secretary of the diocesan tribunal and professor of canon law in the diocesan seminary.

Father McGrath received a doctorate in canon law from the Catholic University of America in 1957. The title of his dissertation was: *Comparative Study of Crime and Its Imputability in Ecclesiastical Criminal Law and in American Criminal Law.* That dissertation might be worth rereading in the light of this past year's focus on priestly misconduct. In January 1958, Fr. McGrath joined the Catholic University faculty as a professor of canon law.

Father McGrath was also one of the first associate priests of the secular institute of Madonna House in Combermere, Ontario founded by the Servant of God Catherine de Hueck Doherty. McGrath helped during the mid-1950s and later with the original constitution and revision of the Madonna House rule and he was a regular supplier of civil and legal advice to that community. McGrath first heard of Madonna House when he went on a two week vacation shortly after being ordained. He was in Toronto and picked up a book written by Eddie Doherty, Catherine's husband. McGrath read the book in one sitting and the very next day took a several hour bus ride to Combermere. He officially became an associate priest on August 15, 1963.[3]

In addition to teaching, Fr. McGrath also served as assistant to the vice-rector for student affairs and from 1958-1960 as administrator of the School of Law of The Catholic University of America. He was the first priest admitted (1955) to practice before the Supreme Court of the United States and the courts of the State of Pennsylvania.[4] He was a staff editor of the *New Catholic Encyclopedia* from

---

[3] September 25, 2002 phone conversation with Bonnie Staib, the archivist of Madonna House, Combermere, Ontario.

[4] Father McGrath was very careful to follow the 1917 *Code of Canon Law.* In accordance with canon 139.3 of the 1917 code, McGrath wrote his chancellor for the bishop's permission to be admitted to the bar of the Supreme Court of the United States. McGrath wrote in a January 15, 1955 letter: "I understand clearly that under canon 139.3 clerics are forbidden to practice the profession of lawyers without proper permission. I shall not file application until I hear the Bishop's decision from you." The chancellor, Monsignor Henry B. O'Donnell, replied on January 18, 1955: "His Excellency has asked me to inform you that he gives you this permission with the understanding that at no time will you practice before the Court." McGrath possessed the capacity to practice before the United States Supreme Court but not the ecclesial permission. This kind of intersection between the worlds of civil law and ecclesial law would be a signature point of McGrath's life as a priest and a canonist. My thanks to Mrs. Linda A. Nichols, Chancellor of the Diocese of Steubenville, for making diocesan McGrath archival material available to me in a July 24, 2002 personal correspondence.

Canon 139.3 reads: "Without the permission of their Ordinary, they [clerics] shall not go into the conduct of goods belonging to lay persons or into secular offices requiring the duty of rendering accounts; they shall not act in the role of procurator or advocate except in ecclesiastical tribunals or in civil [cases] that involve their goods or the goods of their church; in lay criminal trials threatening grave

1963-1966 as well as an associate editor of *The Jurist*. During the summer of 1963, McGrath traveled extensively in Panama, Nicaragua, Costa Rica, Honduras, and El Salvador. His interest in Latin America continued during a Fulbright Scholar sabbatical year (1965-1966) spent teaching at the University of Chile in Santiago, Chile.

In November of 1967, at age 44, McGrath was named the acting president of Saint Mary's College in Notre Dame, Indiana. He took office in January, 1968 and was appointed president in June of 1968. He was installed as the no longer acting president but now actual president on September 29, 1968, the first man to ever lead that all womens' college in its then 124 year history. In May of 1968 he was made a monsignor.

The school newspaper for St. Mary's College, entitled *Crux*, ran a column from the National Catholic News Service that described Fr. McGrath's appointment as acting president this way. I will quote it at some length.

"Father McGrath said he agreed to accept the acting presidency of St. Mary's College with some reluctance, but at the urging of high officials in Catholic education. The officials want Father McGrath to conduct a transfer of control at St. Mary's similar to the reorganizations at St. Louis and at the University of Notre Dame and at other Catholic institutions. Saint Mary's, which enrolls 1000 women students, would then become a model for other small Catholic colleges which want to follow the leaders in granting the public a degree of control of and responsibility for Catholic institutions. [. . .]

Father McGrath is the author of a study on the legal status of Catholic institutions in the United States which will be published by the Catholic University. The study is expected to have major repercussions on the 846 hospitals and 381 colleges and universities conducted under Catholic auspices in the U.S.

---

personal penalties [to the defendant], they shall take no part, not even by offering testimony without necessity." Peters, Dr. Edward, Curator, *The 1917 Pio-Benedictine Code of Canon Law*, (Ignatius Press: San Francisco, CA, 2001): 70. The equivalent but modified 1983 *CIC* canon is 285.

Likewise in a March 19, 1962 letter to his bishop, the Most Reverend John King Mussio, McGrath wrote: "Although a book on American law does not fall within the law of canon 1385 and require an imprimatur before publication, canon 1386 does require a secular cleric to obtain the permission of his Ordinary before publishing a book on a profane subject. I am therefore requesting permission of you to edit the above named book [*Church and State in American Law: Cases and Materials*] and have it published by the Bruce Publishing Co. This work does not discuss the attitude of the Church or the canon law on the Church-State relationship. It is a collection of the relevant American law."

Canon 1386 (1917 *CIC*) reads: "Secular clerics are forbidden, without the consent of their Ordinaries, [and likewise] religious without the permission of their major superiors and local Ordinaries, to edit books that treat of profane things and to write for or supervise newspapers, pamphlets and periodical literature." Peters, p. 466. The equivalent but modified 1983 *CIC* canon is 831.

The study will say that a detailed examination of the charters of most of these institutions shows they were never incorporated under canon law and that their incorporation, and only legal status, came entirely through charters granted them by civil authority. The only two exceptions appear to be The Catholic University of America and Niagara University in New York which received charters from Rome, but even in those cases the original, effective charters were granted by the power of American civil authority.

As a result, the study argues, religious orders which operate colleges, universities, and hospitals have no right to conduct the institutions the way they run their own affairs, with a high degree of arbitrariness and accountability only to the rules of their orders and to Rome. [Notice there is no mention of canon law.] Even though conducted under Catholic auspices, they are in a sense, "public" institutions.

Patrick Cardinal Boyle of Washington recently summoned Father McGrath to a meeting to explain his thesis to a group of Catholic legal experts including William R. Consedine, head of the legal department, United States Catholic Conference, and Joseph Gallagher, lawyer for the archdiocese of Baltimore. The lawyers were reportedly impressed with the priest's scholarship. Father McGrath also spent two days explaining the implications of his study to members of the National Conference of Catholic Bishops at their recent meeting in Washington, and has discussed it at a meeting of the Catholic Hospital Association in Chicago.

The study is expected to provide a legal rationale to religious orders who want to follow the mandate of Vatican II to involve lay men more deeply in the administration of their affairs. Many representatives of religious orders have consulted with Father McGrath during the past year and are expected to make announcements in the near future concerning administration of "Church" property."[5]

It is important to notice in this National Catholic News Service article how McGrath is seen in November, 1967 as an expert on the legal standing of Catholic institutions in the United States.

When asked how he had been selected to be the president of St. Mary's, Fr, McGrath replied: "I had known the sisters since last spring. [1967] I had worked closely with the sisters on the changes in their hospitals concerning the board and trustees. I helped them on their general charter last summer, and I just recently gave a speech here several weeks back."[6] The range of his influence can be seen in the following quote from *The Scholastic*:

---

[5] *Crux*, (November 29, 1967): 3-4, "McGrath Study To Have Major Repercussions," William Ryan, National Catholic News Service.

[6] *The Scholastic*, (January 12, 1968): 10.

"At times, Father McGrath has been quite outspoken in his effort to ensure that Catholic universities meet the requirements of a pluralistic society. In his recently published book, *Catholic Institutions in the United States*, Father McGrath argues that since educational institutions are chartered as corporations under American law and are not owned by the sponsoring body, Catholic colleges are governed by civil and not canon law. Consequently, Catholic colleges are serving the public and not the Church and to serve the public best the board of trustees must be composed of persons from all areas which the institutions serve."[7]

In the winter issue of St. Mary's College alumni communiqué, McGrath was asked: "When did you first come into contact with Saint Mary's?" He replied, "Well my original contact was with the hospitals of the Holy Cross Sisters when I was consulted about their legal status – canon law, American law, and so on. This was the Holy Cross Hospital down at Silver Spring, Maryland. From there I was invited to come speak to the Chapter up here."[8] He was also asked "Have you worked specifically with a women's college before?" McGrath responded "Yes, I did. I did one conference for three days with the Sisters of Mercy-their 21 college presidents and mother superiors and I got quite a bit of experience there. I've been to Fontbonne College. I spent a day with them down in St. Louis. In December I'm going to Detroit and I think we'll have about one hundred college presidents there."[9] McGrath had ample access to the leaders of those institutions. His was a fresh and prominent voice and he had the attentive ears of the leaders of Catholic colleges, universities and hospitals, as well as the ears of religious superiors and bishops.

The interview continues: "You had something to do with the reorganization at Notre Dame and St. Louis?" McGrath: "Notre Dame, certainly not! I've never been on Notre Dame's campus except for a ride. I've never met Father Hesburgh or Dr. Schuster, any of the people they've got over there."[10] It is interesting that Fr. McGrath did not tackle the question of his relationship with St. Louis University. It appears that his consultation with St. Louis was on an informal basis[11] as nothing has been found in that university's archives indicating written

---

[7] Ibid.

[8] *Courier*, (Winter, 1968): 3.

[9] Ibid.

[10] Ibid., 4.

[11] "The reconstruction of our board is one of two major administrative changes recently initiated by the University. The second is the legal separation of the University from the Jesuit community at the University. This move not only emphasizes the role of the new board of trustees, but clarifies the relationship of the authority and assets of the Jesuit order to the institution itself. *In accordance with the strongly supported opinion of many canon lawyers,* such a legal separation highlights the true situation in which our hospitals and educational institutions find themselves in the view point of

77

legal advice from McGrath.[12]

On June 9, 1970, Msgr. McGrath died in South Bend, Indiana following a heart attack. He was buried at the cemetery located on the campus of Saint Mary's College. Father Raymond H. Potvin from The Catholic University of America sociology department preached Msgr. McGrath's funeral sermon. Fr. Potvin said:

> "Father McGrath was absolutely convinced that Holy Orders is a social sacrament that sanctifies a man for the benefit of others. During his years in academic life he never forgot that. He was constantly available to those who needed help and he sought out new ministries to preach the Gospel message. Believing firmly that Christ was his brother and his God, Father McGrath became a priest to proclaim this truth and in some way to make it a reality for all men. [. . .]
>
> "At the center of his priesthood as social sacrament, Father McGrath placed the sacrifice of the Mass, Christ offering himself to his Father as the eternal victim. No confusion here about the sacred nature of this ministry! No compromise here with the supernatural functions of his role. Human, relevant and concerned, Father McGrath made the Gospel meaningful for this life but his priesthood remained a forceful testimony of another life, a life of grace and eternal beatitude. In a sense, this is the both the message of his life and of his death."[13]

American civil law, namely, that religious orders do not "own" these institutions in the legal sense, but that they are in fact a "public trust" to be governed and managed by a board of trustees for the public benefit." Reinert, Paul, S.J., "The Role of Religious in Management," *Hospital Progress*, (September, 1967): 100. Reinert's article was adapted from his address to the annual Catholic Health Association convention in June of 1967. Thus, his influence on the legal reconceptualization and reorganization of Catholic hospitals was extensive. The thinking was obvious and understandable: if this kind of new legal organization is good enough for a large and prominent Jesuit university with a hospital, then it must also be good for us smaller religious communities with our less prominent apostolates.

A featured speaker at the 1968 CHA convention was Father John McGrath. The members of the CHA thus heard in successive years an influential practitioner of the McGrath thesis and the originator of the McGrath thesis.

[12] Personal correspondence from Bridget Fletcher, assistant to the president of Saint Louis University, January 30, 2002. In the article cited in footnote four, William Ryan wrote: "Father Paul J. Reinert, S.J., president of Saint Louis University, consulted Father McGrath prior to the major reorganization of the Jesuit university last spring, involving transfer of control to a board of trustees with a majority of laymen including Protestants and Jews." Page three. Father Reinert died July 23, 2001 at the age of 90. He served as president of Saint Louis University from 1949 to 1974 and as chancellor from 1974 to 1990. Clearly, he was considered one of the leaders not only of Jesuit higher education but of all Catholic higher education in the United States for four decades. If the legal advice McGrath gave made sense to Reinert, then the same advice would have made sense to many other presidents.

[13] *Courier*, (Summer, 1970): 7. *Courier* was the alumnae quarterly of Saint Mary's College, Notre Dame, Indiana.

An example of the pervasiveness of McGrath's influence was his participation in a conference on Governance in American Catholic Higher Education held at Loretto Heights College on February 9-10, 1968 "to mark the inauguration of Sister Patricia Jean Mannion as ninth president of the college. One hundred thirty college and university presidents, members of boards of trustees, and experts in higher education participated."[14] McGrath's talk was entitled "Civil and Canonical Legal Status of Catholic Colleges" and his book *Catholic Institutions in the United States: Canonical and Civil Law Status*[15] was one of the readings sent to participants prior to the conference.[16]

Loretto Sister Helen Sanders attended the above mentioned conference and wrote of her hearing Fr. Paul Reinert, S.J., explain the reorganization of St. Louis University. "One of the seminars I attended was conducted by Paul Reinert, S.J. He explained the governance at St. Louis University thus: the president must be a Jesuit. Of 28 on the board, 10 must be Jesuits. Bylaws can be changed only by a two-thirds vote. Since the University was not regarded as ecclesiastical property, "protecting" it as such is irrelevant. It never really belonged to the Jesuits. St. Louis University proceeded on the assumption of the correctness of Father McGrath's thesis."[17] Sister Helen continues: "Briefly, McGrath's thesis is that U.S. colleges by reason of their separate legal incorporation in a particular state and the right that state invests in them to grant degrees thereby become public trusts and become subject to civil law, no longer to canon law. Because Loretto Heights College also proceeded on the assumption of the validity of this new information, it was spared the long ordeal of applying to "Rome" for 'alienation'."[18] This is an interesting, affirmative example of McGrathian influenced absolution from the necessity of following canon law!

In April, 1969 "he went to Rome as delegate to the Conference on Higher Education. On this occasion, representatives of Catholic colleges and universities throughout the world presented three position papers before the Congregation for Catholic Education, papers clarifying the relationship of Catholic universities to the Church, to the entire university community and to the state."[19] McGrath's legal

---

[14] Sanders, Helen, S.L., *More Than A Renewal: Loretto Before and After Vatican II, 1952-1977*, Sisters of Loretto, (Nerinx, Kentucky, 1982): 155.

[15] McGrath, John, J., *Catholic Institutions in The United States: Canonical and Civil Law Status*, The Catholic University of America Press, Washington, D.C., 1968.

[16] Sanders, 155.

[17] Ibid., 155-156.

[18] Ibid., 156.

[19] *Courier*, (Summer, 1970): 2.

advice and consultation was widespread throughout this time.[20] He even was giving interviews to the Catholic press.[21]

[20] Sister Alice Gallin, O.S.U., in her book on the changes in American Catholic higher education notes that all the presidents of American Catholic universities and colleges who made significant changes in the legal relationship between the founder of the apostolate and the apostolate itself "utilized the legal opinion of Msgr. John McGrath," and that "the decisions were based on an assumption that Msgr. McGrath's explanation of property ownership and control was a valid one." Gallin, *Independence and A New Partnership in Catholic Education*, (Notre Dame, Indiana, University of Notre Dame Press, 1996): xiv and xv.

McGrath's influence on Jesuit educational institutions in the United States was extensive. He spoke to all the American provincials of the Society of Jesus. "The first session of their meeting was devoted entirely to a discussion of the timely and rather involved question of ownership, authority, and responsibility in our universities, colleges and high schools. The discussion was led by John J. McGrath, a priest of the Steubenville diocese, who had practiced law before entering the seminary and as a canonist, was then teaching comparative law at The Catholic University of America. He was considered an expert, and his publication on American institutions had been well received." Fitzgerald, Paul, S.J., *The Governance of Jesuit Colleges in the United States, 1920-1970*, (Notre Dame, Indiana, University of Notre Dame Press, 1984): 203. Fitzgerald cites the minutes from the provincials' meeting. Also see: Conn, James, S.J., *Catholic Universities in the United States and Ecclesiastical Authority*, (Roma, Pontificia Universitas Gregoriana, 1991): 200-205, and Doyle, J.A., *Civil Incorporation of Ecclesiastical Institutions: A Canonical Perspective*, (Saint Paul University, Ottawa, 1989): 173.

The eminent historian of the Catholic Church in the United States, Phillip Gleason, also points McGrath's influences on the leaders of Catholic educational institutions. "McGrath's monograph was not published till 1968, but Catholic educators were familiar with his thesis much earlier, and it seems that the NCEA [National Catholic Educational Association] helped to bring it to publication. Although debatable, it was uncritically-indeed, eagerly-embraced by Catholic educators who were persuaded by the substantive considerations already reviewed that laicization was necessary and desirable. But since it was generally accepted, and so effective in countering objections from recalcitrant members of religious communities, the McGrath thesis has to be regarded as a significant factor in the wholesale shift to autonomous boards." Gleason, Phillip, *Contending With Modernity: Catholic Higher Education in the Twentieth Century*, (New York, New York, Oxford University Press, 1995): 316.

Another historian, Joseph Preville, traces the history of McGrath's thinking and writing on the canonical and civil complications of Catholic institutions in the United States. "The Horace Mann ruling [a 1966 United States Supreme Court case in regard to the constitutionality of government financial aid to church-related universities and colleges] persuaded the National Catholic Educational Association to encourage and sponsor a trenchant legal study of American Catholic institutions by Reverend John J. McGrath, a professor of Comparative law in The Catholic University of America. Although a slim volume of less than fifty pages, McGrath's treatise emerged as the legal cornerstone in the nationwide movement of the laicization of boards of trustees and the separate incorporation of sponsoring religious communities from Catholic educational institutions." Preville, Joseph, "Catholic Colleges, the Courts, and the Constitution: A Tale of Two Cases," *Church History*, 58 (1989): 203-204.

[21] The most interesting interview that McGrath gave is found in *The National Catholic Reporter*. "The American bishops have been satisfied to let these institutions get their juridic personality from the state or the federal government as American law, educational or charitable corporations. Therefore, they must be governed by the American law and not by canon law.

"We're holding that the practice of applying canon law to these institutions was erroneous. Canon law does apply to the personal lives of the religious who conduct these institutions, but not to the institutions themselves.

"Another consequence of this is that the institutions are not owned by the Church, but rather the legal title is in the American law corporation. And the general public has an interest as the beneficiary of

McGrath was trying to give fresh scope to old legal dilemmas in regard to ownership of what appeared on the surface to be church property. He was interested in giving civil juridical dimension and recognition to what had increasingly become the prevalent post Vatican II practice of more direct lay involvement in and responsibility for the various institutional apostolates of the Church.

In some ways it was a question of which egg before which chicken, McGrath's theory influencing the change or the extant change waiting for a canonical theory to catch up with the practice?[22] As shown above, it was much more McGrath galloping around the United States giving a legal foundation for the transformation, than it was the transformers hunting for a canon lawyer to give them permission to change their self-understanding of church property ownership.[23]

For McGrath the ownership dilemma was a legal issue of public trust versus ecclesial trust, the authority of the institution before the public versus the authority of the institution before the Church. If the institution served the public it was a public institution. If the institution served only the Church it was a private institution. If the institution served both the public and the Church simultaneously, then the public beneficiary interest trumped the ecclesial interest.

McGrath drew attention to the potential problems regarding the actual legal ownership of Catholic institutions[24] but he did not offer a correct canonical

---

these corporations. The Church or religious merely conduct them for the benefit of the general public." Balcerak, Carl, "Path to Institutions' Autonomy," *The National Catholic Reporter*, (December 20, 1967): 9.

McGrath incorrectly presumes civil juridic personality to be a substitution for and even an exclusion of canonical juridic personality. His legal reasoning also ignores the fact that even though the general public is free to attend Catholic colleges and universities, the founding reason for these schools was to primarily serve Catholics, not the general public. Also, McGrath gives no attention to the possibility of the Church or religious institute as having a beneficial interest in their own schools! Only the general public seems to have such an interest. We will examine this more in the section on legal and equitable title.

[22] "[...] the scholarly voice of Father John J. McGrath began to penetrate the Roman Catholic community. Father McGrath, as an expert in canon law, maintained that all such Roman Catholic institutions had indeed – with or without ecclesiastical permission – alienated (or made legally secular) the property at the moment the institutions were reincorporated as separate legal corporations. And so, it is now more and more generally maintained that the orders do not own the institutions and, therefore, that the institutions are no longer subject through them to hierarchial control." Grennan, Jacqueline, "Juridical Control by the Church," *Journal of Higher Education*, 40 (February, 1969): 104.

[23] "A number of Catholic institutions have taken, and are taking, this step. If there is any lingering ambiguity on the point of ownership it should be dispelled by the McGrath study." McCluskey, Neil, S.J., *Catholic Education Faces Its Future*, (Garden City, New York, Doubleday and Company, 1968): 230.

[24] "The attitude of the general public is influenced by the way in which Catholic institutions are presented to the community. The assets of the hospital or college may be looked upon as the property of the diocese or religious community, in which case the sponsoring body is thought to be quite wealthy. The same institutions can be presented as public institutions not owned but merely conducted under the

solution. One may be inclined to say his legal advice actually exacerbated the canonical landscape.

The problems could be summed up this way: one set of facts (ownership) but two legal systems, canonical and civil, one game but two sets of rules. While it is not always the case that these two legal systems may contradict, it is the case that they will frequently collide before they ever, if ever, harmonize into any kind of complementarity. In short, sometimes both legal systems cannot be applied equally or at all to the same set of facts. An ecclesial institution thus finds itself with canonical and civil legal questions about ownership but with two sets of rules, two sets of answers and two sets of competing parents. McGrath taught that the civil eclipsed the canonical.

In the 1960s and 1970s many Catholic colleges, universities and hospitals were creating brand new boards of trustees. It is interesting that the phrase "boards of trustees" does not appear in either the 1917 nor the 1983 *Codes of Canon Law.* What were once the equivalent of a small family business had now become a large public concern with many stockholders that required new ways of administering and financing. Newly configured and constituted boards of trustees with a predominantly non-religious membership now seemed the administratively prudent decision to make. And Fr. John J. McGrath had already plowed the soil and planted the legal seeds for a new harvest of ecclesial apostolate administration.

*McGrath's Canonical and Civil Legal Theory*

Monsignor McGrath's canonical influence was pervasive in that he was intensely interested in the civil status of ecclesial institutions with the accent stress always falling in favor of the civil over the ecclesial legal interests. He was the progenitor of a modern way of understanding the intersecting and sometimes conflicting relationship between canon law and civil law in regard to an understanding of institutional ownership of what appeared to be church property. His canonical theory, commonly called the McGrath thesis,[25] was almost prevented

auspices of the diocese or religious community. The image is then one of service, and the meager income of the religious staff is the Church's witness to poverty." McGrath, p. 3. He continues: "It is the thesis of this study that a proper understanding of the *legal status* of these institutions offers the solution to many of these problems." McGrath, p. 4.

Other problems would include the extended and even enormous potential liability for religious communities being held fiscally responsible for their institutions' malpractice.

[25] There is some question as to how accurate this appellation actually is. In the foreword of his book, McGrath writes: "The author is deeply indebted to the Reverend John J. Zemanick of the Society of St. Edmund, and Mr. Donald J. Frickel, who did the basic research in canon law and American law respectively. All three of us are indebted to Miss Carol Baldwin, for her patient typing and reading of the manuscript and endless attention to details." P. viii. Also see the review written by Father Zemanick of McGrath's book for which he served as canon law researcher. "Father McGrath, associate professor of Comparative Law at Catholic University, worked closely with the author of this review on the study

from seeing published daylight.[26]

The simplest way to summarize his thesis is the following: at the moment of an apostolate's civil incorporation, the incorporated institution ceased to be ecclesiastical goods. It was civil law that caused this transformation, not canon law, and therefore canonical permission was not necessary for the civil restructuring.[27] McGrath wanted to examine the dual nature "[. . .] of those

---

of the legal status of Catholic institutions in the U.S." Zemanick, John J., "A Summary Review: Catholic Institutions in the U.S.: Canonical and Civil Legal Status," *Hospital Progress*, (January, 1968): 46. In addition to the conflict of interest found in reviewing a book on which one collaborated, Zemanick's choice of words is quite interesting: McGrath worked closely with the author of this review, not the author of this review worked closely with McGrath. Alice Gallin diplomatically muses: "In the light of Father Robert Kennedy's [found in *The Jurist* 50 (1990): 351-401] critique of McGrath, one wonders if the basic research may have suffered from this delegation to a student." Gallin, Alice, p. 154, note one.

[26] For an interesting look at an attempt to derail or at least delay the publication of McGrath's work, see: Lynch, John E., C.S.P., "Laying Down the (Canon) Law at Catholic University," *The Jurist*, 50 (1990): 39-40. Lynch's research in the faculty minutes revealed that Fr. McGrath reported at a faculty meeting in November, 1967, that John Cardinal Cody of Chicago wanted to delay the publication of McGrath's book. McGrath told the faculty that "no objection whatever to the manuscript was made by the many legal experts who read it or were consulted." Lynch, p. 39. That is an attention grabbing assertion, namely that "many legal experts" would not raise even one objection with McGrath when later McGrath's thesis was so discredited. In McGrath's own words: "Finally, this study is indebted to many consultants too numerous to mention, who gave of their time and knowledge." McGrath, *Catholic Institutions in the United States: Canonical and Civil Legal Status*, (Washington, D.C., The Catholic University Press, 1968): viii. As Lynch puts it, "either the alleged intervention ceased or faculty indignation prevailed," for McGrath's book was published shortly thereafter. Lynch, p. 39.

[27] "Charitable and educational institutions chartered as corporations under America law are not *owned* by the sponsoring body. The legal title to the real and personal property is vested in the corporation. It is the corporation that cares for the sick or grants academic degrees. It is the corporation that buys and sells and borrows money. If anyone *owns* the assets of the charitable or educational institution, it is the general public. Failure to appreciate this fact has led to the mistaken idea that the property of the institution is the property of the sponsoring body." McGrath, p. 33.

William Bassett defines McGrath's thesis this way: "McGrath's thesis was, in substance, that a state-granted civil charter of incorporation created an essentially secular entity, regardless of the religious motivation underlying its creation and operation by the sponsoring church or religious organization." Bassett, William, W., "The American Civil Corporation, the "Incorporation Movement" and the Canon Law of the Catholic Church," *The Journal of College and University Law*, 25 (Spring, 1999): 735. Bassett is a professor of law at the University of San Francisco. He holds, and I concur, that McGrath "was wrong in both canon and civil law. The result of this flawed study, however, was revolutionary. [...] The wish became word." Pp.731-732.

Bassett believes that the fundamental flaw of McGrath's thesis lies at the level of the effects of separate civil incorporation. "Incorporation, in and of itself, has no real effect upon the religious nature of a church organization. Nor should it. The constitutionally-protected right of citizens to assemble and form cooperative ventures is not conditioned or burdened in state law upon abdication of religious faith or mission. To hold otherwise, would fly in the face of the most basic constitutional jurisprudence.

Incorporation itself is religiously and legally neutral. It does not secularize a religious organization, nor within the church itself does it change the canonical status of its assets. Incorporation has no more legal significance in this respect than inclusion of a church in a local fire district.

Incorporation, indeed, is a valuable tool to protect the religious nature of the organization, when

institutions chartered by authority of state or federal law that are conducted under the auspices of the Catholic Church."[28] Catholic institutions were now considered by McGrath as public institutions and not just Catholic institutions. It was as if Catholic institutions were to be considered in the same way as a public utility, serving only the public good.

If McGrath's thesis was legally accurate, then logically one would have had to hold that when the province of a religious institute was civilly incorporated, this province had thereby disassociated itself from the Church, even though the purpose of seeking civil law incorporation was to follow canon law by protecting ecclesiastical goods through civilly valid means.[29] Clearly, the intention of such incorporation would be to remain under canon law with concomitant civil protection of ecclesiastical goods.[30]

However, McGrath's thesis does not allow for this possibility.[31] A strict application of McGrath's thesis would hold that no religious entity could remain a religiously owned entity if it sought civil law protection through civil law incorporation. The realization of civil incorporated ownership requires the sacrifice of religious ownership. Manifestly, that position is clearly contrary to the United States constitutional provision for free exercise of religion, not to mention the codal intention to use civil law when it contradicts neither divine law nor canon law.

Another flaw in McGrath's theory is that he did not point out that canonical ownership does not depend upon civil law recognition of the Church's right to own ecclesiastical goods.[32] Thus, the Church could recognize the validity of civil ownership expressed through civil incorporation, and still claim to retain canonical

---

properly done, to assure by charters and by-laws choices of board members and officers who believe in the charism of the sponsoring, faith-based community, as well as operation of the organization according to the discipline of the church." Pp. 743-744.

[28] McGrath, p. vii.

[29] See canon 1529 from the 1917 code. "Whatever the civil law establishes in a territory concerning contracts, whether in general or in specific, whether nominate or innominate, and about resolution, is to be observed in canon law in ecclesiastical materials with the same effects, unless this is contrary to divine law or canon law provides otherwise." Peters, p. 512. The corresponding canon from the 1983 code is canon 1290.

[30] It is speculatively interesting to wonder what McGrath would have thought in civil law terms in regard to religious who, through vows, canonically relinquish individual ownership of goods.

[31] "The Church has placed its personnel and resources at the service of the general public in a unique manner proper to the American legal system and not foreseen by the canon law." McGrath, p. 32.

[32] Canon 1495: 1. "The Catholic Church and the Apostolic See have the native right freely and independently from any civil power of acquiring, retaining, and administering temporal goods for the pursuit of their own ends. 2. Individual churches and other moral persons that have been erected into juridic personality by ecclesiastical authority have the right , according to the norm of the sacred canons, of acquiring, retaining, and administering temporal goods." Peters, p. 500. The corresponding canon from the 1983 code is canon 1255. Also see canons 1496 (1983 *CIC* c. 1260) and 1499 (1983 *CIC* cc. 1256 and 1259).

ownership of the civilly incorporated apostolate.[33] However, in McGrath's view, the Church could not hold both of these positions simultaneously because he believed that civil incorporation automatically and fully separated the civil corporation from the Church's canon law.

McGrath was trying to explore via a study of civil and canon law the relationship between the public's stake in an institution and the Church's stake in that same institution. His own thinking about this relationship seems to have changed substantially in one decade.[34] McGrath never satisfactorily explains why civil law must always be followed whereas canon law need not always be followed. In fact, McGrath seems to reverse himself in 1968 from an earlier statement he wrote concerning the relationship between civil law and canon law.[35]

## The Difference Between Legal and Equitable Title

Perhaps the most significant key to the McGrath thesis is the distinction he makes between legal and equitable title in regard to the ownership of a corporation.[36] He holds that the equitable title to a charitable corporation is vested

[33] Canon 1489: 1. "Hospitals, orphanages, and other similar institutes destined for works of religion or charity, whether spiritual or temporal, can be erected by the local Ordinary, and by his decree they are constituted juridic persons in the Church." Peters, p. 498. There is no corresponding canon in the 1983 code.

[34] "The purpose of this study is to examine the legal status of these institutions. They are, at the same time, both private and public institutions. They serve the general public and yet are faithful to the ideals and principles of Catholicism. This duality has led to conflicting practices by the administrators of these institutions. The civil law, obviously, must be followed at all times, but the canon law of the Church is often ignored or applied when it is not relevant." McGrath, p. 3.

[35] "In those external matters which affect property or civil rights which flow from or are dependent upon ecclesiastical discipline, the courts are bound to accept as definitive, and enforce, the ecclesiastical law." McGrath, John J., "Canon Law and American Church Law: A Comparative Study," *The Jurist*, 18 (1958): 270.

McGrath even cites at length the following passage from a 1952 landmark United States Supreme Court case, Kedroff vs. St. Nicholas Cathedral: "There are occasions when civil courts must draw lines between the responsibilities of church and state for the disposition or use of property. Even in those cases when the property right follows as an incident from decisions of the church custom or law on ecclesiastical issues, the church rule controls. This under our Constitution necessarily follows in order that there may be free exercise of religion." McGrath, p. 270.

The problem, of course, is that ecclesiastical tribunals are almost never used when questions and problems concerning ecclesiastical goods arise. Where McGrath seems most consistent in his approach is his statement that in the United States "most of the conflicts with the state arise in the field of property, and property rights." P. 275. Thus, the Church faces the situation where the most common conflict with the civil realm is perhaps the least common point of intersection with the canonical realm.

[36] "The ownership of corporation property is in the nature of a trustee relationship. The business corporation holds legal title to the property in its own name, but must use the property for the benefit of its stockholders. The corporation is the trustee; the stockholders are the beneficiaries. The corporation has legal title; the stockholders have equitable title. Equitable ownership gives the stockholder certain rights which the courts will enforce: he can bring suit to prevent the board of

in the general public who is the direct beneficiary of the corporation's existence. Therefore, equitable title is not vested in the ecclesiastical institution that created the charitable corporation. Thus, the selling, merging or giving away of the property is not subject to the canon law of the Church because the equitable title to the property is held by the public and not the Church. "If anyone owns the assets of the charitable or educational institution, it is the general public. Failure to appreciate this fact has led to the mistaken idea that the property of the institution is the property of the sponsoring body."[37]

If McGrath's thesis was indeed not only extensively operative but also legally accurate, then "an adherent to McGrath's thesis could argue that almost all Catholic institutions, in the United States at least, were exempt from ecclesiastical administrative control because of their civil incorporation."[38] One would be hard pressed to conclude that this kind of exemption was the intention of the founders of the apostolates, and that this exemption would be the preferable canonical scenario.

Even if an institution had received canonical juridic personality, McGrath

---

directors from mismanagement of the assets of the corporation; he has a right to share in any profits; he has a right to a proportionate share of the assets if the corporation is dissolved. Members have ownership of whatever stock they hold, which gives them an equitable interest in the assets of the corporation, but *legal title to the corporate property is vested in the corporation.*

"In applying this concept to the charitable corporation, the true ownership of the property of educational institutions and hospitals becomes evident. Legal title to the property is vested in the corporation, just as in a business corporation, but there are no stockholders to hold the equitable title. In a business corporation the equitable title is held by those who are entitled to, and who receive, the *benefit* of the enterprise of the corporation. Who, then, is entitled to and receives the benefit of the enterprise of a charitable corporation? Since the charitable corporation is created to serve the general public, the equitable title to charitable corporate property is vested in the general public.

"In a business corporation the property is distributed, upon dissolution, to its stockholders or members, but the property of a charitable corporation, upon dissolution, is ordinarily distributed by the courts to another charitable corporation of similar purpose. Even in dissolution the public receives the benefit of a charitable corporation's property." McGrath, pp. 8-9

[37] McGrath, p. 33. McGrath makes this idea even more sharply: "The property, real and personal, of Catholic hospitals and educational institutions which have been incorporated as American law corporations is the property of the corporate entity and not the property of the sponsoring body or individuals who conduct the institution. All property must be used in accordance with the corporate purposes as defined in the charter, and any property acquired from a donor who has stipulated a specific use must be used for that purpose.

There is no question of dealing with ecclesiastical property when speaking of the property of Catholic hospitals and higher educational institutions in the United States. The canon law is clear that property is ecclesiastical only when it belongs to some ecclesiastical person. Since the institutions under consideration have not themselves been established as moral persons and, since no other moral person in fact holds title to the property of the institution, their assets are not ecclesiastical property." McGrath, p. 24.

[38] Dunn, Beverly Katherine, *Sponsorship of Catholic Institutions, Particularly Health Care Institutions, By The Sisters of Providence in the Western United States,* 1995, University of Saint Paul, Ottawa, p. 62.

doubted that this would make any significant difference. He mentions that the only two American universities to have been erected as "canonical moral persons," The Catholic University of America (1889) and Niagara University (1956), "[. . .] accepted civil law charters as American corporations prior to their canonical establishment by the Holy See."[39]

His argument seems to be that bestowal and possession of canonical juridic personality which occurs after reception of civil legal personality makes the former subservient to the latter.[40] If that were actually true, then (assuming the law itself has not created the apostolate or institution as a public juridic person) whether or not an apostolate or institution has a decree conferring juridic personality, would be irrelevant when the civil decree of incorporation has preceded the canonical decree of juridic personality. In effect, "McGrath contended that canonical status could not be acquired after civil incorporation, but his analysis did not take into account the numerous situations where canonical status had already been acquired at the time of such incorporation."[41]

While it is clear that subsequent civil incorporation of an extant canonical apostolate would not alter the canonical status of that apostolate if proper alienation procedures had not been followed, it is not clear why canonical status could not be acquired, for the first time, after civil incorporation. Civil incorporation establishes a civil corporation, not a canonical juridic person. Thus, if the canonical parent (who is most probably also a civil corporation) of the apostolate (who is also a civil corporation) and the apostolate itself agree on the feasibility of the apostolate

---

[39] "When any institution receives a charter of incorporation, it enters into a contract with the civil authority obligating itself to fulfill the purpose and terms of such charter. In view of the canon law's recognition of acquired rights and its acceptance of the civil authority's law of contracts it is difficult to see that the canonical establishment of The Catholic University of America and Niagara University produced any real juridical effects. The nature of the institutions could in no way be changed without the intervention of the civil authority which had created them." McGrath, p. 18. If one accepts this argument, then it would seem necessary to also accept that the nature of the institutions could likewise not be changed without the intervention of ecclesiastical authority. Two legal systems would require two legal interventions.

[40] "Curiously, but correctly, McGrath acknowledged that the sponsoring religious body itself may also be, and usually is, civilly incorporated, and hence, in addition to being a creature of ecclesiastical law, is often a creature of civil law as well. But the civil incorporation of religious bodies such as dioceses, parishes, and religious communities is, according to McGrath, subordinate to their essential character as ecclesiastical entities, and such "religious corporations" are an entirely different species of civil-law corporation than is the church-related college, university, or hospital. Nonetheless, McGrath did acknowledge that the religious body under whose auspices an educational or charitable institution is conducted is itself both an ecclesiastical juridic person (subject to canon law) and a civilly-incorporated entity (governed by civil law). It is precisely such a dual legal personality that McGrath denied to a church-related educational or charitable institution." Kennedy, pp. 354-255. Kennedy's critique clearly identifies a contradiction in McGrath's thesis, namely that the parent can have a dual canonical and civil personality, but its child may not.

[41] Horn, Francis, *A Canonical Study of the Ownership of the Property of Malvern Preparatory School*, Washington, D.C., licentiate thesis, The Catholic University of America, 1995, p. 66.

acquiring separate canonical status, how could the civil law prevent this?[42]

McGrath's thesis seems flawed at its very core, namely that civil incorporation of an apostolate which does not already have explicit, independent canonical juridic personality, denies the possibility of the apostolate ever acquiring juridic personality. He taught that the sponsoring Church body of a hospital or college, for example, a diocese or a religious institute, would properly be both canonically and civilly incorporated. Thus, Church and government would mutually confer and recognize the dual ecclesial and civil legal identity of the hospital's sponsor. But in regard to the hospital itself, McGrath held that it "[. . .] is in no sense to be juridically identified with the sponsoring religious body. The former is wholly and solely a creature of civil law; the latter is primarily a creature of ecclesiastical law."[43] Civil law would trump canon law.

Therefore, the offspring apostolate of an ecclesially and civilly mutually recognized sponsor had, in McGrath's opinion, a civilly recognized legal independence from its canonical parent. The offspring would be an entirely secular institution falling completely and solely under civil law. This institution would not be related to the Church in the way children are related to their parents. It would not be a canonically constituted juridical relationship because the offspring is considered by McGrath to be canonically and civilly independent of its founders.

McGrath did not argue that the separately civilly incorporated apostolates should have no relationship with their canonical founders.[44] Nor was he saying separate incorporation meant fully secular.[45] Rather, he held that the relationship

---

[42] "In most of the American jurisdictions each church has some kind of civil corporation which performs civil acts in its name. The corporation is set up according to the requirements of the civil law in order to hold property for the church, to sue and be sued, to borrow money, etc. This civil corporation is not the church, but rather is established to perform legal acts for the church." McGrath, p. 261.

In other words, the civil corporation does not function as the Church; rather, the civil corporation functions as a civil expression of the Church. The Church is the Church and the civil corporation is the civil corporation, but the Church has the civil right to make and own civil corporations to help the Church be the Church. There is no contradiction in either civil law or canon law for the Church to own civil corporations.

[43] Kennedy, p. 354.

[44] "The unique character of American charitable and educational corporations conducted under Catholic auspices demands a unique form of cooperation and separation between the institution and the sponsoring body. When the relationship between them is understood clearly, both the separateness and the cooperation can be achieved." McGrath, p. 36.

[45] "Since the institution and the sponsoring body are two separate and distinct entities, the question arises as to what makes the institution Catholic? The answer to this question lies in the influence over the institution exercised by the sponsoring body. The structure of American corporations provides four vehicles for directing and effectuating this influence: 1.) the charter and by-laws; 2.) the board of trustees; 3.) the administration; and 4.) the staff of the corporation." McGrath, p. 33. Pages 33-36 explicate these four vehicles for making an institution Catholic in spirit though not legally owned by the Catholic Church.

with the Church was not a canonical relationship[46] and therefore change in the apostolic orientation of the ecclesial institution was actually easier to accomplish than previously thought.[47]

McGrath's position had been anticipated, but not at all fully explicated, several years earlier in Jesuit Father Francis Korth's statement: "The advantages of separate incorporation for hospitals have been discussed in recent years."[48] Nowhere else in his book does Korth mention separate incorporation nor does he tease out in any way what those advantages might be. Nor does he mention any possible disadvantages. For Korth, in many ways the canonical question became a consideration of counting. To use 1917 codal language: "How many ecclesiastical moral persons are there in a religious institute? That depends on how many have been constituted as such by the proper ecclesiastical authority."[49]

In effect, McGrath holds that the applicability of canon law is limited by the civil law, whereas the counter argument is that the canonical parent never, via canon law, severed the apostolate from itself, and therefore the apostolate, though civilly incorporated, has never been solely under the control of civil law. Put differently, if the sole source for determining the civil nature of the corporation is the civil charter of incorporation, then the sole source for determining the canonical nature of the corporation is the canon law and canonical tradition of the Church.

McGrath holds that "the property, real and personal, of Catholic hospitals and educational institutions which have been incorporated as American law corporations is the property of the corporate entity and not the property of the sponsoring body or individuals who conduct the institution."[50] Yet McGrath seems

---

[46] In Robert Kennedy' words, for McGrath, "The relationship to the Church is real and important, but it is not juridical; the civilly-incorporated institution is juridically distinct from the Church and from the religious body which founded it and under whose influence its affairs are conducted. As such, it is subject solely to civil law, and dependent exclusively upon that law for the resolution of all questions concerning the ownership of its property." Kennedy, p. 358.

[47] McGrath concluded his monograph by stating: "It has been the purpose of this study to shed light upon the legal status of institutions conducted under Catholic auspices in the hope that apparent obstacles to necessary change may be overcome. All of our problems will not disappear by sound legal thinking, but it does offer a secure base upon which to search for solutions." McGrath, p. 38.

[48] Korth, Francis, S. J., *Canon Law for Hospitals,* St. Louis, Missouri, 1962, The Catholic Health Association, p. 6.

[49] Korth, p. 3. He continues: "A hospital can be set up as an ecclesiastical moral person, that is, an independent religious house; or it might merely be part of, or attached to, some other ecclesiastical moral person or independent house. [. . .] In any of these cases, the proper or temporal possessions of the hospital would actually be ecclesiastical goods or property." Korth, p. 4.

Thus, it appears that for Korth, separate incorporation would mean separate canonical incorporation as a means of matching canonical structure more closely with the civil structure. He gives no evidence or argument for separate civil incorporation as a means of severing and preventing any possible canonical relationships. We might call his undeveloped position "the Korth Thesis," namely, hospitals ought to be separately incorporated, but this incorporation ought to be canonical first before it is civil.

[50] McGrath, p. 24.

to contradict himself by holding that even when property is ecclesiastical property as in the examples of The Catholic University of America and Niagara University, that this reality does not produce any discernible canonical effects if civil personhood existed before canonical personhood.

For McGrath, it is the civil law which carries the most weight, and not canon law, when the issue is the ownership of institutions.[51] His claim is that "the Church has placed its personnel and resources at the service of the general public in a unique manner proper to the American legal system and not foreseen by the canon law."[52] While the Church in the United States may have followed the civil legislation in whatever jurisdiction it found itself, as called for by the code, this is not enough evidence to warrant McGrath's sweeping statement just quoted. His unspoken implication is that because canon law cannot anticipate the demands of the American legal system, therefore civil law, and not canon law, demands the allegiance of the civilly incorporated apostolates. But he ignores the demand of canon law that ecclesiastical goods must not be alienated unless proper canonical procedures are followed.

McGrath's claim seems to ignore the reality that to serve the public does not mean to never have or to sever already existing canonical legal relations between those who serve in the Church's name and the Church itself. He seems to hold that for the Church to serve the public in the United States legal context requires the ecclesial institutions to not be bound by canon law. It is difficult to see that this would be the Church's self-understanding of its mission in the United States: be of service but do not be accountable to the ecclesial institution in whose name you serve.

McGrath writes: "It has been repeatedly emphasized throughout this study that our Catholic institutions of higher education and public health are institutions of

---

[51] "Two important concepts can be educed from the Bradfield case. [This United States Supreme Court case from 1899 dealt with the provision of federal funds for sectarian hospitals.] First, the fact that a sponsoring body is religious or sectarian cannot transform a secular corporation, with clearly defined rights and powers, into a religious or sectarian corporation. Second, the usage of 'under the auspices of' connotes a distinction between the institution itself, on the one hand, and the sponsoring body on the other." McGrath, p. 28. "Charitable and educational institutions chartered as corporations under American law are not owned by the sponsoring body. The legal title to the real and personal property is vested in the corporation. It is the corporation that cares for the sick or grants academic degrees. It is the corporation that buys and sells and borrows money. If anyone *owns* the assets of the charitable or educational institution, it is the general public. Failure to appreciate this fact has led to the mistaken idea that the property of the institution is the property of the sponsoring body." McGrath, p. 33.

[52] McGrath, p. 32. "Thus, from the American law point of view, the legal character of the corporate is solely determined from the charter, which it receives from the state, by whose consent the corporation comes into being. The purposes, powers, and duties enumerated in its charter determine the corporation's legal character. The denominational control by a sponsoring body cannot transform the corporation into a religious or ecclesiastical institution in the eyes of the American law, nor is the sponsoring body to be identified with the institution. Each are separate and distinct entities." P. 29.

90

public trust. Their task is primarily one of service to the general public. [...]"[53] McGrath does not identify at all the first fact that these institutions of higher education and health care come from the heart of the Church. It is only of secondary importance the fact that the apostolate may be directed, even primarily directed, to the service of the general public and not just to members of the Church.

In sum, "McGrath argued that religious had founded these institutions as citizens and not as religious; therefore, such enterprises were subject only to civil law."[54] It is a peculiar civil and canonical position to hold that religious can only function as citizens when they are not functioning as religious.

### A Financial Cause of the McGrath Thesis?

But perhaps the peculiarity is better understood as an attempt by institutions such as hospitals and universities to declare ecclesial independence so as to obtain generous amounts of government funding. If little to no governmental money could be given to religiously based institutions of health care and education, then it would be in the financial interest of those religious institutions to downplay their ecclesial identity.

If a Catholic health care or educational institution is financially ailing, it will be tempted to seek cash-cures from many sources. So, the tension is not first between canonical and civil understandings of property ownership as it is an underlying economic tension. The ecclesial, civil-legal and canonical considerations of the McGrath thesis seemed to have flowed from the need for more intensive amounts of funding.

For example, separate civil incorporation served as a protection against the legal liability of the canonical parent for the actions of their offspring apostolates. Also, separate incorporation made the apostolates more attractive for governmental and other non-sectarian sources of funding.[55] As Phillip Gleason discovered, quoting the then president of Fordham University, Leo McLaughlin, S.J., in regard to the 1960s movement to laicize university boards of trustees: "Putting it bluntly, one reason that changes are being made in the structure of boards of trustees is money. These colleges cannot continue to exist without state aid."[56] Neil

---

[53] McGrath, pp. 34-35.

[54] Hoffman, Francis Joseph, *The Apostolic Constitution Ex Corde Ecclasiae and Catholic Universities in the United States of America,* Roma, Pontificium Athenaeum Sanctae Crucis, 1996, p. 38.

[55] Kennedy, pp. 362-363.

[56] Gleason, p. 316. One of the major federal funding initiatives for higher education in the mid-1960s was grants for student dormitories. John Lynch makes a similar point in that religious institutes, by following McGrath's thesis in order to obtain federal money, secularized their health care and educational apostolates. "Such secularization threatened the Catholic character of these institutions and the canonical safeguarding of millions of dollars of church property." Lynch, John, C.S.P., "Laying

McCluskey, S.J., would disagree with this assessment.[57] Father McCluskey was the secretary[58] of the 1967 Land O'Lakes meeting of representatives of Catholic colleges and university. Apparently, he was also the chief writer of the infamous Land O'Lakes Catholic higher education declaration of independence[59] from the juridical control of the Church.

McGrath found in regard to Catholic hospitals, universities and colleges that it was not "the policy to erect them as canonical moral persons."[60] Therefore, his conclusion was that those institutions did not belong to the Catholic Church. If an institution did not belong to the Church, then it would be reasonable for that

Down the (Canon) Law at Catholic University," *The Jurist,* 50 (1990): 40.

[57] He holds that re-organization along the contours of the McGrath thesis was not caused principally because of monetary reasons, "even though there are Catholic educators who still labor under the illusion that the only problems besetting Catholic higher education are financial. Granted that these problems are enormous and pressing, they are not the critical problems. A blank check on the state treasury or the federal reserve would not solve problems like the dominance of religious orders, reliance on Old World tradition, amateurish administration, shortsighted financial policies, confusion between the pastoral and academic areas, insulation from the main stream of contemporary thought, and lack of definition of purpose. Almost all of these are problems that flow from non recognition of the character of the work of contemporary higher education." McCluskey, p. 233.

It is obvious that for McCluskey there is more at stake than simply money. His desire is for a declaration of total independence, a kind of Catholic higher education Boston Tea Party: be ridden of ecclesiastical interference, but keep all the money.

[58] See Burtchaell, James Tunstead, *The Dying of the Light: The Disengagement of Colleges and Universities from Their Christian Churches,* (1998, William B. Eerdmans Publishing Corporation, Grand Rapids, Michigan): 716.

[59] "To perform its teaching and research functions effectively the Catholic University must have a true autonomy and academic freedom in the face of authority of whatever kind, lay or clerical, external to the academic community itself." The entire Land O'Lakes statement is found in McCluskey, Neil G., *Catholic Education Faces its Future,* (Garden City, New York: Doubleday and Company, 1968): 296-300. This quote is from p. 296.

It is important to note that the statement does not say that a Catholic university is free from governmental authority, but only lay or clerical authority. In effect, the Land O'Lakes statement was a brazen declaration of independence from the Church, and a de facto declaration of dependence upon the government. James Burtchaell's article, "Everything You Need to Know About *Ex Corde Ecclasiae*," Crisis, July-August, 1999, pp. 28-29, identifies no less than 21 governmental agencies to which Catholic universities readily respond. He also identifies at least 15 accrediting agencies which Catholic universities eagerly seek to please. There are also, at minimum, six associations of colleges and universities which set various policies and norms for higher educational institutions. Thus, the statistical evidence (a minimum of 42 groups external to the university, the magisterium not being one of the 42) would seem to indicate that the only institution which Catholic colleges and universities tried to be independent of was the Catholic Church. Also, to claim complete and true autonomy would seem to imply autonomy even from a board of trustees, because such a board is external to the academic community by virtue of being trustees and not teachers. Even public universities do not make such radical claims as the Land O'Lakes participants did. It is obvious that such a wish/declaration of independence can not be made apart from the law of the Church to which such institutions have belonged since their birth. There is no such thing as unilateral secession in the codal tradition.

[60] McGrath, p. 17.

institution to seek secular funding precisely by claiming that it is not a religious institution.

Because Catholic hospitals did not seek moral personhood, moral personhood was never granted them. But these institutions did not seek such recognition because there was no need for it.[61] In order for there not to have been a participation in the parent's moral personhood, it would have been necessary for the religious institute to have clearly decided at the time of the civil establishment of the hospital, that this hospital does not have any kind of canonical connection with the religious institute which founded it. Unless this explicit disavowal of relationship had canonically occurred and could be properly documented, then the fair and reasonable assumption is that the hospital does, in fact and in law, belong to the religious institute.

A two-fold difficulty with the McGrath position is: first, much of the alleged alienation of ecclesiastical goods done under the inspiration of the McGrath Thesis was "alienation" without it being alienation. That is, the civil effects of alienation (sales, mergers, new financial arrangements, and so on) occurred, but the acts

---

[61] The American canonists James Coriden and Frederick McManus believed that McGrath's position had some serious flaws and inadequacies. They summarized their reservations in an appendix of a book devoted to studying legal issues in religiously affiliated higher education. "McGrath surely erred in narrowly construing canon 100 of the [1917] code, which calls for the constitution of ecclesiastical moral persons by the formal decree of the competent ecclesiastical superior. Since explicit, formal decrees of erection had been issued for virtually no Catholic college, hospital, orphanage, etc., McGrath concluded that they were not moral persons canonically. And because church property can only be owned by "moral persons constituted as juridical persons by ecclesiastical authority" (cc. 1495 and 1497), he further concluded that the lands, buildings, equipment, etc., belonging to these institutions were not really church property and not subject to canon law. This simplistic canonical reasoning enabled him to reach the further conclusion at civil law that the general public has equitable title to the property of such institutions because they are chartered as charitable corporations under the authority of the state.

McGrath seems also to have taken insufficient account of certain basic norms of the ecclesiastical law, for example, the underlying responsibility of church administrators to employ the formalities of the civil law in order to protect the property they administer (see c. 1523) or the principle that the intentions of the donors must be respected (see cc. 1513, 1514, and 1523).

It is reasonable to construe less formal documents, appointments, letters, negotiations, etc., which recognize and acknowledge the existence of close and dependent relationships between the college, hospital, orphanage, etc., and the sponsoring diocese or religious community, as the acceptable equivalent of a formal decree. Such institutions created, sponsored, funded, administered, and staffed by a church body should certainly be considered church property in a canonical as well as popular sense." Gaffney, Edward Jr., and Moots, Philip R., *Church and Campus: Legal Issues in Religiously Affiliated Higher Education,* ( 1979, University of Notre Dame Press, Notre Dame, Indiana): 145-146.

McGrath also did not take into account canon 497.3 "In order that a school be built or opened, or [likewise] a hospital or a similar building separated even from an exempt house, it is necessary and sufficient that the special permission of the Ordinary [be had] in writing." Peters, p. 193. One would be hard-pressed to find a school or hospital that had not received such permission from the Ordinary.

leading to those effects never received official canonical ecclesial approval.[62] Second, these non-alienation alienations were sometimes uncompensated alienations in that religious institutes gave away their property for free or sold it for well below fair market value.[63] The Church would thus have been unjustly deprived of revenues that rightly belonged to the Church's health care and educational apostolic endeavors and/or to the stable patrimony of the religious institute or diocese.

McGrath took the contrary viewpoint, namely that the assets of the apostolate belonged to the public and not to the Church.[64] To hold that if a Church-sponsored apostolate, such as a hospital, is sold or closed, that its assets belong to the public and not to the public juridic person, seems to be a conclusion built on McGrath's distinction between the sponsor being a subject of both canon and civil law, and the sponsored offspring being a subject only of civil law. Therefore, when the offspring is sold, the parent has no civil claim to the assets obtained from the sale.

McGrath did not allow for civil law to adopt canon law. Rather, his conclusion was that canon law had to surrender any hope of being recognized by civil law. The church, in her wise legal hypostatic union,[65] allows for both legal systems to protect the Church's interests in as many ways as possible.

*Conclusion*

We have seen at some length and in some detail the wide influence of McGrath's legal theory on the Church's self-understanding of its relationship to the ownership of property.[66] In effect, McGrath's conclusion was that the Church does

[62] That is, canons 1290-1292 were not followed. In the 1917 code, the applicable canons would have been canons 1529 and 1530.

[63] In such cases it is probable that canons 1293, §2 and 1294, §1 also would not have been followed. In the 1917 code, the applicable canons would have been canons 1531 and 1532.

[64] "Since the charitable corporation is created to serve the general public, the equitable title to charitable corporate property is vested in the general public. In a business corporation the property is distributed, upon dissolution, to its stockholders or members, but the property of a charitable corporation, upon dissolution, is ordinarily distributed by the courts to another charitable corporation of similar purpose. Even in dissolution the public receives the benefit of a charitable corporation's property." McGrath, p. 9.

[65] Canon 22 reads: "When the law of the Church remits some issue to the civil law, the latter is to be observed with the same effects in canon law, in so far as it is not contrary to divine law, and provided it is not otherwise stipulated in canon law." For examples of this in the arena of ecclesiastical goods, see canons 1284, 1290 and 1296. One would be hard pressed to argue that civil law is to be considered an equal to canon law in governing the life of the Church. But clearly this canon, which has no counterpart in the 1917 code, is meant to show that civil law has a place in the life of the Church. McGrath seemed to grant too large of a place for civil law.

[66] The Saint Louis University hospital case from the fall of 1997 and the first few months of 1998 would be an interesting example of the application of the conclusions of the McGrath thesis to a misunderstanding of ecclesial ownership of property. The Jesuits of Saint Louis wanted to sell their

not really own her apostolates in their institutionalized expression as property and buildings. Rather, the general public holds the controlling equitable interest.

However, alienation of ecclesiastical goods that belong to a public juridic person must follow proper canonical procedure as well as proper civil procedure. The danger in ignoring canon law is that civil law will seem more important than canon law. The danger in ignoring civil law is that ecclesiastical goods may be needlessly endangered.

By 1973, the McGrath thesis had drawn its share of critics.[67] The most vociferous[68] and public critic[69] was Father Adam Maida, a priest of the Pittsburgh diocese. The Roman Curia weighed in early in 1974 with its own criticisms and rejection of McGrath's legal theory.[70] But by then, several years of reorganizing

hospital to a for-profit health care corporation. The president of Saint Louis University claimed that canonical permission to do so was not needed because since 1967, when the Jesuits had reorganized the Board of Trustees of Saint Louis University from an all Jesuit board to a lay majority board, the hospital had not been considered ecclesiastical property. For more on this, see pages 82-87, 176-178 and 223-224 from my dissertation cited in footnote one.

[67] See pages 106-110 in my dissertation.

[68] "A few years ago, Msgr. John McGrath introduced a theory of both canon and civil law that concerned the ownership of religious institutions. He made some practical conclusions and recommendations, and to this day, to the best of my knowledge, his theories have not been rebutted, his recommendations have received wide acceptance, and the consequences have been most serious for the Church. McGrath has stated: "If any one owns the assets of the charitable or educational institution, it is the general public. Failure to appreciate this fact has led to the mistaken idea that the property of the institution is the property of the sponsoring body." Thus, what Henry VIII did with a sword in England, what Napoleon did with his armies in France, what Lenin did with a political philosophy, McGrath has attempted to do with a legal theory. The unchallenged receptivity of the theory and its conclusions throughout the country is utterly amazing." Maida, Adam, "Civil Law and Canon Law Status of Catholic Hospitals," Hospital Progress, (August, 1973): 54.

[69] "McGrath's proposal seemed a salvation. He recommended changes in corporate charters and bylaws to reflect the 'public' nature of our Catholic institutions; urged that the government and control of these institutions be entrusted to competent lay people representing the broad spectrum of the community; and advocated that the religious congregation or diocese assume a sponsoring rather than an ownership role in its relationship to its institutions. In the judgement of many, this would erase the sectarian character from the nature of our institutions and thus make them available for participation in federal and state aid programs of one nature or another.

"And so it was that many institutions changed their charters and bylaws, changed the character of their institutions, transferred control of their institutions to lay boards, and thus successfully disenfranchised their religious congregations and Church. The various religious congregations which gave birth to these institutions, nurtured them, funded them, staffed them, controlled them, and made them effective witnesses of the love of God for man through religion, now find a witness which has been dissipated, an apostolate which has been lost, an ownership which has been alienated and an experience which has become a nightmare." Ibid., p. 55.

[70] The first document related to the McGrath thesis was issued by the Sacred Congregation for Catholic Education and addressed to the apostolic delegate. It is important to extensively cite this document. "For some time this Sacred Congregation has been anxious about the status of the property and name of the many Catholic colleges and universities in the United States. We have not been unaware of the growing tendency for the ecclesiastical entities that own and operate these institutions to alienate them

had occurred in Catholic colleges, universities, and hospitals throughout the United States. The civil legal toothpaste had been canonically invalidly squeezed from the wrong tube.

It was a legal misunderstanding of a new ecclesiological self-understanding that vaulted the McGrath thesis to such prominence in Catholic legal circles. Perhaps the most important lesson to draw from a study of his legal thought is that bad law will never adequately serve good theology. The law of the Church must never surpass nor ignore what the Church believes and how the Church lives.

from ecclesiastical control and ownership, frequently through civil corporate structural changes (Boards of Trustees, Regents, etc.), often citing the 'McGrath thesis' as justification for this action, an action that takes place without ecclesiastical approbation, indeed, often with the knowledge of Church authorities, who are presented only with a *fait accompli*, alienations that are probably invalid both canonically and civilly.

"It is our genuine concern that millions of dollars of Church property and even the names of these institutions are being lost forever to the Church in this way, not through government confiscation, but by means of a gradual and inexorable drive toward secularization, assisted by the passivity and often tacit approval of Church superiors, by financial and other strains, and by the rather confused situation involving ecclesiastical control and authority in these institutions.

"For this reason, we are considering the possibility of proposing a joint letter with the Sacred Congregation for Religious and Secular Institutes to all U.S. bishops and Major Religious Superiors stating that: 1.) all colleges and universities that are considered Catholic should not be further alienated through civil corporate structural changes without reference first to the Holy See; 2.) the 'McGrath thesis' is not to be used as a pretext for any action in this regard; 3.) each bishop and Major Superior responsible in any way for an institution of higher learning is to send to us appropriate information on how the Catholic character of the institution is being maintained and guaranteed and about the exact civil and canonical status of the institutions." *Canon Law Digest*, 9, pp. 368-369, citing the Sacred Congregation for Catholic Education, Prot. N. 427/70/15; original English text, 2 January, 1974.

The second document, issued by both the Sacred Congregation for Catholic Education and the Sacred Congregation for Religious and Secular Institutes, read: "We believe it necessary, first of all to know which institutions, at the present moment, are or consider themselves Catholic. Once this is known clearly, it should be possible to determine which Bishop and which Major Superior is responsible for the institutions. In the case of those institutions that in the past have always been known as Catholic and which no longer consider themselves such, it would be important to ascertain from the Higher Superiors responsible, the reasons for this change and the steps taken to effect it. We can readily understand the financial pressures in these days of economic stress, but we cannot help wondering whether they are really insuperable to the point where they justify the sacrifice of a value so important in the eyes of the Church as Catholic education for its sons and daughters.

"We would ask the commission to consider the advisability of contacting all such institutions asking them not to make any changes (or further changes, where these have been initiated) in their administrative structure or corporate status, without first informing, and where necessary, obtaining approval from, our Congregations.

"We know that in the course of the study, the influence of the so-called 'McGrath thesis' will emerge as one of the principal bases for the action of some institutions in regard to alienations, etc. we wish to make it clear that this thesis has never been considered valid by our Congregations and has never been accepted." *Canon Law Digest*, 9, p. 370, citing the Sacred Congregations for Catholic Education and for Religious and Secular Institutes, Prot. NN. SCI, 427/70/23 and SCRIS, 300/74; original English text, 7 October, 1974.

# FAVOR OF THE FAITH CASES
# AND
# THE 2001 NORMS OF THE CONGREGATION FOR
# THE DOCTRINE OF THE FAITH

REVEREND MONSIGNOR FREDERICK C. EASTON

## *Introduction*

On April 30, 2001, the Congregation for the Doctrine of the Faith issued a document entitled, *Norms to Complete the Process for the Dissolution of the Matrimonial bond under the Favor of the Faith,* with the incipit *Potestas Ecclesiae.* Sometime after the promulgation of the Norms and after they were published in English by the USCCB, the Congregation issued a four-page document entitled: *Notes regarding the Documentary Procedural Aspects of Favor of the Faith Cases* [hereafter referenced as *Notes*]. At the same time it published a revision of the *cautiones*, that is, the promises to be made by both the Catholic and non-Catholic party when the proposed marriage after the dissolution will be a mixed marriage. A new form for the summary of the acts was also included. The publication of these documents makes it especially opportune for canonists and tribunal workers to again reflect on the nature of these cases and the practical aspects of handling them.

In all of the official documents including the rescripts received from the Congregation, the only terminology used is simply *dissolution of marriage in favor of the Faith.* However many people have used the term *privilege of the Faith* in an obvious parallel to the Pauline Privilege. The term *privilege of the Faith* is found in the code only in canon 1150 (*CCEO,* c. 861): "In a doubtful matter the Privilege of the Faith possesses the favor of the law."

Perhaps, an even more common expression among many authors is the term *Petrine Privilege.* By using this term, authors draw a contrasting parallel between the use of the Pauline Privilege and the dissolution granted by the Pope, the successor of Peter. Some authors believe that it is truly out of place to call this dissolution a *privilege* because the power of the Holy Father is not a privilege granted by Christ to the Church but simply one of the powers or faculties entrusted by Christ to the Church by which it continues its salvific work in the world.[1]

A Brief Historical Background

For anyone interested in the history of the dissolution in favor of the Faith, the preface provided by the Congregation of the Doctrine of the Faith to the 2001 Norms is most helpful. It notes that the practice of granting a dissolution of the bond by the Roman Pontiff in individual cases was introduced only *after* the promulgation of the 1917 code. The preface goes on to explain that prior to the 1917 code the Church bound all the baptized, whether Catholic or not, to the impediment of disparity of worship. The Catholic Church regarded as invalid the marriages between baptized Christians of all denominations and unbaptized people by reason of this impediment. Of course, since neither party of such a marriage was Catholic, there was no occasion to seek a dispensation from the impediment.

Anyone who has taken the time to review some of the old cases in the diocesan tribunal would find a host of affirmative decisions based upon the impediment of disparity of worship between a baptized non-Catholic and an unbaptized person. However, once the 1917 code took effect the impediment of disparity of cult no longer impeded the marriages of baptized non-Catholics with unbaptized persons. As a consequence, there arose a new pastoral situation. This pastoral situation was the context out of which arose the first case of dissolution of marriage in favor of the Faith on April 2, 1924.

A woman named Elizabeth born in 1896 and baptized and educated in a non-Catholic church married Charles, a Jewish man, in 1919 before a civil magistrate. The marriage became unhappy and was dissolved by a civil judge. The woman then converted to the Catholic Faith and wanted to marry a Catholic man. For that reason she petitioned the tribunal for either a declaration of invalidity of her marriage by reason of the impediment of disparity of worship or the permission to use the Pauline Privilege. Of course, by now there was no longer any impediment of disparity of worship standing in the way of a valid marriage for Elizabeth and Charles. Further, canon 1120, §2 of the 1917 code expressly established that the Pauline Privilege would not apply in the case of a marriage of a baptized person and an unbaptized person. Nonetheless, the matter was presented to the Holy See.

The Holy Office responded and Pope Pius XI approved that, in light of the circumstances of the case, the woman could be admitted to a marriage to be contracted with a Catholic man.[2] Therefore, with this case began an era of papal dissolution of marriages *in favor of the Faith*. On May 1, 1934 the Congregation

---

[1] Urban Navarette, "De Termino 'privilegium petrinum' non adhibendo," *Periodica* 53 (1964): 323-327.

[2] X. Ochoa, *Leges Ecclesiae post Codicem Iuris Canonici editae*, II, (Roma, 1966, 1969 and 1980) col. 679-680.

of the Holy Office issued its first instruction on the matter entitled: *Norms to Complete the Process in Cases of Dissolution of the Matrimonial Bond in Favor of the Faith by the Supreme Authority of the Roman Pontiff.* This instruction was sent directly to local ordinaries but not published in the *Acta Apostolicae Sedis.*

After the Second Vatican Council, during the Pontificate of Pope Paul VI, the 1934 Norms were revised, and on December 6, 1973 the Congregation issued a new instruction with procedural norms attached. Now we have the new norms issued in 2001 which will be the focus of this presentation.

## *Nature of a Dissolution of a Marriage in Favor of the Faith*[3]

Important to the understanding of the nature of the papal dissolution is a careful consideration of those three apostolic constitutions which appeared as an appendix to the 1917 *Code of Canon Law*, namely the Constitutions of Paul III *Altitudo*, June 1, 1537, of St. Pius V *Romani Pontificis,* August 2, 1571, and of Gregory XIII, *Populis,*[4] January 25, 1585. As one reads in context these three constitutions referenced by canon 1125 of the 1917 code, one easily concludes that the Roman Pontiffs did not conceive of the dissolution of marriage to be in the nature of a privilege but in the nature of the exercise in concrete cases of the power to dissolve the natural bond of marriage even beyond what is envisioned in 1 Corinthians 7:12-16. The motive behind granting the dissolution was clearly the salvation of souls. The persons touched by the dissolution were not Christian in many instances. Therefore, they could not be the recipients of a privilege. The purpose or value behind granting the dissolution was to promote the Faith, namely, now what we call evangelization. *Favor of the Faith*, therefore, is truly synonymous in this application with the salvation of souls. In the 1983 *Code of Canon Law*, a very important parenthetical statement affirms that the "salvation of souls" […] "must always be the supreme law of the Church."[5] The power of the keys, therefore, was given to Peter and his successors to promote the salvation of souls.

As we well know, the bond of marriage, or as we often refer to it by its Latin term, *ligamen,* forms an impediment to any other subsequent marriage. We are well acquainted with this impediment as we adjudicate documentary invalidity of

---

[3] A good guide to an understanding of the nature of the favor of the Faith dissolutions can be found in the doctoral dissertation of Robertus Rubiyatmoko: "Competenza della Chiesa nello scioglimento del vinculo del matrimonio non sacramentale" (JCD dissertation, Pontifical Gregorian Univesity, Rome, 1998).

[4] Excerpts from these three constitutions are to be found in the appendix of the 1917 *Code of Canon Law*. A translation of these excerpts are to be found in *The 1917 or Pio-Benedictine Code of Canon Law in English Translation*, Dr. Edward N. Peters, Curator (San Francisco: Ignatius Press, 2001): 763-765. The primary sources are: for *Altitudo, Collectanea S. C. de Prop. Fide*, vol. 1, 30; for *Romani Pontificis*, ibid., 493; for *Populis*, ibid., 256.

[5] C. 1952.

marriage cases. The power of the keys gives the Holy Father the faculty to dispense from the divine natural law of the bond of marriage. The result of this dispensation from natural law is the dissolution of the marriage bond such that the person can contract marriage in the Church. This action of the Holy Father is simply the exercise of the power he has in virtue of his office. The petitioner does not have the privilege in any sense. Rather, the petitioner is seeking a spiritual good.

The question often arises of whether or not this papal power is able to be delegated. The more common opinion is that this power is delegable. Felix Cappello[6] and Conte a Coronata[7] affirm this to be true. However Giuseppe Damizia along with A. M. Abate[8] say that it is *not opportune* for the Holy Father to delegate this power in order to protect the validity of its exercise. Although we might like to debate the rationale for reserving to the Holy Father the faculty of dissolving such marriages, this seminar has its principal focus a review of how the cases are to be investigated and presented to the Holy See.

*How a Favor of the Faith Case is Processed*

Since we now have new norms for processing favor of the Faith cases, it would be well for us to journey through the process with a view as to what has been changed, as well as, with an eye to some of the practical aspects of instructing such cases.

Who is Competent to Instruct the Case

The 1973 Norms stated that the process was to be "conducted by the local Ordinary who is competent according to the prescript of the Apostolic Letter, *Causas Matrimoniales* IV, #1."[9] There is no such restriction in the 2001 Norms, which simply state: "The diocesan bishop and those equivalent to him in law, or the eparchial bishop, are competent to instruct the process."[10]

Further, the 1973 Norms stated that the local ordinary would instruct the case "either personally or through another ecclesiastic delegated by him."[11] In the 2001

---

[6] F. M. Cappello, *Tractatus canonico-moralis de sacramentis*, V: *De matrimonio* (Roma, 1961) n. 762, 690-691.

[7] M. Conte a Coronata, *Institutiones iuris canonici: De sacramentis Tractus canonicus,* III, *De matrimonio et de sacramentalibus*, (Roma – Torino, 1957) n. 620, 867.

[8] G. Damizia, "Lo scioglimento del vinculo matrimoniale concesso per delega," *Appollinaris* 39 (1966): 286; A. M. Abate, *Lo scioglimento*, (Roma, 1961): 48.

[9] 1973 Norms for the Process of the Dissolution of Marriage, Art. 1.

[10] 2001 Norms, article 3.

[11] 1973 Norms, Art. 1.

Norms, the instructor no longer needs to be an "ecclesiastic." Article 11 §1 states: "The bishop is either to carry out the instruction of the process personally or is to commit it to an instructor selected from the judges of the tribunal or from persons approved by him for this function." The burden rests upon the diocesan bishop or eparch to ascertain the professional and canonical competency of the person whom he names as the instructor for these cases. The diocesan judges are mentioned first, but someone else who is sufficiently trained – whether lay, religious or cleric, whether male or female – may be appointed as instructor. According to the *Notes* not only may such a person be appointed on a case-by-case basis but also on a permanent basis.

## Preliminary Assessment of the Facts Presented

From personal experience, I have found that it is most important to assess at the outset the likelihood of success of such a case. At this point in the process, anyone working with such a case is heavily dependent upon the petitioner for the information to make such an assessment. Sometimes the instructor, trained persons in the field, or other tribunal staff are involved in making preliminary assessments on what kind of case has hope for success for the petitioner. In any event, it is most important to "begin with the end in mind" as Steven Covey says in his book, *Seven Habits of Highly Effective People.*[12]

It is very helpful always to keep in mind what happens when a case gets to the Holy See. The Congregation for the Doctrine of the Faith assigns these cases to three of their judges. It is the task of these judges to recommend to the Cardinal Prefect of the Congregation whether or not this case should be commended to the Holy Father. More specifically, they are looking to whether or not it is morally certain that one of the parties to the marriage was unbaptized. They are also looking at whether or not the petitioner was the prevailing cause for the breakup of the marriage. In summary, they are evaluating the acts to see if the substantive as well as procedural norms were properly followed in the case.

Thus, it is helpful to have some instrument to help petitioners surface the information needed for a preliminary assessment about the viability of a favor of the Faith case. Many tribunals use a fairly comprehensive instrument that asks for the preliminary information needed in all types of cases. In the cases for the papal dissolution, what is needed are questions or blanks asking for two witnesses who are available to testify. More will be said later about who is a good witness. However, at the outset it is good to remember that witnesses must be knowledgeable about the religious practices of the family of the person alleged to be unbaptized and not simply be able to affirm that he or she truly was unbaptized.

---

[12] Stephen R. Covey, *Seven Habits of Highly Effective People* (New York, NY: Simon and Schuster, 1990).

Unbaptized petitioners and respondents are not considered witnesses because they are not able to attest to events happening in their life before the age of reason. Further, the witnesses must also be in a position to know about the breakup of the marriage. Their testimony needs to give sufficient reason to believe that the petitioner was *not the prevailing cause* of the rupture of the common life of the marriage either on his or her own or by reason of the relationship with the person whom the petitioner wishes to marry.

Many cases for dissolution in favor of the Faith are granted in which the respondent is the unbaptized party. However, in practice, it is often difficult to get respondents and their families to cooperate. I have found that petitioners sometimes are quite naïve about this matter and are easily convinced that the respondent and the respondent's family will take part. Therefore, it seems best to communicate with the petitioner in some detail about what is involved in testifying, namely, about the necessity of being interviewed in person, if at all possible, and of having one's deposition signed either in person before the auditor or by a notary public or other legitimate witness. Some people are very willing to talk to the tribunal over the telephone but become most unwilling to be involved any further and, therefore, often refuse to have their depositions signed and witnessed even before a notary public. I will touch upon this topic later.

### The Commission of the Officers for the Case

After preliminary determination has revealed that such a case is viable, it is important to document immediately the appointment of the instructor for this particular case. Article 11, §2 of the new norms states that this appointment is called a commission and is "to be done in writing and must be evidenced in the Acts." The *Notes* that were issued after the *Norms* states that "the nomination of the instructor, Defender of the Bond and the Notary is to be given in writing, signed by the diocesan bishop, dated and notarized."[13] It states that this can be done either on a case-by-case basis or on a permanent basis. Further it clarifies that the commission is to be established *after* the date of the petition but *before* any testimony is received or any investigation of the case takes place. The 1973 Norms also required such commissioning documents.[14] The determination that the petition should be dated before the commission is a new specification in the procedure.

Thus, in practice, once the preliminary investigation suggests the viability of a favor of the Faith case, the petition ought to be drawn up immediately, signed, and dated. Then the commission or nomination of the officers should be drawn up and signed by the bishop, dated, and notarized. However since it is possible to have a commission on a permanent basis, it may be easier to have the diocesan bishop

---

[13] *Notes regarding the Documentary and Procedural Aspects of Favour of the Faith Cases*, 2.
[14] 1973 Norms, *Ut notum est*, Article 1.

make such an appointment once and for all.  There does not seem to be anything standing in the way of the diocesan bishop appointing more than one instructor, defender of the bond, or notary for these cases.  However if there is already a permanent nomination of a team, then it would seem reasonable that any additional teams would be established on a case-by-case basis.

## The Investigation of the Case

Once the commission is established the investigation can proceed.  As Article 12, §2 notes, "both spouses are to be heard in the instruction."  However, Article 12, §3 notes: "the force of full proof cannot be attributed to the declarations of the parties, unless other elements are present which corroborate them and from which moral certitude can be formed."  This provision is simply a restatement of canon 1536, §2.

### Manner of Questioning of Parties and Witnesses

The *Norms* start with the assumption that all parties and witnesses appear before the instructor.  All are either to take the oath before testifying or confirm by oath the truth of what they have said after they have testified (cf. article 14, §2).  Further it is assumed there is already a questionnaire prepared by either the instructor or by the defender of the bond, but the *Norms* mention that other questions can be added if they are necessary (cf. article 14, §3).  Actually, the rigid or inflexible use of a stock questionnaire without using *ex officio* questions is often not a helpful approach in getting at the truth, particularly when there are some unusual circumstances which can affect the understanding or the evaluation of the evidence.

### Need for Authentication of Testimony

The parties and the witnesses must sign all questionnaires.  Further, these signatures must normally be witnessed by the instructor or a delegated auditor.  However, the *Norms* also give some flexibility when the parties or witnesses are not able to or even refuse to appear at the tribunal to give their deposition.  Article 15 states in that situation "their declarations can be obtained before a Notary (this would also include a notary public) or by any other legitimate method, provided that their genuineness and authenticity are evident.  From my own experience the Congregation for the Doctrine of the Faith always wants the deposition to be signed and witnessed.  There does not seem to be any other way to give evidence of the genuineness and authenticity of the statements.

However, after a case has begun difficulties can arise in obtaining the full cooperation of witnesses, particularly when these people are the family members of the respondent. Further there can also be the same difficulty with family members of the petitioner who are not Catholic and who have considerable suspicion of or perhaps even antipathy towards Catholicism. Sometimes these people are willing to talk to someone over the telephone and have their statements recorded and transcribed. However their willingness to take part may end at this point. Even though they may initially agree to sign their statement once transcribed, when the deposition is mailed to them with the request that they have their signature witnessed by a notary public or by the local Catholic priest, they often simply never respond thereafter. This leads to a quandary concerning what value the telephone deposition will have.

There may be some creative ways of determining the authenticity of those telephone testimonies. Perhaps, one may have obtained from the witness the driver's license number, or maybe one or the other witness was willing to give a social security number, although that is most unlikely. The difficulty with telephone testimony is that it is possible for someone other than the real witness to testify. Further, no civil court will accept such an unsigned deposition as proof in any proceeding.

## Documentation of Delegation of an Auditor

Very often the instructor is not able to personally take all the testimony in a given case. Parish priests and other parish pastoral ministers are often asked to take testimony. The Congregation clearly wants the appointment of any other auditor documented in the acts. There is usually a cover letter sent to those auditors with the questionnaire. A copy of this letter inserted in the acts with the testimony is the simplest way to document that person's appointment.

## Uncooperative Respondents

Respondents, whether they are baptized or not, often do not want to take part in these processes. Article 15, §2 states "The absence of the other party from the process, declared in according to the norm of law, must be evidenced in the Acts." Therefore it is important to keep in mind the provisions in canons 1509-1511 about the citation of the parties. There certainly must be documentation that efforts have been made to communicate with the respondent and to invite him or her into the process.

Canons 1592-1595 speak about what to do when the parties do not appear in a formal case process. These canons are an important guide about what must to be done in order to properly declare the other party absent from the process. From canon 1594 we know that it is important not to simply send one letter to the respondent but to make a second effort to invite the respondent to take part. Further, since the issue of the participation of the respondent is quite similar to what must take place in judicial contentious processes, there must be a decree whereby the instructor explains the efforts made to invite the respondent and documents the fact there was no response and that, as a consequence, the respondent must be considered absent from the process. However, if the respondent chooses to come forward after a decree declaring the absence, the decree no longer has any effect and the respondent's testimony should be taken.

*Profile of a Good Witness for Absence of Baptism*

As I mentioned at the outset, it is important to have the petitioner suggest witnesses who are expected to be knowledgeable. This is in keeping with the mind of Article 16, §2 which states that the *quality* of the witness testimony must be taken in consideration.

Parents are usually the best witnesses to prove the absence of baptism since they are assumed to have been in charge of the religious formation of the person in early childhood. If there had been infant baptism, it would have been the parents who would have presented the child for baptism. However, sometimes parents are either deceased or uncooperative by the time a case comes to the tribunal. In that situation, one is dependent upon other family members. Aunts and uncles of the unbaptized party are often particularly helpful. Younger brothers and sisters are usually less helpful than older siblings. However all siblings can give some testimony to the general religious practices or lack thereof in the family. Occasionally there will be a situation in which someone who is not a family member may have considerable information about the way in which the unbaptized party was reared. Thus, some non-family members might have been in a position to know when and if that person had been baptized.

*Questions regarding Absence of Baptism*

This discussion logically moves us into a consideration of what questions should be used in the inquiry about absence of baptism. Article 16, §3 gives us considerable direction in this matter: "Witnesses are to be questioned not only about the absence of baptism but also about circumstances and indications from which it appears probable that baptism had not be conferred."

Of course, it is important to ask the simple question of whether or not the unbaptized, party had been baptized. However it is also important to ask about the religious practices of each of the parents, whether either of them had been baptized, whether they were going to church when the unbaptized party was an infant or a small child, and whether any of the siblings, if there were any, were baptized. In the event that one or more of the siblings were baptized, it is important to ask why they were baptized and the petitioner or respondent was not baptized.

By questioning the witness about the religious practice of the family of the unbaptized the instructor is able to achieve some assurance that the witness was not mistaken about the principal issue. For example, if the witness says there was very little church attendance, then the statement that there was no baptism is strengthened. On the other hand, if the family was very regular in church attendance and if siblings were baptized, there is reason to wonder why this particular family member was not baptized. When the witness says there was consistent church attendance and especially if siblings were baptized, it is good to ask how it was, then, that the person in question was not baptized.

*Investigation of Church Baptismal Records*

As mentioned above, witnesses should be asked whether the unbaptized party attended any church. Moreover, it is also important to learn the name and the address of the church, if possible. Article 16, §4 of the *Norms* requires there be an investigation, in so far as possible, into the baptismal records of those churches which the unbaptized party attended to ascertain whether or not he or she had been baptized there. Further, the same article goes on to state that even the baptismal records of the church where the marriage was celebrated should also be checked.

Witnesses and parties many times do not give accurate information about the name or the whereabouts of these churches. Sometimes it takes a little effort to identify the church they must mean as the one attended by the unbaptized party. Internet searches for churches are often very helpful in obtaining the names and addresses, as well as, the telephone numbers of these churches. Letters to the churches with the request that they check their records for any evidence of baptism are often met with no reply. However, a second request to a church that has not responded after about a month is important in documenting that the original letter was or was not received. With the expiration of a reasonable time after the second letter was sent with no response, the notary's report that no response was received would be an important documentation that all efforts have been expended in making contact with a particular church.

From time to time I have had a record of a baptism discovered in this search much to the surprise of everyone. This might not mean the end of the favor of the Faith case. In one case it was a situation of mistaken identity. In another, further investigation revealed that the record had been prepared before the baptismal ceremony, but the person "got cold feet" and did not want to be immersed.

*Questions about Cause of the Breakup of the Marriage*

As mentioned at the beginning, one of the other key issues to be investigated is whether or not the petitioner was the prevailing cause for the breakup of the marriage. Therefore, questions about the cause of the separation or divorce must be asked of the parties and the witnesses. Sometimes the breakup of the marriage can be fairly said to be the fault of both parties even if in differing ways. Such evidence should not pose a difficulty for the presentation of the case to the Holy See. However it would be an issue that should be addressed in the bishop's *votum*, about which I will speak later.

On the other hand, not infrequently the respondent will accuse the petitioner of infidelity and even with the person whom he or she now wishes to marry. This allegation will necessitate a more thorough investigation about the matter. I have found that in such cases it usually more effective to meet in person with the petitioner rather than rely on the delegated auditor to properly question the petitioner on these issues. Such a procedure facilitates the asking of additional questions which are germane to the issue, questions which one might not expect the delegated auditor to frame in the course of the session.

Sometimes the additional investigation will surface information which affirms the parties could not have known one another before the breakup of the marriage. At other times the evidence will affirm that they knew one another, perhaps at their common place of employment, but were not seeing each other socially. Witnesses who would not ordinarily be called might be necessary. These would be friends or co-workers who were in a position to know both the petitioner and the intended party or other alleged sexual partner. The questionnaire for such witnesses would consist of special questions appropriate to substantiating or refuting the claims of the respondent.

Sometimes witnesses for absence of baptism are reluctant to speak about the cause of the breakup of the marriage. They feel uncomfortable talking about the matter even though they would have requisite knowledge. In that case other knowledgeable and willing witnesses need to be questioned so that there can be some objective evaluation about this matter.

*Questions about Non-Consummation when the Unbaptized Party was Baptized Later*

Sometimes it happens that the unbaptized party has become baptized but only after the divorce or separation has occurred. This fact does not mean that a favor of the Faith case cannot be pursued. The 1973 Norms addressed this issue as one of the three *sine qua non* conditions for granting a dissolution. In the first article of the 2001 Instruction we read: "A marriage entered by parties, of whom at least one is not baptized, can be dissolved by the Roman Pontiff in favor of the faith, as long as the marriage itself had not been consummated after both spouses received baptism." Later, in the section addressing the process, Article 17 states:

§1. If at the time when the favor of a dissolution is being sought the unbaptized spouse receives baptism, an investigation must be done concerning possible cohabitation after the baptism; witnesses are also to be questioned about this.

§2. The parties themselves in the case are to be questioned whether after their separation they again had some relation between themselves and of what kind, and especially whether they performed the conjugal act.

The provisions quoted above are not essentially new. The focus of such supplementary or additional investigation must be upon any probable cohabitation and sexual intercourse after baptism, that is, consummation of marriage after baptism. The issue of consummation is known first hand only by the parties in question. The witnesses are principally credibility witnesses in this regard.

With regard to the parties, one should mention the date of baptism and then ask whether or not the parties have been alone with each other after that time or renewed marriage by marital intercourse. With regard to the witnesses for this issue, it is perhaps only reasonable to inquire of them whether they would believe the parties if they had stated that there was no renewal of their marriage after the baptism. On this issue, the witnesses are essentially credibility witnesses. However, many times witnesses will volunteer information setting forth the circumstances which would argue against any such consummation of the marriage after baptism.

*Concerning children from the marriage and their support*

In addition to the investigation about the cause of the breakup of the marriage, if possible, according to Article 18, the instructor is to inquire about the present state of life of the respondent and whether the respondent has attempted a new marriage after the divorce.

The Holy See is also interested in knowing whether or not any children were born of the marriage for which a dissolution is being sought. Of course, the Church would be actively interested in having the children born of that marriage baptized and reared as Catholics. However this might not be possible because of civil law, as Article 20 references. If the children are minors, the respondent would have a legitimate interest in making a determination concerning the religious affiliation of the children. Further, it may simply not be possible for the petitioner to arrange for the baptism of these children, especially when the petitioner is *not* a candidate or a catechumen and, therefore, not entering the Catholic Church and is seeking the dissolution only to enable the Catholic party to be married in the Church.

Aside from the issue of the religious education of the children of the marriage for which a dissolution is being sought, Article 20, §2, directs the instructor to inquire about fulfillment of the moral or civil obligations towards the spouse and towards any children that may have been born of the marriage. This norm simply reflects canon 1071, §1, 3°, which states "Except in case of necessity, a person is not to assist without the permission of the local Ordinary at […] a marriage of a person who was bound by a natural obligations toward another party or children arising from a previous union." This provision in the new Instruction, which was also in the 1973 Instruction, Article 12, reflects the norm of canon 1689. This canon directs that in the definitive sentences both in formal cases and documentary cases, that the "parties are to be reminded of their moral and even civil obligations which may bind them both toward one another and toward their children to furnish support and education."

In practice, I have found it suffices to simply ask the witnesses and the parties whether there are any such obligations and whether they are being fulfilled. Sometimes a respondent may claim that the petitioner has not been paying child support payments. In such situations I have found it necessary even to obtain court records of payment of child support. Although this difficulty may not frequently arise, if it is raised, some effort needs to be made to resolve the question before sending the acts of the case to the Holy See.

*Issues concerning catechumens and candidates*

In some cases either the petitioner or the person whom the petitioner wishes to marry in the Church is a catechumen or a candidate. There are a number of issues around this pastoral situation.

It often happens that the preliminary instrument, which is the basis for a petition, indicates that there is some interest on the part of the petitioner in becoming a Catholic. However unless the petitioner will have completed instructions and is still actively interested in entering the Church by the time the case is sent to the Holy See, it would be better to pursue the case on the basis that the petitioner is willing to sign the mixed marriage promises. In that way, the presentation to the Holy See is more reflective of the true reality. If the petitioner later wishes to become a Catholic, there is nothing standing in the way of the conversion even though the case was presented to the Holy See with the request for either mixed religion or dispensation from disparity of worship.

However, if it seems fairly certain that the petitioner or the intended spouse is going to convert, then they need to be questioned about their intention to receive baptism or to become a Catholic (cf. Article 21, §1). Perhaps the more important evidence for a solid intention to become a Catholic comes from the observations and the testimony of the pastor or the priest who is the sponsor for the case at the parish level. Some tribunals may not use a true questionnaire for the pastor or the sponsoring priest but simply ask for a letter from him. However, I have found that all the important issues are more clearly addressed by using the questionnaire.

There are many parishes in our country which are staffed by that person described in canon 517, §2 to whom the bishop has decided that "participation in the exercise of the pastoral care of the parish is to be entrusted." There are various titles which are given to the person holding this position throughout this country. It seems quite important to obtain the testimony of the person described in this canon concerning the issues that would normally be asked of the pastor or the sponsoring priest. However, notwithstanding that these persons are usually more intimately involved with the petitioner and proposed spouse, the Congregation always wants also the testimony of a priest. This priest can be the one mentioned in canon 517, §2, who is "provided with the powers and faculties of a pastor," and "is to direct the pastoral care." However since the *Norms* do not address this issue directly, it would seem also legitimate to use the priest who may be called the *sacramental minister* when this priest is different from the one who "directs the pastoral care" of such a parish. From personal experience, I have found that when I had sent to Rome a case without the testimony of a priest, the Congregation sent back a request that the priest also be heard.

*Documents to be Included*

The 1973 Norms as well the 2001 Norms require certain documents to be included in the acts of the case. In this matter it is helpful to keep in mind the definition of documents in canon 1540, namely, that "[p]ublic ecclesiastical documents are those which a public person has drawn up in the exercise of that person's function in the Church, after the solemnities prescribed by law have been observed. Public civil documents are those which the laws of each place considered to be such. Other documents are private."

In many of these cases there are no public ecclesiastical documents directly concerned with the marriage for which a dissolution is being sought. In the cases in which the marriage is between two people who are not Catholic, which is most often the case, the civil certificate of marriage and decree of divorce are needed. However, a dissolution can be sought from a marriage in the Catholic Church in which one of the parties was unbaptized. Therefore, the following documents from such a marriage should be included:

1. The certificate of marriage drawn from the marriage record register of the Church where the marriage took place.
2. The prenuptial depositions of the parties and, if obtained, of any witnesses.
3. The petition for dispensation from the impediment of disparity of worship including the document of the mixed marriage promises signed by the Catholic party and the rescript or the document granting the dispensation from the impediment of disparity of worship.
4. The certificate of baptism of the Catholic party of such a marriage.

Among the other public ecclesiastical documents required are the certificates of baptism of the children that may have been born of the marriage for which a dissolution is being sought. Also, when the intended spouse of the petitioner is a Catholic, the certificate of that person's baptism is also required.

The petitioners and intended spouses often have entered more than one marriage. Therefore, Article 19, §2 mentions the "inclusion of copies of the dispositive part of the canonical sentence of marriage nullity of any marriages attempted by either intended spouse are to be presented, if they exist."

For example, the petitioner may have entered two or more marriages. If the dissolution of the first marriage is being sought in favor of the Faith, this marriage must be presumed to be valid according to canon 1060. Therefore, the documentary procedure outlined in canon 1686 and the following canons must be used to establish with moral certitude the nullity of any of the subsequent marriages based upon the impediment of *ligamen*.

Further, any such subsequent marriage or marriage preceding the one for which a dissolution is being sought might also be invalid by reason of lack of canonical form. The Pontifical Council for the Interpretation of Legislative Texts determined in 1984 that the only process needed to prove the state of freedom of those who were bound to canonical form yet attempted marriage before a civil official or a non-Catholic minister is the pre-nuptial investigation process mentioned in canons 1066-1067.[15] Nevertheless, since this case is being presented to the Holy See, the instructor or judicial vicar or any other judge should issue a declaration of freedom that the person is free of that marriage by reason of lack of canonical form. Such a document, since it is also a public ecclesiastical document, should be signed by the judicial vicar or judge as well as the notary.

The divorce decree is needed for any marriage of the petitioner which has ended in a divorce. It is needed as well as in the case of the intended spouse if she or he had been previously married and is now ecclesiastically free to marry. Although, as mentioned above, sentences or decrees of nullity of marriage for any subsequent or even prior marriages of the petitioner or the intended spouse must be in the acts, the Congregation also wants to know about the *civil freedom* of the parties. Therefore, in each and every case the decree of divorce must be included.

Since the decree of divorce is truly a public civil document, it must be truly a legitimate decree of divorce. Sometime petitioners simply send what they call "divorce papers." What one receives often are simply the documents which were provided by their attorney which are often simply the property settlement or other matters. What is needed is the decree of divorce that is signed by the judge who issued it and dated by the clerk of the court.

Mentioned earlier was the need for the document which named the officers who are involved in the instruction of the case. However, not infrequently parish priests or other persons involved in pastoral ministry are called upon to interview

---

[15] *AAS* 76 (1984): 747.

witnesses or even the petitioner and the intended spouse. In its procedural jurisprudence, the Congregation has made it clear it wants the instructor to show where he or she has delegated that person to take testimony. This can be easily handled. Any letter which is used to send the questionnaire to the parish priest or pastoral minister contains language which makes it clear that the person is being assigned this task by the instructor. When assembling the acts the instructor needs simply to remember to include this letter with the testimony which was obtained by that person.

## Report of the Instructor

Article 23 makes a brief mention of an "appropriate report to the Defender of the Bond." The *Notes* which were published subsequent to the new norms clarifies that such a report is distinct from the bishop's *votum*. Its content should report on such matters as the following:

a. The quality of the testimony obtained.
b. Why certain witnesses cited by the petitioner did not give formal testimony.
c. Why required searches of baptismal records may not have taken place.
d. Why the respondent was not heard.
e. Why the respondent or witnesses were heard in the manner they were.

Basically this report is designed to explain what elements were included or omitted in the instruction of the case. The report should anticipate any request that might be made by the Congregation "for additional testimony or some other completion of the Acts" (cf. *Notes*, #4, Report of the Instructor). Thus, this report is anything but a formality. I believe that a well designed report, as the *Notes* suggest, can prevent unnecessary delays by properly informing the Congregation what transpired in the instruction of the case which might not seem on the surface to be in total conformity with the *Norms*.

## Animadversions of the Defender of the Bond

Article 23 states that the animadversions are to be sought from "[t]he Defender of the bond who is to find reasons, if they exist, which oppose the dissolution of the bond." Therefore, the defender of the bond should be very familiar with the *Norms* so that he or she can surface any difficulties before the case is submitted for *votum*. If the defender does observe something that is substantial, the instructor must really try to remedy the problem, if possible, before sending the case to Rome. After doing the needed supplementary instruction, especially if it is substantial, it might be well for the instructor to submit an additional report and then submit the case to the defender of the bond for further comment. In such a situation the greater amount of time would always be consumed with trying to fix the problem rather than drafting the supplementary report and supplementary animadversions.

However, there is one caution concerning the role of the defender which also applies to formal cases. The defender of the bond should never argue for the merits of the case but should confine the animadversions to a negative critique of the process and of the testimony presented.

## *Votum* of the Bishop

Article 24 states that the bishop is to produce a *votum* about the case in "which precise reference is to made about the conditions to grant the favor being fulfilled and especially whether the *cautiones* mentioned in Article 5, have been given," where these are necessary. The *votum* is also, according to the same article, to contain reasons "which recommend granting the favor, always adding whether the petitioner has attempted a new marriage in any fashion or lives in concubinage."

The *votum* should not contain a law section. The *votum* is not like a definitive sentence which has to demonstrate the legal basis for a judgment. It is only the Holy Father who can make a judgment in these cases. It is the bishop's task to give an explanation of the merits of the case in his *votum*. Then, it is the task of the Congregation of the Doctrine of the Faith to make examination of the whole case and make a recommendation directly to the Holy Father. Further, there is no need to repeat in the *votum* the matters that were covered in the instructor's report.

## The Summary

Under the 1973 norms, the Congregation for the Doctrine of the Faith eventually provided a form for a summary which was required for every case for dissolution in favor of the Faith being transmitted to them. The 2001 *Norms* also require such a summary. A new form of that summary has now been given by the Congregation at the same time that the *Notes* were published.

There is nothing standing in the way of formatting this summary in a way convenient to the individual tribunal. Thus, to put the summary into a word processing document, for example, is not a problem. The summary is acceptable as long as it contains essentially the same text and sequence of material and is completed with the appropriate and available information.

## Authentication of the Acts

Article 25, §2 makes mention of a sworn affirmation about the faithful transcription of the acts. Likewise, if the local language of the tribunal is not one of those languages recognized for usage in the Roman Curia,[16] then the acts are to be translated. In such a situation there also needs to be a sworn affirmation about the accuracy of the translation.

The norm of Article 25, §2 reflects canon 1474, which states that in cases of appeal that "[a] copy of the acts authenticated by the attestation of a notary is to be sent to a higher tribunal." Thus, a document which is called "authentication of the acts" should be signed in each case by the notary and included at the end of the acts of the case.

## The Index of the Acts

Article 25, §1 mentions the requirement of an index of the material. When we read a case, we all like to have an index. It facilitates our analysis of what we are reading. It facilitates the work of the Congregation as it evaluates whether everything needed has been included in the acts. However some rationale needs to be developed for the arrangement of the material. The *Norms* do not direct any particular arrangement be followed. However, in my experience I have found that a rationale based upon both logic and chronology seems to work best.

Since the *Notes* suggest that the commission of the instructor, defender of the bond and the notary is to be established *after* the date of the petition, it would seem that the petition should be the first document in the acts of the case. It also seems equally logical that the records of marriage and divorce concerning the marriage for which the dissolution is being sought should be included after the petition and before the depositions of the parties or the other witnesses.

Although the petition is chronologically the first document in the case, there is nothing which requires the deposition of the petitioner be taken at the beginning of the instruction of the case. In fact, practical experience sometimes argues that it would be better to hear the petitioner at least after the respondent has been heard. It may happen that the respondent may raise issues concerning the petitioner's role in the breakup of the marriage. Rather than having to hear the petitioner a second time about that matter, it might be more practical simply to delay the questioning of the petitioner until after even all of the witnesses have been heard. Then, if special questions are needed to clarify the cause of the breakup of the marriage, for example, these can be incorporated into the questionnaire.

When a chronological rationale is being used, it might be best to arrange the testimonies as follows: the respondent's testimony or, if absent from the process, the documentation of the respondent's absence; the testimony of the witnesses concerning the absence of baptism and the cause of the breakup of the marriage; reports of the churches who were asked to search their baptismal records for any evidence of baptism of the unbaptized party; the deposition of the petitioner; the

---

[16] *Pastor Bonus*, Apostolic Constitution on the Roman Curia, promulgated June 28, 1988, art. 16.

deposition of the intended spouse; the deposition of the parish priest and any other parish minister who was involved with the petitioner.

Following the testimonies mentioned above should be the report of the instructor, the animadversions of the defender of the bond, and finally the *votum*. The authentication of the acts might well come at the end of the acts of the case. Of course, the index and summary could easily be positioned at the beginning or the end of the acts of the case.

The question might arise about where to place any declarations of nullity or declarations of freedom after a lack of form marriage. When these concern the petitioner, these might well come after the public or ecclesiastical documents concerning the marriage for which a dissolution is being sought. Those pertaining to the intended might be well positioned before or after the deposition of the intended.

However as I mentioned at the beginning, there is no statement in either in the *Norms* or in the *Notes* which mandate any particular order. The overriding consideration is to make the case easy to read for the Congregation. In that regard, I cannot stress enough the importance in eliminating so far as possible any handwritten testimony. This is very difficult to read especially when copied. There may be some occasions when an exception might be appropriate. However, with all the testimony in handwritten form, albeit printed by hand, reading the case would be all that more difficult for the Congregation.

*Special Situations*

Did the petitioner or intended spouse have an earlier favor of the Faith dissolution?

Article 6 notes that the bishop is not even to submit to the Holy See a request for dissolution of a marriage which was contracted only after one of the parties had already received a dissolution in favor of the Faith. Article 6 does not represent a change in the practices of the Holy See. Article 6, part 1 of the 1973 Norms stated, "the dissolution of a valid non-sacramental marriage, which was celebrated or convalidated after a dissolution of a prior valid, non-sacramental marriage had been obtained is not granted." However, under the 1973 Norms there were a number of instances where there was some confusion over the applicability of this norm.

This limitation also applies to any marriages that may have been previously entered by the *intended* party. For example, the intended spouse received a dissolution in favor of the Faith in the past and was thereby permitted to enter a marriage in the Church. However, the married life did not go well, and there was a divorce. Then, the person sought a declaration of nullity of that marriage successfully and so would be free to marry again. However this previous history would, in effect, disbar such a person from sharing in the dissolution in favor of the Faith to be sought by the petitioner. This would also be true if the spouse died

115

whom he or she married after receiving a dissolution. In cases of dissolution in favor of the Faith, both the actual petitioner as well as the intended spouse are in effect "the petitioner" for such a dissolution since they both share in the effects of the favor of the Faith.

Dissolutions of a marriage entered with
dispensation from the impediment of worship

The 1973 Norms also stated that a dissolution in favor of the Faith of a marriage entered with dispensation from the impediment of disparity of cult would not be granted to a Catholic petitioner who is seeking to enter a new marriage with an unbaptized person that was not converting. The same is true under the present norms pursuant to Article 7, §1. A dissolution is granted for the Catholic petitioner if the Catholic party now wishes to enter a new marriage with a baptized person, whether Catholic or not. However the intended spouse's baptism must be a valid, that is a baptism using the formulary "[i]n the name of the Father and the Son and the Holy Spirit."

There is another variation of this situation. When the unbaptized person married a Catholic with dispensation from disparity of worship is now seeking to enter marriage with a Catholic in the Church, he or she cannot petition unless the person is certainly going to be baptized.

General issues involving potential catechumens or candidates

As mentioned earlier, if a petitioning party is not thoroughly convinced that he or she wishes to become a Catholic, it is always best to present the case on the basis that such a person is *not converting* but is nonetheless willing to sign the usual mixed marriage promises. Further, petitioners who are catechumens are not always ready to be baptized when the favorable rescript is received from the Holy See. Article 8 clarifies that in such a situation "[t]he marriage is to be deferred until after baptism." For example, there may be a case in which the petitioner is a catechumen but has not yet completed instructions and is seeking for a grave reason to be married before it is possible to be baptized.

Article 8 states that, if the marriage cannot be deferred until after baptism, the marriage can take place if there are grave reasons and as long as there is "moral certitude that the baptism will be received soon." It would appear rather certain that in such a situation the Holy See would grant a dispensation from disparity of worship so that the marriage could take place without that impediment standing in the way. The *Norms* give no examples of such grave reasons. What might come to mind is the need to convalidate a marriage when the Catholic party is in danger of death.

116

## Catechumens or candidates received into
## the Church but invalidly married to Catholics

This is a very delicate issue. Clearly, the Church cannot condone bringing people into the Church who are not validly married. If the instructor is faced with this *fait accompli*, the case cannot be presented to the Holy See as it stands. The jurisprudence of the Holy See even under the 1973 Norms supports this conclusion. There must be some remedy for the pastoral situation which includes some change in the status of the interested parties that has the effect of bringing their status more into harmony with Church teaching.

There are two possible solutions to make it possible to recommend the case to the Holy See. If the interested parties are able and consent to live as "brother and sister," then they can continue to receive the sacraments and the case may be presented to Rome. However, both the petitioner and the intended must sign sworn depositions that they are both able and willing to live in this manner until they may be able to marry in the Church. In the aforementioned Apostolic Exhortation, the Holy Father mentioned this way of living as a legitimate means for Catholics to return to the sacraments.[17]

The second solution is usually more practical. If the petitioner and intended sign sworn depositions indicating their promise to refrain from receiving the sacraments until they may be able to marry in the Church, the case can go forward. In this situation the interested parties are simply accepting the condition of any divorced and remarried Catholic as the Holy Father also noted in *Familiaris Consortio*.[18]

The advent of the *Rite of Christian Initiation of Adults* engaged many more parishioners in the work of evangelization and the pastoral work of bringing converts into the Church. It is a difficult task to confront the interested inquirer with the need to do a marriage case before he or she can enter the Church. However, *RCIA* is not a program but a process, a process of ascertaining how the life of the interested person can come into harmony with the teaching of the Catholic Church. It would not be honest, at the very least, to overlook the teaching of the Church on marriage in order to make entrance into the Church an easier experience. As the *RCIA* started in this country, the marital status question was sometimes overlooked at the time inquirers registered into the process with the result that it was only sometime in Lent that the oversight was discovered. Sometimes the catechumen or candidate would then be allowed to go forward simply because he or she had progressed that far. However, if a favor of the Faith case is underway to establish the freedom to marry, this situation must be remedied as outlined above.

[17] Ibid.

[18] Ibid.

## Sincerity of Conversion

Questions can arise about the sincerity of conversion of the petitioner and the intended spouse. Article 7, §3 makes it quite clear that the bishop has the responsibility of not recommending a petition to the Congregation if he has a prudent doubt about the sincerity of the petitioner or the intended spouse in becoming a Catholic. This directive to the bishop applies whether or not the petitioner or the intended spouse has already received baptism.

Of course, the presumption would always be in favor of the sincerity of such persons. As mentioned earlier, the word of the parish priest or other parish pastoral minister is a very important for assuring the bishop there is no fear of insincerity. However, there could arise a situation in which the conversion seemed to be motivated solely and exclusively by the idea that this is the only way in which there can be a marriage in the Catholic Church. For that reason, if conversion is not necessary to fulfill the requirements for dissolution in favor of the Faith and there is some doubt about the desire to become a Catholic, it would be, as mentioned earlier, more prudent to avoid the issue by simply seeking the dissolution with no conversion of the petitioner and having both the petitioner and the intended sign the usual mixed marriage promises.

## Question about scandal and the fulfillment of natural obligations from the marriage

There may be special difficulties regarding fear of scandal or fulfillment of obligations arising from the prior marriage. The bishop has the obligation to consult the Congregation concerning fear of scandal if he has any. However the instructor should investigate any claims of scandal before moving the case forward.

The instructor likewise would investigate any claims that there are difficulties regarding the fulfillment of obligations arising from the marriage for which a dissolution is being sought. However, one or the other or both matters may still be in doubt, and yet there is the pastoral need to go forward. In that case the bishop should consult the Congregation about the matter. It would seem likely in such a situation that the case would have been already thoroughly investigated and otherwise ready to be submitted to the Holy See. The acts of the case would be transmitted in the usual way with a cover letter from the bishop or a provisional *votum*, in which he acknowledges the difficult about which he is consulting the Congregation.

## *Conclusion*

Although no marriage case, with the possible exception of the cases of lack of canonical form, is so routine in nature that a favorable and speedy outcome can be predicted, nonetheless, favor of the Faith cases are inherently simple and straightforward. In view of the length of this presentation one might be tempted to think such cases are not so simple and straightforward. However, I have tried to cover as many potential eventualities as possible in this paper.

As mentioned earlier, these cases are usually easier when the unbaptized person is the one petitioning for the dissolution. In many of those cases where the investigation goes smoothly, the instruction phase can be completed within some months and maybe within a few months. As is true with all marriage cases, the speed with which they move has a lot to do with personnel resources as well as with the ready cooperation of the witnesses.

Questionnaires in these cases are such that the instructor can easily sub-delegate a parish priest or others to obtain the testimony so that the old adage can be verified: "Many hands make light work." Many dioceses also have a growing cadre of volunteer persons in the field who could easily be trained as delegates of the instructor in these cases. The only *caveat* is that they should be well instructed on the manner of taking testimony in ecclesiastical proceedings and that documentation of their delegation by the instructor be included in the acts.

The last canon of the *Code of Canon Law* speaks of the fact that the supreme law of the Church is the salvation of souls. Indeed, the whole rationale for the granting of a dissolution in favor of the Faith is indeed a salvation of souls.

There are many tools that we use in our pastoral ministry. I believe that in tribunal ministry a favor of the Faith case is one such very useful and viable means for promoting the supreme law of the Church. The *raison d'etre* for the favor of the Faith has always been the salvation of souls.

CLSA PROCEEDINGS 64 (2002) 121-143

# THE RELATIONSHIP OF PUBLIC AND PRIVATE WORSHIP

VERY REVEREND JOHN J. M. FOSTER, JCL

A few weeks after the Most Reverend Stephen Blaire was installed as the fifth Bishop of Stockton in March of 1999, we were driving to a confirmation liturgy when he said that in his brief time in the diocese he had never seen so many different devotional practices among the people. Devotions he mentioned were those of the Mexican community to honor our Lady of Guadalupe, several Filipino devotions, Eucharistic devotions – both perpetual and periodic – a novena to our Mother of Perpetual Help during a weekday Mass, and numerous exercises surrounding Divine Mercy, just to name a few. The issue for the bishop wasn't the devotions themselves. Rather his concern centered on the fact that many of the devotional practices seemed to be more important to the people than the celebration of the liturgy.

The matter of devotional practices came to a head during the Easter season of 2001. Two weeks after the Second Sunday of Easter, I was given a copy of a program booklet from a parish celebration in honor of the "Feast of Divine Mercy." In addition to a letter from the pastor, the booklet also contained letters from two well-respected priests lauding the "Feast of Divine Mercy." When shown a copy of the booklet, the bishop found problematic not only the misnaming of the celebration but also the fact that the sacrament of penance was scheduled throughout the morning on the Second Sunday of Easter. Soon thereafter, Bishop Blaire asked the Liturgical Commission to begin the process of drafting norms concerning the celebration of devotional practices in the Diocese of Stockton.

The commission formed an *ad hoc* task force to begin the process of drafting norms to assist the clergy and faithful in harmonizing devotions with the liturgy. The task force included members of the commission, some priests from parishes known to have healthy devotional lives as well as some members of ethnic communities in which devotions play an important role. Taking Pope Paul VI's 1974 apostolic exhortation *Marialis cultus* as a starting point, the task force examined the theological foundations of devotional practices. In time, the task force completed its work, and Bishop Blaire promulgated *Norms for the Public Celebration of Devotions in the Diocese of Stockton* on March 6, 2002.

As I've researched the dynamic relationship between liturgy and devotions, especially in light of the *Directory on Popular Piety and the Liturgy: Principles and Guidelines*, recently published by the Congregation for Divine Worship and the Discipline of the Sacraments,[1] I have come to the conclusion that our experience in Stockton is not unique. Indeed, as the fathers at the Second Vatican Council, who took up this subject forty years ago this month, and the latest Roman document show, the dynamic tension between the public and private worship of the Church remains food for our spiritual, theological, and canonical reflection.

In our time together this afternoon, I propose four tasks. First, what do we mean by liturgy and devotions? Second, what are the rights and duties of the Christian faithful concerning liturgy and pious practices? Third, what are the rights and duties of the diocesan bishop with regard to the public and private worship of the Church? And finally, what practical applications might come from these theological and canonical reflections?

### Towards a Definition of Liturgy and Devotions

In baptism, the Christian faithful receive a share in the threefold *munera* of Christ, who is priest, prophet, and king. It is this priestly function, the *munus sanctificandi*, where we find our focus today. The faithful exercise this office of sanctifying in public and private worship. It is helpful to begin then, with a definition of public worship – the liturgy – and private worship – denoted at this point as devotions.[2]

A theological definition of liturgy is found in the Constitution on the Liturgy, *Sacrosanctum Concilium*. Number 7 states:

> the liturgy is considered as an exercise of the priestly office of Jesus Christ. In the liturgy, by means of signs perceptible to the senses, human sanctification is signified and brought about in ways proper to each of these signs; in the liturgy the whole public worship is performed by the Mystical Body of Jesus Christ, that is, by the Head and his members.
>
> From this it follows that every liturgical celebration, because it is an action of Christ the Priest and of his Body which is the Church, is a sacred action surpassing all others; no other action of the Church can equal its efficacy by the same title and to the same degree.[3]

---

[1] Congregation for Divine Worship and the Discipline of the Sacraments, *Directory on Popular Piety and the Liturgy: Principles and Guidelines*, 17 December 2001. While the *Directory* was promulgated in December, it was not released to the public until March 2002. Excerpts from the *Directory* used in this paper are taken from the English translation found at the Vatican's website, www.vatican.va.

[2] As will be shown below, the term "devotions" is shorthand for popular piety and pious exercises.

[3] Second Vatican Council, *Sacrosanctum Concilium*, 4 December 1963, n. 7 [Hereafter *SC*]; Translation from International Commission on English in the Liturgy, *Documents on the Liturgy 1963–1979: Conciliar, Papal, and Curial Texts* (Collegeville: The Liturgical Press, 1982), 1, no. 7. Hereafter

Juridically, the Church spells out its notion of liturgy in canon 834 of the *Code of Canon Law*. Section 1 of the canon presents a summary of the definition just cited from *Sacrosanctum Concilium*. Section 2 states:

> Such worship takes place when it is carried out in the name of the Church by persons legitimately designated and through acts approved by the authority of the Church.[4]

According to this definition, for acts of worship to qualify as liturgy, three conditions apply. First, the activity is "carried out in the name of the Church." The liturgy is the Church's worship of God through Jesus in the Holy Spirit; it isn't the work of Sam and Jenny, Bill and Lucy who meet casually on the street corner. The liturgy – while the action of the total Christ, Head and members – belongs to the entire Church; it is a treasure of the Church. Therefore, for an act to be called liturgy, it is carried out in the name of the Church. Second, acts of liturgy are done "by persons legitimately designated." As Fred McManus points out in his commentary on this canon, the designation referred to here is by baptism. In virtue of dying and rising to new life in Christ through baptism, the faithful not only have a right to full, conscious, and active participation in the liturgy, it is their duty as well.[5] There is also a more specific designation that is stipulated in the ritual books themselves. For example, a priest, deacon, or layperson may bless a new home, but the blessing of a baptistery is reserved to the bishop or delegated priest.[6] Third, acts of worship must be "approved by the authority of the Church" to qualify as liturgy. Relying on article 22 of *Sacrosanctum Concilium*, canon 838 provides three levels of authority for regulating the liturgy: the Apostolic See, the conference of bishops, and the diocesan bishop. In most cases, the rites approved by ecclesiastical authority are found in the approved liturgical books. There may, however, be rites canonically approved by the diocesan bishop for use in his diocese. Examples might include a ritual for the closing of a parish or an order for the blessing of sponsors.[7] To summarize: if an act of worship has been approved by competent authority to be carried out in the name of the Church by persons properly deputed, then it can be properly called liturgy.

"The spiritual life, however, is not limited solely to participation in the

---

citations from *Documents on the Liturgy* will be abbreviated *DOL* followed by the margin reference.

[4] *Code of Canon Law: Latin–English Edition, New English Translation* (Washington, DC: Canon Law Society of America, 1998). Hereafter all English versions of the canons will come this translation.

[5] *SC*, 14; *DOL*, 14.

[6] *Book of Blessings* (1989), n. 661 (for the blessing of a new home) and n. 1087 (for the blessing of a baptistery).

[7] For the latter, see *Order for the Blessing of Sponsors/Orden de la Bendición de Padrinos: Ritual Edition for the Diocese of Stockton* (2001).

liturgy."[8] Indeed, as this quotation from *Sacrosanctum Concilium*, n. 12 states, the *munus sanctificandi* of the Church is not limited to public worship. The conciliar fathers go on:

> Popular devotions of the Christian people are to be highly endorsed, provided they accord with the laws and norms of the Church, above all when they are ordered by the Apostolic See.
> Devotions proper to particular Churches also have a special dignity if they are undertaken by mandate of the bishops according to customs or books lawfully approved.[9]

What the Constitution on the Liturgy calls "devotions" has been refined in the intervening years – first in *Marialis cultus*, and more recently in the *Directory of Popular Piety and Liturgy*. Indeed, the *Directory* provides definitions of pious exercises, devotions, popular piety, and popular religiosity – terms we sometimes throw around without nuance. It may be helpful to think of these terms as concentric circles. In the innermost circle we find pious exercises. Pious exercises can be public or private expressions of Christian piety that are inspired by and in harmony with the liturgy. They may have been established by competent ecclesiastical authority and form part of the cultic patrimony of a particular Church or religious family. Finally, "pious exercises always refer to public divine revelation and to an ecclesial background."[10] Many of those celebrations we call "para-liturgies" would be more properly called pious exercises.

The next larger circle is devotions, here used with a specific meaning. The *Directory* states:

> In the present context, this term is used to describe various external practices (e.g. prayers, hymns, observances attached to particular times or places, insignia, medals, habits or customs). Animated by an attitude of faith, such external practices manifest the particular relationship of the faithful with the Divine Persons, or the Blessed Virgin Mary in her privileges of grace and those of her titles which express them, or with the Saints in their configuration with Christ or in their role in the Church's life.[11]

Popular piety, the next larger circle, covers varied forms of cultic expression – whether private or communal – that find inspiration not in the liturgy primarily

---

[8] *SC*, 12; *DOL*, 12.
[9] *SC*, 13; *DOL*, 12.
[10] *Directory*, 7.
[11] Ibid., 8.

but in a nation, people, or culture. Popular piety speaks of the theological values that underlie the faith in God of a people and spawn interior Christian attitudes.[12] The apparitions of Our Lady of Guadalupe to Blessed Juan Diego, for example, fall within the realm of popular piety.[13]

The outermost circle encompasses popular religiosity. Popular religiosity is common to all people in that all humans have the desire to express their view of the transcendent. Because of the universal nature of popular religiosity, it will not always make reference to Christian revelation.[14] The appeal of television programs such as "Touched by an Angel" demonstrates the inherent power of popular religiosity.

With liturgy and devotions defined, it might be helpful to examine briefly how they relate to one another. *Sacrosanctum Concilium*, n. 13 states that "devotions should be so fashioned that they harmonize with the liturgical seasons, accord with the sacred liturgy, are in some way derived from it, and lead the people to it, since, in fact, the liturgy by its very nature far surpasses any of them."[15]

Based on the teaching found in *Sacrosanctum Concilium*, n. 7, we see it explicitly stated that the liturgical action has a primacy over devotional action. This is rooted in the theological difference of the two actions. The liturgy is an exercise of the priestly ministry of Christ in his passion, death, and resurrection; devotions are not. The *Directory on Popular Piety* states boldly:

> The faithful should be made conscious of the preeminence of the Liturgy over any other possible form of legitimate Christian prayer. While sacramental actions are *necessary* to life in Christ, the various forms of popular piety are properly *optional*. Such is clearly proven by the Church's precept which obliges attendance at Sunday Mass. No such obligation, however, has obtained with regard to pious exercises, notwithstanding their worthiness or their widespread diffusion.[16]

---

[12] Ibid., 9.

[13] See Fanny Cepeda Pedraza, "Hispanic Catholic Identity: The Role of Culture and Faith" *NCCL Catechetical Update* 25 (Spring 2002) 7–8:

The apparitions of Our Lady to Juan Diego in Tepeyac, even if such apparitions were not historical according to modern Western historiography, are still definitely constitutive of the saving truth of the *sensum fidelium* – the faith memory of the people. The full impact of Guadalupe can only be appreciated in the context of salvation history, not just as a Mexican happening. In the year that the natives began their condemnation to humiliation, enslavement, hared labor and destruction, the mother of God brought them a liberating message and Tepeyac became a sacred space in the American continent, where an unlimited diversity of peoples experience a common home.

[14] Ibid., 10.

[15] SC, 13; DOL, 13.

[16] *Directory*, 11. Emphasis in the original.

The *Directory* also frames the theological distinction in this reminder to pastors: "In relation to sacred 'representations' [one form of pious exercises] it is important to instruct the faithful on the difference between a 'representation' which is commemorative, and the 'liturgical actions' which are anamnesis, or mysterious presence of the redemptive event of the Passion."[17] For this reason, Pope John Paul II told the 2001 plenary meeting of the Congregation for Divine Worship and the Discipline of the Sacraments that "the Liturgy is the centre of the Church's life and cannot be substituted by, or placed on a par with, any other form of religious expression."[18]

Not only is there a fundamental theological difference between the liturgy and devotions, the Constitution tells us, there is also a symbiotic relationship. Devotions are derived from the liturgy but also lead people to the liturgy. In the mutual relationship between liturgy and devotions, one must recall that it is popular piety that must be harmonized with the liturgy – not vice versa.[19] This important point is seen throughout the *Directory*. Pious exercises with Sunday as the main chronological point of reference are not to be encouraged.[20] If pious exercises are attentive to the rhythm and demands of the liturgy, especially the liturgical year, hybrid forms of worship wherein liturgy and devotions are mixed, will be eliminated.[21] Ultimately, the *Directory* offers this reminder:

> Thus, it is important that the question of the relationship between popular piety and the Liturgy not be posed in terms of contradiction, equality or, indeed, of substitution. A realization of the primordial importance of the Liturgy, and the quest for its most authentic expressions, should never lead to neglect of the reality of popular piety, or to a lack of appreciation for it, nor any position that would regard it as superfluous to the Church's worship or even injurious to it.[22]

### *Worship and the Christian Faithful: Duties and Rights*

The obligations and rights of all the Christian faithful are enumerated primarily – though not exclusively – in canons 208 to 223, found in Book II, Part I, Title I

---

[17] Ibid., 144.

[18] John Paul II, Address to the Plenary Meeting of the Congregation for Divine Worship and the Discipline of the Sacraments, 21 September 2001. Excerpts from this address are published with the English translation of the *Directory on Popular Piety* on the Vatican web site.

[19] See *Directory*, 58 and 73.

[20] Ibid., 95.

[21] Ibid., 74.

[22] Ibid., 50. See also n. 58.

of the *Code of Canon Law*. We canonists recall that the duties and rights found in these sixteen canons were written by the *coetus* drafting the schema *De Populo Dei* and the *coetus* drafting the *Lex Ecclesiae Fundamentalis*. When the decision was made in 1981 not to publish the *Lex Ecclesiae Fundamentalis*, its listing of obligations and rights was included in Book II along with several canons from the schema *De Populo Dei*.[23]

Before examining the duties and rights of the Christian faithful germane to the sanctifying office, it will also be helpful to bear in mind that the source of rights and duties is found in the human person. As *Gaudium et spes* states, all people

> are endowed with a rational soul and are created in God's image; they have the same nature and origin and, being redeemed by Christ, they enjoy the same divine calling and destiny; there is here a basic equality between all men [and women] and it must be given ever greater recognition.[24]

For the Christian, baptism into Christ endows each member of the Christian faithful with a fundamental equality and dignity. Taken from *Lumen gentium* 32, canon 208 provides the foundation for all the other obligations and duties.

> From their rebirth in Christ, there exists among all the Christian faithful a true equality regarding dignity and action by which all cooperate in the building up of the Body of Christ according to each one's own condition and function.

What is clear from these citations is the development that has occurred over the last century with regard to understanding the source of rights. No longer are rights and obligations considered to be a grant from some external competent authority – as was the case in previous centuries.[25] Rather, rights and duties find their genesis in the human person, and ecclesially, in baptism.

Of course, the Christian faithful do not possess rights and duties for their own sakes. Canon 208 reminds us that the equality we share in Christ is for the purpose of "building up the Body of Christ." Indeed, it is maintaining *communio* that is the

---

[23] See James H. Provost's discussion of this process in *The Code of Canon Law: A Text and Commentary*, James A. Coriden et al., eds. (New York/Mahwah: Paulist Press, 1985), 135–136.

[24] Second Vatican Council, *Gaudium et spes*, 8 December 1965, 29; Translation from Austin Flannery, O.P., ed., *Vatican Council II: The Conciliar and Post Conciliar Documents*, vol. 1 (Northport, New York: Costello Publishing Company, 1984), 929.

[25] Provost, 134.

Christian's primary obligation and right.[26]

Canons 212 to 215 speak directly to the obligations and duties of the Christian faithful concerning the sanctifying office. A word about each canon is in order.

Canon 212, §2 articulates the right of the Christian faithful "to make known to the pastors of the Church their needs, *especially spiritual ones*, and their desires."[27] The fact that spiritual needs are highlighted in this canon is not meant to limit the right of the faithful to make known their other needs. For our purposes here, though, this canon provides a basis for the Christian faithful to approach their pastors with the request to nourish them spiritually from both the liturgical and devotional arenas of the Church's life of worship.

Canon 213 explicates the spiritual needs mentioned in the previous canon: "The Christian faithful have the right to receive assistance from the sacred pastors out of the spiritual goods of the Church, especially the word of God and the sacraments." At first glance, the phrase, "the word of God and the sacraments," might lead one to conclude that the focus of this canon is on the public worship of the Church. However, "the spiritual goods of the Church," while including the word of God and the sacraments, are not limited to them. We can look to canons 834 and 839 to see what "the spiritual goods of the Church" referred to in canon 213 include. In addition to the Church's public worship found in her ritual books prescribed by canon 834, we read in canon 839, §1:

> The Church carries out the function of sanctifying also by other means, both by prayers in which it asks God to sanctify the Christian faithful in truth, and by works of penance and charity which greatly help to root and strengthen the kingdom of Christ in souls and contribute to the salvation of the world.

As we've already seen above, pious exercises and devotions demonstrate another way by which the Christian faithful participate in and access the spiritual goods of the Church. The *Directory on Popular Piety* underscores the fact that the public and private worship of the faithful manifests the spiritual goods of the Church when it says, "the liturgy and popular piety are two forms of worship which are in mutual and fruitful relationship with each other."[28]

While the Christian faithful have the right to receive from their pastors of the spiritual goods of the Church, the obligation falls to the pastors to provide for this

---

[26] Canon 209, §1: "The Christian faithful, even in their own manner of acting, are always obliged to maintain communion with the Church." See Robert J. Kaslyn, S.J.'s excursus on the notion of *communio* as the focus of the duties and rights of the Christian faithful in *New Commentary on the Code of Canon Law*, John P. Beal et al., eds. (New York/Mahwah: Paulist Press, 2000), 254–258.

[27] Emphasis added.

[28] *Directory*, 58.

right. Clearly, pastors have the duty to prepare their people for the celebration of the sacraments and not to deny the sacraments to those properly disposed (c. 843). However, with an ever-increasing dearth of priests to shepherd God's people, the Church's pastors can also provide for the faithful by empowering them to live out their baptismal priesthood. In recent years, we have seen more trained lay ministers presiding over funeral vigils and celebrations of the word of God for catechumens, not to mention Sunday celebrations in the absence of a priest. A large percentage of the blessings contained in the *Book of Blessings* can be celebrated under the presidency of a lay person. Most, if not all, pious exercises and devotions can be led by a lay person.

Canon 214 speaks directly to the right of the Christian faithful to worship God and to follow a form of spiritual life. The canon states:

> The Christian faithful have the right to worship according to the prescripts of their own rite approved by the legitimate pastors of the Church and to follow their own form of spiritual life so long as it is consonant with the doctrine of the Church.

Clearly, the phrase "of their own rite" refers to the Church *sui iuris* into which one is enrolled at the time of baptism or legitimate transfer.[29] However, the text around this phrase, as well as the phrase itself also articulates the right of the faithful to participate in the ritual celebrations according to the approved liturgical books. Canon 846, §1 states the obligations of ministers in this way:

> In celebrating the sacraments the liturgical books approved by competent authority are to be observed faithfully; accordingly, no one is to add, omit, or alter anything in them on one's own authority.

The right guaranteed by canon 214 and the obligation stated in canon 846 remind us that the liturgy is the treasure of the Church, belonging to no one person or group of people. In his commentary on this canon, James Provost raises the possibility of the violation of this right as the subject of a canonical trial when he writes: "Those who fail to do so [follow canon 846, §1] may be denying members of the congregation a basic right."[30]

The second half of canon 214 proclaims the right of the Christian faithful "to follow their own form of spiritual life." This right is qualified, however, as it must be "consonant with the doctrine of the Church." As we will see below, it falls to

---

[29] See Provost in *The Code of Canon Law: A Text and Commentary*, 148; Kaslyn in *New Commentary on the Code of Canon Law*, 269; and Aidan McGrath in the Canon Law Society of Great Britain and Ireland, *The Canon Law: Letter and Spirit* (Collegeville: The Liturgical Press, 1995), 122.

[30] Provost, 148.

local ordinaries to see "that the prayers and pious and sacred exercises of the Christian people are fully in keeping with the norms of the Church."[31]

In leading their own form of spiritual life, the Christian faithful are free to form associations. Canon 215 states:

> The Christian faithful are at liberty freely to found and direct associations for purposes of charity *and piety* or for the promotion of the Christian vocation in the world and to hold meetings for the common pursuit of these purposes.[32]

The *Directory on Popular Piety* refers to associations of the faithful and confraternities throughout its discussion of principles and guidelines. When addressing the subjects of popular piety, the *Directory* asserts:

> Equally important subjects of popular piety are the confraternities and other pious associations of the faithful. [. . .] The Church recognizes the confraternities and grants juridical personality to them, approves their statutes and fosters their cultic ends and activities. They should, however, avoid conflict and isolation by prudent involvement in parochial and diocesan life.[33]

Most pious associations do not possess, nor have they have requested, approval or recognition according to the norms of canons 298 – 329. Rather, they prefer to remain *de facto* associations – small, loose knit groups of clerics and lay people devoted to a specific pious exercise or devotional practice. The *Directory*'s challenge to these associations to avoid conflict and to remain involved in parish and diocesan life is an important one in the Church in the information age. Television and the Internet make it far easier than in years past for groups to be influenced in ways not "consonant with the doctrine of the Church." This appears to be another area where the oversight of local ordinaries is needed.

Finally, while not listed among the duties and rights of the Christian faithful in Book II, the specific role played by the laity in the Church's sanctifying office is found in canon 835, §4:

> The other members of the Christian faithful also have their own part in the function of sanctifying by participating actively in their own way in liturgical celebrations, especially the Eucharist. Parents share in a particular way in this function by leading a conjugal life

---

[31] Canon 839, §2.

[32] Emphasis added.

[33] *Directory*, 69.

in a Christian spirit and by seeing to the Christian education of their children.

The first three sections of this canon – concerning the roles of bishops, presbyters, and deacons in the office of sanctifying – and section 4, save for the final clause, come from the *Lex Ecclesiae Fundamentalis*.[34] Thus, placed in this context in Book IV, the canon proclaims the right of the Christian faithful to participate actively in the Church's worship.

While the first sentence of the canon focuses on the liturgical – and not devotional – role the laity have in the Church's worship, the second sentence concerning the role of parents encompasses the totality of the life of worship in the "Christian spirit." Referring to the final clause on the duty of parents to see to the Christian education of their children, Fred McManus makes this observation:

> [I]t can best be understood as a single and significant illustration of the breadth of the sanctifying function which every Christian believer enjoys in relation to others (children to parents and to their sisters and brothers, spouse to spouse and to other family members, neighbor to neighbor, worker to worker, etc.) not only in the liturgical celebrations of the Church but in every dimension of Christian living.[35]

In summary, the obligations and rights of the faithful concerning Christian worship have their source in the human person and baptism into Christ. The faithful may freely ask for and receive spiritual assistance from the Church. Likewise they possess the right to worship according to their own rite and according to the approved liturgical books as well as to choose a form of spiritual life suitable for themselves. In doing this, they are able to form associations to meet this end.

As we have seen, these rights of the Christian faithful entail obligations on the part of their pastors. Let us now turn to the duties and rights of the diocesan bishop in the sanctifying office.

### Worship and the Diocesan Bishop: Duties and Rights

In the office of sanctifying, bishops exercise the first place. We recall from *Lumen gentium* that

episcopal consecration bestows the fullness of the sacrament of

---

[34] *Lex Ecclesiae Fundamentalis*, c. 67.
[35] Frederick R. McManus in *New Commentary on the Code of Canon Law*, 1009.

orders, that fullness of power, namely, which in both the Church's liturgical practice and the language of the Fathers is called the high priesthood, the summit of the sacred ministry.[36]

Indeed, "the bishop is to be looked on as the high priest of his flock, the faithful's life in Christ in some way deriving from and depending on him."[37] Canon 835, §1 enshrines these foundational principles:

> The bishops in the first place exercise the sanctifying function; they are the high priests, the principal dispensers of the mysteries of God, and the directors, promoters, and guardians of the entire liturgical life in the Church entrusted to them.

These theological insights from the Second Vatican Council resulted in a renewed way of looking at episcopal authority.[38] Whereas the 1917 *Code of Canon Law* prescribed in canon 1257 that the Apostolic See alone regulated the liturgy, and in canons 1259 and 1261 that the local ordinary exercised vigilance over the public and private worship in his diocese, a marked change is found in the present universal law. Canon 838 sets forth the regulation of the liturgy in four sections. Section 1 reads: "The direction of the sacred liturgy depends solely on the authority of the Church which resides in the Apostolic See and, according to the norm of law, the diocesan bishop." Section 2 explicates how the Apostolic See orders the liturgy. The specific role of episcopal conferences in the regulation of the liturgy is the subject of section 3. The final section of the canon reprises the diocesan bishop's function: "Within the limits of his competence, it pertains to the diocesan bishop in the Church entrusted to him to issue liturgical norms which bind everyone."

A first question to be addressed concerns the scope of the diocesan bishop's authority in the liturgical arena. Notice that the phrase in section 1 of canon 838, "according to the norm of law," and the words "within the limits of his competence" in section 4 restrict the authority of the bishop. The qualitative difference between the provisions of canon 838 in the 1983 code and canon 1261 in the former code is one of approach. In the latter norm, the local ordinary was restricted from acting except when he was exercising vigilance concerning the observance of the sacred canons on divine worship. However, in light of *Christus Dominus* 8, the bishop now possesses all ordinary and immediate power to act, except where that power is restricted by law. An example of such a restriction is found in sections 2 and 3 of canon 838. The Apostolic See alone has authority to

---

[36] Second Vatican Council, *Lumen gentium*, 21 November 1964, n. 21; *DOL*, 145.

[37] *SC*, 41; *DOL*, 41.

[38] Second Vatican Council, *Christus Dominus*, 28 October 1965, n. 8.

order the liturgy for the universal Church, to publish liturgical books, and to review their translation. Likewise, conferences of bishops possess the authority to prepare and publish (after receiving the *recognitio*) translations of liturgical books and to adapt them within the limits defined in the books themselves. For a bishop to perform any of these acts would be for him to exceed his authority. Clearly this leaves the diocesan bishop with extensive authority to regulate the liturgy.

At the beginning of this presentation I mentioned the order for the blessing of sponsors. Two years ago, the Christian Initiation Advisory Board of the Diocese of Stockton was looking for a way to publicly recognize those people who serve as sponsors for the catechumens and candidates in the RCIA process. One parish submitted a copy of a ritual it had been using for several years at Sunday Eucharist. Knowing the prescription of canon 846, §1 that "no one is to add, omit, or alter anything in [the approved liturgical books] on one's own authority," the Office for Worship prepared a complete ritual text for the blessing of sponsors modeled on blessings found in the *Book of Blessings*. The order of blessing of sponsors was translated into Spanish and promulgated as the typical edition by Bishop Blaire for liturgical use in the Diocese of Stockton in virtue of the authority granted to him in canon 838, §§1 and 4. This is just one example of a need that surfaced in the diocese where the bishop took the opportunity to regulate the liturgy as the law permits, providing order and preventing parochial accretions from infecting the liturgy.

A second question to be addressed concerns the subjects of the bishop's competence. Section 4 states that any liturgical norms issued by the bishop bind everyone. No one is exempt from the liturgical authority of the diocesan bishop, except those of a different liturgical rite.[39] Because liturgical norms issued by the diocesan bishop are territorial and not personal, they "bind those for whom they were issued as well as those who have a domicile or quasi-domicile there and who at the same time are actually residing there,"[40] including religious.[41] Whereas travelers (*peregrini*) are not bound by particular laws of the territory in which they are present, canon 13, §2, 1° does bind them to observe laws providing for public order. Any liturgical laws issued by the diocesan bishop certainly fall into this category. Transients (*vagi*) are bound by all universal and particular laws in force where they are present.[42]

If canon 838 pertains to the authority of the diocesan bishop concerning the regulation of the public worship of the Church as defined in canon 834, canon 839 speaks to the Church's private worship. Canon 839 states:

---

[39] Ibid., 35.
[40] Canon 12, §3.
[41] Canon 678, §1.
[42] Canon 13, §2, 3°.

§1. The Church carries out the function of sanctifying also by other means, both by prayers in which it asks God to sanctify the Christian faithful in truth, and by works of penance and charity which greatly help to root and strengthen the kingdom of Christ in souls and contribute to the salvation of the world.

§2. Local ordinaries are to take care that the prayers and pious and sacred exercises of the Christian people are fully in keeping with the norms of the Church.

As we have seen already, this canon has its conciliar source in *Sacrosanctum Concilium* 12 and 13. Also, like its predecessor in canon 1259 of the 1917 code, the present canon gives to local ordinaries – and not only the diocesan bishop[43] – a vigilance function with regard to devotional practices. While not derogating from the norm of canon 839, §2 concerning local ordinaries, it is interesting to note the audience to whom the *Directory on Popular Piety* is addressed:

The operative proposals of this Directory, which are intended solely for the Latin Church and primarily for the Roman Rite, are addressed firstly to the Bishops, whose office entails presiding over the worshiping community of the dioceses, promoting the liturgical life and coordinating other forms of worship with it. They are also intended for the Bishops' closest collaborators – their episcopal Vicars, priests, deacons and especially the Rectors of sanctuaries. These proposals are also intended for the major Superiors of the institutes of consecrated life – both male and female, since many forms of popular piety arose within, and were developed by, such institutes, and because the religious and the members of the secular institutes can contribute much to the proper harmonization of the various forms of popular piety with the Liturgy.[44]

The inclusion of priests, deacons, and rectors, along with male and female major superiors, among those who play a role in overseeing popular piety is a helpful step forward in collaborative ministry in the sanctifying office.

In many ways, the *Directory on Popular Piety* is a useful, extended commentary on the local ordinary's authority concerning private worship. It may be helpful to examine briefly three ways in which the *Directory* assists the competent authority to oversee popular piety in the local Church.

First, the *Directory* reminds bishops in ways general and specific of their

---

[43] Canon 134, §§1 and 2 states that local ordinaries are the Roman Pontiff, diocesan bishop and those equivalent to him in law, vicars general, and episcopal vicars.

[44] *Directory*, 5.

responsibility to provide oversight of and direction to the faithful in their private worship. Above all, this means maintaining the clear distinction and proper harmonization between the liturgy and popular piety. Number 21 of the *Directory* states:

> Manifestations of popular piety are subject to the jurisdiction of the local Ordinary. It is for him to regulate such manifestations, to encourage them as a means of assisting the faithful in living the Christian life, and to purify and evangelize them where necessary. He is also to ensure that they do not substitute for the Liturgy nor become part of the liturgical celebrations. The local ordinary also approves the prayers and formulae associated with acts of public piety and devotional practices. The dispositions given by a particular local Ordinary for the territory of his jurisdiction are for the particular Church entrusted to his pastoral care.

In other places, however, the *Directory* prompts bishops or local ordinaries:

- to approve public prayers attached to pious exercises or devotions;[45]
- to ensure that sacred images produced for the faithful – whether for personal use[46] or in churches[47] – do not promote error or superstition; and
- to ascertain that shrines have the appropriate canonical approval because of their cultic importance.[48]

A final note of interest concerning the extent of the episcopal oversight is mention of the conference of bishops. In his September 2001 address to the plenary meeting of the Congregation for Divine Worship and the Discipline of the Sacraments, Pope John Paul II cites popular piety as a fitting sphere for episcopal collegiality. He writes:

> Judgments on these matters is for the diocesan Bishop or for the Bishops of a given territory in which such forms are found. In this case, Bishops should share their experience so as to provide common pastoral guidelines and avoid contradictory positions which can be detrimental for the Christian people. In any event, Bishops

---

[45] Ibid., 16.
[46] Ibid., 18.
[47] Ibid., 244.
[48] Ibid., 264.

should take a positive and encouraging stance with regard to popular religiosity, unless there are patently obvious reasons to the contrary.[49]

The *Directory* itself provides for an episcopal conference role when dealing with "pious exercises widely diffused in a particular country or in a vast region," always observing the competence of the local ordinary or major superior.[50] While such a guideline might be helpful for more homogeneous nations, one can easily foresee in episcopal conferences with many members that no consensus would be reached. Instead, the underutilized canonical institute of the ecclesiastical province or region would be a helpful forum in which to address these concerns.[51]

Second, in providing theological, ecclesiological, and liturgical principles for understanding popular piety, the *Directory* assists bishops and other local ordinaries in promoting effective private worship among the Christian faithful. While located primarily in chapters two and three of the *Directory*, the values of popular piety are found throughout the document. In its presentation of this theological foundation, the *Directory* succeeds admirably in its goal of offering guidelines in a tone that is "positive and constructive."[52] Just a sampling of examples will show how the document underscores these Christian values in popular piety.

- "The Gospel is the measure against which all expressions of Christian piety – both old and new – must be measured."[53]
- A biblical, liturgical, ecumenical, and anthropological spirit must permeate popular piety.[54]
- Popular piety manifests the virtues of patience, trusting abandonment to God, a desire to please God through penance and reparation, detachment from material things, and solidarity with others through friendliness and charity.[55]

Throughout the second part of the *Directory on Popular Piety*, the principles articulated in Part I are used as a framework for discussing popular piety in relation to the liturgical year, the veneration of Mary and the saints, suffrage for the dead, and shrines and pilgrimages. It is here that the congregation raises areas requiring

[49] John Paul II, Address, 5.

[50] *Directory*, 92.

[51] See canons 431, §1 and 433, §1.

[52] *Directory*, 4.

[53] Ibid., 12.

[54] Ibid.

[55] Ibid., 61.

the vigilance of local ordinaries. Bearing in mind that the *Directory* is a document for the entire Church, and not every pious exercise or devotion is practiced everywhere,[56] nor is every cited abuse present everywhere, it will suffice to name but a few examples of areas suitable for ecclesiastical oversight.

- The season of Advent, while apt for devotion to the Mother of God, "cannot be represented merely as a 'Marian month'."[57]
- Devotion to the Cross must always have "its essential reference to the Resurrection of Christ: the Cross, the empty tomb, the Death and Resurrection of Christ are indispensable in the Gospel narrative of God's salvific plan."[58]
- The *Directory* seeks "to ensure that such manifestations of popular piety, either by time or the manner in which the faithful are convoked, do not become a surrogate for the liturgical celebrations of Good Friday."[59]
- "The practice of assigning names to the Holy Angels should be discouraged, except in the cases of Gabriel, Raphael and Michael whose names are contained in Holy Scripture."[60]
- While the names of the *Beati* may be invoked in litanies of the saints, "the names of those whose cult has not received ecclesial recognition should not be used in the litanies."[61]

In a pastoral way, the *Directory* points out areas where pious exercises and devotions have either overstepped their bounds or become isolated from the Christian message. At the same time, the document does a wonderful job of offering suggestions on ways popular piety can be harmonized with the liturgy. For example, the *Directory* suggests:

- At Midnight Mass, the proclamation of the Savior's birth could be sung.[62]
- The *asperges* might be used at Masses on the feast of the Baptism of the Lord.[63]

---

[56] Indeed, the *Directory*, 4 states: "Mention of particular practices or expressions of popular piety is not to be regarded as an invitation to adopt them where they are not already practiced." See also no. 17.

[57] *Directory*, 100.

[58] Ibid., 128.

[59] Ibid., 143.

[60] Ibid., 217.

[61] Ibid., 235.

[62] Ibid., 111.

[63] Ibid., 119.

- When conflicts exist over the celebration of the saints and *Beati*, the norms given in the *Missale Romanum* and Roman Calendar are to be followed.[64]

For those unschooled in the finer points of the liturgy, however, the interweaving of suggestions for liturgical and devotional practices might be confusing. Presumably this should not be a problem for bishops and their collaborators, but the wide distribution the *Directory* has received over the Internet clearly shows the Congregation's interest in catechizing all the Christian faithful.

To summarize, the diocesan bishop enjoys a number of duties and rights connected with his *munus sanctificandi*. Most notably, he has authority, according to the norm of law, to regulate the liturgy in his particular Church. Further, because the sanctifying office is not limited solely to public worship, local ordinaries are charged with the responsibility of seeing that pious practices are in keeping with the norms of the Church. The *Directory on Popular Piety* can be a great help in assisting competent authorities in not only exercising vigilance over the private worship of the faithful but also in providing sound catechesis for that private worship.

### Public and Private Worship: Some Practical Applications

In light of the theological and canonical reflections discussed today, I would like to conclude by examining briefly three practical applications of the dynamic relationship between the liturgy and pious practices.

Nowhere is the nexus of public and private worship better illustrated than in the buildings where the Church is gathered. While these edifices of brick and mortar, stone and wood are erected principally for the celebration of the Church's liturgy, it cannot be denied that sacred spaces also serve as places where Christians of diverse cultures come individually or in groups to praise the Triune God in pious exercises or devotions. The United States Conference of Catholic Bishops recognized the important role played by the church building in the public and private worship of the Christian faithful in their 2000 document *Built of Living Stones: Art, Architecture, and Worship*. Chapter 2 concludes with a section given to the church building and popular devotions. The bishops write:

> Like the liturgy, devotions are rituals. They can involve singing, intercession, thanksgiving, and common postures. Devotional prayer is another way for people to bring the very personal concerns of life to God and to ask the intercession of the saints and of other members of the Christian community. [. . .] The design of the

---

[64] Ibid., 230.

church building can do much to foster devotions and to insure that they enhance and reinforce rather than compete with the liturgical life of the community.[65]

*Built of Living Stones* mentions specifically the Stations of the Cross and sacred images as illustrative of "sacramentals that help the faithful to focus their attention and their prayer."[66] It encourages incorporating symbols of the Trinity, the Blessed Mother, and the saints in windows, murals, frescoes, and statuary when designing a church, since these "can be a source of instruction and catechesis as well as devotion."[67] The document recognizes that

> The placement of images can be a challenge, especially when a number of cultural traditions are part of a single parish community and each has its own devotional life and practices. Restraint in the number and prominence of sacred images is encouraged to help people focus on the liturgical action that is celebrated in the church. Separate alcoves for statues or icons can display a variety of images through the year. Some parishes designate an area as the shrine for an image that is being venerated on a given day or for a period of time, such as the image of a saint on his or her feast day.[68]

We see in these statements how the harmonization of devotions with the liturgy spoken of in *Sacrosanctum Concilium* and reinforced in the *Directory on Popular Piety* is made concrete in the church building. Not only do the bishops articulate the principle that private worship leads to the public worship of the Church, they also provide practical suggestions for incorporating some devotional practices of private worship in the public worship space.

A second application comes from the *Directory of Popular Piety* itself. Earlier, we mentioned some of the theological values that undergird the devotional life of the Christian faithful. The *Directory*, however, touches on other values enfleshed through pious exercises and devotional practices – values sorely lacking in today's increasingly secular world. One such value is the witness popular piety offers during the seasons of Advent and Christmas to the rampant materialism one finds in society.

---

[65] United States Conference of Catholic Bishops, *Built of Living Stones: Art, Architecture, and Worship* (Washington, DC: United States Catholic Conference, 2000), n. 131.

[66] Ibid.

[67] Ibid., n. 135.

[68] Ibid., n. 137.

Popular piety, precisely because it can intuit the values inherent in the mystery of Christ's birth, is called upon to cooperate in preserving the memory of the manifestation of the Lord, so as to ensure that the strong religious tradition surrounding Christmas is not secularized by consumerism or the infiltration of various forms of neopaganism.[69]

In a similar way, the *Directory* notes how popular piety stands as a beacon of faith for a secular society that wants to hide death, or worse, use it for profit. More and more, medical professionals and families "frequently believe that they have a duty to hide the fact of imminent death from the sick who, because of increasing hospitalization, almost always die outside of the home."[70] Traffic congestion puts the funeral cortege on the endangered species list. Urban planning rarely considers setting aside land for cemeteries, relegating them to a distant place. In the face of this secularization, however, the Christian faithful, through pious exercises and devotional practices such as novenas for the dead, visits to cemeteries and the decoration of graves with flowers and lamps, and suffrage for the dead by means of prayers and deeds of charity manifest the Christian belief that death gives way to new life in the resurrection of the Lord. In the words of St. Paul: "Christ has been raised from the dead, the firstfruits of those who have fallen asleep" (1 Cor 15:20).

The final application we will examine comes from the *Norms for the Public Celebration of Devotions in the Diocese of Stockton*.[71] As I mentioned at the beginning of this paper, the Liturgical Commission's *ad hoc* task force established a process whereby priests and lay members of the Christian faithful could have their voices heard and their rights respected as a set of norms was drafted for the bishop's approval. The task force found it enlightening when one priest, speaking of devotional practices surrounding Divine Mercy Sunday, said that what he had witnessed in the diocese in a Filipino community is not what happens in the Philippines. Divine Mercy practices in the United States, he said, have taken on a life of their own, without any connection to their origin at home.

While the catalyst for drafting the norms was abuses surrounding the celebration of Divine Mercy Sunday, the bishop and task force wanted norms that applied to the proper ordering of private and public worship. To this end, the norms apply only to the *public* celebration of devotions, and here, chiefly in churches, oratories, or parish facilities. Second, the norms provide guidance for the proper celebration of devotional practices in accord with the liturgical year. Public celebrations of novenas are not permitted during the Easter Triduum, and

---

[69] *Directory*, 108; see also n. 105.

[70] Ibid., 259.

[71] The complete text is found in the appendix.

communal celebrations of the sacrament of penance cannot be scheduled on the Sundays in the Easter season. Third, the norms underscore the liturgy's preeminence over devotional practices. For example, the recitation of the Rosary is not to replace the funeral vigil. Finally, the laity are encouraged to assume various roles in the celebration of pious exercises and devotions, including those of presider, reader, cantor, et al.

The Church's sanctifying office includes the public celebration of the liturgy and the private worship of the Christian faithful. While the faithful enjoy duties and rights with regard to their spiritual lives, bishops and other local ordinaries are charged with guarding, promoting, and moderating the entire worship life of the particular Churches entrusted to their care. In most cases there exists little if any tension in the exercise of these respective rights. Nevertheless, as the *Directory on Popular Piety* makes clear, when deviations or abuses infiltrate the private worship of the Christian faithful, hierarchic action is warranted to preserve the faith and tradition of the Church.

*Appendix: Norms for the Public Celebration of Devotions in the Diocese of Stockton*

1. The devotional life of the Christian faithful is an essential part of the spirituality of each member of the body of Christ. While "the liturgy is the summit toward which the activity of the Church is directed [and] at the same time [. . .] the font from which all her power flows" (*Sacrosanctum Concilium*, 10), the liturgy does not exhaust the Church's life, nor especially her sanctifying office. "Popular devotions of the Christian people are to be highly commended, provided they accord with the laws and norms of the Church, above all when they are ordered by the Apostolic See" (*SC*, 13).

As important as devotions are for the personal spirituality of the faithful, they must be understood and promoted in their proper relationship to the liturgy.

> Devotions should be so drawn up that they harmonize with the liturgical seasons, accord with the sacred liturgy, are in some fashion derived from it, and lead the people to it, since, in fact, the liturgy by its very nature far surpasses any of them (*SC*, 13).

As the ecclesial action of the Church united to Christ her Head, the liturgy makes present the one, eternal sacrifice of the Lord. Popular devotions lead the faithful to a more fruitful celebration of the liturgy, at the same time that the liturgical celebration spurs them on to greater piety and holiness.

2. In his apostolic exhortation on Marian devotion *Marialis cultus*, Pope Paul VI outlined several characteristics of devotion to the Blessed Virgin Mary that apply

equally to all popular devotions. First, true devotions are Trinitarian in nature, praying to the Father through the Son in the Holy Spirit. Second, they are rooted in the mystery of the Word made flesh, Jesus the Lord. Third, while devotions do not possess the preeminence of the liturgy, they do nevertheless help the faithful to exercise their baptismal priesthood through pious exercises, an activity always done in and through one's membership in the body of Christ, the Church.

The Liturgy and Devotions

3. Even though the liturgy far surpasses any popular devotion, the dynamic relationship between the liturgy and devotions cannot be understated. On the one hand, some understand the liturgical reforms of *Sacrosanctum Concilium* to diminish the need for and importance of popular devotions. This thinking contradicts the strong commendation of devotions by the conciliar fathers. On the other hand, one cannot mix the liturgy and devotions to form some hybrid rite, as when pious exercises are inserted into the Eucharistic celebration. "This creates the danger that the Lord's Memorial Rite, instead of being the culmination of the meeting of the Christian community, becomes the occasion, as it were, for devotional practices" (*Marialis cultus*, 31).

The Liturgical Year and Devotions

4. The entire cycle of the Christian Mystery is set forth in the liturgical year. Through the seasons of the temporal cycle, "the Church celebrates the whole mystery of Christ, from his incarnation until the day of Pentecost and the expectation of his coming again" (*General Norms for the Liturgical Year and Calendar*, 17). Popular devotions must, in their own way, promote the unfolding of the Christian Mystery for the faithful. Thus, they can never diminish – or far less, contravene – the seasonal liturgical celebration of the Paschal Mystery.

The Easter Triduum and Easter Season hold first place among the seasons of the liturgical year. This "culmination of the entire liturgical year" gives Easter "the same kind of preeminence in the liturgical year that Sunday has in the week" (*GNLYC*, 18). For this reason, any communal celebration of popular devotions must give way to the celebration of the liturgy on these most important days.

General Norms

5. The following General Norms are promulgated as particular law for the Diocese of Stockton to ensure a proper balance between the celebration of the liturgy and the public celebration of devotions.

a. Public celebrations of devotions are permitted in churches, with the consent of the pastor, and in oratories, with the consent of the superior.

b. Public celebrations of novenas are not permitted in churches, oratories, or parish facilities during the Easter Triduum.

c. On the Sundays of Easter, communal celebrations of the Sacrament of Penance are not permitted. Likewise, it is not in keeping with the joy of the Lord's resurrection to schedule any celebrations of the Sacrament of Penance on the Sundays of Easter.

d. Devotional practices cannot replace or curtail liturgical celebrations, e.g., replacing the Funeral Vigil with the Rosary, or eliminating the reception of the body at the door of the church because the Rosary immediately precedes the Funeral Mass.

e. Only the competent ecclesiastical authority can approve liturgical texts. Therefore, devotional prayers are not to be added to the liturgy.

f. When the faithful gather to celebrate devotions publicly, lay persons are encouraged to exercise their baptismal priesthood in roles as the presider, reader, cantor, et al.

As diocesan bishop, I hereby decree that these norms will take effect on 19 March 2002, the solemnity of St. Joseph, as particular law for the Diocese of Stockton.

+ Stephen E. Blaire
Bishop of Stockton

Barbara Thiella, SND de Namur
Chancellor

Given at the Chancery
of the Diocese of Stockton
on this 6th day of March, 2002.

CLSA PROCEEDINGS 64 (2002) 145-155

# HOSTILITY IN THE TRIBUNAL CONTEXT

REVEREND PETER G. GORI, O.S.A., JCD

*I. The Meaning of Hostility*

In order to approach this subject of "hostility" I thought that it would be helpful first to inquire into its etymology. I am somewhat fascinated by etymology and have often found the origins of words to be both instructive and amusing. I already knew that the Latin root, *hostis*, gave us the English word. This Latin word, so familiar to anyone with a glancing acquaintance with *Caesar's Gallic Wars*, means "enemy." Now that is certainly a powerful word, enemy.

My enemy is the person or persons who oppose me, threaten me, and even attack me. My enemy places me or mine in jeopardy. My enemy is a threat to my wellbeing, physically or otherwise. My enemy is more that just an adversary. An adversary is a legitimate opponent in a contest or competition. Mutually accepted regulations and legitimate authority govern such a contest or competition. It usually concludes with a winner and a loser. The presence of an enemy evokes images of violence, even warfare. It often concludes with triumph for one side and defeat for the other.

There is another meaning attached to the root, *hostis*, and that is "stranger." A stranger may or may not pose a threat. A stranger may or may not be an enemy as well. Perhaps it is fair to consider a stranger as a "potential threat." The reverse is also possible, namely the stranger, because he/she is a stranger, may feel threatened.

Most any rational person would agree that hostility is a negative, undesirable emotion, even if all too familiar. In a situation of hostility we are reduced to an "us-and-them" scenario. A good part of this relates to experience, context and perceptions.

Our topic, "Hostility in the Tribunal Context" includes all of the foregoing aspects. If any party is going to exhibit or experience hostility it most likely will be the Respondent in a tribunal proceeding. This is natural. It is rare to encounter a Petitioner who is hostile [...] until he or she is faced with the disappointment of a negative decision. However, that is really not the same thing. The negative reaction of a Petitioner is more likely the anger that results from disappointment. I have been known to contrast the Petitioners and Respondents by using the images of trained circus poodles and German shepherds respectively. (Meaning no disrespect to the persons or the breeds, of course!) "I never asked for this!" is a typical Respondent point of view.

I need to be clear about something at this point. Not every Respondent is hostile. Just because a Respondent may have expressed opposition does not equate with the description, hostile.

I would say that the source of most hostility that I have experienced on the part of Respondents in the tribunal context has been caused by them feeling as though they are threatened, under attack and strange. Oddly enough, the tribunal context itself can be a major source of hostility for some Respondents.

## II. Tribunal Context

In his very well received book, *Annulment – The Wedding that Was*, Monsignor Michael Smith Foster introduces the section on Tribunal Personnel with a picturesque description from the Wizard of OZ:

> In the film adaptation of L. Frank Baum's, The Wizard of Oz, Dorothy approaches the Great and Wonderful Wizard with palpable fear, trepidation and hope. The grandeur of the hall heightens her fear! The unknown sounds and voices deepen her trepidation! And a dread that her request and those of her friends will be denied almost causes her to lose hope! Many who approach the tribunal can identify with that scene as well as with Dorothy's emotions.[1]

Various aspects coalesce to constitute the tribunal context. There is, first of all, *the place* itself. For most every Respondent the tribunal is shrouded in mystery or at least mystique. "Tribunal" is no more than a crossword puzzle word or part of the return address on an equally perplexing piece of mail recently received, namely the citation. The name itself conjures images of courthouses, high benches, authority, and trouble. The first correspondence bearing this return address and received by the Respondent is the citation. It may be about as welcome as a traffic citation or a summons to jury duty. The resulting reaction, often mixed with surprise, may be an angry or hostile one. All too often the Respondent is still smarting from the last go-round with the civil courts during the divorce proceedings. There is an understandable sense of, "Oh, no! Not again!" The image is not necessarily a neutral one in the Respondent's mind.

The correspondence begins to introduce new people, *the Tribunal personnel*, with authoritative titles – Advocate, Judge, Expert, Auditor, Defender, etc. It may begin to sound like an army is assembled and it is poised to march over my marriage and me. "Who are all these people and why are they intruding into the

---

[1] Michael Smith Foster, *Annulment: The Wedding that Was* (New York, NY: Paulist Press, 1999): 111.

privacy of my life?," questions the Respondent. Again, there arises a sense of being a stranger among strangers. "Are these enemies, posing a threat to me," wonders the Respondent.

How important it is for the tribunal staff to remember that what and whom we find so familiar because of our daily exposure and contact is not so for the Respondent. Equally important for the tribunal staff person to remember is that hostility provokes hostility.

The contacts that the Respondent has with the tribunal can all be occasions for heightened hostility or diminished hostility. The letters that accompany decrees and questionnaires ought to be respectful, informative, professional, but as non-threatening as possible. To include the invitation to make a telephone call or to refer the party to someone specific for further assistance helps to encourage participation. It simultaneously diminishes the sense of threat.

Telephone conversations are likewise important in this regard. It is good to remember that for many people it takes a certain amount of courage to initiate such a telephone call to such a place about such matter, which is intensely personal. That is why the tone of respect is so very important. Patience and understanding cannot be overvalued. There should be someone the Respondent can ask for by name when she or he calls the tribunal. It is disturbing and frustrating to have to explain one's personal circumstances repeatedly to different people. That alone can provoke hostility unnecessarily.

When the Respondent should come to the tribunal in person, she or he should be received with the same graciousness as the Petitioner and made to feel welcome and respected. Even though he or she may be on record as "opposed" to a declaration of nullity, that does not make him or her a threat, much less an enemy of the tribunal.

Careful record of each and every contact with the Respondent should be made. The kind of contact (telephone conversation, visit, written communication) should be noted and readily accessible. How much more respectful is it to be able to say, "Yes, I know you called this office last week while I was away." It is a simple thing, but it helps to build trust and ideally, cooperation and to diminish the potential for hostility.

The *reputation and image* of a Marriage Tribunal is a big part of the context. The tribunal is the court of the Catholic Church. Many people find it puzzling why the Church would even need to have a court, any more than it would need a police force or jails or such things that are associated with the civil justice system.

Most unfortunately the events and revelations of the past ten months relative to sexual abuse to minors by clergy have done plenty to answer justify their existence. I should think that an entire convention could be built around the negative ramifications of the current clergy sexual abuse crisis for church work of all kinds. We have to take that into consideration. It is not an exaggeration to say that our image right now as Church is not good. Anything that would imply

147

condescension or superiority must be avoided. At the same time, we cannot attempt to be the grand apologist for all the evils in the world. It is part of our current context and, as such, it may influence the preconceived image that someone may have about what they will encounter at the tribunal. Our present context is one that is ripe for hostility and suspicion.

Tribunals are *courts*, plain and simple. They are the places where controversies are weighed and settled. They are the place to which we go to vindicate rights, to impose sentences on criminals in punishment for offenses. They are associated in the mind of the general public with the same kind of activities one would have in a civil court: contesting traffic tickets, restraining orders, divorce and child custody settlements, criminal arraignments and trials. These are not exactly pleasant associations! Almost always these are occasions characterized by hostility that accompanies adversarial contests.

To all of this we add the *Church*. For most practicing Catholics, until recently, the Church has always been associated with the positive aspects of life. The Church is where our babies are baptized, where we worship on Sundays, where we marry and where we bury our loved ones. The Church is where we go for comfort, guidance, spiritual assistance, the sacraments, community celebrations, and reconciliation.

Tribunals, as Church Courts, need to combine the images and associations to the best advantage of the mission. The parties – Petitioner and Respondent – will combine the images and associations anyway. Rather than have the concept of Church Court develop into a contradictory, fearsome construct in someone's imagination, it is far better for the tribunal personnel to promote and project a good, true image. The place where the rights of parties are vindicated by means of a legal tradition that has the Gospel as its foundation is a far better image to promote and project.

The parties themselves form part of the tribunal context. This is obvious to us, but not to them. Who are they? It can be a type of minefield experience just to use the acceptable references to the parties. We call them "Petitioner" and "Respondent." Now isn't that friendly! Some parties are offended from the start by the fact that the case name will bear her maiden name. A hostile Respondent will complain that obviously you have already made your decision. One should patiently explain that the manner of record keeping in the Church always conserves the party's names this way. Even their marriage record is retained that way. When confronted with this kind of complaint it is helpful to remember that the real concern here is trust, not the name. Therefore, it is helpful to first reply, with an affirmation of the parties point, "I see what you mean." Then follow with the calm explanation. I find it helps to point out the simple fact that this manner of entitling the case makes it easy for us to see who introduced the case. "It doesn't really matter," I explain, "whether the case is called Smith-Jones or Jones-Smith, but if it were called Smith-Smith, we wouldn't be able to tell who was who. We wouldn't be able to tell you from your ex-spouse. You both have equal rights in the case. If it had been you who introduced the case then your name would be listed first." In this way I try to disarm the distrust while assuring the Respondent of the objectivity of the process. Mistakes happen. Sometimes mistakes contribute to the rise of hostility. For example, the Petitioner doesn't give the tribunal the address of the Respondent. We contact her in care of her mother's address. This makes her angry because she has personal issues with her mother. Perhaps the Petitioner did this inadvertently or perhaps he did this out of spite, knowing that it would irritate her. She suspects the latter. What to do? Get defensive? Pass the blame on to the Petitioner? No. Apologize; correct the information and thank her for bringing it to our attention. Such an instance may even be an opportunity to encourage participation by submitting testimony. It is certainly the opportunity to communicate that the tribunal cares and is interested in her input, even on something as simple as the correct address. She does not necessarily need to know all the canonical details about citation and competent forum. However, she may have provided information pertinent to those canonical details simply by voicing her complaint.

What does the Respondent want to be called? Is she using her married name, maiden name or a name from a subsequent union? Practically speaking the initial form should provide the information from her. It is not always reliable to depend on the Petitioner to supply this information accurately. The party herself should be invited to supply this information about herself.

The parties deserve to be spoken about with respect, even if they do not do so themselves. I usually refer to the other party by name instead of "your ex-wife," or "ex-husband" or just "ex." This is part of the minefield to which I referred. If we say "husband," we may get a quick reminder that they are divorced. If we say "ex-husband," we may get a quick accusation that we have already annulled the marriage. In our written communications at the Boston Tribunal we usually refer to the "former spouse." When I receive questions or complaints about that I explain that it is only acknowledging the civil divorce status, without implying any premature judgment by the tribunal. We never know how much animosity may be present, so it is better to tread softly. In one meeting with a Respondent I once compared the tribunal study of the marriage to the performance of an autopsy. She replied, "At least with an autopsy you get to bury the b------!" You never know! Although they are not parties to the case, the children of a marriage under study can also be a source around which hostility can arise. The children themselves may be a major concern of the Respondent, as in the perennial misconception about legitimacy. When minor children are involved it is very helpful to have additional resources and referrals available to help the parent help the child understand. Usually it is no more and no less than the stress and trauma of coping with the separation and divorce. The annulment fits right in, adding to the anguish. The anguish is often exacerbated because it is the Church doing this. "Everybody understands divorce," they sometimes say.

*III. The Respondent "as is"*

Sometimes the Respondent is *cooperative*. She or he could have just as easily been the Petitioner. She wants the annulment and sees it as justified. If there is hostility present, it is usually directed not at the tribunal or the process, but merely at the Petitioner. It is important to respect that, but never to participate in it, nor to encourage any "bashing" of the Petitioner. To do so would impugn the integrity of the process. It is unprofessional. To be empathetic and respectful is what is appropriate. The cooperative Respondent, not infrequently, provides the testimony critical to substantiating the case.

If there is going to be any hostility it is likely to come from a Respondent who has registered his or her opposition. That is not to say that opposition in and of itself is the same as hostility. (I have found that the categories available in some tribunal-use computer software are limited in this regard.) The Respondent has a legal right to oppose the contention that the marriage is null. This is done by submitting testimony and with the assistance provided by an advocate.

It has been my experience that opposition on the part of a Respondent takes many forms, not all of which are strictly speaking, canonical. It is very often in the context of these various modes of opposition that the hostility manifests itself. It may involve several of these modes.

The Respondent may be opposed to the very concept of a declaration of nullity. This can be the position taken by a Roman Catholic or one who is not Roman Catholic. "I don't believe in annulments" is the usual expression. This is an early indication that we are dealing with someone on the verge of hostility at least! With such a person it is important and helpful to review not canon law, but the theology of marriage that gives rise to the canon law. Without a foundational understanding of the theology of marriage the canon law references are trivial.

The Catholic Church understands marriage as one of the seven sacraments and, as such, includes the essential qualities of unity and indissolubility. It is a covenant relationship in which the spouses make a mutual gift of the whole person to each other (c. 1057, based on *Gaudium et spes*). This is the creation of the communion of life and love, which we call the sacrament of matrimony. Sometimes a patient review of matrimonial catechesis is all that is necessary to dissipate hostility. Sometimes it isn't.

Most often, I find that the real target for hostility is the Petitioner. It is quite often that in this circumstance that the Respondent can be persuaded to testify. I try to help the Respondent distinguish between opposition to the ex-spouse and what is truly legal or canonical opposition. Many times the person will calm down if they feel that they are being respected and understood on that emotional level. I ask them outright to tell me what is it that they object to. Then I explain that legally speaking, opposition means that you are convinced that this was a good, strong, valid, sacramental marriage as the Catholic Church defines marriage and that maybe even the divorce was a mistake. If the Respondent agrees with that statement then we have genuine, legal opposition. It has been very effective in getting clarification.

More likely now because of all the present scandal and controversy in the Church the Respondent may be opposed to the Church itself. You may encounter someone who is sadly disillusioned with the Church, or even someone who suffered abuse – of whatever kind – committed by a cleric or other Church related person. Non-Catholics can be quite offended, even hostile at times, by the very idea that the Catholic Church is meddling in the private matters related to their marriage.

Often people are under the impression that the valid form of marriage is the equivalent of validity. If the wedding took place in a church, before a priest, deacon or bishop and with two witnesses, then it must be a sacrament. I never cease to be amazed by the shallow level of catechesis prevalent. Very few Catholics know that the spouses themselves are the ministers of this sacrament.

The Respondent may if fact be truly opposed on legal grounds to the declaration of nullity. The source of this person's hostility could be any of the various modes. Again, opposition and hostility are not equivalent. It is very helpful when a truly opposed Respondent can be persuaded to participate by offering testimony. In cases of adultery or abandonment, with no other grounds, their testimony is very important. Stressing that point of how important it is that the tribunal hear from them about the marriage under study helps to defuse hostility and build cooperation.

This is the Respondent to whom the various rights available in the process can be explained reasonably. Such a Respondent will want to participate responsibly in the process. Surprisingly enough, even when the final decision may be rendered in the affirmative, with the absence of hostility, that decision is far more likely to be accepted by him and even understood. I have had many Respondents who have dropped their opposition when I was able to first assist them in dropping their hostility.

It does not always prove successful. I would not want to give the impression that there is any guarantee here. It can and does happen that the Respondent is going to be hostile to you because of what he or she thinks you represent. Never take it personally; I have had many a Respondent excoriate me only to have them tell me by the end of the conversation that they appreciated the fact that I listened to them! After the person had discharged all that anger they were in a better position to listen themselves [. . .] or they just hung up the phone!

Some people are inclined to oppose everything. They will be contentious with every person at the tribunal, with the former spouse, with the advocate, the judge and the receptionist. That happens and there is really nothing that can be done about it. They deserve the same respect and rights as anyone else involved in the tribunal process. It is not unusual to discover that their testimony was essential in substantiating the grounds of the case.

I would like to say a bit more about the uninformed Respondent. Lack of information or ability to understand the information provided could lead to a sense of fear and distrust that quickly manifests itself as hostility. The antidote is found in the cause. What I call remedial catechesis goes a long way to filling the gap of knowledge about marriage. Only when there is some appreciation for the Catholic teaching about marriage as a sacrament will the concept of an invalid marriage have a chance of making any sense.

Indeed, because marriage is a sacrament the Church has takes rightful responsibility for and interest in its validity, its celebration, and its vitality. Likewise, the Church has a responsible interest in those marriages that fail or whose validity is impugned. It helps to explain the role of the state as distinguished from that of the Church in marriage. The state sees marriage exclusively on the level of a contract. Likewise the state claims the right to dissolve the contract by means of divorce. It is very straightforward and all too familiar. The Church, by contrast, takes the marriage contract to a higher level, that of the sacramental bond, *foedus*, covenant. The more descriptive one gets in detailing the Catholic theology of marriage the more impressive and beautiful it is seen to be. Sadly, many Respondents, and Petitioners for that matter, in our tribunals have never had this explained to them. Occasionally I have had a Respondent exclaim, "my marriage was never like *that*!" So much for opposition!

The process is not meant to mimic that of the divorce proceeding, which, for all too many people is a very painful and humiliating experience. The marriage is what is on trial here, not him or her. I explain that the marriage is treated in this process as though it were a person, with rights. That leads to explanation of the presumption of validity enshrined in canon 1060. Very rarely does a Respondent know this fact. The more prevalent presumption is that the tribunal study begins in a neutral position. Then there is the introduction of the Defender of the Bond, as the marriage's attorney, so to speak.

It is very rare to have a Respondent who is cognizant of his or her rights in the tribunal process. I have included in the handout a summary listing of the rights of the Respondent. I usually explain to the person about the process in general, the various stages and requirements without getting too technical. The process is a foreign one; the language, terms and procedures can be threatening. To allay fears by providing access to information and guidance helps the process, helps the Respondent and furthers the search for truth by creating a more receptive context in which to instruct the case.

Information about the effects of a declaration of nullity can help to allay fear and, hopefully, hostility. Will the parties now be able to marry again in the Church? Will an abusive spouse be able to repeat the pattern? How will the legitimacy of children be affected? We may hear such questions over and over again, but we must remember that for this particular Respondent they are new and pertinent questions.

Confidentiality is a significant matter. Assurances need to be given about how the sensitive and personal information is protected. This is an area in which I often explain that his and her confidentiality is equally important and protected. That is why certain protocols are observed for everyone's protection. It is appropriate to explain that the archives are secured.

*Conclusion*

Hostility is not usually a deliberately chosen stance. It flows very naturally from human emotions. When the emotional cause is cared for successfully, then the hostility just as naturally abates. It has been my experience in tribunal work in which I have served directly and almost exclusively on behalf of Respondents as an Advocate, that hostility is a frequently occurring hazard. To ignore it will usually increase it. I have found that the following are typical emotions contributing to hostility. The responses are effective measures. When there is fear, counter with respect; when there is suspicion reply with information; when there is anger, meet it with empathy; when there is revenge, try suggesting reason; when there is defensiveness, trust.

I have not yet heard of anyone perpetrating physical violence against tribunal personnel. That is a good thing! Yet, it could happen in an increasingly violent society such as ours that anger becomes rage and results in such an act. Someone should be available, willing and able to respond to the legitimate needs of the Respondent from the time of the citation to the decision. The response ought to be that of the Church, not just that of an ecclesiastical court or an impersonal office. The parties to a broken marriage may be helped, legally, emotionally and spiritually by participation in the tribunal process. They certainly should never be at risk for further harm, for that would be against the law, the supreme law, the salvation of souls.

## The Rights of the Respondent
## in a Marriage Nullity Case

1. The Right of Defense  (c. 1598, §1)
   a.  Denial of which causes irremediable nullity (c. 1620, 7°)

2. The Right to be consulted by one's own Judicial Vicar (as determined by domicile) when determining the forum of competency, provided that both parties reside within the territory of the same Episcopal Conference. (c. 1673, 3°)

3. The right to standing in court, unless a Curator has been appointed by the judge. (Cc. 1476-79; 1620, 5°; 99; 1508, §3; 1528)

4. The right to be cited and therefore notified of judicial acts. (cc. 1507-12; 1686) The related obligation to respond (cc. 1476; 1530; 1531). The Respondent who refuses to accept the citation document or who prevents its delivery is considered to have been legitimately cited. (c. 1510).

5. The right to know the grounds for nullity posited by the Petitioner (c. 1508, §1). The *libellus*/petition is to be attached to the citation unless, for grave reasons, the judge determines that the petition is not to be made known to the Respondent before the Respondent submits a deposition (c. 1508, §2).

6. The right to have appointed an Advocate and/or Procurator  (cc. 1477; 1481, §1; 1490). The Advocate gives legal advice and pleads the cause before the tribunal. The Procurator acts as proxy on behalf of the Respondent. Both require a mandate.

7. The right to nominate witnesses (cc. 1547; 1551; 1593, §1).

8. The right to know the names of the witnesses presented by the Petitioner either before they are examined or at least before the publication of the testimony (c. 1554).

9. The right to raise objections against the witnesses, experts, the judge, the defender of the bond, or any other officer of the court. (cc. 1555; 1576; 1449).

10. The right to inspect the Acts of the case, under penalty of nullity (c. 1598, §1).
    – NB: In cases pertaining to the public good, the judge may exclude some part or parts of the Acts to avoid very serious dangers. (c. 1598, §1)
    – The Respondent who is judged absent from the trial waives the right to

154

inspect the Acts of the case. (c. 1592)

11. After examination of the Acts, the right to propose other items of proof (cc. 1598, §2; 1593; 1601).

12. The right to plead and to respond to pleadings and observations (cc. 1603; 1606)

13. The right to be aware of the contents of the sentence and the means by which it may be challenged (c. 1614).

14. The right to challenge a sentence, even if he/she did not appear or respond before a decision was reached (c. 1593, §2).
    - By formal appeal to the tribunal of second instance (cc. 1628; 1630; 1687, §2; 1637).
    - This recourse may be made even after two conforming sentences, provided that there is new and serious evidence. (cc. 1643; 1644)
    - By a plaint of nullity due to some substantial defect (c. 1626).

(Compiled by Rev. Robert Gavotto, O.S.A.; edited and used with permission. See also, Robert M. McGuckin, "The Respondent's Rights in a Matrimonial Nullity Case," *Studia Canonica*, 18 [1984]: 457-481.)

CLSA PROCEEDINGS 64 (2002) 157-175

# FROM WORDS TO DEEDS: INCLUSIVITY IN MINISTRY

Sister Lynn Jarrell, OSU
Reverend Daniel J. Ward, OSB

The inclusion of laity in jurisdictional positions in ministry is a matter of substantive justice which has not been addressed with concrete steps in most cases. The issue, while having been studied extensively in recent years especially concerning the status of women, is now in need of a far more serious and verifiable response by those exercising the power of governance within the Catholic Church. Our times urge action in light of the reality of the situation for both male and female lay members of the Christian faithful.

### Context of the Topic

When speaking of the inclusion of the laity within the jurisdictional ministry of the Church, most of the recent official documents on this topic have focused on the concerns of women and how women could be more included in this work. However, the documents can easily be applied to all of the laity since the concerns are similar for both male and female.[1]

Pope John Paul II in his Apostolic Constitution, *The Vocation and Mission of the Lay Faithful in the Church and in the World (Christifideles Laici)* in 1988 speaks of the role of women within the Church.[2] In this document he called for the promotion of women to the fullest extent. Clearly, the tone of his text emphasizes the urgency to do more than talk about the discriminatory manner women have been prevented from using their talents in a equal and respectful sense in the Church's mission.

This same theme and urging to promote the role of women in the Church has been repeated on many occasions by the Pope in recent years. In particular, the pressing need to address the treatment of women within the Church was

---

[1] One such study is the following: "Report on Catholic Men's Ministries" by the Bishops' Committee on Marriage and Family and the Bishop's Committee on Evangelization, *Origins* 29:11 (September, 1998): 178-180.

[2] John Paul II, apostolic exhortation *Christifideles laici,* December 30, 1988 *AAS* 81 (1989): 393-521; *The Vocation and Mission of the Lay Faithful in the Church and in the World (Christifideles Laici)* (Washington: USCC, 1988). See especially Section #49.

emphasized in his 1995 *Letter to Women* when he called for there to be a movement from simply stating the situation in words to the empowering of women by deeds.[3]

Following in the path of their 1994 document on the concerns of women, the Bishops' Committee on Women in Society and in the Church issued in 1998 a document entitled "From Words to Deeds, Continuing Reflections on the Role of Women in the Church." This new document was the committee's way of giving concrete expression to the strong, repeated urgings of the Pope to promote the role of women within the Church. The underlining intention was to keep the state of laity, especially women, in the Catholic Church in the forefront of the thinking of the American Church.[4] Strong encouragement is given by the text to the bishops of the United States to create increased movement within their dioceses around the many concerns raised previously as well as currently by women. In order to do this it was decided that another detailed study and more statistics would not necessarily advance the conversation or demonstrate how each bishop could address the issues in his diocese. Rather, the committee concluded that "urgings to act" with suggested ways in which to respond would be most helpful to the bishops and the members of the Christian Faithful. The study charges each diocesan bishop within his local Church to identify concrete ways to support and empower women to their rightful place among the Body of Believers through following the three-fold path of:

(1) Appreciating publicly the giftedness of women.
(2) Appointing women to positions of jurisdiction.
(3) Collaborating with women in significant ways.[5]

At other gatherings of bishops beyond the boundaries of the United States or through their episcopal conferences, a similar promotion of the laity has occurred. For example Cardinal Carlo Martini of Milan raised in his address on October 11, 1999, to the Special Assembly for Europe of the Synod of Bishops his concerns about the role women in society and in the Church. In his view it is an institutional problem that is of the upmost importance. Cardinal Pierre Yet of Bordeaux, France, affirmed this intervention of Cardinal Martini in his remarks on December

---

[3] John Paul II, "Letter to Women," in English in *Origins* 25:9 (July, 1995): 138-143.

[4] Committee on Women in Society and in the Church of the United States Conference of Catholic Bishops, *From Words to Deeds* (Washington, DC: United States Catholic Conference, 1998). This committee has undertaken for over a decade the task of studying and raising the concerns of women. Previous members of the committee published in 1994, *Strengthening the Bonds of Peace*, a pastoral reflection on women. This 1998 document is meant to build on the 1994 document which had stressed the need for "the continuing priority of women's participation in the life of the Church."

[5] Ibid., 4. This three-fold recommendation has equal application to laymen although the document was written specifically on women.

9, 2000.

On various occasions the end result generally has been an open-ended conclusion that the diocesan bishop has and can exercise the authority to appoint women to positions to which jurisdiction is attached. Yet, at this point in time, there is still such hesitation and actual prejudice in many cases about competent laity, in particular women, exercising the power of governance within the Church.

## Historical Underpinnings

*Introduction*

History is a good place to start when discussing the underpinnings of the call of all to ministry. History enhances our vision of the present, both by showing us a range of possibilities that existed at various times, and also showing us the path of limitations during the centuries. History itself, of course, can be skewed by the writer, the interpreter, and by our culturally determined hindsight. Nevertheless, even with its limitations, history can help shed some light on past realities that could become present possibilities.

History, however, presents a particular problem for Americans. First, we tend not to take a long view of things; rather we expect things to happen today or tomorrow. Perhaps this is because of our own relatively short history as a country. Second, our experience of life is one of rapid changes in lifestyles and possibilities. This experience is especially vivid for Catholics. In the aftermath of the Second Vatican Council, our life story has compressed into a few decades fundamental changes of a sort that used to take centuries. Third, we tend to be a people of law and structure. Thus, to let things just happen and develop is generally not our *modus operandi.* We desire to hurry to planning programming and codification.

Despite these drawbacks, history provides us with a vision of ministry that presents many possibilities for the present and the future. History, I believe, demonstrates a number of things:

- In the Church over the centuries there was a much broader vision of ministry, even if not named such;
- Ministry often developed outside of existing Church structures and only later was incorporated into the structures and law;
- During some periods in history the ministry of leadership was much broader than it is today;
- Culture has played a great role in determining who can share in what ministries;
- There was a much broader and divergent view of various ministries than may be present today;
- What I call "the refining of the theology of ministry" has not always been

159

positive.

Therefore, let us look very briefly at some history of the Church and ministry.

*Ministry in the Early Church*

The New Testament presents to us a picture of Church in which ministry is not limited to one class or group of persons. Mary Magdalene, I posit, is the paradigm of the change in ministry that took place after the Resurrection. She received the message of the resurrection first and was commissioned to take the message to the apostles. This, I think, dramatically delineates a difference between Judaism and Christianity. Women are included and have a significant role in the way of Jesus Christ.[6]

Both Paul and Luke name women who minister in the early Christian communities. The delineation between an ordained class and a lay class of ministers is not evidenced in these writings.

In the early Church, the monastic movement was a lay movement. In fact, clerics were not always welcome in early monastic communities. Spiritual leadership among the early monastic was not limited to males, although later, male-dominated society generally preserved only the records of the great male leaders and teachers. Researchers today are unearthing the treasures of the early women spiritual leaders.

The Canon Law of America study on women and the diaconate evidences that ordination was more inclusive than is it today. This seems to have been true both in the Roman and the Byzantine Churches. Tradition in the Celtic Church portrays women as ordained.

*The Medieval European Church*

In the medieval European Church, ministry of leadership was not only entrusted to those who were ordained. Both within the continental Church and the Celtic Church abbesses exercised jurisdiction over both women and men. Abbesses had jurisdiction over the clerics of their monasteries.

However, the watershed of change seems to have been around the twelfth and thirteenth centuries when European society changed from the feudal system to an urban economic system. The position of women was dramatically altered from one

---

[6] As a side note, I am amused at the Roman Liturgy of Hours petition at Evening Prayer II for the common of an apostle. It reads, "Father, you wanted your Son to be seen first by the apostles after the Resurrection from the dead." The petition was either an attempt to alter the historical reality of the post-Resurrection appearances or it was to demonstrate a new theological insight into God, namely that not even God always gets what God wishes.

of equality to one of inequality. This had profound effects on the role of women within the Church. It also promoted male clericalism within the Church and society. We still live under many of the ecclesiastical attitudes developed during the high medieval period.

Nevertheless, even during this era, groups continued to emerge that did not limit themselves to official ecclesiastical structures and recognition. One of the most important groups was the Beguinnes, a lay women's religious movement of the thirteenth century. These woman lived lives of poverty and chastity. They worked among the poor and the sick in imitation of Christ. Although Pope Honorius III did grant them a dispensation in 1215 so that they could live as single women unharmed in their community, the Beguinnes were not an institutionally recognized way of life and ministry. They were women who were often times being rejected by the ecclesiastical and civil leadership. Their spirituality was not to seek acceptance by the "system" but rather to follow Christ in humility.

During this era, other women wished to minister within some form of ecclesial recognition and structure. For instance, Saint Frances of Rome, with the help of a male monastic community, became an "oblate sister." Thus she received some official standing within the Church but was not bound to cloister. She could serve the needs of the poor of Rome. Hers was a creative way to stay within the system, and also change the system. However, as we know, subsequent history was not always so kind to creative movements. The Visitation sisters who first lived a non-cloistered life were eventually cloistered.

During this period, women ministered within the Church, often times by criticizing and resisting hierarchical authority. Whether by writing, preaching or teaching, women were often the leading reformers of the Church. Mechthild of Helfta, Joan of Arc, Hildegard of Bingen, Theresa of Avila are only four of the many women who put their commitment to the gospel above hierarchical obedience and acceptance.

*The Seventeenth-Twentieth Centuries*

Perhaps history teaches us a great lesson when we recognize that necessity and the practices resulting from the necessities cause systems to change. The seventeenth through nineteenth centuries clearly evidence this. The necessities required to minister during the Industrial Revolution and the flow of immigrants to the Americas rapidly changed ministries and lifted restrictions, especially for women. European political changes and laws against religious orders brought into existence new forms of ecclesiastically recognized communities living the evangelical counsels. Not only were persons living religious life with solemn vows, but also perpetual vows and some even without vows. Some were not living in community. Women were "released" from the cloisters to minister to the social needs of the society and as in former times traveled great distances to bring the

161

gospel and God's love to people in new lands.

In the roles of ministers of the gospel, women religious not only built the schools, hospitals, orphanages and spiritual centers, but they also financed and managed them. While excluded from governance within the hierarchical structures, women religious, perhaps even more than their lay counterparts, held the leadership positions of major institutions. These women religious demonstrated that the notion of "the weaker sex" was a cultural bias rather than a fact.

*The Present*

Today within the Church, who can minister and in what capacity within the church are major issues. Limiting official ministry to clerics and persons who make life-time commitments of the evangelical counsels is giving way to a much broader vision of ministry than has existed officially for centuries in the Western Church. Leadership long limited to ordained male celibates with the power of jurisdiction is starting to give way to more inclusive ministry as was practiced in earlier times. Cultural conditions and events are causing a system of power and authority vested in a single individual to give way to collaborative ministry, shared responsibility and consensus decision-making.

Nevertheless, while the landscape of who can minister is broadening, there is disagreement about the theological underpinning of inclusive ministry. Does ministry exercised by a lay person derive from baptism and recognition by the ecclesial community or is it ministry delegated to the laity by the ordained? The debate, of course, brings into question whether or not the Church, and therefore ministry, must be hierarchical. Is the notion of a hierarchical Church of divine origin or merely culturally determined? Can there be another vision or model of the Church?

History, I believe, demonstrates that the structures and barriers limiting in most certain position of authority within the Church to celibate ordained males are cultural based. In Europe we need only to compare the development of the ecclesiastical system in Roman society with the development of ecclesiastical system in Celtic societies. The eventual domination of the Roman system over the Celtic does not attest to the orthodoxy of the Roman system, but rather to many factors, not least of which were politics and power.[7]

The demands of our times and the practices that are developing can perhaps find roots in the past if our vision of the past is long enough, broad enough, and not colored by our present cultural and theological perspectives. History is not so

---

[7] Some months ago a high-ranking Vatican official told me that Americans are trying to impose American culture on the Church. This must be resisted, he said, because the Church is above culture. The Church is a-cultural. I found this an odd comment in light of the fact that he was a member of the *Roman* Catholic Church.

narrow and straight laced, lined as we are sometimes led to believe by those who wish to maintain the "status quo." We must educate ourselves in the broader vision of Church, as it has existed through the ages and in different parts of the world. For the Church was, is and must be greater than the late medieval European Church.

## Theological and Canonical Underpinnings

As demonstrated by various benchmark studies and analyses of the state of affairs, the current reality is that the successful carrying out of much of the day-in and day-out ministry of the Church is highly dependent on the efforts of competent, non-ordained laity, male and female.[8] The findings from these studies indicate that consistently the laity are the backbone of the Church's work of carrying out the mission of Jesus Christ. In addition, the laity are increasingly assuming some roles that have traditionally had the power of governance attached to them.[9]

Yet, the inclusion of the laity in the Church's ministry in positions of responsibility remains a fragile and highly subjective matter. For some the attitude exists that the use of laity in roles which exercise any element of jurisdiction, whether delegated specifically to a lay person or proper to the individual as the result of holding a particular office, is a temporary situation due to the shortage of available clergy.[10] Such reasoning presumes that the inclusion of the laity in any full sense is not desirable.

As a result there is on-going questioning about laity being appointed to certain positions. The questioning raises, on one hand, the strong argument that laity should not and actually cannot be named to certain roles since they are unable to

---

[8] It was reported in 1998 by the NCCB Lay Ministry Committee that 29,137 lay persons were enrolled in lay ministry studies. Over 61% were women. About 20,000 lay person, including non-ordained religious, were working in paid positions in parishes that required twenty or more hours a week. These individuals were in 19,000 parishes. The numbers do not include all the lay persons who make up parish school and maintenance staffs as well as the large number of laity who volunteer in endless ways in parishes. As of 1998 85% of all new ministers were women, with only four of every ten of these being members of religious institutes. For an excellent discussion of the legal issues these statistics raise, see Lynda Robitaille, "A Subtext in the Canonical Discussion of Clergy/Laity Issues: Gender," *Studia Canonica* 34 (2000): 467-488.

[9] In this discussion jurisdiction and the power of governance are being used as they are in canon 129. It involves the capacity and authority attached to an office or appointment to make a decision and to act in a given situation. For a comprehensive study of specifically identified roles and offices in the Church to trance if there has been movement in this area see Anne Munley, IHM, Rosemary Smith, SC, Helen Maher Garvey, BVM, Lois MacGillivray, SNJM, and Mary Milligan, RSHM, "Women and Jurisdiction And Unfolding Reality," (Leadership Conference of Women Religious, 2001).

[10] Much of this question comes out of the weighing of the text of canon 517 and the practice that has developed since then in the American Church. For a thorough discussion of the question see James A. Provost, "Temporary Replacements of New Forms of Ministry: Lay Persons with Pastoral Care of Parishes," *In Diversitate Unitas* (University of Leuven: Msgr. W. Onclin Lecture, 1997).

exercise the jurisdiction necessary for fulfilling the obligations which follow.  On the other hand, the questioning points out that the laity cannot and should not be asked to assume certain positions unless they also have the accompanying jurisdiction prescribed in the law that is part of the role in order to carry out their duties.

Underpinning this questioning are two fundamental aspects of the law: the development of custom and the interpretation of what the *Code of Canon Law* says about the relationship between the laity and the power of governance.  Both aspects present a basis for allowing lay men and women, who are competent and duly appointed, to exercise jurisdiction in the Church.

Concerning the developments in custom around the practice of laity exercising jurisdiction, much has been occurring in recent years.  The practice in some parts of the Church, including many dioceses in the United States, has been to appoint the laity according to the pastoral needs of the local Church.[11]  The evolution of this practice is based on a conviction that the diocesan bishop possesses the power to appoint individuals according to their competence, rather than whether they are ordained or not.  Also, he has the duty to take the appropriate steps to provide for the pastoral care of the Christian faithful who are part of his diocese.  Always this practice remains respectfully within the limits set in the universal law around the need for the ordained to hold offices and to exercise the jurisdiction necessary in the full care of souls.[12]

Fundamental to this expansion in practice are the texts of two canons in the *Code of Canon Law*: canons 129 and 145.  Much has been written on both of these canons since 1983.[13]  These canons combine to establish the possible legal basis for the baptized to be part of the Church's work of evangelization according to their condition and function.  While the ordained are named as the only group who can exercise jurisdiction, the laity are said to be able to cooperate (the first draft said "participate") in the power of governance in the public life of the Church.[14]  The extent of this cooperation is connected to who can hold an office.  The only specifications for who can hold an office are that one be in communion, possess

---

[11] *Women and Jurisdiction*, 99-103, and *Benchmarks for Church Leadership Roles for Women* (Leadership Conference of Women Religious, 1996): 69-80.

[12] See canon 150.

[13] Comprehensive discussions of these canons can be founded in NCCB Lay Ministry Subcommittee, "Lay Ecclesial Ministry: State of the Question," in *Origins* 29:31 (January 20, 2000): 497-512; and in John P. Beal, James A. Coriden, and Thomas J. Green, editors, *New Commentary on the Code of Canon Law*, (Paulist Press: Mahwah, NJ, 2000).

[14] See canon 129. The word "cooperate" is not defined in the scope of the code or in the sources from which the canon comes. Since the publication of the code in 1983 in response to a variety of parochial and diocesan situations, especially around available clerical personnel, a pastoral practice has been unfolding that is giving meaning to this word.

the necessary qualifications, and be appropriately appointed.[15]

The expansion around who can potentially hold jurisdictional positions and how the power of governance is exercised follows from the theological position taken in the 1983 code that all are equal by baptism.[16] This inherent equality among the members of the Church implies rights and obligations that all the Christian faithful possess depending on preserving communion and according to one's condition and function. Concerning the matter of communion this remains a difficult criterion to judge unless the parameters set in the law are overtly violated.[17] At the same time, there is no reason to question the ability of the laity any more than the clergy to maintain the necessary level of communion needed to hold positions of authority in the Church's public life.

Concerning condition, or the capacity to be empowered in the Church's apostolate, it follows both from the individual's abilities and from having the appropriate training the individual may have obtained. The *Code of Canon Law* specifics that appropriate training is to be provided to both the laity[18] and the clergy.[19] The supervision of such formation falls to the local ordinary for those within his territory.

Concerning function, or the assuming of ministry within the Church, it needs to be considered as a range of possibilities which follows from one's baptism and condition.[20] The range encompasses the three sources of ministry in the Church. The first source of ministry is the type of evangelization which belongs to a member of the Christian faithful by baptism or that person's common ministry. The second source is the various roles available to any person who is a member of the Christian faithful or each individual's potential for public ministry as a result of being in communion. The third source is the eligibility of members of the Christian faithful to be named to positions which exercise the power of governance or jurisdictional ministry.[21] It is the last of these three, jurisdictional ministry, from which the laity, women especially, have been historically barred and in practice still are despite the changes in the content of the canons. The impact and the basis for the continuation of this exclusion are at the focal point of this study.

---

[15] See canon 145.

[16] See canon 208; Vatican II, dogmatic constitution *Lumen gentium, AAS* 57 (1965), No. 32; Vatican II, pastoral constitution *Gaudium et spes, AAS* 58 (1966), No. 49 & 61.

[17] Canon 205 specifies that each member of the Christian faithful maintains communion by means of the bonds of the profession of faith, the sacraments, and the observance of ecclesiastical governance.

[18] See canon 229.

[19] See canons 244-245.

[20] See canon 208.

[21] *Benchmarks*, 52-58.

*Present Reality: General Obstacles in Current*
*Practices Within Church Ministry*

*Introduction*

In the NCCB Lay Ministry Subcommittee report on "Lay Ecclesial Ministry: State of the Question" the statement is made: "In fact, it is beneficial that the practice has a chance to develop before it is codified too tightly."[22] I believe that it is important to remember this principle as we move into the future. Changes will happen as the practices develop, followed by later codification and recognized structures. Of course, this is not the way ecclesiastical bureaucrats like things to happen since they lose control. On the other hand, some of us do not do this either because we would like to codify immediately less we lose any progress. But I do not think that either is good or wise. Let things happen as the committee report suggests.

*Limitations and Hindrances*

As we look to inclusivity in ministry, we need to recognize the challenges, that is, limitations and hindrances that will cause hurdles to development of inclusivity.

The first is the dualism that permeates our Church's worldview. As Barbara Fiand writes:

> For the dualistic mind what is different is seen as contradictory and irreconcilable; what is weak can never be strong; what is dark can never be light; what is bad is never good; what is female never male.[23]

Such dualistic thinking categorizes opposites such as clerical and lay, and then creates walls around each. The walls not only define each opposite but are also made impermeable. Dualism prevents us from thinking in new ways, prevents us from the discipleship of dying to self and opening self to why Jesus first appeared to Mary Magdalene after the Resurrection and made her the apostle to the apostles.

Second, despite ecclesial statements, our ecclesiastical polity still operates too often from a stance of monarchial power and authority rather than from a sense of mutual *communio*. At times the Vatican dycasteries use *communio* to mean being in a hierarchical communion with Rome. *Communio* is a one-way street. There is not an understanding of a mutuality of *communio*.

Third, we are limited because our institutional structures limit the possibility of

---

[22] *Origins* 20:31 (January 20, 2000): 500.

[23] Barbara Fiand, *Releasement: Spirituality for Ministry*, (New York, 1991): 56.

truly inclusive leadership. This is a much broader issue than ordination of women and married persons. It also encompasses cultural narrowest, loyalty to selective theological viewpoints, and the holding of absolute truths in a dynamic, evolving, and perhaps transitory creation.

Fourth, the institutional structures are hierarchical, and thus leadership on each level rests in one person. Except in a few defined cases of consent (a negative power), participation in leadership is advisory.

Fifth, because of our dualistic worldview, attempts to include those not ordained in ministry have led to the question of the meaning of ordination. Is the ministry of ordination about celebrating only certain sacraments? Is the ministry of ordination about the ability to have and exercise jurisdiction? Is lay ecclesial ministry a delegated ministry from the ordained who are the only persons able to have fully the power of orders and the power of jurisdiction? Perhaps the medieval issues of the power of orders and the power of jurisdiction have emerged again. The development of inclusive ministry will impact the meaning and the place of the ordained within the Church.

Sixth, and perhaps the most difficult, is the system already in place. Persons in power do not easily change nor are they readily willing to share authority as seemed evident in the decision regarding the selection a priest as the general secretary of the USCCB because tradition requires the general secretary to be ordained. The sexual abuse by clergy in the United States perhaps is partially a result of an unwillingness of the holders of power to change "the good old boys" system. The system and its holders must be protected at all costs. Too often leaders and bureaucrats seem programmed to prevent change and growth. Change requires adjustment that is not always easy.

*What is needed?*

What is needed, I believe, is for us to move forward with a new vision of leadership and ministry within the Church. Recall in Matthew's gospel when Jesus tells his disciples:

> If any want to become my followers, let them deny themselves and take up their cross and follow me. For those who want to save their life will lose it, and those who lose their life for my sake will find it. (Matthew 16:24-25)

One commentary sees in these verses that Jesus is teaching that "there can be no renewal without a dying to the old way of thinking."[24]

I think this is what Barbara Fiand meant when she called for a conversation to

---

[24] *International Bible Commentary*, William R. Farmer, editor, (Collegeville, 1998): 1305.

androgynous ministry. She writes:

> [...] it becomes possible to see reality generally as androgynous.
> By this is meant that all of it belongs to humankind and was released
> to us for our shepherding. Its diversity in all its fullness was
> created, and continues to be created, for and through man and
> woman as the image of God, as the channels of meaning.[25]

For change to happen in ministry, there must be a profound conversion to a new way of thinking.

### Present Reality: Gender Limitations

In 1994 the United States bishops wrote about in their document entitled "Strengthening the Bonds of Peace" the unnecessary but real restrictions put on lay women. They noted that there is fundamental equality among women and men. To think or act otherwise is against what Jesus Christ taught. They go on to reject all aspects of sexism.[26] It was their position that alternative means of leadership need to be identified in order to empower women.

Again, in the document, "From Words to Deeds" and the accompanying update since 1998 on what progress has been made, the Bishops' Committee on Women in Society and in the Church emphasized that women are being unjustly held back from assuming their rightful role in the Church. The origin of this barring of women from exercising jurisdiction comes from discrimination based on gender rather than on the competence of women.

While some areas of confusion remain around what "to cooperate" in the exercise of jurisdiction means, there are no actual norms in the Church's law to justify the overall pattern of prohibition that all too often continues to occur in our times.[27] The basis for the pattern of discrimination appears to flow from a subconscious prejudice towards and a fear of the feminine gender.

This prejudice penetrates the structural life of the Church, leaving a difficult imbalance in practice and in attitude among the Christian faithful. It results in non-inclusion, if not total exclusion, of women from the decision-making and shaping of the Church solely because of their gender. Regardless of whether it is subtle or overt, the end result is a powerlessness and voicelessness in a whole range of

---

[25] Fiand, 78.

[26] National Conference of Catholic Bishops, "Pastoral Reflection: Strengthening the Bonds of Peace," November 16, 1994, in *Origins* 24:25 (December 1, 1994): 420-421. The bishops speak of the concerns of women under the categories of leadership, equality, and the diversity of gifts in the Christian faithful.

[27] Robitaille, 480.

ministries of the Church.[28]  Such prejudice about woman is unfounded in the text of the *Code of Canon Law*, which potentially opens the door to the increased equality among the sexes in the life and ministry of the Church.  Yet the discrimination continues, an injustice causing pain to individuals and to the overall life of the Church.

### The Future: Mindset Shift Leading to Possibilities

There are some possibilities we can think about and maybe even act upon now that will at least begin to change the structures, laws, and practices of ministry in the Church, practices that could advance "From Words to Deeds" not only for women but all members of the Church; practices that will help change our ecclesial reality.

First, the aftermath of the bishops' 2002 June meeting in Dallas says that in diocesan leadership there must be more than "the good old boys system." It seems to me that by structuring the review boards as they did, the bishops recognized that broad participation not controlled by the clergy is necessary in the governance of the Church.  And the way these boards are developing, they seem more than merely advisory to a bishop.  Whatever we think of the system, it is recognition that broad participation not controlled by the clergy is possible within present Church structures.

Second, the structure of the USCCB could be changed so that there is inclusivity at the national level.  Presently, only bishops are members of committees, other participants are advisory.  However, in the past this was not true.  For some time the committee on religious life was composed of both bishops and religious.  Politics seemed to have changed this.  Now only bishops can be members of committees.  But the fact remains; membership on committees has not always been exclusively episcopal.

Third, Roch Pagé has suggested that on the diocesan level there be established the "pastoral ministers council," composed of priests, lay persons, religious and permanent deacons.  The council would represent the "various ministers and ordained ministries, recognized or baptismal, working full-time in the diocese."[29] While not replacing the canonically required presbyteral council, the pastoral ministers council would be more representative of ministers within the diocese and would deal with many of the issues presently considered by the presbyteral council.

Fourth, parish leadership could be reconfigured so that collaborative ministry becomes the norm on the parish level.  Canon 517, §2 could become the preferred

---

[28] Ibid., 485; Joseph Koury, "Part II: The Code and Collaboration: Recent Literature," *CLSA Proceedings* 54 (1992): 170.

[29] Roch Pagé, "Full-Time Pastoral Ministers and Diocesan Governance," *Canon Law Between Interpretation and Imagination*, W. Onclin, chair, (Leuven, 2001).

model for establishing pastoral governance of a parish. The canon seems open-ended enough to allow for development of inclusivity in ministry.

Finally, we can now celebrate more widely in dioceses, parishes and on the national level the diversity of ministry present within the ecclesial community. We can acknowledge that ministry is not limited to organizations listed in *The Official Catholic Directory* nor to the exclusive listing of only ecclesial ministers who are ordained priests or bishops.[30] We can develop and encourage liturgical rituals that recognize, celebrate and entrust people with ministry flowing not only from delegation but from baptism and community recognition or community appointment. Rituals not only celebrate but also raise the consciousness of people. This is a way by practice to change the awareness, the attitudes and eventually the structures and the laws of the People of God. From words to deeds will happen, ministry will become more and more inclusive, changes will happen as we raise the consciousness of the entire People of God.

The future of inclusivity in ministry depends on our present willingness to undertake new ways of thinking and acting now. As quoted earlier "There can be no renewal without a dying to the old way of thinking."[31]

*Urgings for the CLSA to Address this Situation*

The primary question for the Canon Law Society of America on this topic is: How can it, as an organization of professional canonists, assist in addressing the areas of concerns raised by the Bishops' Committee on Women in Society and in the Church and respond to the invitation issued by Pope John Paul II to promote the role of the laity, in particular women, in the Church? In other words, what action can be taken in order that the discrimination against the laity, especially women, can be replaced with far more inclusivity in jurisdictional ministry based on one's condition and function?

There are many suggested "urgings to act" which have been published in the last ten years based on the findings of various benchmark studies. To spark the conversation this paper will highlight two of these proposals of how to address the current situation. Each one states a plan in need of being acted upon at this time. The CLSA would be in the position to promote the implementation in part or in total of such plans because of the numerous administrative positions with jurisdiction that its members hold throughout the dioceses of the United States and beyond.

---

[30] It is certainly interesting that in *The Official Catholic Directory*, only the priests are listed for a religious institute composed of both priests and brothers. Further, there is no listing of the membership of women religious communities. While only a book, *The Official Catholic Directory* portrays a mindset that is still very dominate in the clerical Church

[31] Farmer, 1305.

The first of these plans is the one proposed by the Bishops' Committee on Women in Society and in the Church in 1998. It calls for the following areas of action:

A. *Appreciate and Incorporate the Gifts of Women in the Church by Looking for Ways to Provide*:

    1. opportunities to educate all the Christian faithful, especially those who hold or are preparing for pastoral leadership positions, about the Church's teaching regarding women's gifts, women's equality with men, and the implications of that teaching.

    2. incorporation of the above teachings on women into the programs and policies of the diocese.

    3. review of parish, diocesan, and organizational programs to ensure cultural and gender awareness and sensitivity.

    4. inclusion of the contribution of the laity in the history of the parishes, diocese, and organizations.[32]

B. *Appoint Women to Church Leadership Positions by*:

    1. naming qualified women to decision-making roles as the law allows.

    2. establishing ways to assist women, both financially and organizationally, in getting the necessary preparation and on-going professional development.

    3. employing women as spokespersons for the Local Church.

    4. creating an advisory committee to track and evaluate the progress in this area, both on the parish and diocesan levels.[33]

C. *Promote Collaboration between Men and Women in the Church by Focusing on the Practical Steps of*:

    1. confronting those beliefs and behaviors which hinder the Local Church's ability to collaborate with the laity.

---

[32] *From Words to Deeds*, 10-11.
[33] Ibid., 15.

   – this may call for taking time for healing and reconciliation among individuals or groups.

2. being open to discernment and affirmation of the individual's gifts by the group, be this the parish or diocese or an organization.

3. clarifying roles and responsibilities to avoid struggles around the extent of one's authority.

4. developing the needed skills of healthy communication and conflict resolution plus the ability to work with groups and the ability to deal with diversity in various forms.

5. nurturing the spiritual foundation of collaboration in ministry through individual and group prayer, time for reflection and faith sharing, and attentive listening to the Spirit in the group's midst.[34]

The Bishops' Committee on Women in Society and in the Church hoped that its plan would be implemented in each local Church in order to promote respect for and just treatment of the laity, especially women, in the Church.

A second proposal contains the plan developed by the Executive Committee of the Leadership Conference of Women Religious in 1996. This proposal was envisioned as:

> "[…] some practical ways of responding to the question (of the treatment of women in the Church) […] fifteen recommendations for action, which […] are modest steps, all possible within current Church practice; in fact several are called for by Church law."[35]

The plan identifies these steps:

A. *Promotion of Church Leadership Roles for Women*:

1. Historical Contribution of Women: Inclusion of the role of women when teaching the history of the American Church, emphasizing the equality of women; this should be done in all levels of education (primary grades through Church-related graduate degrees.)

2. Leadership Positions: Appointment of qualified women to positions

---

[34] Ibid., 19-21.
[35] *Benchmarks*, 85.

172

traditionally reserved to clergy and/or lay men.

3. Media Coverage of Women: Assessment of the media's coverage and of convention programs; take steps to feature and/or include women on convention programs or in media coverage on a more equal basis.

B. *Protection of Rights*:

1. Due Process: Encouragement that local Church employers publish the procedures for settling grievances.

2. Advocates: Training of religious institutes' personnel to serve as advocates.

3. Negotiating Skills: Preparation of members of religious institutes in negotiating skills and conflict resolutions as a primary means to protect rights and resolve conflicts.

4. Personnel Policies: Development of personnel policies by Church employers that are based on competence, applying equally to clergy and laity, women and men.

C. *Education and Formation*:

1. Availability of Requisite Education: Allocation of the Church's resources to lay ministers, especially women, equal to that available to those studying for the priesthood.

2. Appropriate Training of Personnel: Need for religious institutes to encourage members to undertake serious study in preparation for leadership positions within the Church.

   – this may mean joint funding by a diocese and a religious institute of a degree program for an institute's member.

3. Women in Seminary Education: Challenge dioceses to either continue to or to begin to employ competent women as part of the formation of seminarians so they are better prepared to work with women.

4. Women as Spiritual Directors: Employment of competent women as spiritual directors by dioceses, religious institutes, and parishes.

D. *Just Compensation*:

> Requirement of all Church employers to provide just compensation and benefits to their employees.

E. *Equitable Representation*:

1. Representation on Consultative Bodies: Requirement that both women and men be equitably represented in all Church consultative bodies.

2. Inclusion of Women within the Quinquennial Reports: Ask USA bishops to include in their quinquennial reports, perhaps in the section on the laity, a description of the progress each diocese has made in promoting women in the public ministry of the Church.[36]

The two above proposals present concrete, measurable ways in which a shift to fuller inclusion of the laity in the life of the Church can occur within the legal norms that currently exist. It is only with the recognition and active movement in the above areas that laity can contribute to the life and ministry of the Church in a collaborative style.[37]

*Conclusion*

Women who already hold positions of jurisdiction state they are permeated with a deep sense of the call to service and to the meaning that comes from being in the midst of their vocation of ministry in the Church. They desire thorough formation in the spiritual life and in leadership skills as well as the opportunity to dialogue about their giftedness.[38]

The members of the CLSA have an invaluable role and responsibility to work for the just treatment of all the Christian faithful. Just treatment entails allowing the laity, male and female, to assume those positions and roles available to them in the norms of the law. Any other approach is a far more restrictive interpretation of the canons than the actual texts specify. Without the full inclusion of all the Christian faithful in the jurisdictional ministry of the Church, a core part of the Body of Christ continues to be suppressed.

---

[36] Ibid., 89-101.

[37] Women need to take advantage of those areas legitimately open to them and to be willing to advocate for the opening of such available ministries to all of the laity who are competent and willing to serve in this manner in the Church. Sharon Euart, RSM, "Woman in the Church in a New Millennium," *Origins* 29:43 (April, 2000): 698-703.

[38] *Women and Jurisdiction*, 103-104.

174

The American bishops expressed in "Strengthening the Bonds of Peace" that "[…] the true face of the Church appears only when and if we recognize the equal dignity of men and women and consistently act on that recognition." May these "urgings to act" be responded to for the sake of justice which is long over due among all the Christian faithful[39]

---

[39] *Origins* 24:25 (December 1, 1994): 421.

CLSA PROCEEDINGS 64 (2002) 177-190

# THE ISLAMIC LEGAL TRADITION: AN OVERVIEW

DOCTOR JANE DAMMEN MCAULFFE, PH.D.

Law is the central intellectual achievement of the Islamic religious tradition. The most esteemed Muslim scholars, whether of the classical or the contemporary period, are those who speak with a deeply educated authority about the law. In conceptualizing and codifying the law, Muslim jurisprudents can be considered collaborators in a divine-human project. For like that of the other monotheistic traditions, Islamic law has two agents, God and the human intellect. It is the human attempt to understand the divine disclosure that creates the category of law and it is the continuing endeavor to modify and readjust that understanding that gives Islamic law its range and vitality.

The topic of Islamic law is, however, enough to fill several lifetimes of study and research, so my remarks today will simply get us started on this subject and I would like to group those remarks around four key questions: (1) What are the sources of Islamic law? (2) How did legal scholars derive law from these sources? (3) What does the classically developed system cover? (4) In what areas do Muslims often face difficulty in adapting to the norms and practices of North American life?

Before tackling these four questions, I will venture a word or two about terminology. To begin with, let's look at the English word "law" and the Arabic word "*sharī'a*." My Webster's first defines "law" as "a binding custom or practice of a community" and as "the whole body of such customs, practices and rules." That definition works well enough for our contemporary American understanding of law, shaped by the founding documents of this nation, and their emphasis on the "consent of the governed." It makes no sense, however, when trying to understand the word "*sharī'a*." That word itself has a very humble etymology: it means "a watering hole" or, more precisely, "the path to a watering hole." By extension, it eventually came to connote the path to God, comprising the totality of God's precepts relating to human life and human activities. Put most simply, it is God's guidance for humankind. Most broadly, it can signify the whole of God's own religion, Islam.

The range of meaning associated with the Arabic word "*sharī'a*" offers a far different understanding of law than the one found in that first Webster's definition. But letting my eyes roam down that dictionary page, I find another understanding of the word "law": "the revelation of the will of God set forth in the Old

Testament." Exactly. Law, in Islam, is not a human creation; it is a divine one. In Muslim eyes, God is the only real lawgiver. Humans do not make law. They discover, explain and codify the law revealed by God in his final revelation, the Qur'ān, and embodied in the life and words of his final prophet, Muhammad.

## What are the Sources of Islamic Law?

With that final sentence, I have started to answer the first of the four questions which I am raising with you today: What are the sources of Islamic law? From what do Muslims derive their understanding of God's will for humankind? In the first place, they find it in the Qur'ān. Now, if you pick up a copy of the Qur'ān in your local library or at a nearby bookstore, you'll note that it's not a very long document and if you flip through it, even casually, you'll see that it is certainly not a law code. What, then, is the best way to describe or characterize the Qur'ān? The simple statement, "God's own words" provides both the most apt description of the Qur'ān and the key to understanding its importance for Islamic law.

According to the Muslim biographical literature on Muhammad, which dates from the late 8th and early 9th century, this future prophet was raised in the west Arabian trading center of Mecca and worked as a caravan director and business man for the first part of his adult life. Yet these same sources portray him as a man of strong spiritual sensitivity, what we might today call a "religious seeker." He would withdraw for periods from the daily rush and devote himself to prayer and to night vigils. During one of these vigils he was startled by an angelic visitor, a visitor whom the tradition identifies as the angel Gabriel, and told to "Recite in the name of your Lord who created, created man from a blood clot; recite by the name of your most noble Lord who taught by the pen, taught man what he did not know" (Q 96:1-5). Over a period of about twenty years, Muhammad experienced subsequent intervals of revelation, usually conveyed through an angelic intermediary, that Muslims understand to be God's very words as expressed in a perfect form of Arabic.

As the imperative "recite" signals, Muhammad quickly realized, albeit with some considerable personal concern, that God was not initiating some sort of private spiritual dialogue. Rather he was calling this Arab business man to an entirely new role and vocation, that of acting as God's prophet to the people of his area and era – and to those well beyond such temporal and geographical boundaries. The revelations dated to the earlier years of Muhammad's prophethood are often succinct and strong warnings about the final judgment to be visited upon those Meccans who persist in polytheistic idolatry and various forms of social immorality. The tone is demanding; the message is urgent. In the years after the *hijra* – Muhammad's forced emigration from Mecca to Medina – both the content and the form of qur'ānic revelation changes considerably. As the Prophet began to broaden his religious leadership to include political, juridical and military supremacy, what was "sent down" by God became more concerned with matters of community organization, social behavior and ritual performance.

In neither period does the Qur'ān represent itself as divorced from other, prior forms of divine revelation. The salvation history expressed in the Qur'ān speaks specifically of earlier messengers and prophets who had carried God's words to their respective peoples. In a number of passages it refers by name to the Torah (*Tawrāh*) and the Gospel (*Injīl*) and recognizes these as forms of divine disclosure to the Jews and Christians, respectively. With the culminating revelation offered in the Qur'ān, God was doing for the Arab "believers" what he had already done for these earlier groups. Through Muhammad he was giving this people access to the gift of his guidance. But through this prophet and these people, God was also confirming his earlier disclosures and providing a final revelation for all humankind, present and future. Later theological reflection would develop qur'ānic references to "the well-protected tablet" (*al-lawh al-mahfūz*) or "the mother of the book" (*umm al-kitāb*) as indicating that all of these revelations, at least in their original, pristine formulations, were the temporal reproductions of an uncreated and eternal archetype.

The final assessment, however, that the Qur'ān directs towards earlier revelations is that of "abrogation." As God's final disclosure the Qur'ān effectively nullifies any abiding authority that earlier revelations might hope to claim. The concept of abrogation also operates within the Qur'ān itself and has proven to be an important element in the development of Islamic law. Certain passages (Q 2:106, 13:39, 16:101, 17:86 and 87:6-7) make clear that the divine self-revelation to Muhammad was sequential and that God would occasionally rescind or cause his prophet to forget an earlier passage. What complicates this intra-textual notion of abrogation, however, is that abrogation does not necessarily mean erasure. As explicated in the later works of Islamic jurisprudence, the qur'ānic text continues to carry injunctions that have been abrogated by other parts of the revelation. The classical example of this, and one upon which I wrote one of my earliest articles, is the successive abrogation of wine. Through a series of three different verses (Q 2:219, 4:43, 5:90-91) an initial divine distaste for wine (as being more sinful than useful) is transmuted into an unequivocal prohibition. Just as a side note: the prohibition ends on earth; wine is one of the promised beverages of Paradise and Q 56:19 assures us that it will not even cause headaches.

Recent scholarship on the Qur'ān has placed necessary emphasis on the primacy of the Qur'ān's orality, i.e. the fact that Muslims more often experience the Qur'ān by hearing and reciting than by reading. When reciting the Qur'ān, Muslims believe that they are repeating God's very words. The act of qur'ānic recitation is itself a rigorously disciplined art form, requiring the mastery of complex rules of pronounciation, vocal and consonantal assimilation and prolongation as well as intra-verse pauses or continuations. The effort expended on recitation – and becoming a truly educated and adept *qāri'* can take years of instruction and practice – demonstrates both the high priority placed on the absolutely accurate verbal conveyance of the Qur'ān as well as the reverence that should accompany the human articulation of God's words. The deep Muslim belief in the accuracy of this transmission from generation to generation grounds itself in the extraordinary care taken by those who devote themselves to these meticulous processes of qur'ānic recitation and memorization. The reverence associated with qur'ānic recitation extends to the written text (*mushaf*) as well. Pious Muslims are careful to keep the Qur'ān away from anything that will dirty or disfigure it and will perform mandated ablutions before touching the Qur'ān.

As God's final guidance for humankind the Qur'ān stands indisputably as the primary source of Islamic law, broadly conceived, yet it actually contains relatively little that can be understood and applied as unmediated legal prescription and proscription. Fortunately, early Muslim legal scholars had recourse to another source of pre-eminent authority, the *sunna* of the prophet Muhammad. The term *sunna* simply means the "way" or the "habitual practice" and encompasses all the tradition can tell us about what Muhammad said and how he acted, about those things of which he approved and those of which he did not. The Prophet's words and actions were noted during his lifetime by his closest companions and taken as a model for all human thought and behavior. These companions passed the information, usually in the form of individual statements or anecdotes, each of which is known as a *hadīth*, to those who followed them. Eventually these *hadīth*, which by the ninth century numbered in the tens of thousands, were collected, assessed and organized in written form and, in their totality, they represent the other major source of Islamic law.

### How did Legal Scholars Derive Law from these Sources?

The second question that I will pose this afternoon takes us from sources to processes, shifting our gaze from God and his prophet Muhammad to the human intellectual activities of searching these sources in order to extract from them as comprehensive an understanding as possible of what constitutes divinely-guided human behavior. Very soon after the death of the prophet Muhammad, situations arose which could not be addressed by explicit recourse to either the Qur'ān or the *sunna*. With the rapid military migration of the first Islamic century, the early Muslims had to develop or adapt administrative and governance structures that were far more complex than those known to the earliest members of the community. Only gradually did a systematized legal procedure evolve out of efforts of the first generations to accommodate to new environments and rapidly changing circumstances. Scholars who study the history of this evolution postulate that the initial periods of religious and cultural adaptation were very fluid. Customs and practices characteristic of the regions that were coming under Muslim hegemony were appropriated and ratified with implicit or explicit reference to the primary religious texts. The word used to describe this effort to make sensible judgments about circumstances not directly addressed by the Qur'ān or the *sunna* is *ra'y*, often translated as "personal opinion" but better rendered as "informed personal judgment."

As might be expected, the results of such early intellectual efforts generated an ever-widening spectrum of diverse and even conflictual judgments. Concern about the communal consequences of such contradictions pushed the first scholars of the law to construct a more refined methodology, a process of analogical reasoning that is termed *qiyās*. Where the Qur'ān and the *sunna* failed to provide a clear and unequivocal judgment, juridical recourse was had to a procedure of controlled extrapolation. It starts with the (at least implicit) acknowledgement that the divine guidance provided by the Qur'ān and the exemplary life of the prophet Muhammad was context specific and could not be expected to apply to all possible future circumstances. The jurist, therefore, had to make a considered connection between the foundational texts and the new situation. This he did by isolating the feature – Islamic jurisprudence uses the word "cause" (*'illa*) – common to the two cases. Let me use the most frequently-cited example to demonstrate this.

I have already mentioned the qur'ānic prohibition of wine and the series of verses which culminated in Q 5:90-91, "O you who believe, wine and games of chance and idols and divining arrows are an abomination from the work of Satan. Turn aside from it so that you may know happiness." The word used here is *khamr*, the Arabic term for fermented grape juice. But a more common beverage in the time and region was the fermented juice of dates, *nabīdh*. Naturally the question arose, "Since only wine is explicitly forbidden by the qur'ānic verse, is it permissible to drink *nabīdh*?" The jurists were therefore obliged to ascertain the legal status of an unmentioned drink. They did so by finding the basis or "cause" for the prohibition of wine, i.e. its intoxicating effects. In a manner analogous to wine, they reasoned, *nabīdh* is forbidden because it, too, causes intoxication.

While careful analogical reasoning of this sort became accepted during the classical and medieval periods by most Muslim jurisprudents, its acceptance was never universal. A minority group known as the "literalists" (*zāhirī*) rejected this methodology, as did most Shī'ī jurisprudents. The dangers of straying too far from the textual sources of divine guidance, the ever-present fear of human fallibility – whether deliberate or inadvertant – served as a cautionary circumscription.

Nevertheless, the necessity of human intellection in the development of the law was never denied. Repeated attempts to address particular cases through the use of *qiyās*/analogy led inexorably to the formulation of more general concepts and principles and to the evolving systematization of the law. The effort involved in this intellectual activity was given a name – *ijtihād*. *Ijtihād* is related to an Arabic word that has entered more general English parlance, i.e., *jihād*. Both terms carry a core sense of striving, struggling, exerting oneself to the utmost. Legal *ijtihād*, while closely allied to *qiyās*, is a more general designation, one which subsumes various forms of legal reasoning. As legal theory became more systematized and elaborated, *ijtihād* was defined as the intellectual effort expended to find a solution or create a ruling (*hukm*) on a religious matter. It operated in those areas where the textual sources did not provide a clear and unambiguous stipulation of divine judgment and its effective operation required training and education in those sources.

Those who acquired such training and education were (and are) known as *mujtahids*. In English, these could be called the "strivers," the "toilers," or to use the principle of analogy, the canon lawyers. The classical works of Muslim jurisprudence make clear that the strenuous effort which must be applied to legal matters is part of the divine plan. Had all the work been done by God, there would be no reason for human endeavor and no basis upon which to reward that endeavor. Ascertaining the law requires human activity and provides its practitioners with an arena in which to compete for divine approval. (It is worth noting that the same argument was used by commentators on the Qur'ān to justify the work needed to become an exegete and to function effectively as one.)

Now, in a bit more detail, what did that work involve? The training and tasks can be divided into the "pre-legal" and the "legal." The "pre-legal" tasks include acquiring a sound and sophisticated knowledge of Arabic lexicography and grammar. No one could assume the mantle of *mujtahid* whose command of the language was less than secure. Language, of course, is a subtle and malleable human product. The educated speaker of any language must be able to recognize the multiple forms of language use and to identify statements as, for example, metaphorical, imperative, ambiguous and of general or particular applicability.

The pre-legal activities also involved ascertaining the reliability of the texts which lay before the *mujtahid*. The Qur'ān presented no problem. Its inviolability had been assured by the doctrine of its flawless transmission (*tawātur*). With the *sunna* and its expression in the massive accumulation of *hadīth*, however, questions of authenticity were ever-present. A large corpus of biographical literature was created to assist the *mujtahid* in his assessments. These were biographies of those whose names were found in the transmission history that prefaces each *hadīth*. In these biographies particular attention was paid to the quality of the teachers with whom an individual had studied and to his own reputation for integrity and pious living. The quality of a *hadīth*, i.e., its authenticity or doubtfulness, was, in large part, a function of the quality of the lives and scholarship of those who passed it on from one generation to another.

Even having assured himself of the authenticity and the reliability of the texts before him, a *mujtahid* had to ask whether any of those pertinent to his particular case had been abrogated by others. You will recall my earlier mention of "abrogation" as an intra-qur'ānic function. It was only after such extensive preliminaries that the *mujtahid* could apply the processes of *ijtihād*, including analogy/*qiyās*, to his sources in order to extract from them an adequate and well-grounded ruling (*hukm*).

The collective results of generations of such legal "toil" coalesced in the final foundation of Islamic jurisprudence, *ijmā'* or consensus. A famous *hadīth* of the prophet Muhammad proclaims, "my community will never agree on error" and this has served as the primary textual justification for this doctrine of consensus. Other *hadīths* as well as various qur'ānic passages (Q 4:115, 2:143, 3:110, 9:16 and 31:15) were used to buttress this argument. But who constitutes the "community" whose collective judgment is error-free? Certainly not all Muslims, not even all adult Muslims. Consensus on legal matters is reserved to the *mujtahids* and it is discovered retrospectively. In other words, when one generation of scholars, looking back at the work of its predecessors, discovers unanimous or near-unanimous agreement on a particular point of law, that matter enters the category of consensus. In effect, it then moves from the realm of probability to that of certainty and can operate as a textual source in the same way that the Qur'ān and the *sunna* do. The conceptual correlations between this notion of consensus/*ijmā'* and the Roman Catholic teaching of infallibility are intriguing.

Reconceptualizations of both consensus/*ijmā'* and of intellectual struggle/*ijtihād* have been a potent force for religious renewal in the 20th and 21st centuries. Muhammad Rashīd Ridā (d. 1935), an Egyptian scholar who collaborated on an important Qur'ān commentary and whose writings addressed many forms of social and political renewal, called for a restriction of the notion of *ijmā'* by both time and topic. Temporal restriction pushed it back to the very first years of Islam: only those matters upon which the prophet Muhammad's companions had reached consensus could be considered binding. Topical restriction reduced the range of *ijmā'* to matters of worship only. Reining in the scope of *ijmā'* was, of course, a way of reopening for debate and decision a host of issues with major political and social consequences. It was a way of moving towards processes of legislative consultation (*shūrā*) built on representative forms of government.

Reopening issues for discussion and debate amounts to a call for renewed *ijtihād*. Those scholars who felt that the burden of traditional interpretations had become an intolerable impediment to religious and social advancement urged that Islamic teachings be rethought with direct reference to the Qur'ān and the *sunna* themselves. Where these sources offer explicit direction on matters of faith, religious practice and personal status, the matter is permanently settled. But all other instances, everything else that affects the Muslim community in its private or public forums, are potentially subject to reconsideration and reinterpretation.

One famous example of the results of such reinterpretation is the Tunisian Law of Personal Status which was passed in 1957. As I am sure you know, traditional Islamic law allows a man to marry up to four wives. The pertinent qur'ānic verse for this is Q 4:3. The fourth *sūra* of the Qur'ān is entitled *al-Nisā'*, "The Women," and contains a number of passages relating to matters of personal status, such as marriage and inheritance. Q 4:3 contains the clause, "marry from among women such as are lawful to you, [even] two, or three or four. But if you fear that you cannot treat them fairly, then one. [. . .]" Using the process of *ijtihād*, the Tunisian legislators reasoned that a second marriage (or third, or fourth) was permissible only if a man could treat each wife with complete equality. Given contemporary social conditions and the constraints of human psychology, they argued, this is a practical impossibility. The condition imposed – equal treatment – nullifies the permission and polygynous marriage is therefore proscribed. In effect, the second part of the verse was deemed to have abrogated the first.

*What does the Classically Developed System Cover?*

Turning now from process to product, we can ask, "What does the classically developed system cover?" Classical compendiums ordinarily divide the topics of Muslim law into two categories, matters of ritual, i.e., the duties incumbent upon a servant of God (*'ibādāt*) and matters of social behavior, i.e., the duties involved in human interactions (*mu'āmalāt*). The books always begin with the first because one's obligations to God are of primary importance. A brief summary of the topics addressed in the many volumes of law (*fiqh*) and the commentaries upon them provides a good indication of the range achieved by combining the foundational sources of Islamic law with the generations of legal reasoning exercised by Muslim scholars. As mentioned, the first concerns are the duties of divine worship. Observant Muslims, as I am sure you know, pray five times a day. Before praying a Muslim must enter a state of ritual purity by performing prescribed ablutions. The precise requirements vary depending upon the degree of ritual impurity which the worshiper must redress. The law books, therefore, begin with the detail necessary to cleanse oneself correctly in preparation for prayer. Water, whether still or flowing, used or unused, is discussed, as are those elements that render it impure. The human conditions that necessitate ablution include the normal bodily functions of urination, excretion, passing wind, sleeping, fainting and male and female orgasm. Menstruation renders a woman exempt from the prescribed prayer. In fact, she should not enter a mosque during her menses or touch the script of the Qur'ān. As in Jewish law, sexual intercourse is forbidden during the days of menstruation.

Ablution itself is a precisely detailed performance that addresses the degree of an individual's pollution. While some forms of pollution are externally generated, such as contact with the discharges of animals, other forms are the consequence of human acts or experiences. Most of the bodily functions just mentioned require a form of washing known as *wudū'*. Q 5:6 provides the locus for this requirement: "O believers, when you stand up to pray, wash your faces, and your hands up to the elbows, and wipe your heads, and your feet up to the ankles. If you are defiled, purify yourselves. But if you are sick or on a journey, or if any of you comes from the privy, or you have touched women, and you can find no water, then have recourse to wholesome sand and wipe your faces and your hands with it." In the performance of this ablution, the right side of the body is addressed first and short prayers are usually uttered at each step.

The major pollution occasioned by intercourse, menstruation and postpartum bleeding cannot be removed by *wudū'*, the ritual washing of face, hands and feet. It requires a full bath (*ghusl*) whose various elements are carefully described in the law books. As the qur'ānic verse that I have just recited indicates, clean sand or dust can be substituted for the minor ablution when a person needs to meet a required prayer time but has no access to clean water.

I have expended some time and attention on these matters of pollution and ablution for two reasons: (1) they are an important part of Muslim life and religious observance that has no real counterpart in contemporary Catholic practice and (2) because they present a good example of the kind of fine detail to which the law books addressed themselves.

Naturally, the ritual prayer itself is the next major topic to which these law books turn and here, too, the specificity regarding performance practice and the conditions that validate or invalidate prayer is noteworthy. So, too, it is with the sections that follow, those devoted to the prescribed fast and the acts of pilgrimage. Fasting during the month of Ramadān requires absention from food, drink and sexual intercourse between daybreak and sunset on each day of the month. But the law books deal explicitly with extenuating circumstances, such as the situation of a woman who is in the final stages of pregnancy or who is a nursing mother. According to most of the schools of law a woman can break her fast during such periods if she fears harm to her own health or that of her child. The schools differ on whether she must make up the days of dispensation at another time but this, too, they lay out in detail.

The pilgrimage itself, which is incumbent only upon those Muslims who have the physical and financial capacity to sustain it, occupies a large section of these books. Matters of timing, preparation, travel, appropriate body covering, prayer formulas and ablution surround the principal activities: entering the sacred precincts of Mecca, circumambulating the *Ka'ba*, running or walking the long corridor between the two small hills of Safā and Marwa, moving on to the vast plain called 'Arafāt for the long afternoon and evening of prayer and praise (*wuqūf*), the return to Mecca with the halt at Muzdalifa and then Minā and the concluding commemoration of Abraham's willingness to sacrifice his son in the great communal Feast of Sacrifice (*'īd al-adhā*), and the final circumambulations of the Ka'ba. As even this very cursory summary indicates, this is a large and complex series of rituals whose every aspect generated intense legal discussion and stipulation.

But this covers only the first part of the law books, that dedicated to the duties incumbent upon each mature Muslim in his/her relations with God. These compendia must also address all of the areas of human interaction for which God has provided guidance, such as financial matters and regulations pertinent to personal status. Legally prescribed almsgiving or *zakāt* is often linked with *salāt*, the Arabic term for ritual prayer, in qur'ānic verses that summon humans to the fundamental practices of a pious life. Worship God and care for others – this is the basic moral message of the Qur'ān. Caring for others takes several forms in Islam. One is acts of charity (*sadaqa*), whether by deeds or dollars, while another is establishing endowments or endowing properties (mosques, cemeteries, water fountains) that will serve the community long after one's death. Both of these are voluntary but *zakāt* is a requirement and operates a as kind of tax on various forms of personal property, e.g., cash, including gold and silver, cattle, crops, and merchandise used in trade or business. There are minimum holdings in each category before the tax becomes applicable and the rate of taxation varies depending on the category. For example, the tax on mercantile commodities is 2.5% while for cattle it is one mature animal for every 30 in a herd. For much of Muslim history, particularly that of the pre-colonial period, *zakāt* was collected by the government and allocated to those classes of people eligible to receive it – yes, these, too, are specified in the law books. With, however, the introduction of non-Muslim legal codes in many parts of the Muslim world, the institutionalization of *zakāt* has been lost and it has become a matter of personal initiative. Countries such as Saudi Arabia, Sudan, Pakistan, Malaysia, Iran and Libya have reinstituted a government apparatus for collection and distribution.

Laws pertaining to inheritance bridge the groupings of financial and personal status. They are far too complex to describe in any detail but it is worth noting the limitations entailed. Only one-third of an individual's estate may be bequeathed by personal discretion. The rest is encumbered by the specified inheritance rights of one's spouse, parents and descendents. Islamic inheritance laws (*mīrāth*) have a strong qur'ānic base and the Qur'ān provides greater specificity in the regulation of inheritance than in most other matters of personal status. They have, therefore, been more resistant to change in the post-colonial legal reforms of various Muslim countries than other areas of the *sharī'a*.

Marriage and divorce regulations offer another area in which Islamic practice differs markedly from that of Christianity. In Islam, marriage is a contractual relation and an expected part of one's life as an adult. Celibacy is neither encouraged nor admired. The bride is represented by her guardian (*walī*) who is ordinarily her father or another close, male relative and in most Muslim countries, marriages are usually arranged between the bride's family and the groom's. The contract itself entails conveyance of a gift or dowry (*mahr*), often a substantial transfer of assets, from the groom's family to the bride. The qur'ānic mandate for this is Q 4:4, "And give women their marriage portions in the spirit of a gift." Conveyance of the entire bride gift need not be completed at the time of contract. The marriage contract can stipulate an amount that will be paid only if the husband initiates a divorce. This functions as a legal and financial mechanism to forestall the hasty disruption of a marriage. Here, too, a qur'ānic specification operates: Q 4:20, "But if you desire to give up a wife and to take another in her stead, do not take away anything of what you have given the first one, however much it may have been."

The conditions and procedures of divorce are given considerable attention in the classical compendia of Islamic law. These mandate the correct circumstances, the period between initiation and irrevocable closure and the necessary waiting period – three menstrual periods – before either party is free to remarry. While men have much more power to initiate divorce, women have recourse to certain legal stratagems. For example, in a form of divorce known as *al-khul*, a woman can pay her husband to divorce her. Yet another basis for divorce has garnered international attention in recent years. Apostasy, the renunciation of Islam by either husband or wife, invalidates the marriage bond. A group of Islamist lawyers in Egypt charged a professor at Cairo University, Nasr Hāmid Abū Zayd, with apostasy, insisting that his publications, particularly those on the Qur'ān, demonstrated that he was no longer a Muslim. An Egyptian Appellate Court then ruled that Abū Zayd be forcibly divorced from his wife on the grounds of his apostasy and because a Muslim woman cannot be married to a non-Muslim man. Nasr and his wife left Egypt, with both fear and reluctance, and now live in The Netherlands.

Two final topics before we leave this quick overview of what the Muslim legal system covers: *hudūd* punishments and *jihād*. The *hudūd* are a category of punishment and discussion of them takes us from the realm of religious and civil law – to use Western categories – to that of criminal law. The punishments that most often receive attention in the Western press are those for stealing and those for adultery and fornication. The latter have been the cause of recent international attention focused on a court case in northern Nigeria. Based on Q 5:38-39, theft merits amputation of the hand, on the first offense, and further amputation with a second offense. For fornication, an unmarried person is sentenced to 100 lashes (Q 24:2), a married person to death by stoning. This latter punishment does not have a qur'ānic warrant but is based upon a prophetic *hadīth*. While there is no denying the horrible severity of these punishment, they are by no means commonplace. Strict rules of evidence apply; for adultery or fornication, these mandate four eyewitnesses to the act itself or a voluntary act of confession. The *false accusation* of unlawful intercourse is itself subject to 80 lashes. Nor is there much evidence of the actual application of these punishments in the contemporary period. While they remain part of the penal codes of some Muslim countries – Saudi Arabia, Pakistan, Sudan, Yemen, Iran, and Nigeria – relatively few cases have been documented. Some executions for adultery or fornication that have reached public attention are instances of "honor" killings committed by male relatives.

Perhaps no Arabic term has garnered as much recent media attention as the word "*jihād*." Its base meaning of struggle or striving and, by extension, trying to better oneself in the eyes of God and to promote Islam, is now widely known. The ways of doing this can be private spiritual and ascetical practices or active proselytization. But this "greater *jihād*" does not claim our attention. It is the "lesser *jihād*," the so-called "holy war" that is the subject of great concern. Muslims do consider it their duty to defend Islam even if this means taking up arms. Q 22:39-40 proclaims, "Permission is given to those who fight because they have been wronged – surely God is able to help them – those who were driven from their homes without justification, but only because they say, 'Our Lord is God'." Interestingly, the concluding phrases of this passage seems to assume that forms of defense are common to all religions: "For, if God had not enabled people to defend themselves against one another, monasteries and churches and synagogues and mosques – in [all of] which the name of God is mentioned often – would have been destroyed." This passage, and several others in the Qur'ān (Q 2:190 and Q 9:13), place the emphasis on defensive warfare. But other verses (e.g., Q 9:5 and 9:29) have traditionally been understood to underwrite a broader warrant and to have abrogated the more restrictive verses. Further complicating any appraisal of this topic are verses like Q 2:256, "There shall be no compulsion in religion." Undeniably, however, pronouncing a military effort a "*jihād*" has profound resonance within the Muslim world and its consequences can be traced through the whole course of Islamic history. That history will show, however, particularly in its 19th and 20th century chapters, that wars of *jihād* are most often declared by one Muslim ruler against another or by a political adversary who seeks to overthrow the current regime. To justify this – since Muslims are forbidden to fight each other – the one opposed must be declared an unbeliever. Within the Muslim world, forms of social and political resistance have often represented themselves as movements to "purify" Islam, to remove the current government and install a more "authentically Islamic" one.

### *In What Areas Do Muslims Often Face Difficulty in Adapting to the Norms and Practices of North American Life?*

I wanted to conclude this lecture on a more practical note, with some remarks that will sensitize you to the difficulties Muslims experience on this multireligious, multicultural, non-Muslim continent. Obviously, more recent immigrants deal with all of the usual struggles surrounding the relationship of faith to national identity, including questions of assimilation and integration as opposed to maintaining strongly separatist boundaries. For those who are trying to negotiate these boundaries, adherence to Islamic law, at least to the extent it was possible in the countries of origin, becomes fraught with difficulties here. For example, Muslim congregational worship occurs on Friday but our business and industrial schedules, as well as our educational schedules, can accommodate only Saturday and Sunday sabbath observance. Imagine trying to pray during the mandated times for each of the five daily prayers, while working on a factory floor or in a high-rise office building. Imagine trying to perform the ablutions requisite to the proper execution of these prayer periods.

Muslim meat, like that eaten by orthodox Jews, must be slaughtered in a religiously appropriate fashion. Muslims in large urban areas can either patronize Muslim butchers or, as often happens, kosher ones. Those in small towns are usually out of luck. The proscription of pork presents yet another problem. This is not just a matter of avoiding ham on a buffet table or asking for eggs without the bacon. Lard – a major pork product – is used in many kinds of food. I've seen Muslim college students patiently studying the list of ingredients on a box of cookies to see whether it could be considered *halāl*.

Muslim children in public or private schools must address an assortment of challenges: cafeteria food, as I have just indicated, represents one of these. So do co-ed gym classes and sporting events. In many families Muslim girls are encouraged to wear "Islamic dress" (*hijāb*) even before reaching the age of puberty. While this ordinarily does not present a legal problem here – unlike the situations that have developed in France and Quebec – it does present a social problem. As these children become teenagers, the tensions of peer expectations about dating can conflict strongly with the more conservative attitudes of many Muslim parents.

## Concluding Remarks

In trying to answer – or begin to answer – four basic questions about Islamic law, we have covered a lot of territory this afternoon. I hope that even this brief survey has given you some sense of the powerful place that law occupies within the thought world of classical and contemporary Islam. To conclude where we began: the entire structure of Islamic belief and practice is built on the fundamental assertion that God has given clear guidance to humankind. The revelation of his own words and the exemplary life of his final prophet provide humans with the information and insight necessary to live lives that are in conformity with the divine will. As both a process and a product, Islamic law is the mechanism that translates those words and that prophetic example into specific prescriptions and proscriptions. In their totality, all of these precepts pave the pathway to God, what the Qur'ān calls "the straight path," *al-sirāt al-mustaqīm*.

## Suggested Readings

Al-Zwaini, Laila and Rudolph Peters. *A Bibliography of Islamic Law, 1980-1993.* Leiden, 1994.
Anderson, J. N.D. *Law Reform in the Muslim World.* London, 1976.

An-Na'im, Abdullahi Ahmed. *Toward an Islamic Reformation: Civil Liberties, Human Rights, and International Law.* Syracuse, 1990.

Bakhtiar, Laleh, ed. *Encyclopedia of Islamic Law: A Compendium of the Major Schools.* Chicago: 1996.

Coulson, N. J. *A History of Islamic Law.* Edinburgh, 1964.

Dupret, Baudouin, et al. *Legal Pluralism in the Arab World.* The Hague, 1999.

Esposito, John. *Women in Muslim Family Law*, 2nd edition. Syracuse, 2001.

Hallaq, Wael. *A History of Islamic Legal Theories.* New York, 1997.

Khadduri, M. *Islamic Jurisprudence.* Baltimore, 1961.

Peters, Rudolph. *Islam and Colonialism: The Doctrine of Jihad in Modern History.* The Hague, 1979.

Schacht, Joseph. *The Origins of Muhammadan Jurisprudence.* Oxford, 1950. *An Introduction to Islamic Law.* Oxford, 1964.

Weiss, Bernard. *The Spirit of Islamic Law.* Athens, 1998

Ziadeh, Farhat. *Lawyers, the Rule of Law, and Liberalism in Modern Egypt.* Stanford, 1968.

CLSA PROCEEDINGS 64 (2002) 191-208

# THE PRINCIPLE OF SUBSIDIARITY REVISITED

REVEREND MONSIGNOR ROCH PAGÉ

## Introduction

It is indeed a privilege for me to be able, once again, to address the members of the Canon Law Society of America. I hope that our time together today will be both fruitful and interesting. Since this presentation is called a "Seminar," this means that I am expected to put points on the table that can lead to discussion. I do not expect that you will agree with everything that I mention. Indeed, this is one of the advantages of our meeting – it affords each of us an opportunity to listen to the ideas of others and review our own thoughts on issues affecting Canon Law and the life of the Church.

This presentation was originally titled: *Subsidiarity: State of the Question.* However, after having read the Holy See's documents that address the issue, as well as numerous studies which deal with subsidiarity, I decided that the time is ripe to re-examine the question as a whole. One of the articles that pushed me to this view was the excellent article by John Burkhard found in *The Jurist*,[1] entitled: "The Interpretation and Application of Subsidiarity in Ecclesiology: an Overview of the Theological and Canonical Literature." There have also been doctoral studies done on the question. In particular, I'm thinking of the one prepared by Sister Rachel Harrington in 1997.[2] In addition, there is the final report from the extraordinary synod of bishops from 1985 in which the Synod Fathers recommended "that a study be made to examine whether the principle of subsidiarity in use in human society can be applied to the Church and to what degree and in what sense such an application can and should be made."[3] A year later Pope John Paul II highlighted this recommendation.

It is important to note that this Synod took place in 1985, twenty years after the Council and more than fifty years after Pius XI formulated the principle of

---

[1] *The Jurist* 58 (1998): 279-342

[2] R. Harrington, *The Applicability of the Principle of Subsidiarity according to the Code of Canon Law*, (Ottawa, Saint Paul University, 1997), iii-322.

[3] Synod of bishops, "The Final Report," in *Origins* 15 (1985-1986): 449.

subsidiarity without, however, mentioning its possible application in the Church. It is even more surprising to read that some authors were certain that the principle of subsidiarity has been applied in the formulation of the 1983 code. And yet, the legislator himself, three years after the promulgation of the code, accepted the recommendation of the Extraordinary Synod to study whether the principle of subsidiarity should be applied in the Church. And what has happened since that time? Burkhard concludes his study stating: "It would seem that there are almost as many understandings of the principle of subsidiarity as there are interpreters."[4] This statement, among others, convinced me to change the direction of the presentation whose title has **now** become: *The Principle of Subsidiarity Revisited.*

Since, in a certain way, I wish to "re-visit" the principle of subsidiarity, it would be important first to "visit" it, to see where it has come from, what it usually means in the light of the present code, and how it seems to have been applied in recent documents. From there, we will ask ourselves whether there might be an important aspect of the principle that has been neglected if not forgotten.

## I. The Development of the Recognition of Subsidiarity in Church Teachings

### A. The term "subsidiarity"[5]

The term "subsidiarity" derives from the Latin word *subsidium*, a military expression used to refer to a group of soldiers held in reserve to replace those who were tired. In other words, they were there to step into the battle in case of necessity, to be a support when needed. The word has since come to mean *assistance*. Although assistance can come from the outside, *subsidium* comes from within the ranks; it is a reserve force in case of necessity. It is important to recall the original meaning of the term. Etymologically "to be subsidiary" is to take someone's place. But we will see that the principle of subsidiarity is applied when the role of each person, each institution, or each community is respected by the higher level of authority. The higher level must not take over more than its proper role.

In fact, the term "subsidiarity" must be applied to the one who offers assistance to a principal party, or to that which strengthens a principal party. The subsidiary is there to help, and is an accidental accessory when the principal agent is unable

---

[4] "The Interpretation and Application of Subsidiarity in Ecclesiology," 331.

[5] Many of the ideas in this section are taken from G. LeSage, "Le principe de subsidiarité et l'état religieux," in *Studia canonica* 2 (1968): 99-123. See also, R. Metz, "La subsidiarité, principe régulateur des tensions dans l'Église," in *Revue de droit canonique* 22 (1972): 155-176. See also D.A. Bosnich, "The Principle of Subsidiarity in Catholic Social Thought," in *Religion and Liberty* 6 (1996), No. 4, as on Internet site.

to assume responsibilities. In its proper sense, then, subsidiarity is the quality of being subsidiary.

## B. *Initial magisterial statements regarding the rule of subsidiarity*

We should not look to Canon Law for the development of Church usage of the term. Rather, its origins are to be found in the social doctrine of the Church.

Leo XIII, in *Rerum novarum* (May 16, 1891) spoke of the intervention of the State when it was necessary to promote and protect the common good. He used the principles of distributive justice as a basis for this teaching.

Pius XI, in *Quadragesimo anno* (May 15, 1931), noted that the natural object of any intervention of the State in social matters had as its purpose to assist the citizens, and not to destroy or absorb them. It might be worthwhile to quote his text at length, since it is fundamental to our study.

> 79. As history abundantly proves, it is true that on account of changed conditions many things which were done by small associations in former times cannot be done now save by large associations. Still, that most weighty principle, which cannot be set aside or changed, remains fixed and unshaken in social philosophy: *just as it is gravely wrong to take from individuals what they can accomplish by their own initiative and industry and give it to the community, so also it is an injustice and at the same time a grave evil and disturbance of right order to assign to a greater and higher association what lesser and subordinate organizations can do.* For every social activity ought of its very nature to furnish help to the members of the body social, and never destroy and absorb them.

> 80. The supreme authority of the State ought, therefore, to let subordinate groups handle matters and concerns of lesser importance, which would otherwise dissipate its efforts greatly. Thereby the State will more freely, powerfully, and effectively do all those things that belong to it alone because it alone can do them: directing, watching, urging, restraining, as occasion requires and necessity demands. Therefore, those in power should be sure that the more perfectly a graduated order is kept among the various associations, in observance of the principle of "subsidiary function," the stronger social authority and effectiveness will be, the happier and more prosperous the condition of the State.[6]

We notice, though, that Pius XI made no reference to the Church in this regard. It was Pius XII, in his allocution to the new cardinals (February 20, 1946), who

---

[6] English translation taken from Vatican website: www.vatican.va.

indirectly mentioned the possibility of applying the principle of subsidiarity in the Church.[7] At the same time, he proclaimed what has come to be known as the superiority of the individual over the collectivity. John XXIII, in *Mater et Magistra* (May 15, 1961) reminded us that the activities of the State should not suppress the freedom of action of individuals. Rather, in virtue of the principle of subsidiarity, the State should favour and assist private initiatives in the economic sphere (No. 152).

## C. Vatican II

It is interesting to note that Vatican II referred explicitly to the term subsidiarity on three occasions, and, each time, used it in a slightly different meaning.

In *Gravissimum educationis* (No. 3), the Council says that part of the State's duty is to promote the education of youth. It fulfills this responsibility "*by implementing the principle of subsidiarity* and completing the task of education, with attention to parental wishes, whenever the efforts of parents and of other groups are insufficient."[8]

In the same document (No. 6), the Council again refers to subsidiarity when speaking of educational possibilities offered by the State: "It must keep in mind the principle of subsidiarity, so that no kind of school monopoly arises, for such a monopoly would militate against the native rights of the human person, the development and spread of culture itself, the peaceful association of citizens, and the pluralism which exists today in many societies."[9]

Finally, the third reference to the principle is found in *Gaudium et spes* (No. 86). Speaking of the international community, the Fathers note that it "should regulate economic relations throughout the world so that they can unfold in such a way which is fair. In so doing, however, the community should honour the principle of subsidiarity."[10]

If we examine these references closely, we can see that there are three distinct meanings that could be given to the term:

1) the intervention of the State should not deprive citizens of their natural rights;

---

[7] See Pius XII, Allocation, February 20, 1946, in *AAS* 38 (1946): 145. French text in *Documents pontificaux de Sa Sainteté Pie XII, 1946*, Saint-Maurice, (Éd. Saint-Augustin, 1963), Vol. VIII, 69-80, at p. 73. After quoting the words of Pius XI noted above, Pius XII adds: "Paroles vraiment lumineuses, qui valent pour la vie sociale à tous ses degrés et aussi pour la vie de l'Église, sans préjudice à son organisation hiérarchique."

[8] English translation taken from W. Abbott, ed., *The Documents of Vatican II*, (London, Chapman, 1966): 642.

[9] Ibid., 644.

[10] Ibid., 300.

2) appropriate decentralization should be fostered;

3) decisions should be taken at the most appropriate level.

We can see that the term has come to be used in reference to the State's intervention when individual citizens are unable to provide for their personal needs and for those of persons immediately around them. Nevertheless, because of the confusion arising from the different nuances given to the term, we still find today that the word is used in various meanings. This, of course, can lead to misunderstandings.

## II. Subsidiarity and the 1983 Code of Canon Law

### A. The Code Commission

When the 1967 Synod of Bishops met to approve the principles guiding the revision of the *Code of Canon Law*, not surprisingly, one of the ten accepted guidelines concerned the principle of subsidiarity. However, if we look at the approved text, we note that there is still some confusion as to the understanding of the term.[11]

The Synodal document begins by referring to the application of the principle to church legislation. It gives a description of the principle:

> The function of this principle of subsidiarity is to strengthen and confirm legislative unity in all the fundamental and major pronouncements of law of any society that is complete and compactly structured within itself. The principle of subsidiarity also has the function of defending the reasonableness or need especially of individual institutions to provide for their own advantage by particular law enacted by themselves as well as by a reasonable amount of autonomous executive power and authority.

We note already two different functions given to the term: providing for legislative unity, and allowing for particular law.

The text goes on to describe the function of unity:

> The system of Canon Law must be one unified system for the whole Church with regard to basic principles, with regard to the fundamental

---

[11] See *Communicationes*, "Principia quae Codicis iuris canonici recognitionem dirigant," 1 (1969): 77-85, esp. pp. 80-82. For an English translation of this document, see "Principles Which Govern the Revision of the Code of Canon Law," trans. R. Schoenbechler, OSB, in J. Hite and D.J. Ward, *Readings, Cases, Materials in Canon Law. A Textbook for Ministerial Students* (Collegeville, Liturgical Press, 1990): 84-92, esp. pp. 87-89.

institutions of the Church, as also with regard to the description of the means proper to the Church for attaining its supernatural end. The system of Canon Law must finally be one with regard to legislative technique. All these proposals are offered as being most fitting for the common good of the Church.

We note that the text provides four characteristics of legislative unity:

1) the basic principles are the same;
2) the fundamental institutions are the same;
3) the description of the means for attaining the end of the Church are the same;
4) the legislative technique must be one.

When it comes to different cultures and their application of the legal principles, there is usually not too much trouble with the first three of these characteristics. It is the last one – *legislative technique* – which causes concern at times, particularly if we compare a common law world mentality with that of a continental or civil law mentality. This leads to practical differences, which the Synod itself recognized when it spoke later of the unity of procedural law:

> We must, therefore, think of broadening the procedural law in the new *Code of Canon Law*, giving it a more general and universal form and leaving to the respective regional authorities the faculty to enact rules or norms to be observed in the tribunals of justice. Thus they would determine what pertains to the constitution of the tribunals, to the office of the judges and of other officials of the tribunal. The regional authorities would also adapt the laws of the code to the character and style of the laws prevailing in their respective regions. In this matter very often the court procedures of the land can serve as an example.

It could be mentioned in passing that, with the exception of the canons relating to means of avoiding trials (cc. 1713-1716), the principles of adaptation outlined in this passage were not applied too consistently in the 1983 code.

Again speaking of tribunals, the Synodal document has another passage that concerns us and that can be of importance in interpreting the present code:

> In regard to procedural law, grave doubts have arisen as to whether or not decentralization (as it is called) in this matter should be admitted to a greater extent than is now practised – that is, so that decentralization would extend to autonomy of the regional and national tribunals.

Here, we notice that the Synod refers to the principle in terms of "decentralization." In other words, we find in this document the same ambiguity as we found in the three Council passages. The principle can, then, mean three things which are inter-related, but which are quite different in their approach:

1)  decentralization;
2)  recourse to other types of law to supplement the canon law;
3)  allowing decisions to be taken at the most appropriate level by providing for "greater broadness of power and autonomy... for particular legislation."

## B.  *The proposed Oriental Code*

We could also note in passing that a similar principle was approved for the revision of the Oriental Law.  It is worthwhile quoting the statement at length:

1. Thanks to their traditional structure within the One Church of Christ, the Oriental Churches have, to a certain extent, adhered to the *principle of subsidiarity* all through the ages, even if without explicit reference to it. For a more extensive and more effective application of this principle, the following criteria must be borne in mind.

2. The new code should limit itself to the codification of the discipline common to all the Oriental Churches, leaving to the competent authorities of these Churches the power to regulate by particular law all other matters not reserved to the Holy See.

3.  That which the individual bishops are empowered to do in their respective dioceses should not be withdrawn from them, since their "power, which they exercise personally in Christ's name, is proper, ordinary and immediate, although its exercise is ultimately regulated by the supreme authority of the Church, and can be circumscribed by certain limits, for the advantage of the Church or of the faithful."

4. In the same manner, also, it must be borne in mind that, ordinarily, the bishop should not do that which others in his diocese are in a position to carry out; on the contrary, he should be careful to respect the legitimate competence of others, grant his cooperators the requisite faculties of which they are in need, and support the rightful initiatives both of individuals and of groups.[12]

---

[12] The text of the Oriental Principles for revision can be found in *Canon Law Digest* Vol. VIII, 29-39, esp. pp. 34-35.

*C. Application of the principle in the drafts of the Latin Code*

In a paper presented to the Canon Law Society of America at its 1981 convention in Chicago, Frank Morrisey commented on the application of the principle in the drafts of the code, as they stood at that moment – just before the final meeting of the Code Commission.[13]

He noted in passing that an immediate level of authority presupposes corresponding levels of responsibility, and that the code was prepared for an adult Church, one where the fullness of faith is presumed to exist.

Although the principle of subsidiarity has as one of its purposes to relax tensions, its application can give rise to new ones. For instance,

> episcopal conferences operate in such a way that it often takes a considerable amount of time for consensus to be reached on controversial issues, especially if the conference is numerous. It can take two or more years for decisions to be ratified, and then they still have to be implemented. Since a number of the points in the new law that require decisions from the conferences could have direct and immediate bearing on the lives of the faithful, there will be a tendency here and there to proceed on a local level before the appropriate groundwork has been laid by the conferences.[14]

The Code Commission had a serious juggling act to perform when it came to distributing the levels of decision-making. In general, there were three levels, each with internal subdivisions: the Holy See, the Conference of Bishops, the diocesan bishop. At the level of the Holy See, for instance, some decisions were reserved personally to the Holy Father,[15] others to the "Supreme authority of the Church" (see c. 373), and still others to the various curial offices.[16] At the level of the Conference of Bishops, some decisions were reserved to the bishops of an ecclesiastical province, while others were taken by the entire conference.[17] The code also provides for many possible examples of inter-diocesan cooperation.[18]

---

[13] See F.G. Morrisey, "The New Code of Canon Law. 1. The Importance of Particular Law," in *Origins* 11 (1981-1982): 421, 423-430, esp. pp. 423-427. See also "The Significance of Particular Law in the Proposed New Code of Canon Law," in CLSA *Proceedings* 43 (1981): 1-17.

[14] ID, in *Origins* 424.

[15] For instance, see canons 291 (dispensation from clerical celibacy); canon 377 (the appointment of bishops); canon 1698 (dissolution of ratified non-consummated marriages), etc.

[16] Compare the wording of canon 1698, §1 with that of §2, to note the distinction between the prerogatives of the Roman Curia and those of the Roman Pontiff personally.

[17] See canons 952 (Mass stipends); 1264 (offerings on the occasion of the administration of sacraments or sacramentals.

[18] For instance, see canons 237 (inter-diocesan seminaries), 1274 (inter-diocesan retirement and security funds), 1423 (inter-diocesan tribunals).

Lastly, at the diocesan level: the diocesan bishop can take some decisions on his own; for others, he needs the intervention of various councils.

If we compare the various drafts of the Code with the promulgated version, we see that a number of points which, at one time, were entrusted to the Conference of bishops have now been placed either at the level of the diocesan bishop, or at that of the Holy See. It was important to respect the conciliar principle (see *Christus Dominus*, No. 8) that the diocesan bishop has all the ordinary, proper and immediate authority necessary to carry out his task, except where such has been reserved to a higher authority (see c. 381). If there were over 100 instances where it was necessary to have recourse to the Conference of Bishops or to the Holy See, the broad principle outlined by the Council and repeated in canon 381 would become meaningless.

So, as the Commission attempted to determine the most appropriate level for decision-making, in a number of instances a somewhat arbitrary distribution of authority had to be provided for. There is no problem with this, provided we keep in mind that the present distribution of powers is not written in stone. In the final text, eighty-four canons allowed for some form of particular legislation at the level of the Conference of bishops.

Indeed, the tendency today is perhaps to return to a form of centralization. As Frank Morrisey noted in the presentation mentioned above:

> Even though particular law is being given great importance [in the new code], the various mechanisms for review and confirmation create a feeling of lack of confidence in local legislation – not always without reason, of course. It is to be hoped that the Church won't revert to a highly centralized system that could for all intents and purposes stifle any initiatives. Indeed, if such were the case, many would simply ignore it.[19]

It will be interesting to see whether this warning was heeded in the years following the promulgation of the code.

### D. Subsidiarity in the 1983 Code

While it is evident that great efforts were made to allow for the three levels of application of the law, without mentioning the term "subsidiarity," there are nevertheless in the Code some instances where decisions are reserved to a higher authority, and yet where it does not seem necessary for the unity of the Church to have such types of recourse prescribed.

Three examples will suffice.

Canon 237, §2 speaks of the establishment of a seminary for more than one

---

[19] See *Origins loc. cit.*, 430.

diocese. In such instances, the prior consent of the Holy See is required. Possibly this is because a bishop will henceforth share his authority with another bishop, but it really does not seem necessary to have this type of recourse, especially since canon 1274 on inter-diocesan funds does not require such prior authorization.

A similar example is found in canon 1423, where the approval of the Holy See is required for two or more bishops to come together to operate a tribunal.

Perhaps the most interesting case of reservation is to be found in the law for religious institutes, canon 684, §5 on transfers. The canon provides that while religious can transfer from one institute to another without having to approach the Holy See, the same does not apply when transferring to or from a secular institute or a society of apostolic life. In such instances, the permission of the Holy See is required and its instructions are to be observed. However, a recent case giving such "instructions" shows that there really is nothing special there that we would not expect to find when a person is transferring from one religious institute to another. The rescript reads as follows:

> The Congregation for Institutes of Consecrated Life and Societies of Apostolic Life, having given careful attention to the petition, and taking into account the consent of the Superior General of the Society of origin and of the Superior General of the Institute of Consecrated Life, grants the requested permission as required by canons 684 and 744 of the *Code of Canon Law*.
>
> During the specific period of probation which will last for three years, the Institute of Consecrated Life must verify that N.N. is living according to the vocation proper of the Institute, and at the conclusion of this period it may admit him to definitive incorporation, observing canons 684, §2 and 685.
>
> The Society of origin will be informed of the decision concerning his admission to definitive incorporation...[20]

If the permission is granted that readily, we could ask whether the reservation is really necessary. A similar situation occurred a number of years ago, when the prior permission of the Apostolic Signatura was required before executing an affirmative decision in a marriage case of Orthodox Christians based on a defect of sacred rite. On June 6, 1977, it was declared that this permission was no longer required.[21]

These are but examples of reservations to a higher authority, but they suffice to show that the distribution of powers was not always as clear cut as some would

---

[20] See CICLSAL, Rescript No. 45359/2000, August 4, 2000.

[21] Text in *Canon Law Digest* Vol. IX, 15-16. See also *Canon Law Digest* Vol. 7, 15, requiring the intervention of the Apostolic Signatura.

have wanted it to be.

We can now shift our attention to a few post-code decisions and documents.

## III. Some Post-Code Decisions and Documents

### A. Decrees of the Conferences of bishops

While the code allows Conferences of bishops to enact decrees in those instances where the law provides for it, we also note that a certain uniformity seems to be imposed these days on Conferences that wish to pass decrees. If the decrees are to be the same, then we could ask whether the purpose of leaving decisions to the Conferences is being fulfilled.

Two examples come to mind immediately: the holy days of obligations, and the term of office of parish priests.

Conferences that now wish to have different days established for holy days, partly because of the seasons in their part of the world, are being told to adopt the ones accepted by other places. Likewise, the term of office of parish priests has been fixed in practice at six years, renewable. For example, in the United States, the decree of the conference of bishops applying canon 522 was corrected by the Holy See so that the term of office would be six years, which had not been in the text voted upon by the assembled bishops of the conference.[22]

### B. Diocesan synods

One of the most important provisions of the new code was to allow for greater forms of participation in diocesan synods. It was primarily at this level that particular diocesan legislation would be elaborated and eventually approved by the diocesan bishop.

However, in a document issued July 8, 1997, the Congregation for Bishops and the Congregation for the Evangelization of Peoples – "to be of assistance to those involved in the preparation of diocesan synods" – it is now prescribed that the diocesan bishop is to provide a copy of the decisions to the Metropolitan and to the Conference. Also, through the Pontifical representative, "a copy of the synodal documentation [is to be transmitted] to the Congregation for Bishops or to the Congregation for the Evangelization of Peoples, for their information."[23]

It could be asked why it is necessary to submit copies of the documentation to the Holy See. Even if just the decrees were to be transmitted, this would be less surprising.

---

[22] See USCCB, Complementary Norms, February 28, 2002, canon 522.

[23] See Cong. for Bishops – Cog. for Evangelization of Peoples, "Instruction on Diocesan Synods,"July 8, 1997, in *Origins* 27 (1997-1998): 324-331, at p. 329.

## C. Catholic Universities

On June 7, 2000, it was announced that the Holy See had approved the USA norms implementing *Ex Corde Ecclesiae*, the Papal constitution on Catholic Universities and Colleges.[24]

In the norms we find a number of provisions relating to the intervention of competent ecclesiastical authorities. We could ask ourselves whether it is really necessary to have such controls. If we establish a University or a College, we should be able to trust the persons involved in its operations.

## D. Penal trials

The document of the Congregation for the Doctrine of the Faith, May 18, 2001, on the handling of certain grave offenses, takes away from diocesan bishops the right to implement penal law on their own. In a sense, the document, by requiring that the Ordinary indicate to the Congregation that a case is to be processed and await particular "instructions," seriously restricts a bishop's coercive power and centralizes a good portion of it at a higher level. Since the "instructions" are now publicly available on the Internet, it seems of little avail to have the reservation maintained.[25]

## E. General absolution

The Apostolic Letter, *"Misericordia Dei"* of Pope John Paul II, April 7, 2002,[26] raises a number of serious issues in regard to the application of the principle of subsidiarity today. For instance, while a number of years ago, in urgent cases a confessor could determine whether the conditions necessary for imparting general absolution existed.[27] This was then restricted in canon 961, §2 to the diocesan bishop, "mindful of the criteria agreed with the other members of the Bishops' Conference."

The new document, however, considerably conditions the power of the bishop as well as that of the conference, and places it, at least indirectly, at the level of the Holy See. The text provides:

> Given the fundamental importance of full harmony among the bishops'

---

[24] See texts in *Origins* 30 (2000-2001): 65, 67-75.

[25] See text in *Origins* 31 (2001-2002): 528-529, and related articles.

[26] See text in *Origins* 32 (2002-2003): 13-16.

[27] See Cong. for the Doctrine of the Faith, *"Normae pastorales circa absolutionem sacramentalem generali modo impertiendam,"* June 16, 1972, in *AAS* 64 (1972): 511, n. III, as repeated in the *Ordo Paenitentiae*, December 2, 1973, 21.

Conferences of the world in a matter so essential to the life of the Church, the various Conferences, observing canon 455, §2 of the *Code of Canon Law*, shall send as soon as possible to the Congregation for Divine Worship and the Discipline of the Sacraments the text of the norms which they intend to issue or update in the light of this *motu proprio* on the application of canon 961. This will help to foster an ever greater communion among the bishops of the Church as they encourage the faithful everywhere to draw abundantly from the fountains of divine mercy which flow unceasingly in the sacrament of reconciliation.

The document continues by asking that each bishop inform his Conference whether or not cases of grave necessity have occurred in his diocese. The Conference, in turn, will then inform the Holy See about the situation.

It is interesting to see how what was probably one of the only new approaches to the sacrament of penance that was really working – since it usually drew the faithful in the hundreds, even in the thousands – is being withdrawn, and the decisions centralized at the level of the Holy See. Time will tell how these provisions will be applied.

*F. English translation of liturgical texts*

The Instruction *Liturgiam authenticam* (March 28, 2001), on the translation of liturgical texts,[28] addresses a number of issues relating to the translation of liturgical texts. Rather than having liturgical texts translated by persons who know and speak the language, henceforth, "when it may be deemed appropriate by the Congregation [...] a text will be prepared after consultation with the bishops called a *ratio translationis*."

Furthermore, the document requires that if there are foreigners in the place who use an approved liturgical text from their original country, the diocesan bishop is to report this to the Holy See, describing the circumstances, the number of participants and the editions used. It could be asked whether such a provision is necessary, since the liturgical texts have already been approved by the Holy See.

The document also provides for the Holy See to establish "mixed commissions," applicable to a number of conferences. In other words, the bishops themselves from several Conferences where the same language is spoken, can no longer agree informally to work together to prepare a text in their language. Of

---

[28] Cong. For Divine Worship and the Discipline of the Sacraments, Instruction, *Liturgian authenticam*, (March 28, 2001), in *Origins* 31 (2001-2002): 17, 19-32.

course, we cannot help but think of ICEL and *Vox Clara* in such circumstances.[29]

*IV. The Forgotten Aspect of the Principle of Subsidiarity*

We know that in the 1917 code (c. 1040) only the pope could dispense from the diriment matrimonial impediments which were of ecclesiastical law. In practice, the bishops were able to grant dispensations by reason of the special indults they received (usually the quinquennial faculties); in other words, by reason of delegated power.

In 1963, near the end of the second session of the Council (November 30), the *motu proprio Pastorale munus* gave to diocesan bishops the power to dispense from most of the matrimonial impediments of ecclesiastical law – as well as many other faculties – and it gave them this power in virtue of their office. I do not remember hearing or reading at the time that this was an application of the principle of subsidiarity. Rather, this was considered to be an instance of decentralisation. Three years later (June 15, 1966), six months after the closing of the Council, the *motu proprio De episcoporum muneribus* legislated for the dispensing power of the bishops, at the same time reserving certain dispensations to the Holy See. Even then, I do not recall hearing of the principle of subsidiarity, neither when considering the power of the bishops that came to them by virtue of their office, nor in considering the fact that the Holy See was reserving certain cases to itself.

We do have here, though, in this one document, an application of the principle of subsidiarity seen under both its negative and positive aspects.[30]

> *a) Negatively,* the principle of subsidiarity requires that a society not fulfill those functions that an individual is able to accomplish, or that a hierarchically superior institution not carry out those functions that a hierarchically inferior one could accomplish. The principle is usually considered in this light.

> *b) Positively,* the principle of subsidiarity is applied when an individual member of the faithful or a small community, or even a hierarchically inferior institution cannot adequately accomplish certain tasks, or when these tasks are beyond their capacity. In this case, the community allows the individual to blossom forth, or the larger community intervenes in order to provide for the smaller one, or the higher institution provides for the hierarchically inferior

---

[29] See letter of John Paul II, April 20, 2002, regarding the establishment of "Vox Clara" (text available on Vatican web site). See also M. Gilchrist, "New English Missal: Archbishop Pell to Chair International Vox Clara Committee," in *AD 2000*, 15 (2002), No. 5, p. 3, as on www.adoremus.org website. For information regarding the status of ICEL, see Cardinal J. Medina Estevez's letter of October 26, 1999, in *Origins* 29 (1999-2000): 488-490.

[30] Cf. R. Metz, p. 159 and J. Burkhard, p. 333.

one. This would be an instance of being subsidiary in the etymological sense of the term.

In my opinion, this is the neglected and forgotten aspect of the principle of subsidiarity. And yet, at the same time, it is the aspect that should concern us the most. Too often and for too long we have confused decentralisation and the principle of subsidiarity. For example, we could consider that most of the tasks entrusted to the Conferences of bishops by the Holy See are applications of the principle of subsidiarity, but we must go further and ask ourselves whether the task which has been entrusted to the Conference could not be adequately accomplished by the diocesan bishop, or even by the bishops of the ecclesiastical province? If the task could be fulfilled only by the conference of bishops, it would be an application of both aspects of the principle of subsidiarity: the function is being exercised at the appropriate level, neither by the Holy See or by the diocesan bishop.

I wonder if there is not at the present time a tendency to abuse the principle of subsidiarity under its positive aspect, i.e., under the aspect of substitution or replacing. Let us come back to some examples already highlighted above.

*i) The term of office of a parish priest.* Since the Holy See usually gives its *recognitio* only to a decree of an episcopal conference that fixes the term of office at six years,[31] we could certainly say that it intervenes in the decision-making power of the episcopal Conference, which the Conference has in virtue of the law itself (cf. c. 522), and thus it applies the principle of subsidiarity under its positive aspect in something that ought to remain the domain of local jurisdiction. Does it act in this fashion to preserve unity? Granted, there is certainly uniformity.

*ii) The Diocesan Synod.* The code prescribes (cf. c. 467) that the declarations and decrees of a diocesan synod are to be communicated to the Metropolitan as well as to the conference of bishops. Yet, neither has real jurisdiction over the diocese. This prescription can be understood only as fulfilling a desire for unity and perhaps as aiding a future *receptio* by other dioceses in the same territory. The fact that the 1997 instruction on diocesan synods requires that synodal documents be sent to the Holy See constitutes not only a new norm, but, in my opinion, a particular application of the principle of subsidiarity. We must examine the decision to see if it is founded on the incapacity of the diocese to adapt its pastoral plan and its legislation to its particular situation, or whether it is founded on the desire for unity, or perhaps whether it is nothing more than a means for the Holy See to exercise vigilance.

---

[31] However, the decree of the conference of bishops of the Indian Ocean reads: "this term of office will not be less than five years."

205

*iii) Penal law.* One cannot deny that the document published in May 2001 by the Congregation for the Doctrine of the Faith on the treatment of certain criminal delicts diminished the diocesan bishop's exercise of power in applying the norms of penal law. Here again, in my opinion, we must consider the application of the principle of subsidiarity in its positive aspect, giving aid or assistance. Is it appropriate in this case? I doubted this myself until June 2002 when I read the norms prepared in Dallas on zero tolerance in cases of sexual abuse. In the light of the provisions of this controversial document, I believe that we should not be surprised to see that the Holy See intensifies its vigilance over the activities not only of episcopal conferences, but also of diocesan bishops. We also know that vigilance can be exercised by receiving administrative recourses or other types of cases.

*iv) General absolution.* The *motu proprio Misericordia Dei*, 7 April 2002, introduces what could become a new way of applying the principle of subsidiarity. It requires that each diocesan bishop inform his episcopal conference if cases of grave necessity exist in his diocese. The Conference, in turn, must inform the Holy See of the situation in its territory. The Conference is being used as a level between the bishop and the Holy See. And yet, most recently on 6 October 2001, Cardinal Ratzinger himself stated the following which would lead one to conclude the contrary:

> The bishop must have the courage to decide and judge with authority in this struggle for the Gospel. If the bishops take hold of their mission as judges in matters of faith and doctrine, the desired decentralization will be realized automatically. It is obvious that the episcopal conference must help the bishop through a good doctrinal commission and with unanimity in the struggle for the faith. But familiarity with the subtleties of modern theology is not necessary for the bishop's decision making. The bishop does not decide on the questions of specialists; he decides on the recognition of baptismal faith, the foundation of every theology. And if sometimes it can be just to tolerate a minor evil for the peace of the Church, let us not forget that a peace paid for with loss of the truth would be a false peace, an empty peace.[32]

The Conference of bishops should not become a vehicle for supervising diocesan bishops.

---

[32] Card. J. Ratzinger, "Returning with Clarity to the Jesus of the Gospels," October 6, 2001, in *Origins* 31 (2001-2002): 453.

## Conclusion

As I conclude this "revisiting" of the principle of subsidiarity, I have some conclusions to draw.

1. The principle of subsidiarity does not apply only in those instances where the superior authority does not impede the individual or the hierarchically inferior institution from doing what it can do on its own. It also applies when the hierarchically superior institution or the larger community provides assistance for the individual or the smaller community. Both aspects are part of the principle of subsidiarity.[33]

2. We frequently still confuse the application of the principle of subsidiarity and decentralisation. This is easily understood when we recall that when it was believed that the principle could be applied in the Church, we still had to request an indult from the Holy See for practically everything.

3. If we rejoiced every time rights were recognized as belonging to a level other than the Holy See, this should not prevent us from questioning the subsequent centralisation of certain faculties and rights which had previously been recognized at other levels. If this is considered to be an application of the principle of subsidiarity, we must ask ourselves whether such an application is appropriate.

4. Finally, the abundant literature and differing interpretations and opinions lead to the inevitable question: is the principle of subsidiarity fully applicable in the Church? *Fully*, i.e., not only in its positive aspect in the sense that the central authority reserves something to itself, but also in its negative aspect, i.e., by not impeding the other levels of government from doing what they have the capacity to do.

Since at the end of the 1985 Synod of Bishops John Paul II recalled that the principle of subsidiarity "is a subtle question which takes its origin from problems of a social, not ecclesial, nature," and he added: "My predecessors Pius XI and Pius XII accepted it as a valid principle for social life, whereas for the life of the Church they pointed out that any application must be made 'without compromising the Church's hierarchical structure',"[34] it has appeared evident that in the Pope's opinion the principle of subsidiarity is not fully applicable in the Church. It seems to me that it has never really been applied and will never be so, except by analogy to civil society. We know that two realities are analogous when there are similarities and differences between them. If the two societies – the Church and civil society – resemble each other in that they are composed of human persons in

---

[33] See Burkhard, p. 333.

[34] John Paul II, Address to the Roman Curia, "Implementing the 1985 Synod," in *Origins* 16 (1986-1987): 195.

interrelationships and seek a common goal, nevertheless they are distinct from each other essentially by the hierarchical structure of the ecclesial society, whose existence is not based on a social contract established among the members, but on the will of its Founder. Consequently, the mission of its leaders is to conduct the members toward unity and toward communion in the larger Church, which will be always considered its final goal.

CLSA PROCEEDINGS 64 (2002) 209-239

# PARISHES ENTRUSTED TO THE CARE OF RELIGIOUS:
# STARTING AFRESH FROM CHRIST

REVEREND MONSIGNOR ALEXANDER J. PALMIERI, JCL

*Introduction*

In a message presented to the Plenary Session of the Congregation for Institutes of Consecrated Life and for Societies of Apostolic Life [CICLSAL], just ten days after the terrorist attack on the United States of America, Pope John Paul II encouraged all consecrated persons to recall that, especially at critical times such as these:

> [. . .] [t]he Church counts on the continual dedication of this chosen company of her sons and daughters, on their longing for holiness, and on their service, as a means of promoting and supporting every Christian's striving for perfection and to reinforce the solidarity with one's neighbor, especially the most needy. In this way, they witness to the living impact of Christ's love among men and women.[1]

Two months later, in an address to Caritas Italiana on the day before he canonized four women and men religious as saints, our Holy Father reflected on the need for authentic signs of hope in the midst of a world plunged into despair at this beginning of the Third Millennium of Christianity. He described our world as one in which "[. . .] not only are technology and economy globalized, but also insecurity and fear, crime and violence, injustices and war."[2]

There can be no doubt that we live in a world forever changed by the tragic events of September 11, 2001, a world filled with despair and hopelessness, a world in which we are warned to be increasingly suspicious of our neighbor, a world where a "striving for perfection" in any vocation or lifestyle is ridiculed by many people who view such striving as an impossible ideal and a waste of time and

---

[1] John Paul II, Message to the Plenary Session of CICLSAL (September 21, 2001), in *L'Osservatore Romano*, English Edition (October 10, 2001): 13.

[2] John Paul II, Address to Caritas Italiana (November 24, 2001), in *L'Osservatore Romano* (November 25, 2001): 4.

energy. Yet, this era is supposed to be a new springtime for the Church, the beginning of a new millennium of Christianity, which was initiated with the urgent appeal of the Bishop of Rome to "put out into the deep" (*"Duc in altum!"*) [Luke 5:4], so that we might cast our nets anew! These words "[. . .] invite us to remember the past with gratitude, to live the present with enthusiasm, [. . .] to look forward to the future with confidence,"[3] and to proclaim that our future is, in fact, "Jesus Christ, the same yesterday, today, and forever" [Hebrews 13:8].

Of all the institutional structures of the Catholic Church, the one which is best suited to respond to the needs of all women and men in this new millennium is that of the parish. "It is through the parish that the Catholic comes in contact with the Church; it is the place where he [or she] is nourished with word and sacrament. Every individual is formed initially through the influence of the local parish community."[4]

While the canonical description of a parish as a "certain community of the Christian faithful stably constituted in a particular church whose pastoral care is entrusted to a *parochus* as its proper *pastor* under the authority of the diocesan bishop" [c. 515][5] appears somewhat static, mainly because of its nature as a juridical norm, the ideal to which every parish is to strive in reality is a much more dynamic and life-giving entity. Again, in the words of our Holy Father,

> [i]t is essentially the parish which gives the Church concrete life, so that she may be open to all. Whatever its size, it is not merely an association. It must be a home where the members of the Body of Christ gather together, open to meeting God, [. . .] and ready to accept their brothers and sisters with fraternal love, whatever their condition or origins. The parish institution is meant to provide the Church's great services: prayer in common and the reading of God's Word, celebrations, especially that of the Eucharist, catechesis for children and the adult catechumenate, the ongoing formation of the faithful, communications designed to make the Christian message known, services of charity and solidarity and the local work of movements. [. . .] [The parish is] a body to bring to life and develop together, a community where God's gifts are received and where the baptized generously make their response of faith, hope, and love to

---

[3] Pope John Paul II, Apostolic Letter *Novo Millennio Ineunte* [*NMI*] (January 6, 2001), translated in *Origins* 30:31 (January 18, 2001): 489-491.

[4] Rev. John E. Lynch, C.S.P., "The Parochial Ministry in the New Code of Canon Law," in *The Jurist* 42 (1982): 383.

[5] All citations from the *Code of Canon Law* are taken from *Code of Canon Law: Latin-English Edition, New English Translation*, by the Canon Law Society of America (Washington, DC: 1999).

the call of the Gospel.[6]

When considering the many and varied ministries in which women and men religious[7] serve today, the one *locus* which seems to bring together most if not all their good works is the parish. It is in the parish where "[p]eople are desperately searching for a sense of belonging, an identity, an escape from the numbing isolation in which they find themselves. Their spiritual well-being requires more than a station dispensing the sacraments conducive to salvation. They are looking not merely for a support system for their individual concerns, but for a religious experience where faith may be shared and values affirmed."[8]

This fact finds renewed emphasis throughout the most recent curial document on the consecrated life, entitled *Starting Afresh From Christ: A Renewed Commitment to Consecrated Life in the Third Millennium* [*SAFC*]. This work, which is not a directory or an instruction but which is simply designated as a "document" of CICLSAL, was approved by the Holy Father on May 16, 2002, and published on May 19, 2002. It serves more as a reflection on the reception of the post-synodal apostolic exhortation *Vita Consecrata* [*VC*], celebrating the fifth anniversary of the publication of that important text. While specific mention of the parochial ministry of consecrated persons is not made anywhere in this document, the application to this apostolate is easily deduced throughout this work.

> The most important challenge [for consecrated persons] today is that of a renewed commitment to the spiritual life, starting afresh from Christ in adhering to the Gospel and living the spirituality of communion in a unique way [. . .] on the streets of the world where Christ walked and today is present, where the Church proclaims him as Savior of the world, where the Trinitarian life spreads communion in a renewed mission.[9]

---

[6] Pope John Paul II, Address to a group of bishops from France on their visit *ad limina Apostolorum* (January 25, 1997), in *L'Osservatore Romano*, English edition (February 5, 1997): 5.

[7] For this presentation, the term "women and men religious" includes members of religious institutes of consecrated life and societies of apostolic life. "The entrustment of a parish to the care of religious," however, refers solely to clerical religious institutes of consecrated life and clerical societies of apostolic life.

[8] Lynch, 386.

[9] Congregation for Institutes of Consecrated Life and for Societies of Apostolic Life [CICLSAL], *Starting Afresh From Christ: A Renewed Commitment to Consecrated Life in the Third Millennium* [*SAFC*] (May 19, 2002): 4.

*Scope and Limitations of this Presentation[10]*

Using *SAFC* as a backdrop, the scope of this presentation will encompass the following elements: the process of the entrustment of a parish to the care of religious; the written agreement that is to be executed between the diocese and the institute or society; the importance of the charism of the institute or society in the life of the parish; and, the provision for the office of pastor.[11] Next, there will be a consideration of the particular experience of entrusting parishes to the care of religious in the Archdiocese of Philadelphia, including some of the benefits and/or tensions that can arise from such an act of entrustment. Finally, attached as appendices to this presentation are a sample written agreement between a diocese and a religious institute or society of apostolic life, and a sample program regarding the charism of the institute or society and the life of the parish.

Since this topic concerns the "entrustment" of a parish to the care of religious, this presentation will be limited to a consideration of specific forms of consecrated life, namely, to clerical religious institutes of consecrated life and to clerical societies of apostolic life (cf. c. 520, §1). Excluded from this presentation as outside its scope, therefore, is any consideration of the entrustment of "participation in the exercise of the pastoral care of a parish [. . .] to a deacon, to another person who is not a priest, or to a community of persons" due to "lack of priests," in which case the diocesan bishop appoints "some priest who, provided with the powers and faculties of a pastor, is to direct the pastoral care" (c. 517, §2). Such an inclusion, particularly regarding religious sisters or brothers who adeptly exercise such parochial offices in priest-less parishes of many dioceses in our nation, would certainly appear to be consonant with the theme of this convention ("Colleagues in Service: Clergy and Laity in the Church"); however, this is outside the scope of the topic at hand.

With the exception of select pertinent canons dealing with the apostolate of institutes or societies, canons 673-683 and canon 738 will not be examined in depth, since such an examination was more than adequately accomplished at last year's convention in Albuquerque, New Mexico.[12] Finally, this paper will not consider the special circumstance of a religious priest who is appointed as a pastor or parochial vicar in a parish which has not been entrusted to a clerical religious institute or to a clerical society of apostolic life.

---

[10] For further examination of the topic of this paper, cf. Velasio DePaolis, "De paroeciis institutis religiosis commissis vel committendis," in *Periodica* 74 (1985): 389-417.

[11] The principal source for all these canons is Pope Paul VI's motu proprio *Ecclesiae Sanctae* [*ES*] I, August 6, 1966, on the implementation of the Second Vatican Council's decree *Christus Dominus* [*CD*].

[12] Cf. Rev. James J. Conn, S.J., "Bishops and the Apostolates of Religious," in *Canon Law Society of America Proceedings* 63 (2001): 49-83.

> Consecrated persons extend a persuasive invitation to reflect upon the primacy of grace and to respond to it through a generous spiritual commitment. Despite widespread secularization, there is a widespread demand for spirituality which is often expressed as a renewed need for prayer. Life's events, even in their ordinariness, present themselves as challenges which should be seen in light of conversion. The dedication of consecrated persons to the service of an evangelical quality of life contributes to keeping alive in many ways the spiritual practices among the Christian people. Religious communities increasingly seek to be places for hearing and sharing the Word, for liturgical celebration, for the teaching of prayer, and for accompaniment through spiritual direction. Thus, even without realizing it, this help given to others offers mutual advantages.[13]

Such mutually advantageous assistance between consecrated persons and the people whom they serve is preeminently evident in the parish as "the family of families." While no institute or society can erect a parish on its own authority,[14] even in one of its churches or oratories, a parish can be entrusted "to a clerical religious institute or a clerical society of apostolic life" (c. 520, §1). This action of entrustment, however, can only be executed by the diocesan bishop himself. Canon 520, §1 explicitly excludes the diocesan administrator, that is, the "one who is to govern the diocese temporarily" (cc. 414 & 421, §1), as one capable of entrusting a parish to the care of religious. This is clearly in accord with the canonical principle that "[w]hen a see is vacant, nothing is to be altered" (c. 428, §1). Implicitly included is one who "is equivalent in law to a diocesan bishop," that is, one who presides over the other particular churches likened to a diocese, as mentioned in canon 368.[15] Implicitly excluded as among those capable of entrusting a parish are the vicars general and the episcopal vicars, who, like the diocesan bishop, are "local ordinaries," (c. 134, §2), but who are not "equivalent in law to a diocesan bishop" (c. 134, §3).

The ability of the diocesan bishop to entrust a parish to the care of religious is a qualified one, since the bishop is required to receive "the consent of the competent superior," which consent is required for the validity of the act (cf. c. 127, §2, 1°). It is unimaginable, both from a theoretical and a practical standpoint, that a diocesan bishop would ever attempt such an important action as entrusting

---

[13] *SAFC* 8.

[14] Canon 515, §2: "It is only for the diocesan bishop to erect, suppress, or alter parishes [. . .]"

[15] The other particular churches are: "[. . .] a territorial prelature and territorial abbacy, an apostolic vicariate and apostolic prefecture, and an apostolic administration erected in a stable manner" (c. 368).

a parish to a religious institute or society of apostolic life without the consent of the superior competent to give consent according to the proper law of his institute or society. With such consent, the diocesan bishop is also empowered to entrust a parish to the care of religious "even by erecting it in a church of the institute or society" (c. 520, §1), in such a way that the institute's or society's church becomes the parish church as well.[16]

Other than the provision for the office of pastor, and the agreement to be executed regarding the entrustment of a parish to the care of religious, the code is silent on the specifics of the act of entrustment, with one exception, namely, that the entrusting of a parish to an institute or a society "[. . .] can be made either perpetually or for a specific, predetermined time" (c. 520, §2). To entrust a parish "perpetually" is, in itself, a relative notion, implying that the arrangement is "irrevocable until such a time as the competent authority or one's successor(s) determine(s) otherwise."[17] A situation could inevitably arise wherein the leadership of the institute or society determines that it lacks sufficient personnel to staff the parish, especially in those communities which require two or more members living together in order to establish a local community. Or, another scenario could exist wherein the diocesan bishop decides to "twin"[18] such a parish with a neighboring parish, or, after having heard the presbyteral council on the matter (cf. c. 515, §2), to suppress the parish which had been perpetually entrusted to the institute or society. It appears that the entrustment of a parish to the care of religious "for a specific, predetermined time" is the wiser of the two options.

Two final issues regarding the process of entrustment, which are not codified but which emanate more from the practical realm, are the initiator of the process and the persons from whom advice is to be sought regarding the matter. As far as the one to begin the process, the invitation to accept a parish could be made by the diocesan bishop to the competent major superior, or the major superior could request consideration from the diocesan bishop to entrust a parish to his institute or society.

[16] Old Saint Joseph's Parish, located at Willings Alley in the City of Philadelphia, is a good example of such an arrangement. While a chapel, and soon afterwards a church, of the Society of Jesus was erected on this site in 1733 (becoming the place where public Catholic Mass has been celebrated continuously for the longest period of time in the English-speaking world), it was not until much later that the Bishop of Philadelphia erected a parish at this church.

[17] Joseph A. Janicki, "Parishes, Pastors, and Parochial Vicars (cc. 515-552)," in *The Code of Canon Law: A Text and Commentary*, James A. Coriden, Thomas J. Green, and Donald E. Heintschel, eds. (Paulist Press, New York/Mahwah, NJ: 1985): 421.

[18] The term, "twinned parishes," which is commonly used in many dioceses, is a misnomer. A better term would be "twinned pastorates," which emphasizes that the two parishes remain as two separate juridic persons, but that the care of souls for both parishes is entrusted to one and the same *parochus*.

The Church documents of the past ten years have constantly taken up the conciliar style which invites the bishops to evaluate the specific charisms [of consecrated life] in the overall pastoral picture. At the same time, they encourage consecrated persons to make known and to offer, clearly and confidently, their own proposals for presence and work in conformity with their specific vocation.[19]

Regarding those from whom advice is to be sought concerning the entrustment of a parish to the care of religious, the common law itself is silent; however, the proper laws of many clerical religious institutes and clerical societies of apostolic life place the decision in the hands of the provincial superior, with the prior consent of his council, not simply his council's advice. While the 1917 code did require the diocesan bishop to obtain prior consultation with the college of consultors and prior consent of the Apostolic See in order to "give a parish to a religious organization" (cf. 1917 *CIC* cc. 452 & 1425),[20] there is no such requirement in the present code.

One can cite canon 515, §2 which states that the diocesan bishop is not to "alter notably parishes unless he has heard the presbyteral council," and that this requirement is for validity; however, an argument could also be made as to whether entrusting a parish to the care of religious actually "alters notably" the parish itself. Despite the apparent doubt surrounding this issue, it still seems to be the best approach for the diocesan bishop to consult his presbyteral council on this matter, as well as the diocesan pastoral council, if one exists, and the particular parish pastoral council. In this way, the entrustment of the parish would have more widespread acceptance in the local Church, and the religious members assigned to the parochial ministry would feel more welcomed.

While the context for the one canon on the entrustment of a parish (c. 520) is within the code's Book II ("The People of God"), Part II ("Hierarchical Constitution of the Church"), Title III ("The Internal Ordering of Particular Churches"), there is a complementary canon in Part III of Book II ("Institutes of Consecrated Life and Societies of Apostolic Life"), regarding all works entrusted to religious by the diocesan bishop. Such apostolic works, including parishes, "[. . .] are subject to the authority and direction of the same bishop, without prejudice to the right of religious superiors according to the norm of canon 678, §§2 and 3" (c. 681, §1). This canon attempts to balance the rightful autonomy of the institute or society with the rightful authority of the diocesan bishop, an element which will

---

[19] *SAFC* 32.

[20] The union of a parish with a religious congregation in full right (*plene iure*) required prior consultation with the consultors because such a union entailed an alienation of property. Cf. Stanislaus Woywood and Callistus Smith, *A Practical Commentary on the Code of Canon Law* (Joseph F. Wagner, Inc., New York: 1952): 185.

be considered further in the next section regarding the written agreement.

*The Written Agreement Between the Diocese and the Institute or Society*

> Relationships within the whole Christian community are improving with a mutual and complementary interchange of gifts among the various ecclesial vocations. It is in fact within the local Churches that concrete pastoral plans which respond to Christ's challenges to reach out to people, to mold communities and to have a deep and incisive influence in bringing Gospel values to bear in society and culture, can be established. From simple formal relationships, one willingly moves to a communion lived in mutual charismatic enrichment. This effort can be helpful to all God's people, since the spirituality of communion supplies institutional reality with a soul by prompting a trust and openness wholly in accord with the dignity and responsibility of every baptized person.[21]

The written agreement between a diocese and an institute or society, which is meant to define specific matters regulating the entrustment of a parish, is a clear example of such a "simple formal relationship." Such an agreement, however, will be nothing more than a pseudo-legalistic document unless it gives rise to, and is an expression of, that "communion lived in mutual charismatic enrichment."

It is important to note that it is not the mind of the legislator that this agreement be executed according to the fashion of a legally binding contract, as is evident by the use of the word *conventio* (agreement) rather than the word *contractus* (contract).[22] As an "agreement," there is a recognition of the fact that unforeseen circumstances, such as those previously mentioned in this paper, may lead either of the parties to the cancellation of the arrangement prior to the end of its stated term. Further, an agreement implies a certain amount of trust between the parties, a mutuality which respects the fact that the diocese and the institute or society are not merely corporate entities but ecclesial entities, conferring upon the agreement a significance which is more profound than that of a contract.[23]

In two canons contained in two distinct sections of the code,[24] the common law

---

[21] *SAFC* 7.

[22] This is clear both in the meaning of the words themselves as well as in their parallel uses in the code. For the use of *conventio*, cf. cc. 271, 296, & 790, §1, 2°; for the use of *contractus*, cf. cc. 639 & 1290.

[23] Cf. DePaolis, 410.

[24] Canon 520, §2: "The entrustment of a parish [. . .] is to be made by means of a written agreement between the diocesan bishop and the competent superior of the institute or society, which expressly and accurately defines, among other things, the work to be accomplished, the persons to be assigned to the parish, and the financial arrangements."
Canon 681, §2: ". . . [T]he diocesan bishop and the competent superior of the institute are to draw

is very clear that the execution of a written agreement between the diocesan bishop and the competent major superior is not an optional item.[25]   Rendering this agreement in writing can additionally be viewed as a great advantage "to both the bishop and the institute [or society] in clarifying the duties and responsibilities of each."[26]   Although the list is not a taxative one, there are three elements which every parish agreement must contain, namely, a description of the apostolic work, the priests and other members of the institute or society who are to be assigned to the parish, and the financial arrangements between the diocese and the institute or society.

In describing the work to be accomplished, it is usually sufficient to state that the institute or society will administer the parish in all spiritual and temporal matters, in accord with the code, with diocesan particular law, and with religious proper law.[27]   Since the code adequately delineates the obligations of the pastor of every parish (cf. cc. 528-530) as well as the duties of the parochial vicar(s) (cf. c. 548), there is no need to specify each and every aspect of the parochial ministry, such as visiting the sick, preparing couples for marriage, celebrating Mass, etc., in order to fulfill the requirement of describing the apostolic work.

There can be particular situations, nevertheless, which warrant a "special mission in addition to the normal pastoral duties prescribed by law"[28] to be included in the parochial ministry.  For example, the parish priests could be responsible for the pastoral care of a non-Catholic hospital or nursing center located within the territory of the parish, but lacking its own Catholic chaplain; or, the parish could be responsible for the administration of its parochial high school. In these and similar instances, it seems wise to state explicitly what is included in the apostolic work of the parish over and above the usual affairs.

Regarding the personnel from the institute or society to be assigned to the parish, the number of priests and brothers to be involved in the parochial ministry is to be defined.  Yet, this definition is not to be so precise as to appear to be a guarantee, since the institute or society may not be able to retain this specific commitment of personnel over the course of the agreement.  It is better for the diocese and the institute or society to agree on a minimum number of priests who will share in the parochial apostolate under the supervision of the pastor, or as part of the team of priests to whom the parish has been entrusted *in solidum*, in accord with canon 517, §1.

Reaching a mutual agreement on the maximum number of priests is equally

---

up a written agreement which, among other things, is to define expressly and accurately those things which pertain to the work to be accomplished, the members to be devoted to it, and economic matters."

[25] DePaolis, 410.

[26] Jordan Hite, "The Apostolate of Institutes (cc. 673-683)," in Coriden, 510.

[27] Cf. item #2 in "Appendix I" of this paper.

[28] Janicki, 421.

important, so that the major superior is aware that he cannot simply assign an unlimited number of his members to service at the parish, when such a number is not necessary for the pastoral care of the parishioners, when it could present a financial hardship to the parish as far as compensation and benefits are concerned, and when parishes of a similar size in the diocese have less priests assigned to them. The same arrangement is operative for the assignment of religious brothers to assist in the parish work. The agreement ought to state that any additional religious priests or brothers assigned "in residence" at the parish, as part of the local community, are the financial responsibility of the institute or society.[29]

The final necessary element in a parish agreement is the financial arrangements, whereby "provision must be made so that a just and equitable plan is agreed as between the needs of the diocese and those of the institute [or society] involved."[30] Since most if not all dioceses in the United States have uniform plans for compensation and benefits for religious, with these plans undergoing revision every fiscal year, and since the term of the parish agreement is often for more than one year (usually for three years), it is prudent simply to cite the plan in the agreement and then to add the appropriate schedule by way of an attachment prior to the beginning of each new fiscal year.[31] The agreement is to state clearly that it is the priests and brothers who are actually assigned to the parochial ministry who are entitled to the compensation and benefits from the parish.

Other financial considerations in the form of benefits, in addition to health benefits, include, but are not limited to, housing, transportation, retirement benefits, vacation, sick leave, workshops, retreat, etc. When the parish agreement is not specific enough regarding these financial matters, "inequities and misunderstandings can occur for either or both the diocese and the religious institute [or society]. Such agreements assure justice and clarity for both the bishop entrusting the work and the competent superior who missions the religious."[32]

In addition to a description of the apostolic work, the personnel assigned, and the financial matters as required by law for inclusion in the agreement, there are other matters which must be also considered for good order and for the preservation of good relations between the diocese and the institute or society. The ownership of the parish property is a primary example. The agreement should specify whether the parish buildings, and the land upon which they are erected, are

---

[29] Many dioceses, however, welcome the retired religious members to reside in a parish house without any reimbursement to the parish.

[30] Enid Williamson, "Cann. 573-746," in *The Canon Law: Letter and Spirit,*" Gerard Sheehy et al., eds. (The Liturgical Press, Collegeville, Minnesota: 1995): 380.

[31] Cf. item #8 & item #10 in "Appendix I" of this paper.

[32] Rose M. McDermott, "The Apostolate of Institutes [cc. 673-683]," in *New Commentary on the Code of Canon Law,* John P. Beal, James A. Coriden, and Thomas J. Green, eds. (Paulist Press, New York, NY/Mahwah, NJ: 2000): 848.

owned by the parish, or by the institute or society, or by both in an equitable fashion.[33] For example, in the case of a parish which has been erected in a church of a religious institute or society, the latter remains the public juridic person which owns the church property, while the public juridic person of the parish has the right to acquire, own, administer, and alienate its own property which it may acquire from the moment of its canonical erection. In any case, experience often proves that there needs to be a careful investigation and examination of the issue of ownership, particularly through a professional title search, in order to determine rightful ownership prior to the inclusion of any such statement in a written agreement.

Although it may seem obvious, the parties to the agreement, namely, the diocese and the religious institute or society, are to be explicitly mentioned in the written document, along with the names of their representatives (the diocesan bishop and the competent major superior), who will be the signatories to the agreement. The term of the agreement is also to be articulated, with mention of the date the agreement becomes effective and the date when it expires. Along these same lines, mention should be made of the period of time prior to the expiration of the agreement which is necessary for either party to state his intention not to renew the agreement for another term, or to renew with revisions, or simply to remain silent and allow the agreement to be automatically renewed; also, there ought to be a statement as to whose consent is required in order to terminate the agreement prior to the expiration date.[34]

Finally, among other matters which ought to be delineated, the following are worthy of mention: a statement which recognizes and seeks to balance "the authority and direction of the [diocesan] bishop, without prejudice to the right of religious superiors according to the norm of canon 678, §§2 & 3" (c. 681, §1);[35] responsibility for repairs to parish property;[36] responsibility for past indebtedness;[37] whether or not the local community is erected as a religious house (or a house of the society);[38] and, method of deleting, adding, or revising any provision of the agreement.[39]

One general note which cannot be overlooked or ignored in establishing the written agreement when a parish is to be entrusted to the care of religious is that the agreement, as well as its individual provisions, can never be unilaterally imposed; instead, it is absolutely imperative that the diocesan bishop and the religious

---

[33] Cf. item #3 in "Appendix I" of this paper.

[34] Ibid., item #14.

[35] Ibid., item #2.

[36] Ibid., item #3.

[37] Ibid., item #5.

[38] Ibid., item #6.

[39] Ibid., item #16.

superior engage in fruitful mutual dialogue (c. 678, §3). This is a concrete way in which "the mutual relations between bishops and religious, conducted with sincerity and good will, will express in clear and realistic terms the dynamism and vitality of the Church-Sacrament in its admirable mission of salvation."[40]

*The Importance of the Charism of the Institute or Society in the Life of the Parish*

> [T]oday, thanks to an ever increasing formation of the laity, there can be a mutual assistance which fosters an understanding of the specificity and beauty of each state of life. Communion and mutuality in the Church are never one way streets. In this new climate of ecclesial communion, priests, religious and laity, far from ignoring each other or coming together only for a common activity, can once again find the just relationships of communion and a renewed experience of evangelical communion and mutual charismatic esteem resulting in a complementarity which respects the differences. This ecclesial dynamic will be helpful to the renewal and identity of consecrated life. As the understanding of the charism deepens, ever new ways of carrying it out will be discovered.[41]

It would be an error to view the charism of the religious institute or society as not having any impact on the life of the parish. Equally erroneous is the view that the parishioners' understanding of and appreciation for the religious charism has no influence on the deepening of living that charism by the religious members. To share either or both of these outlooks is to fail miserably in recognition of one of the most important reasons for entrusting a parish to the care of religious.

That importance does not rest primarily in the need for more priests to staff parishes, although often times this is the catalyst for entrustment. Rather, it lies in the need for the Church to live, at every level, the reality of *communio*, a "working together" in which every member of the Christian faithful – cleric, religious, and lay – shares his or her own gifts with all, working toward the one goal of striving to bring the Church toward its perfection, which is the Love of God Himself. That is, in effect, the theme of this convention, that we are all "colleagues in service [. . ] in the Church."

It is most fortunate that "many institutes have come to the conclusion that their charism can be shared with the laity. The laity are therefore invited to share more intensely in the spirituality and mission of these institutes. We may say that [. . .]

---

[40] Sacred Congregation for Bishops and Sacred Congregation for Religious and Secular Institutes, decree *Mutuae Relationes* [*MR*] (May 14, 1978) Conclusion.

[41] *SAFC* 31.

a new chapter, rich in hope, has begun in the history of relations between consecrated persons and the laity."[42] But what constitutes the distinct "charism," or "gift of the Spirit," which is unique to every institute of consecrated life and society of apostolic life?

While the law on consecrated life omits any explicit use of the word "charism," canon 578 provides an adequate description: "[. . .] the mind and designs of the founders regarding the nature, purpose, spirit, and character of an institute, which have been sanctioned by competent ecclesiastical authority, and its sound traditions, [. . .] constitute the patrimony of the same institute."[43] The necessary complementarity of charism and apostolic action is also made clear in canon 675, §1: "Apostolic action belongs to the very nature of institutes dedicated to works of the apostolate. Accordingly, the whole life of the members is to be imbued with an apostolic spirit; indeed the whole apostolic action is to be informed by a religious spirit."

An excellent example of a concerted effort on the part of a religious institute or society to share its particular charism with the people it serves, especially in parishes entrusted to it, is one formulated in July, 2001 by the Order of the Brothers of Saint Augustine, Province of Saint Thomas of Villanova, whose provincialate is located in the Archdiocese of Philadelphia. This program, entitled "The Rule: Augustinian Spirituality for Parochial Ministry,"[44] is a concrete expression of the importance of the charism of the institute or society in the life of the parish. It originated in a presentation on "Augustine and Church" by an Augustinian friar, Reverend Thomas Martin, O.S.A., who suggested "that there are many elements of the Rule that could, perhaps, be used to indicate how a parish served by Augustinians may be different from other parishes."[45]

Using the Rule of Saint Augustine as its point of reference, the document outlines twelve principles which can be utilized in forming and serving Augustinian parish communities.[46] Suggested uses of the document include: sharing sessions with parish staff and school staff; study groups; parish renewals; days of

---

[42] Pope John Paul II, post-synodal apostolic exhortation *Vita Consecrata* [*VC*], (March 25, 1996): 54.

[43] The *coetus* for the revision of the law on consecrated life, in its third session, established guidelines which supplemented the principles for revision of the code as formulated by the 1967 Synod of Bishops. While the working group removed the word "charism," it retained the notion in the law. These charisms or "diverse gifts of the Spirit," as recognized by Vatican II in the decree *Perfectae Caritatis* [*PC*], include the components mentioned in canon 578, with "sound traditions" denoting the institute's or society's spirituality, prayer, and government. All of these elements constitute its unique spiritual heritage or patrimony. Cf. *Communicationes* 2 (1970): 170 ff.

[44] Cf. Appendix II (reprinted here with the permission of the Reverend John Rotelle, O.S.A., then Provincial Secretary, now deceased, of Saint Thomas of Villanova Province of the Augustinians.

[45] Ibid., under "History."

[46] The twelve principles are: unity and harmony; stewardship; care and respect for the individual; worship; moderation and self-denial; mutual care; humility; the common good; reconciliation; authority and obedience as service; ongoing conversion; and, freedom under grace. Cf. Appendix II.

recollection; RCIA; Sunday homilies, etc. This program can serve as a model for other institutes or societies to whose care a parish has been entrusted.

There are differences between parishes staffed by diocesan priests and those staffed by religious priests. Without attempting to stress the importance of one over the other, it is to the mutual advantage of clergy, religious, and lay faithful alike that the differences be demonstrated in word and in action, for the sole purpose of helping to build up the Body of Christ as a communion of persons with a variety of gifts.

*Provision for the Office of Pastor*

> Today there is a greater freedom in the exercise of the apostolates, a flourishing with greater awareness, a solidarity expressed through knowing how to stand with the people, assuming their problems, in order to respond to them, paying close attention to the signs of the times, and to their needs. [. . .] [Therefore, t]he first task which must be assumed with enthusiasm is the proclamation of Christ to all. This task falls especially to consecrated persons who bring the message to the growing number of those who ignore it.[47]

Canon 528, which delineates in two lengthy paragraphs the obligations of the pastor of a parish, lists as his first duty "to make provision so that the word of God is proclaimed in its entirety to those living in the parish.[. . .]" It is apparent from these citations from *SAFC* and from the code that a parallel exists between the primary obligation of consecrated religious in general, and of those priests, religious and diocesan, who hold the office of parish pastor in particular.

The code makes it evident that the office of pastor must be held by a physical person (or group of persons *in solidum*, as mentioned in canon 517, §1), but not by a juridic person. While the 1917 code permitted a religious institute, which is a public juridic person by the law itself, to become the pastor of a parish with an indult from the Apostolic See,[48] this is expressly prohibited in canon 520, §1 of the present code. Further, the law requires for validity that the physical person who is appointed as pastor must be a presbyter (c. 521, §1).

Since the office of pastor is an ecclesiastical office as defined in canon 145, §1, provision for this office must be made in accord with one of the four methods outlined in canons 146 – 183, namely, by free conferral, presentation, election, or postulation. However, canon 523 further restricts this matter by stating that "[w]ithout prejudice to the prescript of canon 682, §1, the provision of the office of pastor belongs to the diocesan bishop, and indeed by free conferral, unless

---

[47] *SAFC* 36-37.
[48] 1917 *CIC* canons 452 & 1423.

someone has the right of presentation or election."

The aforementioned "prescript of canon 682, §1" which pertains to an ecclesiastical office being conferred upon a religious, is, then, an exception to the principle of free conferral established in canon 523. It states that, in this case, "the diocesan bishop appoints the religious, with the competent superior making the presentation, or at least assenting to the appointment." Here, it is the major superior who presents or nominates the priest, recommending that this priest be appointed as pastor; then, if the diocesan bishop finds the one nominated to be suitable, the bishop appoints him as pastor. "Frequently enough, however, a particular religious will be known by the bishop or have come to his attention as a candidate for [pastor]. [. . .] While he may request the assignment of this religious, he cannot appoint him [. . .] without the consent of the major superior."[49] Once again, as with the establishment of a written agreement when a parish is entrusted to the care of religious, collaboration is required between the diocesan bishop and the major superior.

The norm for the removal of a religious priest from the office of pastor, or indeed from any ecclesiastical office in a diocese, as stated in canon 682, §2 is a unique one and is meant as a recognition of the dual authority of the diocesan bishop and of the major superior (cf. also, c. 538, §2). It states that either authority can remove the religious from office "after having informed" the other party, with neither the diocesan bishop nor the major superior requiring the consent of the other authority.

This norm is unique because there is no stated need for a just cause for removal, although it is difficult to imagine such an action being taken without a just cause. In addition, the removal of a religious priest from the office of pastor is not subject to the norms of the special process for the removal of a pastor, as found in canons 1740-1747. While the causes for the removal can vary from incompetency, to grave neglect of pastoral duties, to a need for the services of this priest in another apostolic work of the institute or society, one thing is certain: arbitrariness is to be avoided at all costs and mutual consultation is to precede all such decisions affecting the diocese and the religious institute or society, as well as the parishioners and the individual religious members assigned to the parish.

> Arbitrary administrative changes by competent superiors or diocesan bishops without appropriate consultation with the parties involved offer poor witness of ecclesial communion, cause instability in service to the diocese, and contribute to lack of trust and poor relations between the bishop and religious. The pastoral care and

---

[49] Richard A. Hill, "The Apostolate of Institutes: Canons 673-683," in *A Handbook on Canons 573-746*, Jordan Hite, Sharon Holland, and Daniel Ward, eds. (The Liturgical Press, Collegeville, MN: 1985): 214.

spiritual needs of people must always be the ultimate concern of those responsible for missioning or appointing others to sacred ministry or apostolic service.[50]

## The Particular Experience in the Archdiocese of Philadelphia

It is therefore essential to make use of all initiatives which foster greater mutual knowledge and esteem. Only in harmony with the spirituality of communion and with the teaching outlined in *Novo Millennio Ineunte* can the Holy Spirit's gifts to the Church through the charisms of consecrated life be recognized. The coexistence in the life of the Church between the charismatic elements and the hierarchical elements, which John Paul II often mentioned when referring to new ecclesial movements, also holds true, in a special way, for consecrated life. Love and service in the Church must always be lived in a reciprocity of mutual charity.[51]

Entrusting parishes to the care of religious in the Archdiocese of Philadelphia has been and continues to be an expression of that "spirituality of communion," with a mutual exercise of love and service between and among diocesan clergy, religious clergy, and the lay Christian faithful including men and women religious. The local experience of entrustment is a long-standing one and has generally been very positive and rewarding both for the archdiocese and for the institute or society. Some of the oldest parishes in the archdiocese are those staffed by religious priests.[52] Presently, of a total of 282 archdiocesan parishes, there are twenty-two parishes which are entrusted to the care of eight religious institutes,[53] one society of apostolic life,[54] and one public association of the Christian faithful awaiting approval as a religious institute.[55]

---

[50] McDermott, 849.

[51] *SAFC* 32.

[52] Most notable among these are Old Saint Joseph's (founded by the Jesuits in 1733) and Old Saint Augustine's (founded by the Augustinians in 1796), both located in the "Olde City" of Philadelphia. These parishes predate the founding of the Diocese of Philadelphia in 1808.

[53] Congregation of the Most Holy Redeemer (C.Ss.R.) [Redemptorists], Baltimore Province; Missionaries of the Sacred Heart (M.S.C.), United States Province; Order of Friars Minor Capuchin (O.F.M., Cap.), Province of Saint Augustine; Canons Regular of Prémontré (O.Praem.) [Norbertines], Our Lady of Daylesford Canonry; Order of the Brothers of Saint Augustine (O.S.A.) [Augustinians], Saint Thomas of Villanova Province; Oblates of Saint Francis de Sales (O.S.F.S.), Wilmington-Philadelphia Province; Order of the Most Holy Trinity (O.SS.T.) [Trinitarians], Immaculate Heart of Mary Province; and, Society of Jesus (S.J.) [Jesuits], Maryland Province.

[54] Congregation of the Mission of Saint Vincent de Paul (C.M.) [Vincentians], Eastern Province.

[55] Institute of the Incarnate Word (I.V.E.), United States Province.

224

The priests of these parishes are responsible for the pastoral care of approximately 53,000 Catholics. Seventeen of the parishes are in an urban setting, of which twelve are considered inner-city, and five are suburban parishes. The smallest of these is a German personal parish in the city of Philadelphia with less than 350 parishioners, while the largest, also an urban parish, has 9,500 parishioners, mainly of Puerto Rican ancestry. While the majority of these parishes is territorial, five are personal parishes, although the ethnic communities for which these parishes were originally erected have generally migrated out of those areas.

In the past ten years, religious institutes or societies have assumed the pastoral care of six parishes formerly staffed by diocesan priests. In fact, several major superiors have expressed an interest in assuming the pastoral care of additional parishes, as their members increasingly voice a desire to leave their traditional apostolic works, such as staffing or teaching in archdiocesan high schools, and undertake parochial ministry instead. A few major superiors, whose institutes or societies do not presently have a house or ministry in the Archdiocese of Philadelphia, have shown an interest in exploring the possibility of accepting the entrustment of a parish.

In the necessary process of mutual collaboration between the diocesan bishop and the major superior, it is important for both authorities to be well-informed before the entrustment is executed. If an institute or society does not presently staff a parish in the diocese, experience has shown that it is best for the diocesan bishop, through his episcopal vicar or delegate for religious, or episcopal vicar for clergy, etc., to conduct a confidential inquiry with the corresponding authority in any diocese in the United States where parishes are presently entrusted to religious from the particular institute or society. This inquiry should be fairly general and focused upon an evaluation of the effectiveness of these religious priests in parish ministry.

Likewise, the major superior should request of the diocesan bishop all pertinent information regarding the parish being considered for entrustment, such as its demographics, and its most recent annual pastoral reports and annual financial reports. The diocesan bishop should be open and honest with the major superior in sharing any information regarding unique problematic situations in the parish.

The benefits that have arisen in the archdiocese from the entrustment of parishes to the care of religious are manifold. They include: a greater awareness of the consecrated life by diocesan clergy and laity alike; the experience of a variety and diversity of charisms; the unique insights garnered from the religious pastors concerning pastoral planning for neighboring parishes and for the archdiocese in general; the input from the charismatic perspective offered by pastors who are religious and who serve on various archdiocesan councils, such as the presbyteral council and the archdiocesan synod; the fulfillment of the need for sufficient priests to minister to the "care of souls" in parishes; and, the living witness of the special consecration of religious as parish priests following in a special way in the footsteps of the chaste, poor, and obedient Christ.

Tensions that have arisen, which are certainly few in number, center on two areas. First, there have been a few individual religious serving as parish priests who at times ignore the particular laws of the archdiocese regarding the administration of the sacraments, or liturgical norms, or policies concerning capital projects. Second, there have been two instances of a religious institute withdrawing from a parish prior to the expiration date of the agreement, with little notification to the diocesan bishop and a minimal statement of just cause. It must be emphasized, however, that the benefits far outweigh any tensions.

Some tension has also been experienced by the religious priests when dealing with the perceived "bureaucracy" of the archdiocesan curia. However, this is no different in the case of diocesan clergy, who view the service of the various curial offices in a positive vein when they easily receive the assistance or action they are seeking, but in a negative vein when any question is raised regarding their request! In a brief survey sent to all religious priests serving as pastors in the Archdiocese of Philadelphia, most agreed that there are many beneficial areas of cooperation with the archdiocese, and few, if any, tensions. They also recognized a fine working relationship, as well as a characteristic camaraderie, between the religious and diocesan clergy who staff parishes.

*Conclusion*

Let me conclude by citing once again the recent document from CICLSAL, from a section which seems to be addressed directly to the situation of parishes entrusted to the care of religious. The mutual spiritual value which emerges from this arrangement, for the individual religious priests, for the parishioners, for the religious institute or society, and for the diocese and all its members, clergy and laity, cannot be overemphasized.

> The experience of communion among consecrated persons results in an even greater openness to all other members of the Church. The command to love one another, experienced in the internal life of the community, must be transferred from the personal level to that of the different ecclesial realities. Only in an integrated ecclesiology, wherein the various vocations are gathered together as the one people of God, can the vocation to consecrated life once again find its specific identity as sign and witness.[56]

[56] *SAFC* 31.

---

## AGREEMENT BETWEEN
## THE ROMAN CATHOLIC ARCHDIOCESE OF PHILADELPHIA
## OF THE LATINS AND THE

---

_____ PROVINCE

The Roman Catholic Archdiocese of Philadelphia of the Latins (hereinafter referred to as the ARCHDIOCESE) represented by His Eminence, Anthony Cardinal Bevilacqua, Archbishop, and the _____, _____ Province, a religious institute of consecrated life of pontifical right (hereinafter referred to as the INSTITUTE) *[OR a society of apostolic life of pontifical right (hereinafter referred to as the SOCIETY), OR a public association of the Christian faithful of diocesan right (hereinafter referred to as the ASSOCIATION]* represented by Very Reverend _____, Provincial Superior, hereby accept the following terms of an agreement between them relating to the Parish of _____, _____ (hereinafter referred to as the PARISH).

1. After consultation with the Council of Priests of the ARCHDIOCESE, and with the consent of the Provincial Superior, the Archbishop of Philadelphia entrusts to the INSTITUTE *[or SOCIETY or ASSOCIATION]* in accordance with this agreement the PARISH of _____, located at _____, in _____, Pennsylvania.

2. The INSTITUTE *[or SOCIETY or ASSOCIATION]* will administer the PARISH in spiritual and temporal matters in accordance with the prescriptions of canon law and Archdiocesan norms, directives, and practices, except in what concerns the particular norms of observance according to the nature and purpose of the INSTITUTE *[or SOCIETY or ASSOCIATION]* as specified in its proper law.

3. The PARISH with all its temporalities and property, real and personal, is simply entrusted to the INSTITUTE *[or SOCIETY or ASSOCIATION]* in

accordance with the terms of this agreement. Attached to this agreement is an inventory of PARISH property. The PARISH with all its temporalities and property, real and personal, remains an Archdiocesan entity in accordance with the existing canon law as well as in accordance with the civil law of the Commonwealth of Pennsylvania. Repairs needed for the adequate preparation and maintenance of living quarters for the members of the INSTITUTE *[or SOCIETY or ASSOCIATION]* assigned to the PARISH will be provided by the PARISH. Modifications needed for the work of the members of the INSTI-TUTE *[or SOCIETY or ASSOCIATION]* "in residence" will be provided by the INSTITUTE *[or SOCIETY or ASSOCIATION]*, all necessary permissions having been previously obtained from the ARCHDIOCESE.[57]

4. All income from any PARISH functions, PARISH related activities, or bequests/legacies to the PARISH, belongs to the PARISH. The INSTITUTE *[or SOCIETY or ASSOCIATION]* may appeal to the parishioners for one special collection each year, not to conflict with the schedule of Archdiocesan collections or regular PARISH collections. The INSTITUTE *[or SOCIETY or ASSOCIATION]* agrees not to engage in any other solicitation of funds, bequests or legacies, direct or indirect, for the INSTITUTE *[or SOCIETY or ASSOCIATION]* itself without the specific authorization of the Archbishop.

5. The INSTITUTE *[or SOCIETY or ASSOCIATION]* as such does not assume

---

[57] In those parishes where the entire property (land and buildings) is owned by the INSTITUTE *[or SOCIETY or ASSOCIATION]*, paragraph "3" is replaced with the following: "The PARISH with all its temporalities and property, real and personal, is owned by the INSTITUTE *[or SOCIETY or ASSOCIATION]*, while the apostolic work of the parish is entrusted to the INSTITUTE *[or SOCIETY or ASSOCIATION]* by the Archbishop." In those parishes where the ownership is mixed, that is, where some or all of the land and/or some or all of the buildings are owned by the PARISH and by the INSTITUTE *[or SOCIETY or ASSOCIATION]*, paragraph "3" is replaced with the following, e.g.: "The PARISH with all its temporalities and property, real and personal, is simply entrusted to the INSTITUTE *[or SOCIETY or ASSOCIATION]* in accordance with the terms of this agreement. Attached to this agreement is an inventory of PARISH property. The PARISH with all its temporalities and property, real and personal, remains an Archdiocesan entity in accordance with the existing canon law as well as in accordance with the civil law of the Commonwealth of Pennsylvania; however, the PARISH real estate is owned equitably by the PARISH and the INSTITUTE *[or SOCIETY or ASSOCIATION]*, except for that land upon which the church is built, which is owned solely by the PARISH. Repairs needed for the adequate preparation and maintenance of living quarters for the members of the INSTITUTE *[or SOCIETY or ASSOCIATION]* assigned to the PARISH will be provided by the PARISH. Modifications needed for the non-parochial work of the members of the INSTITUTE *[or SOCIETY or ASSOCIATION]* "in residence" will be provided by the INSTITUTE *[or SOCIETY or ASSOCIATION]*, all necessary permissions having been previously obtained from the ARCHDIOCESE."

the responsibility for past or future debts of the PARISH. Neither does the PARISH as such assume the responsibility for any past or future debts of the INSTITUTE *[or SOCIETY or ASSOCIATION]*.

6. Notwithstanding the precise canonical nature of the establishment of the local community in a canonically erected religious house as defined in canon 609, §1 of the *Code of Canon Law*, henceforth the PARISH House shall be called "_ _____ Rectory *[or Friary or Priory]*."[58] The internal affairs of the INSTITUTE *[or SOCIETY or ASSOCIATION]* shall be carried out according to the *Code of Canon Law* and the specifications contained in the proper law of the INSTITUTE *[or SOCIETY or ASSOCIATION]*.

7. The INSTITUTE *[or SOCIETY or ASSOCIATION]* agrees to staff the PARISH with a minimum of one and a maximum of two full-time priests.[59] One of the priests will serve as pastor. The appointment of the pastor and parochial vicar(s) as well as the termination of their assignment will be in accordance with the prescriptions of canon law.

8. Each of the full-time priests assigned to the PARISH will be entitled to compensation and benefits provided for religious priests who serve as pastors or parochial vicars. Schedule is attached to this agreement.

9. According to PARISH needs and resources, the INSTITUTE *[or SOCIETY or ASSOCIATION]* may assign a maximum of two brothers to the PARISH staff for general and particular work of the PARISH ministry.

10. Full-time brother(s) assigned to the PARISH will be entitled to the compensation and benefits provided to religious brothers assigned to the ARCHDIOCESE. Schedule is attached to this agreement.

---

[58] In those parishes entrusted to a society of apostolic life, this sentence is to read: "Notwithstanding the precise canonical nature of the establishment of the local community in a canonically erected house of the society as defined in canon 733, §1 of the *Code of Canon Law*, henceforth the PARISH House shall be called "_____ Rectory *[or Friary or Priory]*." In those parishes entrusted to a public association of the Christian faithful, this sentence is omitted.

[59] In the Archdiocese of Philadelphia, depending upon the number of parishioners, this may read: "a minimum of two and a maximum of four. [. . .]"

11. The INSTITUTE *[or SOCIETY or ASSOCIATION]* is permitted to assign, in accordance with the prescriptions of canon law, additional members of the INSTITUTE *[or SOCIETY or ASSOCIATION]* to the community at the PARISH. The maintenance and support of any additional personnel shall totally and solely be the responsibility of the INSTITUTE *[or SOCIETY or ASSOCIATION]*.

12. One automobile to be used by the staff solely for parochial services may be purchased and maintained by the PARISH.[60] Premiums for the insurance for PARISH-owned automobile*(s)* will also be the responsibility of the PARISH. Except for this *(these)* automobile*(s)*, all other vehicles utilized by the staff are the responsibility of the INSTITUTE *[or SOCIETY or ASSOCIATION]*.

13. Any item not included in this Agreement relative to the administration of the PARISH shall be regulated in accordance with the prescriptions of canon law as well as by Archdiocesan norms, regulations and practices.

14. This Agreement between the ARCHDIOCESE and the INSTITUTE *[or SOCIETY or ASSOCIATION]* shall be binding for a period of three years beginning as of July 1, ___ and ending on June 30,____. It can be terminated at any time only by the consent of both parties. It shall be renewed automatically every three years, unless written notice be given by either party six months before the original or any subsequent renewal date of the Agreement.

15. The interpretation or application of any part of the Agreement is to be made without prejudice to the canon law of the Church, Archdiocesan norms, regulations and practices, and the proper law of the INSTITUTE *[or SOCIETY or ASSOCIATION]*.

16. Should either party desire a deletion, addition or change in any of the provisions of the Agreement, the revision may be effected with the consent of both parties, to the extent allowed by canon law and the respective norms, regulations and practices of both parties.

---

[60] If there are more than two priests/brothers assigned to parish ministry, two automobiles may be purchased and maintained by the parish.

For the ROMAN CATHOLIC ARCHDIOCESE OF PHILADELPHIA OF THE LATINS:

Archbishop of Philadelphia

**SEAL**

_____
Date

For the _____, PROVINCE:

_____
Provincial Superior

**SEAL**

_____
Date

*Appendix II*
Sample Program Regarding the Charism of the Institute or
Society and the Life of the Parish

---

THE RULE
AUGUSTINIAN SPIRITUALITY FOR PAROCHIAL MINISTRY

The Province of Saint Thomas of Villanova
Order of Saint Augustine

*[reprinted with permission]*

July, 2001

At the Parochial Conference of October 2000, a Committee was charged to produce a document which would show how the Rule might be used to teach Augustinian spirituality in the parishes where we serve.

Quotations from the Rule are found in the document which embody a principle of Augustine Spirituality. Those verses labeled with a "P" are taken from the translation of Fr. Russell, the numbered verses are from the translation of Dr. Canning.

**History**: Tomas Martin, OSA, in his presentation of "Augustine and Church" suggested that there are many elements in the Rule that could, perhaps, be used to indicate how a parish served by Augustinians may be different from other parishes. We share our own values and spirituality with the people we serve. The Rule is central in our formation and spiritual development. It is the sharing of those values found in the Rule that makes our parishes different. In departure celebrations, people frequently identified, as characteristic of our presence, elements and values found in the Rule. Why not be pro-active in teaching these values in the parishes where we serve, consciously sharing our heritage with the staff working alongside us so that they also can model the same values.

**Method**: During the discussions at the parochial conference, the friars attending added to the list suggested by Tom Martin. These topics were examined by the Committee and after much discussion, twelve elements were identified as key elements. Each member of the committee then wrote a commentary on each of the twelve elements. The results were shared with one another. The group met several times and reduced the seven commentaries to a single unified statement.

232

**Intention**: The document is meant to stimulate discussion among the friars and to be a plan for discussion and teaching Augustinian values to the staff and parishioners. It can be used as a plan for sharing Augustinian Spirituality with staff over a period of time. It might be the basis of a lesson plan for each of the different values.

**Not intended**: This document is not an attempt to cover all of Augustine's theology and spirituality, only some point of the Rule. It may be a starting point for further reading and study, but that depends on those using it.

**Hoped for results**: As you read and use this document, you may refine it or develop ways of using or teaching the material. Please offer feedback to the committee so that your good insights can be shared. The committee is willing to serve to focus your feedback so that our Spirituality may be better transmitted to those we serve. We the committee have enjoyed doing this work you requested. It is our hope that the document will be helpful in transmitting our heritage to the people of the parishes in which we serve.

The Committee: Dennis Harten, OSA, Francis Doyle, OSA, Edward Dixey, OSA, James Martinez, OSA, Joseph Genito OSA, Peter Gori, OSA, Arthur Johnson, OSA.

---

## The Rule: AUGUSTINIAN SPIRITUALITY FOR PAROCHIAL MINISTRY

*Introduction:*

*Before all else, dear brothers, love God and then your neighbor, because these are the chief commandments given to us.* P1

All followers of Jesus are called to love God and our neighbor. Augustine's synthesis of the gospel and how it can be lived is found in his Rule or Way of Life.

We can use these principles, found in the Rule, in our ministry of service. As religious, we can be a model of community to those parish communities that we form and serve.

*Principle One:* Unity and Harmony

*Live harmoniously in your house, intent upon God in oneness of mind and heart.* (P3)

*Live together in harmony, being of one mind and heart on the way to God.* (1.2)

St. Augustine, reflecting on the Christian community described in the Acts of the Apostles, realistically expects diversity. He likewise promotes harmony, by which differences are respected and, under influence of grace, the community approaches unity. Our unity as a community of faith is not self-centered, nor is it an end in itself. It is fundamentally outward directed toward God as the goal.

*Principle two:* Stewardship

*Call nothing your own, but let everything be yours in common.* (P4)

*Those who owned possessions in the world should readily agree that, from the moment they enter the religious life, these things become the property of the community.* (1.4)

Like the community of Acts, we are called to be wise stewards of our time, treasure and talents – both material and spiritual goods. Freed from the burden of possessiveness, Augustine encourages us to abandon self-seeking in order to find joy in sharing with others God's manifold gifts. The community (Church) can hold goods in common and from this storehouse share whatever is necessary for those in need. Our parish communities advance this way of life by embracing steward-ship, returning a share of what we have and focusing our mission on the genuine concern for those who are in need.

*Principle three:* Care and respect for the individual

*Food and clothing shall be distributed to you by the superior, not equally to all, for all do not enjoy equal health, but rather according to each one's need.* (P4 also P6 and P37)

*Your superior should see to it that each person is provided with food and clothing. He does not have to give exactly the same to everyone, for you are not equally strong, but each person should be given what he personally needs.* (1.3 also 1.6 and 5.3 & 8)

When common resources are joyfully shared to meet individual needs, the community itself is strengthened. Both the person providing the resource and the one receiving it benefits.

This reflects the life of our Trinitarian God in our imitation of God's own generosity and sharing. The core teaching of the gospel and the first principle of social justice is that every human person is a child of God, worthy of respect and dignity. A parish encourages each person in the use of his/her God-given gifts in service to the community. The parish is also to be open to the differences of individuals as a means of witnessing to the community through each person's uniqueness and diverse gifts.

*Principle four:* Worship

*Be assiduous in prayer, at the hours and times appointed.* (P10 also P11, 12)

*Persevere faithfully in prayer at the hours and times appointed.* (2.1 also 2.2 & 2.3)

The community should always have an outward focus, seeing and finding Christ in others. Allowance must be made for personal and private prayer so that the God who dwells within can be found. Prayer and liturgy (as the work of the people) encourage a peaceful and harmonious community. For authentic community life to exist in a parish there must be a faith-based sharing of one's interior life as we journey on our way to God. Our prayer together must come from the heart, contemplating in our hearts what is said by our lips.

*Principle five:* Moderation and Self-Denial

*Subdue the flesh, so far as your health permits, by fasting and abstinence from food and drink.* (P13 also 12, 14, 15, 16, 17, 18)

*As far as your health allows, keep your bodily appetites in check by fasting and abstinence from food and drink.* (3.1 also 3.2 to 3.5)

Fasting, abstinence, sacrifice, self-denial are all necessary for spiritual growth but they are means, not ends in themselves. St. Augustine urges moderation in all things, advising spiritual discipline "so far as your health permits." These practices are meant to lead us to God and to live a simple lifestyle, rejecting materialism and consumerism and being in solidarity with the poor.

In the words of St. Augustine: "It is better for us to want a little than to have too much."

*Principle six:* Mutual Care

*In all actions, let nothing occur to give offense, but only what becomes your holy state of life.* (P19 through 29)

*Whatever you are doing, your behavior should in no way cause offense to anyone, but should rather be in keeping with the holiness of your way of life.* (4.1 thru 11)

God cares for us when we are cared for by another in love. One clear manifestation of such care is the obligation to speak fraternally to another who is in danger of straying into sin. Ultimately, such admonishment must always manifest the tender mercy and forgiveness of God. When in need of assistance we must graciously accept the help given. We must humbly accept fraternal correction, which is based on truth and offered in a charitable spirit.

*Principle seven:* Humility

*Monasteries will come to serve a useful purpose of the rich and not the poor, if the rich are humbled there and the poor are puffed up with pride.* (P6, 7, 8)

*If, in the religious life, rich people were to become humble and poor people haughty, then this style of life would seem to be of value only to the rich and not the poor.* (1, 6, 7, 8)

Augustine contends that there is no possibility of true community of mind and heart without the virtue of humility. It is the primary virtue for common life. Conversely, pride, which lurks even in good works, is the beginning and origin of all sin.

Just as Christ emptied himself, so too ought we to guard against pride which can undermine a good work and distort motivation.

Social status, education, possessions and high achievements do not make us who we are except when pride dominates. The Incarnation of the Word is God's humility. When we imitate Christ in His humility, we are formed in His image by loving God and others more than self. We depend on God for all that we are and what we have.

*Principle eight:* The Common Good

*Whenever you show greater concern for the common good than for your own, you may know that you are growing in charity.* (P31)

*Love puts the interest of the community before personal advantage, and not the other way around.* (5.2)

Charity grows whenever the individual or the community freely chooses to place the greater good ahead of one's own.

We are called to build the kingdom of God, not our own. Cooperation, collaboration and the recognition of the gifts of others enhance the growth of community. The measure of our growth in charity is found in our placing the community interest (parish) before our own.

*Principle nine:* Reconciliation

*Whoever has injured another by open insult, or by abusive or incriminating language, must remember to repair the injury as quickly as possible by an apology, and he who suffered the injury must also forgive, without further wrangling.* (P41, 42, 43)

*If you have hurt a person by abusing him, or by cursing or grossly accusing him, be careful to make amends for the harm you have done, as quickly as possible, by apologizing to him. And the one who has been hurt should be ready in his to forgive you without wrangling.* (6.2)

A community of life without conflicts is impossible. Living and interacting together is bound to create conflicts and Augustine in the Rule offers us a way to respond to these situations. Disputes are to be addressed quickly, directly, and with compassion. The one who has been offended must be ready to forgive. Here again, forgiveness must come from the heart and not just the lips. To forgive from the heart requires humility.

Augustine makes it eminently clear that a community will be strong only if its members interact honestly and lovingly. Reconciliation is based on true concern for each other's welfare. An Augustinian parish ought to model open, forthright and loving confrontation in pointing out what is truly harmful to individual persons and to the community for the welfare of all.

*Principle ten:* Authority and obedience as service

*The superior, for his part, must not think himself fortunate in his exercise of authority but in his rule as one serving you in love.* (P44, 46-47)

*Your superior must not think himself fortunate in having power to lord it over you, but in the love with which he shall serve you.* (7.1-4)

For Augustine, authority is an act of loving service. A designated authority figure or leader is not placed above others but remains a part of the community (parish) with special responsibilities and duties toward others. Guiding the community toward the fulfillment of the Gospel ideals and being an example to others are two of the most important aspects of the role of authority (pastor).

Every member, however, must take responsibility for the progress toward these ideals and the discernment of the community's direction.

Likewise, obedience shows a loving compassion for the leader who bears greater responsibility for the community and a willingness to listen and cooperate for the common good. This certainly shapes our New Testament understanding of authority as counter-cultural as proclaimed by Jesus. Such authority remains gentle and humble because it is always perceived as in service to God, whose servants are thereby served.

*Principle eleven:* Ongoing conversion

*And that you may see yourselves in this little book, as in a mirror, have it read to you once a week so as to neglect no point through forgetfulness.* (P49)

*This little book is to be read to you once a week. As in a mirror, you will be able to see in it whether there is anything you are neglecting or forgetting.* (8.2)

Augustine encourages us to look into the gospel and Rule as in a mirror to assess how well we are approaching our goals. Thus, we can monitor our progress in the Christian life, a gradual process of ongoing conversion in Christ. Conversion is a life-long process. Frequent personal communal evaluations help us focus on the journey toward God in oneness of mind and heart. Augustine's words alert us that on our journey as the pilgrim people of God we cannot be complacent. Regular review of the process can stimulate renewal and strengthen commitment and fervor.

*Principle twelve:* Freedom under grace

*The Lord grant that you may observe these precepts . . . not as slaves living under the law but as men living in freedom under grace.* (P48)

*Live in such a way that you spread abroad the life-giving aroma of Christ. Do not be weighed down like slaves straining under the law, but live as free men under grace.* (8.1)

While striving to live in oneness of mind and heart intent upon God as proposed by Augustine, we must remember that God gives us the grace needed to succeed. It is this grace, freely given by God, that grants us the freedom to choose to love one another as Jesus did and reject the enslavement of sin.  Grace gives us the freedom and the responsibility to find God in ourselves an in one another.

*Suggested use of the document*

- Personal reflections
- Local House Chapter
- With Parish Staff
- With School Staff
- Study Groups in the Parish
- Parish Renewal
- Day of Recollection
- R.C.I.A. (Confession and Rule)
- Reflection guide or use with Augustinian Volunteers
- Retreat experiences
- Share with other ministries of the Province

*Suggested aids for use of the document*

- Develop a series of concrete questions based on the document to focus discussion.
- Increase specific application to Parish Community to meet local needs.
- Share any developed materials and uses with the committee for distribution.

CLSA PROCEEDINGS 64 (2002) 241-252

# AN INTRODUCTION TO LITURGICAL LAW:
## SOURCES AND INTERPRETATION

### SISTER ANN REHRAUER, OSF

Liturgical Law is part of ecclesiastical law and therefore part of canon law in the broad sense. In addition to the disclaimer in canon 2, a number of canons refer to the elements that affect the celebration of sacraments, as well as govern sacred times and places. As an integral part of the Church's law, liturgical law provides the rules governing public liturgical celebrations including those governing the words and actions of celebrant and participants, the environment, and the circumstances of the celebration.

*Similarities with other Ecclesiastical Law*

Like other ecclesiastical law, liturgical law follows the principles which establish who enjoys legislative authority. It has both a universal and particular dimension, a specific purpose, and there are specific sources where the law is found. Within the scripting of the liturgical law one finds a variety of literary forms.

Legislators: Unlike *CIC* 1275, canon 838 of the 1983 *Code of Canon Law* provides for three levels of legislators in the area of liturgical law: a) the Apostolic See (the Pope, the college of bishops, and/or an ecumenical council) which orders the sacred liturgy, publishes liturgical books, reviews vernacular translations, and sees that the norms are observed; b) the conference of bishops in a particular country (which prepares and approves the translations and, within their competence, approves the minor adaptations for vernacular typical editions of liturgical books); and c) an individual diocesan bishop, within his competence, who issues liturgical norms for his diocese.

In 1963 the Second Vatican Council issued *Sacrosanctum concilium*, the apostolic constitution which provided major legislation and guidance in the area of liturgical celebration. Besides calling for a revision of liturgical rites, the constitution specified who possessed the power to govern the liturgy (*SC* 22, 64), how future cultural adaptation would be handled (*SC* 37-40) and provided specific norms for celebration. Many of these provisions were incorporated into the introductory canons (cc. 834-839) of the 1983 code.

Although the actual work of revising the various rites was done by the Concilium (a subcommittee of the Congregation of Rites) and the staff of the Congregation charged with overseeing liturgical celebrations (now the Congregation for Divine Worship and the Discipline of the Sacraments), the Holy Father himself usually promulgates the apostolic constitution which declares a particular revision to be the typical (official) edition of the liturgical book. It is he who directly reviews and approves any change in the matter and formulae for the celebration of the sacraments. Occasionally the Holy Father will issue a *motu proprio* in liturgical areas as well.

The Episcopal Conference has legislative competence in some liturgical areas. It is theirs to prepare and approve the translation of liturgical texts and to promulgate the vernacular typical edition (*SC* 22). The translation approved by the Conference requires the *recognitio* from the appropriate Roman dicastery (*SC* 35). While *this recognitio* adds juridical and moral weight to their decision, the translation is issued by the authority of the Episcopal Conference. In addition, the Conference can make adaptations when this is specified in the liturgical book or document. The most evident expression of this adaptation is the recently revised American Appendix to the *Institutio Generalis Missalis Romani* which I will discuss later in this article. The *Institutio* specified a number of areas where the Conference was encouraged to legislate or offer further specifications in the areas of liturgical music, furnishings, vessels and vestments, feast days and days of penance, and liturgical ministries. Where the ability to make adaptations is not given to the Conference, the bishops can request further adaptations by indult or privilege.

The individual bishop also has some (but more limited) legislative authority in the area of liturgical law for his diocese. While most bishops issue guidelines and policies, some bishops enact particular law, for example, with regard to the age of liturgical ministers, determining the meaning of "evening" and the time at which the Sunday Mass may be celebrated on Saturday.

Interpreters: Just as there are legislators for canon law and for liturgical law, there are also interpreters. The legislator is an authentic interpreter of liturgical law. The Commission for the interpretation of legislative texts also has competence over liturgical provisions in canon law. In fact, they have provided the interpretation of *iterum* (again) in canon 917, stating that a person may receive Holy Communion a second time on the same day during the celebration of the Eucharist in which he/she participates. The Commission also clarified when *extraordinary ministers of Holy Communion* may or may not exercise their role when *ordinary* ministers are present. In addition to these authentic interpreters, we have the benefit of private responses from the Congregation for Divine Worship and the Discipline of the Sacraments (CDWDS), and responses to queries published in *Notitiae*, the official journal of CDWDS.

Dispensation: Like many of the canons in the code, some liturgical laws are subject to the general canonical principles of dispensation found in canons 87 and 88. Thus, merely ecclesiastical disciplinary laws can be dispensed by the diocesan bishop and the local ordinary when certain criteria are met constitutive law, however, cannot be dispensed nor can those laws which specifically prohibit dispensation by a lower level of authority. Clearly a bishop or vicar general cannot dispense from the matter and form of the sacraments, from the requirement of faculties or jurisdiction, and from provisions like the requirement of baptism before reception of the other sacraments.

Universal and Particular Dimension: Like other ecclesiastical law, liturgical law has a universal and a particular dimension. Universal liturgical law applies to all the Christian faithful or to all the members of a particular group. The *Praenotanda* to the typical edition of liturgical books like the *Institutio Generalis Missalis Romani*, the determination of the matter and form of the sacraments, general provisions regarding liturgical translation, such as *Liturgiam Authenticam*,[1] are universal in nature. Particular law includes (but is not limited to) the vernacular typical edition of liturgical books with the appropriate cultural adaptations, decrees of the Episcopal conference in liturgical areas and statutes governing liturgical issues (such as the USA Statutes for the Rite of Christian Initiation of Adults).

Purpose: The basic purpose of liturgical law is consonant with the purpose of all ecclesiastical law – the salvation of people. In addition, liturgical law helps facilitate good worship and offers a kind of "quality control," protecting the rights of the faithful (from the whims of a celebrant, of liturgical ministers, or other individuals in the congregation), and promoting harmony and unity in the external life of the Church.

Literary Forms: Just as there are a variety of literary forms in the *Code of Canon Law*, so are there different literary forms in liturgical legislation. One finds theological statements, admonitions and exhortations, prescriptive language (of greater or lesser weight), and facultative or optional provisions.

---

[1] The fifth Instruction on the Right Implementation of the Constitution on the Sacred Liturgy of the Second Vatican Council, *Liturgiam authenticam*: on the Use of Vernacular Languages in the Publication of the Books of the Roman Liturgy, March 28, 2001.

Sources: Unlike other areas of ecclesiastical law, most liturgical laws are not found in the code. There are, however, some canons which, although not strictly liturgical law, affect liturgical law. Book IV of the code contains the majority of laws governing the liturgical area. It includes general principles on who may legislate and on celebration (cc. 834-839), some determinations for sacraments and sacramentals (cc. 840-1172), the celebration of the liturgy of the hours (cc. 1173-1175), funeral rites (cc. 1176-1185), relics and images, sacred places and sacred times (cc. 1205-1253). Book III contains some canons which govern liturgical preaching, specifically the homily at Mass (cc. 762-772). Book I contains the disclaimer found in canon 2 (the code does not define the rites used in liturgical celebrations) and the specifications for installed and otherwise deputed liturgical ministers (c. 230). But the general principles in Book I, such as that of revocation of contrary laws, also applies to liturgical law.[2] In Book V one finds canons regulating Mass stipends and funds for liturgical celebrations left in wills and bequests (cc.1299-1310).

But the largest number of liturgical laws are found outside the *Code of Canon Law*. Liturgical laws with binding force are found in the liturgical books such as the Roman Missal (the *Sacramentary* and the *Lectionary*), the *Roman Pontifical*, the *Ritual* (the Book of Blessings), the individual ritual books, and the *General Norms for the Calendar*. Within each of these books there are three major components. The first is the introduction or *Praenotanda,* which contains the theological foundation for what follows and the specific liturgical norms and directives for that ritual celebration.[3] The second component includes the actual euchological or prayer texts – the actual words recited by the various participants. The third component is the set of rubrics – the more detailed directions. These are printed in red and are liturgical law – and therefore subject to the principles of interpretation and dispensation.

In addition to reviewing liturgical books, one searches for liturgical law in other kinds of documents. In determining whether an ecclesiastical document is legislative, it may be helpful to note that usually, provisions contained in apostolic constitutions and in decrees are legislative. Usually those contained in *declarations* and *messages* are offering policy statements or exhortations. Ordinarily the content of an apostolic letter, a decretal letter and an apostolic exhortation are not

---

[2] When the 1983 code was promulgated, a specific set of emendations to existing liturgical norms was issued on 9/21/83 to bring the liturgical books into conformity with the new code.

[3] For example, the *Praenotanda* to the Lectionary #22 prescribes that the responsorial psalm is sung or recited at the ambo; #23 directs that the alleluia or verse before the Gospel is sung or not used; #36 of the *Institutio Generalis* (GIRM) prescribes the proper posture for the congregation at various times during the Mass.

legislative. Since the second Vatican Council, the Apostolic See has issued over 400 documents concerning the liturgy, and about half of them are juridic in nature.

Dicasteries of the Roman Curia enjoy only executive power (not legislative power) unless legislative authority has been delegated to them. They can, however, issue binding documents if their norms are in accord with the law.

Liturgical Law is also subject to the same general canonical principles regarding the promulgation. In general, the dicasteries of the Apostolic See receive a general type approval from the Holy Father to issue norms and provisions. Like the other congregations, in the liturgical area the Congregation for Divine Worship and the Discipline of the Sacraments can also draft decrees which become law by papal approbation. If the Holy Father chooses to make the provision papal law, it is issued *in forma specifica.*[4]

Manner of Promulgation: We look to publication in the *Acta Apostolicae Sedis* (*AAS*) as the normal manner of promulgating law. However, with liturgical law, there is a special form of promulgation. The Holy Father issues an apostolic constitution to declare the new edition of the liturgical book to be the typical (official) edition and (usually) to determine the date for the first use of the new edition, and the date for mandatory use.

For the vernacular typical edition, the text must first be approved by a 2/3 majority of the *de iure* members[5] of the Episcopal conference, and then the text (translation and adaptations) is confirmed by the Congregation for Divine Worship and the Discipline of the Sacraments. In the United States, after the *recognitio* is received, the President of the USCCB promulgates the text by decree and usually includes a date for its *first use* and a date for its *mandatory use,* allowing the *vacatio legis* to prepare people for the changes and to provide time for the printers and publishers to have the books ready for use.

Codification: There is no definitive collection or codification of liturgical law. By reviewing the *Acta* (*AAS*) and *Notitiae* one can find much of the legislative documentation. Then one turns to the liturgical books themselves. In addition, two unofficial collections are very helpful. *Documents on the Liturgy*, edited by the International Commission on English in the Liturgy (ICEL) was published in 1982 and contains the post conciliar documentation and legislation through. In addition, Reiner Kaczynski has provided us with the *Enchiridion documentorum*

---

[4] Like the recent *Instruction on Certain Questions Regarding the Collaboration of the Non-Ordained Faithful in the Sacred Ministry of Priests* (8/15/97).

[5] In the United States, these are the active Latin bishops (and those comparable) but not the bishops of the Eastern Churches.

*instaurationes liturgicae*, published in 1988.[6]

Types of Documents: As noted above, it is essential to know the type of document with which you are dealing.[7]

Apostolic Constitutions are legislative documents and are the usual means the Holy Father uses to promulgate a new or revised liturgical book. Thus, they contain papal law. This is the most solemn form of a document issued by the Pope in his own name and is reserved for more weighty issues of a doctrinal or disciplinary nature and is issued as universal law. In 1966 Pope Paul VI issued *Paenitemini* which revised the discipline of fast and abstinence for Lent and Fridays of the year. More recently we received *Sacra Unctionem infirmorum* (the Anointing of the Sick) which revised the matter and form for the sacrament. The new rite allows the priest to bless the oil during the administration of the sacrament, and prescribes olive oil *or any plant oil.*

Apostolic letters *motu proprio* are also issued by the Holy Father. There have been over fifty since the Second Vatican Council. This is the most common source of canonical legislation after the code itself. They are written by the Pope on his own initiative and they are mostly legislative in nature and are directed to the Church at large. *Ministeria quaedam* suppressed the minor orders and resulted in the installed or instituted ministries of acolyte and lector. The provisions of this *motu proprio* have made their way into canon 230 of the 1983 code. *Mysterii paschalis* in 1969 promulgated the norms for the liturgical year, and the most recent *motu proprio, Misericordia Dei,* altered the previous practice to allow confessions to be heard during the celebration of the Eucharist (abrogating the pertinent provision of *Eucharisticum mysterium* of 1967). In *Misericordia Dei* the Holy Father also directed that Rite III of the Rite of Penance be placed in an appendix to the Rite.

General Decrees. The Congregation for Divine Worship and the Discipline of the Sacraments has been given the mandate and the approval of the Holy Father to issue general degrees.

While most of the directives of the Episcopal conference are developed as guidelines or policies, some are also done by decree, which gives them the status of law.

---

[6] Cf. *Documents on the Liturgy 1963-1979, Conciliar, Papal and Curial Texts.* Prepared by the International Commission on English in the Liturgy (Collegeville: Liturgical Press, 1982) and Volumes I and II of the *Enchiridion documentorum instaurationes liturgicae,* edited by Reiner Kaczynski, Turin, 1988.

[7] For a more thorough treatment of this aspect, please refer to the article by John Huels, *Assessing the Weight of Documents on the Liturgy* in the March issue of Worship (2002) and Francis G. Morrisey's *Papal and Curial Pronouncements: Their Canonical Significance in Light of the* Code of Canon Law (Ottawa, 1995).

The Episcopal conference may enact disciplinary laws within the areas of its competence (c. 455, §1). In recent years the Episcopal conference in the United States (USCCB) has legislated on the age of confirmation (c. 891), approved statutes for the catechumenate (c. 788, §3), further determined Holy Days of obligation for the United States, including the determination of when the Ascension would be celebrated (c. 1246), established the ages for fast and abstinence, the age for instituted acolytes, and established the norms for preaching by lay persons, which took effect January 15, 2002. The recently revised *Institutio Generalis* (GIRM) specifies areas where the episcopal conference can adapt or make further determinations in the *Roman Missal.*

General Executory Decrees also have binding force, and usually contain binding administrative norms. These give guidelines for the application of accepted principles and assist the faithful in practical matters. The *Ecumenical Directory* of 1993, issued by the Pontifical Council for Promoting Christian Unity, contains provisions to guide a priest or minister who is celebrating a wedding. When there is a conflict or variation between a directory and the rite found in the liturgical book, the provisions of the rite take precedence. Other directories issued in recent years include the *Directory for Sunday Celebrations in the Absence of a Priest*, and the *Directory for Masses with Children issued by the Congregation for Divine Worship in 1973.*

Instructions issued by the Roman Curia are usually explanations which clarify the prescriptions of laws and elaborate on approaches for implementation. They clarify and interpret law that is clear (not law requiring an official interpretation), and they encourage its observance. These are usually directed to administrators. Two of the more recent instructions pertaining to the liturgy are the 1994 instruction on *Inculturation and the Roman Liturgy* (1/25/94 CDWDS) and the 2001 CDWDS instruction on the translation of liturgical texts, *Liturgiam authenicam.*

The Circular Letter is a relatively new form of document used by the Curia. It outlines procedures and sometimes indicates new obligations, but it is more exhortative in scope. Its purpose is usually to explain the intention and purpose of the law or the rules. The *Circular Letter on the Preparation and Celebration of the Easter Feasts*, issued in 1988 did not create any new directives but clarified and restated the provisions of the revised Roman Missal that pertain to the celebrations of the Triduum.

In addition to the documents noted above, there are guidelines of the Episcopal conference (in the United States, the USCCB). These are not legislative documents per se, but they sometimes quote provisions of universal or particular law, and *those elements* remain binding because their source is legislative. In recent years the Conference has issued *Guidelines for Televising the Liturgy* (1987), *Guidelines for the Reception of Holy Communion by Non-Catholics*, and *Built of Living Stones*, national guidelines for art and architecture (2000). While a bishop could make any of these documents law within his diocese, most bishops use them as guidelines to set the context for their further specifications.

## *Interpretation of Liturgical Law*

For liturgical law, as in other areas of canon law, interpretation is necessary. Authentic or authoritative interpreters are the lawmakers (the pope, the ecumenical council, the conference of bishops, and individual bishops of their dioceses) and the Commission for the Interpretation of Legislative texts. Interpreters of liturgical law follow the same principles of interpretation as do interpreters for other areas of ecclesiastical law: laws which restrict the rights of others or contain an exception to the law are to be strictly interpreted (c. 18) and laws which are more favorable are to be broadly interpreted. Universal law does not derogate from particular law unless it specifically says so. In interpreting liturgical law, the interpreter considers the weight of the law, the literary form, the meaning of the words in text and context, and his/her own prejudice. If possible, we look for the historical and cultural context out of which the law developed, the purpose of the law and the values it seeks to protect, and whether it was part of a compromise. In approaching a text, it is important to determine whether this is primarily a juridic document (is it an apostolic exhortation or an apostolic constitution?), the authorship (from the Holy Father, a congregation but approved *in forma specifica*, a diocesan bishop), the audience to whom it is addressed (the Christian faithful, bishops, priests), and whether it is binding or advisory.

When a liturgical law is lacking in an instance, we look to similar circumstances, general principles of law, the jurisprudence and practice of the Roman Curia, and the common and constant opinion of learned persons. However, in those cases, there is still no law.[8]

## *Current Issues Related to Liturgical Law*

This final section does not pertain specifically to the sources and interpretation of Liturgical Law, but is meant to update the members on recent activities in the liturgical area.

---

[8] The most frequently used example in this area is the essay on liturgical dance which appeared in *Notitiae* in 1975 and later in the *Newsletter of the Bishops' Committee on the Liturgy*, volume 18 [1982]. While the article is to be considered an authoritative point of reference for any discussion on the topic – but there is still no law on this issue.

Third Edition of the Roman Missal: The long awaited third edition of the Roman Missal has been promulgated by apostolic constitution and decree of the CDWDS. The *Praenotanda* (*Institutio Generalis Missalis Romani*) was released early and an informal translation had been provided by the Bishops' Committee on the Liturgy, prompting some questions and confusion about when the law went into effect.

Knowing the changes that the GIRM would introduce, the bishops of the United States, through their Committee on the Liturgy, prepared particular legislation in areas provided for by the GIRM, and requested three indults in areas where the GIRM did not allow them to legislate.

The Appendix to the *Institutio Generalis* for the United States of America contains legislation approved by 2/3 of the Latin bishops of the USCCB on November 14, 2001 and subsequently confirmed by CDWDS on April 17, 2002. These changes became effective for dioceses of the United States on April 25, 2002. However, a number of bishops have not yet implemented the changes in their dioceses since there has been no preparation of their people. The following is a list of the areas in which the USCCB legislated for the United States.[9]

- Posture during Mass (43, 2) after communion people *may sit or kneel.*

- We kneel from the *Sanctus* until after the Eucharistic Prayer except when prevented *on Occasion* by reasons of health, lack of space . . . .

- The faithful kneel after the *Agnus Dei* unless the diocesan bishop determines otherwise.

- Options for the Introit (48): there are four options: antiphon and psalm from the gradual of the Roman Missal, a seasonal antiphon and psalm, a song from another collection of songs and antiphons approved by the USCCB or the diocesan bishop (including a responsorial or metrical form), or a suitable song chosen in accord with GIRM 47

- Responsorial Psalm (61, 4): In place of the psalm assigned in the *Lectionary,* we may use a proper or seasonal antiphon and psalm from the *Lectionary,* an antiphon and psalm from another collection (including a metrical setting) if it is approved by the USCCB or the diocesan bishop. *Songs or hymns may not be used in place of the responsorial psalm.*

---

[9] The numbers in parentheses refer to the sections of the *Institutio Generalis* that are being modified or further specified. For the exact wording of the changes and a more complete presentation, cf. the website of the United States Conference of Catholic Bishops (www.usccb.org). On the main page select "departments" and choose "Liturgy." Then choose the documents on the Roman Missal.

- The Sign of Peace (154, 2): *For good reason, on special occasions (funeral, wedding civic leaders present) the priest may offer a sign of peace to a few of the faithful near the sanctuary.*

- Communion Song (87, 1): The same four options are those given for the Introit but the reference here is *in keeping with GIRM 86.*

- Distribution of Holy Communion (160, 2). The normative posture for the reception of Holy Communion is *standing.* However, we may not deny Holy Communion to people who do not follow the norm and kneel. We are to deal with this pastorally by giving them catechesis.

   *When receiving Holy Communion standing, the communicant bows his/her head before the sacrament as a gesture of reverence and receives the Body of the Lord from the minister. The consecrated host may be received either on the tongue or in the hand at the discretion of each communicant. When Holy Communion is received under both kinds, the sign of reverence is also made before receiving the Precious Blood.*

- Communion under both kinds (283, 3). We are referred to the USA norms found in *This Holy and Living Sacrifice.*

- Materials for Fixed Altars (301). In the United States, *wood* which is worthy, solid, and well crafted may be used, provided that the altar is structurally immobile.

- Color of altar cloths (304): If there are cloths in addition to the white cloth, they may be of other colors (based on festive significance or local usage) as long as the uppermost cloth covering the *mensa* (i.e. the altar cloth itself) is always white.

- Materials for furnishings (326): These materials may include wood, stone or metal which are solid and appropriate to the purpose for which it is used.

- Materials for Sacred Vessels: [added] sacred vessels may also be made from other solid materials that, according to the common estimation in each region, are precious, for example, ebony or other hard woods, provided that such materials are suitable for sacred use and do not break easily or deteriorate. This applies to all vessels which hold the hosts such as the paten, the ciborium, the pyx, the monstrance, and other things of this kind.

- Vesture for Lay Ministers (339): acolytes, altar servers, readers, and other lay ministers wear the alb or other suitable vesture or other appropriate and dignified clothing.

- Color of Sacred Vestments (346). For funerals and other offices and masses for the dead, the options for color are violet, white, and black. Gold *or silver* maybe warn on more solemn occasions.

- Readings for Mass (362) Adaptations to the OLM (ordo) as contained in the Lectionary for Mass for the USA should be carefully observed

- Special Days of Prayer (373): added to the present adaptations: In the United States, January $22^{nd}$ is to be observed as a particular day of penance for the violation to the dignity of the human person through abortion, and a day of prayer for the full restoration of the legal guarantee of the right to life. We are to use the Mass for Peace and Justice (various needs #21) and violet vestments are worn.

- Instruments and musical settings (393): All musical settings of the texts for the people's responses and acclamations in the Order of Mass and for special rites that occur in the course of the liturgical year must be submitted to the USCCB Secretariat for the Liturgy for review and approval prior to publication. (This does not refer to hymn texts).

    While the organ is accorded pride of place, other wind, stringed, percussion instruments may be used in liturgical services according to the longstanding local usage, provided they are truly apt for sacred use or can be rendered apt.

*Current Status of the USA Sacramentary*

In summer of 2000 we received an early release of the *Praenotanda* to the third edition of the Roman Missal (the *Institutio Generalis Missalis Romani*) and expected that we might receive the rest of the text later that year. A copy of the third edition of the Missal has been promulgated and published and was released to the press on March 25, 2002. The provisions of the *Institutio* (GIRM) are now in effect.

The Latin members of the episcopal conference of the United States (USCCB) approved USA adaptations to the GIRM. These were confirmed by CDWDS and became effective (by decree of the President of the USCCB) on April 25, 2002 so they are in force.

As noted above, most bishops have not yet implemented this legislation in their dioceses.

The Latin members of the USCCB approved *Norms for the Distribution and*

*Reception of Holy Communion under Both Kinds in the Dioceses of the United States of America.*[10] These were subsequently confirmed by CDWDS and were promulgated with an effective date of April 7, 2002, so they, too, are now in force. A final English translation of the *Institutio* (GIRM) will be going to the members of the USCCB for approval in November 2002.

Once the translation is approved and confirmed , we will have the *Praenotanda* (GIRM) and the USA adaptations to the GIRM in English and in force. However, the other elements of the third edition of the *Roman Missal* – all the prayer texts and the USA adaptations to those rites are still awaiting confirmation. The major adaptations include the optional placement of the gesture of peace, a three year cycle of opening prayers, and the revised penitential rite with its options.

The new prayers added to the third edition of the Missal will need to be translated and approved. The translation of prayer texts already approved by the USCCB and awaiting confirmation, will have to be revised in light of the new provisions of *Liturgiam authenticam.* The translation of the new texts and the revision of the already approved translations will take some time.

ICEL and VOX CLARA

In recent days we received news that Cardinal Arinze, has been appointed the new prefect of the Congregation for Divine Worship and the Discipline of the Sacraments.

Vox Clara is a commission formed by the Congregation (CDWDS) to help with the process of translating the third edition of the Roman Missal into English. Four bishops from the United States serve on Vox Clara: Archbishop Oscar Lipscomb of Mobile, Archbishop Justin Rigali of St. Louis (who serves as treasurer), Cardinal Francis George of Chicago, and Archbishop Alfred Hughes of New Orleans. The Commission is chaired by Archbishop George Pell of Sydney. The members of Vox Clara have committed themselves to produce translations that are "precise, theologically faithful, and effectively proclaimable." They met April 21-24, 2002 and began to work on the ordination rites.

ICEL, the International Commission on English in the Liturgy, has elected a new Chairperson of the Episcopal Board. Bishop Arthur Roche, coadjutor of Leeds, England serves as the new Chairperson of the governing board. Reverend Bruce Harbert of Birmingham, England has been appointed the new Executive Director of the ICEL Secretariat. Cardinal Francis George of Chicago serves as the Treasurer of ICEL. Presently the ICEL staff and Episcopal Board are working on a revised translation of the GIRM because it had not been done according to the principles of *Liturgiam authenticam.*

---

[10] These Norms replace the earlier directory, *This Holy and Living Sacrifice.*

# PRESIDENTIAL REPORT

## REV. KEVIN E. MCKENNA

As I conclude my term as President of the Canon Law Society of America, I would like to express my gratitude for the opportunity that was given to me to offer service in leadership this past year. I was richly blessed with committed colleagues who served on the Board and I have appreciated their guidance and support. This report would not be possible without their cooperation and assistance.

### 2001 CONVENTION RESOLUTIONS

We have been described as a "resolution driven" Society. The formation and implementation of resolutions that advance the mission of our Society are an important part of our focus. Five resolutions were passed at our last convention held in October in Albuquerque, New Mexico:

*First Resolution*: "Be it resolved that the membership of the Canon Law Society express support for this effort [by canon law students at Catholic University] by contributing the requested $5,000.00 to the fund to endow the James H. Provost Memorial Lecture, an annual event at The Catholic University of America." $5,000.00 has been donated by the Society that will honor an extremely distinguished contributor to our Society.

*Second Resolution*: "Be it resolved that the membership recommend to the Board of Governors that it provide a seminar at the 2002 or, at the latest, the 2003 Convention to address how the principle of subsidiarity is understood by the bishops and curial officials and in what ways it has or has not been manifested. The seminar should address the canonical principles of subsidiarity and the substantive and procedural ways it has been or could be implemented." Msgr. Roch Pagé, dean of the faculty of canon law at St. Paul University has graciously accepted the invitation to present this seminar at the 2002 Convention.

*Third Resolution*: "Be it resolved that the BOG be directed to re-constitute a Committee on Consecrated Life and Societies of Apostolic Life as an on-going committee no later than February 2002;

Be it further resolved that by the 2002 CLSA Convention, the Committee on Institutes of Consecrated Life and Societies of Apostolic Life propose to the BOG specific tasks or studies to be undertaken for the next five years." The Committee on Consecrated Life and Societies of Apostolic Life has been reconstituted, chaired by Sr. Rosemary Smith, with members Sr. Nancy Reynolds and Rev. Warren

Brown. The committee has submitted a five-year plan to the BOG.

*Fourth Resolution*: "Be it resolved that the Board of Governors take into consideration all the discussion on this proposal on a Catholic-Muslim Dialog on Legal Tradition and plan one or more concrete sessions on this topic at next year's convention;

Be it further resolved that the Board of Governors, if it seems fitting, make a new proposal on this topic at next year's convention." Dr. Jane Dammen McAuliffe graciously consented to present "Islamic Legal Tradition: An Overview" at this year's convention. The BOG will await feedback and a possible recommendation from the floor concerning the need for another similar topic for next year's convention.

*Fifth Resolution*: "Be it resolved that the Board of Governors establish a task force, composed of experts in family law, immigration law, constitutional law, canon law and pastoral ministry, to address issues related to ecclesiastical marriages for undocumented persons and persons seeking to regularize their immigration status when those marriages cannot be recognized or celebrated according to the norm of civil law, namely to:

1. identify and examine basic human rights issues, such as the right to marry
2. identify and examine legal and pastoral issues
3. prepare a legal and canonical analysis
4. prepare a canonical and pastoral guide
5. propose actions to be taken by the CLSA;

Be it further resolved that the task force be in consultation with the USCCB and other appropriate organizations;

Be it further resolved that the task force make recommendations to the membership at the 2003 Convention." Thomas Paprocki was appointed chair of the task force, with members Mark Bartchak and Vicente De LaCruz who will enlist the further assistance of other experts as mentioned in resolution.

## COMMITTEES

Much of the work of the Board and its meetings is spent reviewing the progress and direction of the many committees and projects that are currently underway. As President, I replaced a number of committee members whose term had expired or for some other reason were unable to continue serving, as well as renewing the appointments of some terms.

## New Committee/Projects Appointments
2001-2002

| *Committee* | *Member* |
|---|---|
| Convention Planning | Michael Souckar (2004) |
| Nominations | Paul Counce (2004) |
| Professional Responsibility | Greg Bittner (chair) |
| Hearing Officers | Tom Brundage (2004) |
| | Kevin McDonough (2004) |
| Civil and Canon Law | Diane Barr (chair, 2003) |
| | Tom Paprocki (2004) |
| Electronic Media | Paul Hartmann (chair, 2004) |
| | Peter Vere (2004) |
| Investment Review | Margaret Stallmeyer (2004) |
| Roman Replies | F. Stephen Pedone, chair  (2004) |
| | Rose McDermott (2004) |
| Scholarship Fund | Langes Silva (2004) |
| | Louis Sirianni (2004) |
| Advisory Opinions | James Donlon, (chair, 2004) |
| | Ann Keevan (2004) |
| Canon Law Digest XIII | John Renken (2004) |
| Canon Law Digest XIV | Ronny Jenkins (2004) |
| Canon Law Digest XV | Fred Easton (2004) |
| Convention Liturgies | Ron Krisman (2004) |

COMMITTEE APPOINTMENTS:

As a result of the 2001 Convention, and as a follow-up to our BOG meetings, I made the following committee/project appointments:

Lay Ministry Handbook:      Linda Weigel (chair)
                                        Zabrina Decker
                                        Steve Osborn
                                        Ronald Gainer

Task Force on Issues Related  Tom Paprocki (Chair)
To Marriage and               Mark Bartchak
Undocumented Persons      Vicente DeLa Cruz

Marriage Procedures        Dan Smilanic (Chair)
Handbook                      Victoria Vondenberger
                                        Larry Price

| Institutes of Consecrated | Rosemary Smith (Chair) |
|---|---|
| Life and Societies of | Nancy Reynolds |
| Apostolic Life | Warren Brown |

We can be especially grateful for the many members of our Society who contribute so much of their time and talent working on these various committees and projects. I am particularly grateful to Vice-President Lawrence O'Keefe for his work in serving as liaison for the BOG with the various committees and projects during the course of the year. He carried out this responsibility admirably.

PUBLICATIONS

One of the key areas where our Society fulfills its responsibility for providing canonical education is in the area of publications. This year several publications were completed. Our Executive Coordinator, Rev. Arthur Espelage, OFM, completed the 2nd compilation of *Advisory Opinions: 1994-2000* that is now available for purchase. Msgr. Fred Easton completed work on the *festschrift* in honor of Rev. Lawrence Wrenn, *The Art of the Good and Equitable* that will be presented to Father Wrenn at this convention, in gratitude for his many dedicated years of service to our Society through his much appreciated publications.

I am also happy to report that the long-awaited publication of *Canon Law Digest XII* is imminent, thanks to the work of the CLD committee and our Executive Coordinator. The BOG will be restructuring the CLD committee and its work in the hopes that a reasonable time frame can be assembled for future editions.

Two marriage related publications were completed and will soon be available: *Jurisprudence: A Collection of U.S. Tribunal Decisions* and another work on Rotal decisions and marriage consent, prepared by the Marriage Research Committee. Both publications are welcomed additions to our extensive publications on marriage and tribunal ministry and will provide new updated resources. In addition a project that evolved as a result of one of our convention resolutions was completed with the publication of *Canonical Standards for Parishes: A Self-Evaluation Instrument*, which is being distributed at this year's Convention.

Two new publications are in the works: A Lay Ministry Handbook and a Marriage Procedures Handbook. The committees for these projects were appointed this year, and hopefully these works will be published soon.

This year I had the opportunity of attending two international canon law society conventions and a number of regional meetings:

*The Canadian Canon Law Society*
October 15-18, 2001
36th Annual Congress
Hôtel Loews Le Concorde
Quebec City, Canada

Most Rev. Ernest Leger: *Droits des fideles*
Rev. Ron Bourque, *Relations between Ordained and Non-ordained Ministers – Collaboration*
Rev. Pasquale Stilla, *Administration of Parishes/Canonical Issues*
L'abbe Marc Pelchar, *Les nouveaux ministères dans l'Église*
Rev. John M. Huels, *The New General Instruction of the Roman Missal: Subsidiarity or Uniformity?*
Rev. Ladislas Örsy, *The Future of Canon Law*

The Canadian Conference of Catholic Bishops is now studying the possibility of establishing some national board for conciliation procedures. The Canon Law/Inter-Rite Commission of the C.C.C.B. has prepared several drafts of an "alternative judicial method" for resolving ecclesiastical conflicts that are traditionally reserved to a canonical administrative procedure or civil procedure. I asked one of the members of the C.C.L.S. who is working on this project to keep our Society informed of the progress of this work. They are aware of our work in Administrative Tribunals and Due Process.

I extended greetings from our own Society during the business meeting and shared in summary the resolutions passed at our own convention as well as information about the new translation of the *Code of Canons of the Eastern Churches*.

*Floyd Begin Law Lecture*
Cleveland, Ohio
Tuesday, October 23, 2001
John Carroll University

The Tribunal of the Diocese of Cleveland in conjunction with John Carroll University sponsors this lecture series, presented on an annual basis. The President of the Canon Law Society is traditionally invited to attend. The lecture is dedicated to the memory of Floyd Begin, the late bishop of Oakland and former officialis and auxiliary bishop of the Diocese of Cleveland. It attempts to make canon law accessible to a wider public. This year's presentation was "Let the Children Come to Me: The Law in Service to Children" by Michael Smith Foster, J.C.D. of the Archdiocese of Boston.

Before the lecture I had the opportunity to meet Bishop A. James Quinn, auxiliary bishop of the Diocese of Cleveland. Bishop Quinn is the chair of the Canonical Affairs Committee of the USCCB and I reminded him of the availability of the Canon Law Society of America to be of assistance to the committee or to the conference as needed. I followed up later that week with a letter to Bishop Quinn, again reminding him of the availability of our Society to the Canonical Affairs Committee.

*Conference of Chancery And Tribunal Officials*
*Provinces of New Orleans and Mobile*
November 27 – 29, 2001
*Fiftieth Anniversary*
Fairmont Hotel, University Place, New Orleans, Louisiana

This Conference consists of the two Provinces of New Orleans and Mobile: the archdioceses of New Orleans and Mobile, the dioceses of Alexandria, Baton Rouge, Houma-Thibodaux, Lafayette, Lake Charles, Shreveport, Biloxi, Birmingham, and Jackson.

"Administrative and Judicial Work as Ecclesial Ministry" presented by Rev. Robert T. Kennedy, J.U.D., The Catholic University of America

Session 1: Discovering Spirituality in Administration
Session 2: Church Governance in the Service of Justice
Session 3: The Canonical Form of Marriage: Nuisance or Necessity?
Session 4: Responsible Stewardship in the Alienation of Church Property and
    Related Transactions

As part of the opening session, Most Rev. Alfred C. Hughes, Coadjutor Archbishop of New Orleans gave a report on the November USCCB meeting, which included: updates on the proposed Catechism for Young Adults; the Conference and the document *Authenticam Liturgicam*; the updating of the Pro-Life Pastoral Plan; solidarity between the Conference and the Church in Africa; a re-examination of the "Just War" theory in light of the present world developments, and norms that have been developed for lay preaching and for those representing the Church to the media.

As part of the program, I was also given the opportunity during the course of the Conference to give a report on the work of the Canon Law Society. Materials were available, relating to our publications, as well as membership applications.

To celebrate the milestone of fifty years for the conference, a special banquet was held at the Pavilion of the Two Sisters in Oaks-City Park, hosted by Archbishop Francis B. Schulte of New Orleans. Also, as part of the festivities participants were given the opportunity for a Mississippi River cruise aboard the John James Audubon Riverboat.

*Visit to Louvain and Rome by The President,*
*Vice President and Executive Coordinator*
January 30 – February 10, 2002

American College, Leuven

An increasing and significant number of new members of the CLSA are coming to the Society as graduates from the Catholic University of Louvain. The Officers and Executive Coordinator decided this year, on the way to the biennial visits to the offices of the Holy See, to stop first at Leuven to meet with representatives of the University of Louvain as well as students engaged in canon law study. We were warmly welcomed to the American College by Very Reverend Kevin A. Codd, rector and his administrative assistant, Mr. John Steffen.

It was our pleasure to meet with students from the canon law department from a diversity of countries, including India, China, Latvia and the United States. We discussed with them the work of our Society. We were strongly impressed by the quality of the students that we met and their commitment to canonical studies. We were also grateful for the kind hospitality of Prof. Rik Torfs, dean of the canon law department and department staff member Kurt Martens who graciously offered us a tour of the University Theological Library as well as the beautiful Central Library.

Visits to the Offices of the Holy See
February 4 – 9, 2002

This year the Vice-President and Executive Coordinator joined me for the biennial visits to the Dicasteries, Tribunals and Councils of the Holy See. Our visits included:

Divine Worship and the Discipline of the Sacraments
Institutes of Consecrated Life and Societies of Apostolic Life
Congregation for the Doctrine of the Faith
Congregation for Education
Congregation for the Clergy
Congregation for Bishops
Congregation of the Saints
Congregation for Eastern Churches
Pontifical Council for the Laity
Council for the Interpretation of Legislative Texts
Roman Rota
Apostolic Signatura

We were warmly welcomed at each of the Offices we visited. Great interest was shown in our publications and the work of our Society and many helpful suggestions were made about various areas of interest. Rev. Michael Hilbert, S.J. was an invaluable resource in setting up our appointments and in translation. The highlight was the opportunity to present the Holy Father at an audience a copy of the new CLSA translation of the *Code of Canons of the Eastern Churches*.

.

*Texas Catholic Conference – Judicial Vicars Department*
*27th Annual Spring Conference*
February 19 – 20, 2002
Oblate Renewal Center
San Antonio, Texas

Speaker: Dr. Linda Robitaille, Professor of Canon Law, St. Paul University, Ottawa

- Psychological Incapacity or Simulation?
- The Positive Act of the Will
- Exclusion of Children
- Procedural Concerns in Marriage Cases

Speaker: Rev. David-Maria A. Jaeger, OFM, JCD, Professor of Canon Law, Pontifical Athenaeum "Antonianum", Rome; Consultor to the Pontifical Council for Legislative Texts and Congregation for Eastern Churches

- The Holy See and the Holy Land

I was offered the opportunity to make a presentation to the assembly concerning the present work of the Society and solicit possible new membership. I also included in my presentation, a brief report of the officers' visit to the Roman Dicasteries.

*St. Paul University, Ottawa, Canada*
February 25 – 26, 2002

Traditionally, the President of the Canon Law Society is invited by the dean of the canon law department at St. Paul University to visit the canon law students and faculty. In 1889, Leo XIII granted a charter to what is now known as St. Paul University. On May 24, 1931 the faculty of Canon Law was established as distinct from the Faculty of Theology. Ecclesiastical degrees are granted in virtue of the charter granted in 1889; civil degrees are granted jointly by the Senate of St. Paul University in virtue of its 1866 civil charter and by the Senate of the University of Ottawa, which is federated with St. Paul University.

The president is also invited to give the Glasmacher lecture on a canonical topic. This year I presented a lecture on "Canonical Ministry in Service to the Church."

I also had the opportunity to visit with Rev. Pierre Allard, S.M. at the Appeal Tribunal of Canada, which offices are in Ottawa and to meet with the staff of the Tribunal. Pierre Allard also serves as the President of the Canadian Canon Law Society.

I was given the opportunity to meet with the canon law students to share with them the work of the Canon Law Society. We received six applications for CLSA membership.

*Western Regional CLSA Convention*
Doubletree Alana Waikiki Hotel
Honolulu, Hawaii
March 4 – 6, 2002

Speaker: Rev. Michael Hilbert, S.J., Vice-Rector, Gregorian University, Rome.

- Clergy sexual misconduct: rights and obligations, bishops, clerics, Christian faithful
- *Delicta Graviora*: the norms

- Review of present diocesan clergy misconduct protocols

Speakers: Carol Ignacio and Cheryl Ramos

- Ethnic diversity

I was offered the opportunity to make a presentation to the assembly concerning the present work of the Society and to solicit possible new membership. I also included in my presentation, a brief report of the officers' visit to the Roman Dicasteries.

*Meeting with Apostolic Nuncio*
*Archbishop Gabriel Montalvo*
March 11, 2002

On Monday, March 11, Rev. Espelage and I had the pleasure of meeting with Archbishop Montalvo, Apostolic Nuncio to the United States at the Nunciature in Washington for the traditional meeting with the President of the CLSA. The Archbishop was extremely gracious and welcoming. He expressed great interest in our work and especially encouraged the Society in terms of the present situation of sexual misconduct by clergy. We shared with him our concern that priests' rights are observed and correct processes be followed in any penal sanctions or other actions being taken against priests. He expressed concern about the relations between bishops and their priests given the present climate and its impact upon the laity. He also wondered about the motivation of the press in their coverage of this difficult situation. We took the opportunity of our visit to reaffirm the commitment of the Society to any assistance needed by the Nuncio or the Holy See.

*Catholic University of America*
Washington, DC
March 12, 2002

Frs. Larry O'Keefe and Steve Pedone who were in Washington for our evaluation of the Executive Coordinator joined me in meeting with the faculty and students of the canon law Department of Catholic University on March 12. I had the opportunity traditionally afforded the President to give a lecture. I presented a talk on "Canonical Ministry in Service to the Church".

*Northwest Regional Canon Law Convention*
West Coast Yakima Center Hotel
Yakima, Washington
April 8 – 11, 2002

Speaker: Father Tom Brundage

- "What About My Rights? Obligations and Rights in the Church"
- "Structural Engineering: Church Structures for the Vindication of Rights"
- "What is the Real Story?" Case Studies

Diane Barr

- "Comparison of Civil Law and Canon law, Rights of Individuals"

Jane Villanueva & Matt Adams

- "Respect Life/ Social Justice; Northwest Immigrants Project, Impact of Immigration on Families"

*Midwest Regional Conference*
April 29 – May 1, 2002
Springfield, Illinois

Speakers:

- Msgr. Anthony McDade, "Issues Involving Clergy Personnel in Today's Church"
- Rev. Ronny Jenkins, "Recent Rotal Decisions on Condition and Error"

Again it was my privilege to present a report on the work of our Society and to invite interested parties to join us as new members.

*Eastern Regional Conference*
May 6 – 8, 2002
Harrisburg, Pennsylvania

Speakers:

- Msgr. Brian Ferme, "Graviora Delicta", New norms regarding delicts reserved to the Congregation for the Doctrine of the Faith"
"The New Norms for Marriage Cases 'In Favorem Fidei' "

- Patricia Dugan, Philip Murren, Richard Connell, Sr. Marlene Weisenbeck, "Emerging Movements and New Initiatives"
- Sr. Elizabeth McDonough, "Looking Ahead: The Council and the Code"

This region is "re-grouping" and is working hard to reorganize and revitalize as an effective canonical regional meeting.

*Canon Law Society of Great Britain and Ireland*
Dean Park Hotel Renfrew, Scotland
May 13 – 17, 2002

It was my pleasure and honor to represent the Canon Law Society of America at this international convention held in Scotland. I was particularly grateful for the warm hospitality extended to me by the President, Rev. John Conneely and the other participants. I also appreciated the opportunity to extend greetings from our Society and to share some of the work that we are presently engaged in.

Speakers:

- Rev. Pasquale Stilla, "The Permanent Diaconate: Theological and Canonical Considerations"
- Rev. Lawrence Wrenn, "Sacramentality and the Invalidity of Marriage"
- Rev. Nicholas Gosnell, "Marriage and the Military"
- Msgr. Charles Scicluna, "Recourse against singular or particular administrative acts of the Diocesan Bishop"
- Very Rev. Dr. Ireneu Craciun, "Elements of canonical organization, synodality and primacy in the Orthodox Church"
- Rev. James Conn, S.J., "Parishes-of-Choice: Canonical, Theological and Pastoral Considerations"

*Tribunal Workshop of the Province of Oklahoma City*
Tulsa, Oklahoma
August 6 – 7, 2002

Speaker:

- Deacon Gerald T. Jorgenson, "The Use of Psychological Experts in Decree of Nullity Petitions."

I had the opportunity of presenting the good wishes of the Society and sharing with the participants the work within the Society and the current status of many of our projects.

I wrote on October 30 to Bishop Joseph Fiorenza, President of the USCCB and Archbishop Gabriel Montalvo of the Apostolic Nunciature, offering the services of the Canon Law Society of America, wherever needed. I also wrote to Dr. Peter Phan, of Catholic University of America, President of the Catholic Theological Society of America, inviting joint participation on projects of common concern. I wrote as well to John Conneely, President of the Canon Law Society of Great Britain and Ireland, Pierre Allard, President of the Canon Law Society of Canada and Robert McGuckin, President of the Canon Law Society of Australia and New Zealand, offering our services in any collaboration on projects of mutual interest. I also wrote to Bishop Wilton Gregory, congratulating him on his election as President of the USCCB and offering the services of our Society to the Conference and Canonical Affairs Committee.

I later wrote again to Bishop Wilton Gregory of the USCCB in which I forwarded a copy of the full press release that the Vice-President and I had issued concerning sexual misconduct by priests and the protection of rights. I also included in that letter an offer on behalf of the Society to help as needed. I also sent a copy of the press release to Archbishop Montalvo who had expressed interest in any help the Society could offer when Fr. Espelage and I met with him in March.

### SEXUAL MISCONDUCT AND CLERGY ISSUES

The situation that has emerged over the last several months in regards to sexual misconduct and clergy and church personnel has occupied much of my time as well as the Board of Governors. Some of the concerns relate to the issue of how well and to what extent the rights of all parties were being observed. In March, the Vice-President and myself wrote a statement thanking the bishops for their solicitude extended to victims and respectfully asking them to observe canonical procedures especially as they deal with the removal of priests from parishes and allegations that have surfaced from a number of years past. In addition, at our April meeting the BOG prepared a formal statement expanding on our March statement, reaffirming a recognition of the of the heinous nature of the crime of sexual abuse by clergy and church workers, and reminding of the importance of certain canonical principles needed to guide an effective response to this crisis. This statement was sent to all the bishops of the USCCB and to our members through the June CLSA newsletter.

After consulting with the Board of Governors, I also wrote to the chair of the USCCB committee, Archbishop Harry Flynn, who prepared draft guidelines for the

June meeting of the Dallas bishops. In my communication I shared with him and his committee some of the canonical concerns that had been discussed in regards to the proposed guidelines that became the Charter and Essential Norms. As you are aware, a Presidential Hearing has been scheduled at this Convention to assist our Society in coordinating an effective, long-term strategy to assist where we can in the procedures that will ultimately evolve from the bishops.

## CONCLUSION

This has been an exhilarating year to serve as President. I am particularly grateful for the kind hospitality I received at the regional meetings I attended. I was reminded continually of the large number of members of our society who are actively involved in canonical ministry and sharing their gifts in service to the Church. The meetings with the other national canon law societies were also extremely helpful, both in the presentations I was privileged to hear and the insights afforded as to the role of canon law in the universal Church today.

I am grateful for the assistance provided me by the Board of Governors by their insightful recommendations and participation in our meetings. Our Vice-President Larry O'Keefe and our Past President, Robert Deeley gave invaluable assistance with wise counsel and helpful suggestions during the course of this past year. Our Executive Coordinator, Art Espelage, was always willing to be of assistance when asked and with the help of Jennifer Miller and Kay Winner provides exceptional service to our membership from our office in Washington, D.C. The Board of Governors was unanimous in their desire to renew the contract for Fr. Espelage for another three-year term and look forward to his continued excellent service to our Society.

I am also most grateful to St. Cecilia Parish in Rochester, where I am privileged to pastor for their kind understanding as I traveled this past year. Without the assistance of the staff and priests of the parish, the responsibilities of the presidency would not have been possible.

Finally, my deepest thanks to the Society that entrusted me with the responsibility of the presidency. I was humbled by your confidence and grateful for the opportunity to serve such an outstanding Society that provides such an important and needed ministry to the Church today.

# REPORT OF THE TREASURER

REV. MSGR. ALEXANDER J. PALMIERI

I am pleased to present to the membership the Annual Financial Report for Fiscal Year 2001-2002, as well as the Approved Budget for Fiscal Year 2002-2003. These reports reflect the diligent work of several individuals. In particular, appreciation is extended to Reverend Arthur Espelage, Executive Coordinator, to his administrative assistant, Mrs. Jennifer Miller, and to our bookkeeper, Mrs. Kay Winner. Their daily attention to the responsible administration of the society's finances, always executed in an expert and skillful manner, is certainly commendable.

Gratitude is also extended: to Mr. Joseph Godbout, C.P.A., for his ongoing professional assistance; to the Board of Governors, particularly its president, Reverend Kevin McKenna, for their continued direction and help; to Sister Margaret Stallmeyer, for her insights and generous willingness to be of assistance to me; and, to the members of the Budget Committee and the Investment Review Committee, for their input in these two important areas. The hard work of all these persons throughout the year, and their availability to me in my capacity as treasurer, were indispensable to the preservation of the financial health of the society.

As noted in the Report of the Investment Review Committee, during this past fiscal year it became necessary to withdraw $30,000 from investments held in the general "CLSA Account," in order to pay bills which resulted from the shortfall of anticipated income, due to the fact that several publications, which had been previously budgeted for income, were not ready to be published. An additional factor was the lower market returns on our investments, due to the present volatility in that sector and not as a result of the policies of the investment manager.

Two reports are attached to this item. The first report is the end-of-year account with the auditor's review (note that a full audit is only conducted every other year). This report begins with the consolidated statement of financial position, consisting of all the assets and liabilities of the society as of June 30, 2002. In comparison with Fiscal Year 2000-2001, the total net assets of the society decreased by $29,573, due primarily to the realized and unrealized loss on our investments, as well as the increased costs at Professional Mailing and Distribution Services (PMDS), for the outsourcing and warehousing of our publications. A summary of income and expenses for each of the four funds (general operations, publications, convention, and scholarship) is found at the end of the account report.

The second report contains the summary of the approved budget for the present fiscal year. This report begins with an overview of the four funds, which indicates that each fund, with the possible exception of general operations, is anticipated to operate in the black. There are many variables to be taken into consideration, not the least of which are the number of anticipated publications and the income derived from dues, particularly from prospective new members. With this in mind, the approved budget is both realistic and fiscally responsible.

# PART I

INDEPENDENT AUDITOR'S REPORT

To the Board of Governors
and Executive Coordinator
Canon Law Society of America
Washington, D.C.

I have reviewed the accompanying statement of financial position of Canon Law Society of America (a District of Columbia not-for-profit professional organization) as of June 30, 2002, and the related statements of activities and changes in net assets and cash flows for the year then ended in accordance with Statements on Standards for Accounting and Review Services issued by the American Institute of Certified Public Accountants. All information included in these financial statements is the representation of the management of Canon Law Society of America.

A review consists principally of inquiries of company personnel and analytical procedures applied to financial data. It is substantially less in scope than an audit in accordance with generally accepted auditing standards, the objective of which is the expression of an opinion regarding the financial statements taken as a whole. Accordingly, I do not express such an opinion.

Based on my review, I am not aware of any material modifications that should be made to the accompanying financial statements in order for them to be in conformity with generally accepted accounting principles.

My review was made for the purpose of expressing limited assurance that there are no material modifications that should be made to the financial statements in order for them to be in conformity with generally accepted accounting principles. The information included in the accompanying schedules is presented for supplementary analysis purposes. Such information has been subjected to the same inquiry and analytical procedures applied in the review of the basic financial statements, and I am not aware of any material modifications that should be made to these schedules.

The financial statements for the year ended June 30, 2001 were audited by me and I expressed an unqualified opinion on them in my report dated August 30, 2001, but I have not performed any auditing procedures since that date.

JOSEPH E. GODBOUT
Certified Public Accountant

Silver Spring, Maryland
August 14, 2002

CANON LAW SOCIETY OF AMERICA
STATEMENTS OF FINANCIAL POSITION

June 30, 2002

with comparative figures for June 30, 2001

**ASSETS**

|  | June 30, 2002 (Unaudited) | June 30, 2001 (Audited) |
|---|---|---|
| *Current Assets:* | | |
| Cash and cash equivalents | $ 75,728 | $102,9082 |
| Accounts receivable-book sales | 8,259 | 6,211 |
| Royalties receivable | 9,400 | 3,859 |
| Accounts receivable-dues | 1,575 | 400 |
| Accrued interest receivable | 761 | 1,354 |
| Miscellaneous receivables | -0- | 2,127 |
| Current inventory of books and publications, at cost (Note 3) | 16,304 | 15,974 |
| Prepaid postage | 3,443 | 1,240 |
| Prepaid insurance | 413 | 341 |
| Prepaid book costs (Note 6) | -0- | 12,914 |
| Prepaid expenses, other | 6,213 | 609 |
| Total Current Assets | 122,096 | 148,011 |
| *Non-current Assets:* | | |
| Furniture and equipment, at cost, less accumulated depreciation of $13,952 ($14,474 at June 30, 2001) | 7,850 | 10,173 |
| Long-term inventory of books and publications, at cost (Note 3) | 181,322 | 138,334 |
| Investments (cost $144,207- $181,378 at 6/30/01, at market value (Note 4) | 160,380 | 216,876 |
| Investments (cost $257,199 - $243,727 at 6/30/01), at market value, temporarily restricted in Scholarship Fund (Note 5) | 264,872 | 268,008 |
| Total Non-current Assets | 614,424 | 633,391 |
| Total Assets | $736,520 | $781,402 |

270

## LIABILITIES AND NET ASSETS

|  | June 30, 2002 (Unaudited) | June 30, 2001 (Audited) |
|---|---|---|
| *Current Liabilities:* | | |
| Accounts payable | $ 15,006 | $ 17,375 |
| Royalties payable | 15,859 | 8,616 |
| Deferred revenue - book sales | 4,231 | 22,316 |
| Deferred revenue - convention | 34,665 | 34,838 |
| Deferred revenue - membership dues | 700 | 2,625 |
| Total Current Liabilities | 70,461 | 85,770 |
| *Net Assets:* (Statement-page 29) | | |
| Unrestricted | | |
| Board designated restricted reserve fund (Note 8) | 55,412 | 55,412 |
| Board designated for special projects (Note 9) | 88,591 | 75,082 |
| Other unrestricted | 257,184 | 297,130 |
| Total unrestricted | 401,187 | 427,624 |
| Temporarily restricted-scholarship fund | 264,872 | 268,008 |
| Permanently restricted | NONE | NONE |
| Total Net Assets (Statement-page 25) | 666,059 | 695,632 |
| Total Liabilities and Net Assets | $736,520 | $781,402 |

The accompanying notes are an integral part of these financial statements.

# CANON LAW SOCIETY OF AMERICA

## STATEMENTS OF ACTIVITIES AND CHANGES IN NET ASSETS

for the year ended June 30, 2002

with comparative figures for the year ended June 30, 2001

|  | June 30, 2002 (Unaudited) | June 30, 2001 (Audited) |
|---|---|---|
| Changes in unrestricted net assets: | | |
| Revenues and Gains: | | |
| Membership dues | $158,195 | $154,710 |
| Investment income (Note 13) | 5,761 | 7,956 |
| Sales of publications and books | 178,917 | 138,832 |
| Royalties | 16,142 | 39,618 |
| Convention and pre-convention workshops fees | 96,977 | 93,582 |
| Other income | 3,007 | 1,775 |
| Total unrestricted revenues and gains | 458,999 | 436,473 |
| Net assets released from restrictions: | | |
| Satisfaction of scholarship restrictions | 13,179 | 8,049 |
| Total unrestricted revenues, gains, and other support | 472,178 | 444,522 |
| Expenses: | | |
| Program services (Schedules-pages 26 & 27) | 346,404 | 376,773 |
| Supporting services (Schedule-page 28) | 132,365 | 120,044 |
| Net realize loss on sale of investments (Note 13) | 3,642 | 26,694 |
| Net unrealized loss on investments (Note 13) | 16,204 | 10,601 |
| Total expenses and losses | 498,615 | 534,112 |
| Increase/(decrease) in unrestricted net assets | (26,437) | (89,590) |

|                                                     | June 30, 2002 (Unaudited) | June 30, 2001 (Audited) |
|-----------------------------------------------------|---------------------------|-------------------------|
| Changes in temporarily restricted net assets:       |                           |                         |
| Contributions to the scholarship fund               | $ 24,848                  | $ 12,161                |
| One time transfer from general operations           | -0-                       | 41,351                  |
| Income on long-term investments (Note 13)           | 8,156                     | 8,168                   |
| Net realized gain/(loss) on sale of investments (Note 13) | (6,099)             | (30,824)                |
| Net unrealized gain/(loss) on appreciation of investments (Note 13) | (16,862)    | (11,108)                |
| Net assets released from restriction (Page 27)      | (13,179)                  | (8,049)                 |
| Increase (decrease) in temporarily restricted net assets | (3,136)              | 11,699                  |
| Changes in permanently restricted net assets:       | NONE                      | NONE                    |
| **INCREASE/(DECREASE) IN NET ASSETS**               | (29,573)                  | (77,891)                |
| Net Assets at Beginning of Year                     | 695,632                   | 773,523                 |
| Net Assets at End of Year                           | $666,059                  | $695,632                |

The accompanying notes are an integral part of these financial statements.

# CANON LAW SOCIETY OF AMERICA

## SCHEDULES OF PROGRAM SERVICES

for the year ended June 30, 2002

with comparative figures for the year ended June 30, 2001

|  | June 30, 2002 (Unaudited) | June 30, 2001 (Audited) |
|---|---|---|
| Publications |  |  |
| Cost of publications | $ 36,146 | $ 58,523 |
| Loss on inventory reduction | 1,090 | 4,079 |
| Executive expenses | 59,103 | 48,800 |
| Royalty expense | 7,243 | 4,375 |
| Depreciation | 2,572 | 2,740 |
| Bad debts | 2,713 | (7,589) |
| Advertising | 8,815 | 15,635 |
| PMDS | 57,880 | 50,483 |
| Total Publication Expenses | 175,562 | 177,046 |
| Convention and Pre-convention Workshops |  |  |
| Coordination (Note 13) | 28,181 | -0- |
| Pre convention expenses | 13,141 | 12,079 |
| Food service | 27,251 | 38,137 |
| Honoraria | 3,800 | 3,400 |
| Travel | 1,480 | 325 |
| Printing | 9,000 | 7,502 |
| Lodging | 2,764 | 5,095 |
| Freight | 1,795 | 27 |
| Other | 1,467 | 1,263 |
| Postage | 2,731 | 2,015 |
| Convention Chair | 425 | -0- |
| Liturgy | 2,079 | 3,295 |
| Supplies | 5,150 | 11,034 |
| Convention planning | 2,299 | 2,165 |
| CUA Day | -0- | 6,946 |
| Audio Visuals | 2,237 | -0- |
| Total Convention and Pre-convention Workshops | 103,800 | 93,283 |

The accompanying notes are an integral part of these financial statements.

*Projects*

| | | |
|---|---|---|
| Gift to Scholarship Fund | -0- | 2,500 |
| Canon Law Digest - Vol. 12 | 104 | 119 |
| Consecrated Life | 2 | 1,340 |
| Use of Third Form | -0- | 53 |
| CCEO Translation | -0- | 1,290 |
| Canonical Education | -0- | 1,790 |
| Advisory Opinions | -0- | -0- |
| Reception at convention | 8,840 | -0- |
| American Jurisprudence | 68 | -0- |
| Other | -0- | 61 |
| Total Projects Expenses | 9,014 | 7,153 |

*Membership Services*

| | | |
|---|---|---|
| Postage | 4,865 | 14,550 |
| Printing | 7,670 | 15,616 |
| Newsletter | 16,031 | 14,352 |
| Total Membership Services | 28,566 | 44,518 |

*Committees*

| | | |
|---|---|---|
| Nominations | 3,022 | 4,643 |
| Marriage research | 2,031 | -0- |
| Selection of Bishops | 417 | -0- |
| Canonical Advocacy | 640 | -0- |
| Parish Viability | 397 | 492 |
| BOG designated committees | 60 | 238 |
| Advisory Opinions | 93 | -0- |
| Total Committees | 6,660 | 5,373 |

| | | |
|---|---|---|
| *Visit to Holy See* | 4,623 | -0- |
| | | |
| *One Time Contribution - Scholarship Fund* | -0- | 41,351 |
| | | |
| *Provost Memorial* | 5,000 | -0- |

*Scholarship Fund*

| | | |
|---|---|---|
| Scholarships paid | 6,500 | 5,000 |
| Scholarship expenses | 6,679 | 3,049 |
| Total Scholarship Fund | 13,179 | 8,049 |
| | | |
| Total Program Services | $346,404 | $376,773 |

The accompanying notes are an integral part of these financial statements.

# CANON LAW SOCIETY OF AMERICA

## SCHEDULES OF SUPPORTING SERVICES

for the year ended June 30, 2002

with comparative figures for the year ended June 30, 2001

|  | June 30, 2002 (Unaudited) | June 30, 2001 (Audited) |
|---|---|---|
| Board of Governors |  |  |
| Rental housing | $13,149 | $13,000 |
| Travel | 11,807 | 6,868 |
| Food service | 5,882 | 6,761 |
| Other expenses | 1,207 | 988 |
| President | 11,359 | 7,800 |
| Vice President | 1,056 | 853 |
| Treasurer | 605 | 1,981 |
| Secretary | -0- | -0- |
| Executive Coordinator Office | 85,251 | 79,164 |
| Depreciation expense | 2,049 | 2,629 |
| Total Supporting Service | $132,365 | $120,044 |

The accompanying notes are an integral part of these financial statements.

# CANON LAW SOCIETY OF AMERICA

## STATEMENT OF CHANGES IN NET ASSETS BY FUND

### for the year ended June 30, 2002

| | Special Projects Fund | Restricted Reserve Fund | Scholar- ship Fund | Other Unrest- ricted | Total |
|---|---|---|---|---|---|
| Balance, July 1, 2001 | $75,08 | $55,412 | $268,008 | $297,130 | $695,632 |
| **Add: Increases** | | | | | |
| Membership dues | | | | 158,195 | 158,195 |
| Investment income | 19 | | 8,156 | 5,742 | 13,917 |
| Sales of publications | 178,917 | | | | 178,917 |
| Royalties | 16,142 | | | | 16,142 |
| Convention, workshops | | | | 96,977 | 96,977 |
| Other income | 3,007 | | | | 3,007 |
| Contributions | | | 24,848 | | 24,848 |
| | 198,085 | -0- | 33,004 | 260,914 | 492,003 |
| **Less: Decreases** | | | | | |
| Publication expenses | (175,562) | | | | (175,562) |
| Convention, workshops | | | | (103,800) | (103,800) |
| Projects expenses | (9,014) | | | | (9,014) |
| Membership services, committees and other | | | (13,179) | (44,849) | (58,028) |
| Supporting services | | | | (132,365) | (132,365) |
| Losses on investments | | | (22,961) | (19,846) | (42,807) |
| | (184,576) | -0- | (36,140) | (300,860) | (521,576) |
| Balance, June 30, 2002 | $ 88,591 | $55,412 | $264,872 | $257,184 | $666,059 |

The accompanying notes are an integral part of these financial statements.

CANON LAW SOCIETY OF AMERICA

STATEMENTS OF CASH FLOWS

for the year ended June 30, 2002

with comparative figures for the year ended June 30, 2001

|  | June 30, 2002 (Unaudited) | June 30, 2001 (Audited) |
|---|---|---|
| Cash Flows From Operating Activities: | | |
| Membership dues | $155,095 | $156,935 |
| Publications and book sales | 158,198 | 173,526 |
| Convention and workshops | 96,804 | 101,780 |
| Royalties | 10,601 | 23,936 |
| Investment income | 6,354 | 7,752 |
| Other income | 3,007 | 2,374 |
|  | 430,059 | 466,303 |
| Less: Cash paid to suppliers and employees | (491,665) | (436,015) |
| Net Cash From/(Used In) Operations | (61,606) | 30,288 |
| Cash Flows From Investing Activities: | | |
| Purchase of furniture and equipment | (2,297) | (3,691) |
| Purchase of investments | (57,618) | (48,006) |
| Proceeds from sales of investments | 94,267 | 38,640 |
| Net Cash From/(Used In) Investing Activities | 34,352 | (13,057) |
| Cash Flows From Financing Activities: | NONE | NONE |
| Increase/(Decrease) During Year | (27,254) | 17,231 |
| Cash and Cash Equivalents at Beginning of Year | 102,982 | 85,751 |
| Cash and Cash Equivalents at End of Year | $ 75,728 | $102,982 |

278

|                                                                          | June 30, 2002 (Unaudited) | June 30, 2001 (Audited) |
|--------------------------------------------------------------------------|-------------:|-------------:|
| Reconciliation of Increase/(Decrease) in Net Assets to Net Cash Provided By/(Used In) Operating Activities: Increase/(decrease) in Net Assets (Statement-page 25) | $(29,573) | $(77,891) |
| Adjustments to Reconcile: | | |
| Depreciation | 4,621 | 5,369 |
| Gains/losses on long-term investments | 42,807 | 79,227 |
| Contributions to the scholarship fund | (24,848) | (12,161) |
| Investment income – scholarship fund | (8,156) | (8,168) |
| Loss on inventory reduction | 1,090 | 4,079 |
| Bad debts | 2,713 | (7,589) |
| (Increase)/decrease in accounts receivable – book sales | (4,761) | 12,755 |
| (Increase)/decrease in royalties receivable | (5,541) | (682) |
| (Increase)/decrease in accounts receivable – dues | (1,175) | 200 |
| (Increase)/decrease in accrued interest receivable | 593 | (204) |
| (Increase)/decrease in miscellaneous receivables | 2,127 | (1,286) |
| (Increase)/decrease in inventory of books | (44,408) | (15,085) |
| (Increase)/decrease in prepaid postage | (2,203) | (555) |
| (Increase)/decrease in prepaid insurance | (72) | (22) |
| (Increase)/decrease in prepaid book costs | 12,914 | 19,199 |
| (Increase)/decrease in prepaid expenses, other | (5,604) | 10,396 |
| Increase/(decrease) in accounts payable | (2,369) | (7,232) |
| Increase/(decrease) in royalties payable | 7,243 | 4,375 |
| Increase/(decrease) in deferred revenue – book sales | (18,085) | 22,316 |
| Increase/(decrease) in deferred revenue – convention | (173) | 8,198 |
| Increase/(decrease) in deferred revenue – membership dues | (1,925) | 2,000 |
| Increase/(decrease) in deferred revenue – royalties | -0- | (15,000) |
| Expenses paid from scholarship fund | 13,179 | 8,049 |
| Net Cash From/(Used In) Operations | $(61,606) | $30,288 |

The accompanying notes to are an integral part of these financial statements.

CANON LAW SOCIETY OF AMERICA

NOTES TO FINANCIAL STATEMENTS

June 30, 2002
and
June 30, 2001

Note 1. Summary of Significant Accounting Policies

This summary of significant accounting policies of Canon Law Society of
America (CLSA), a District of Columbia not-for-profit professional
organization, is presented to assist in understanding the financial statements.
The financial statements and notes are representations of the organization's
management, who is responsible for their integrity and objectivity. These
accounting policies conform to generally accepted accounting principles and
have been consistently applied in the preparation of the financial statements.

*Accounting Basis*
CLSA prepares its financial statements on the accrual basis of accounting;
that is, income is recognized when earned and expenses are recognized when
the obligation is incurred.

*Accounts Receivable – Books and Publications*
Books and publication receivables are considered uncollectible if not
collected within 90 days after sale.

*Accounts Receivable – Dues*
Dues are billed to members at the beginning of each fiscal year (July 1).
CLSA records dues income on the basis of dues actually collected. Dues not
collected by the issue date of the annual report are considered uncollectible
and are written off.

*Deferred Revenue*
Membership dues, book sales, workshop and convention registrations
collected in advance have been included in deferred revenue in the
accompanying balance sheets under current liabilities. This deferred revenue
is all recognizable within one year.

*Inventory of Books and Publications*
The inventory of books and publications is valued at cost, on the first-in,
first-out method. CLSA carries a 5 year supply of some books and

280

publications. Because of this long-term supply, there is the possibility that part of the inventory will become obsolete and never be sold. The inventory has been separated on the balance sheet between the estimated current portion which management believes will be sold in the next twelve months and the estimated long-term portion which management expects will be sold in the remaining four years as detailed in Note 3.

The write off for obsolete inventory for the fiscal year ended June 30, 2002 was $1,090, and June 30, 2001 was $4,079.

*Capitalization and Depreciation Policy*

Expenditures for fixed assets of $300 or more per item are capitalized and depreciated using the straight-line method over the estimated useful lives of the assets of five years. Depreciation is computed for six months on assets additions during the year. Fully depreciation assets and their related reserves are removed from the accounts. Repairs are expensed as incurred.

Fixed assets additions during 2000-2002 were:

| 2001-2002 | | 2000-2001 | |
|---|---|---|---|
| Server & Backup | $2,297 | Notebook computer | $2,641 |
| | | Draperies | $1,050 |
| | | | $3,691 |

Depreciation expense for the years ended June 30, 2002 and June 30, 2001, was $4,621 and $5,369, respectively.

*Investments*

Investments are carried at their fair market value on the balance sheet date. Gain or loss on investments during the year is measured by the difference between the sales price or the fair market value at the end of the year and their cost if acquired during the year or their fair market value at the end of the preceding year.

*Restricted Funds*

Restricted funds are recorded as either temporarily or permanently restricted in the net assets. Temporarily restricted gifts are reclassified to unrestricted net assets and reported in the statement of activities as net assets released from restrictions when the stipulated restriction is accomplished.

*Board Designated Net Assets*

The Board has designated that part of the unrestricted net assets be set aside for special purposes as described in Notes 8 & 9 below.

*Expenses for Convention and Workshops*

Expenses for the convention and workshops have been charged with direct costs only, and do not include overhead costs which may be associated with these functions.

*Income Taxes*

CLSA is a nonprofit organization exempt from federal income taxes under Section 501 (c) (3) of the Internal Revenue Code, and contributions to it are deductible by donors for income tax purposes. The organization is also exempt from state income taxes.

*Cash Equivalents*

For purposes of the statement of cash flows, CLSA considers only highly liquid investments with an original maturity of three months or less at the time of purchase to be cash equivalents.

*Current Assets and Current Liabilities*

Current assets and current liabilities are those items expected to be or which may be realized or liquidated during the next twelve-month period.

*Fund Accounting*

CLSA uses fund accounting because this method allows the organization to readily keep track of the various monies under its control and the purposes of those funds.

*Use of Estimates*

The preparation of financial statements in conformity with generally accepted accounting principles requires the use of management estimates and assumptions. Accordingly, actual results may differ from those estimates.

Note 2. Organization

The Canon Law Society of America (CLSA) is a national, not-for-profit, professional association, established in November, 1939 in Washington, DC to promote canonical and pastoral approaches to significant issues within the Roman Catholic Church. In addition to a publication service, CLSA convenes an annual convention and other symposia to promote a better understanding of church law and its pastoral applications. Major sources of gross income are from membership dues (35%), sales of publications and books (39%) and annual convention (21%).

Note 3. Inventory

Total inventory at June 30, 2002, at cost, was $197,627 ($154,308 at June 30, 2001) of which $16,304 ($15,974 at June 30, 2001) is reported on the statement of financial position under current assets as the estimated portion of the inventory which management believes will be sold in the coming fiscal year. The balance of the inventory of $181,322 ($138,334 at June 30, 2001) is reported under non-current assets. Four recent publications make up 76% of this long-term portion.

Note 4. Investments-Canon Law Society

These investments are subject to market risks, and their values fluctuate daily. They are held in a Schwab Institutional account as follows:

|  | 2002 | | 2001 | |
| --- | --- | --- | --- | --- |
|  | Cost | Value | Cost | Value |
| Stocks | $ 83,837 | $ 98,519 | $105,699 | $140,510 |
| Corporate bonds | 45,319 | 46,763 | 60,668 | 60,973 |
| Government bonds | 15,051 | 15,098 | 15,011 | 15,393 |
|  | $144,207 | $160,380 | $181,378 | $216,876 |

Note 5. Investments-Scholarship Fund

These investments are subject to market risks, and their values fluctuate daily. They are held in a Schwab Institutional account restricted for use by the Scholarship Fund as follows:

|  | 2002 | | 2001 | |
| --- | --- | --- | --- | --- |
|  | Cost | Value | Cost | Value |
| Cash | $ 26,132 | $ 26,132 | $ 12,098 | $ 12,098 |
| Stocks | 109,352 | 115,595 | 114,585 | 137,191 |
| Corporate bonds | 20,024 | 20,750 | 55,379 | 55,623 |
| Government bonds | 99,996 | 100,700 | 59,969 | 61,400 |
| Pledge receivable | -0- | -0- | 25 | 25 |
| Accrued interest | 2,008 | 2,008 | 2,021 | 2,021 |
| Less: Accounts payable | (313) | (313) | (350) | (350) |
|  | $ 257,199 | $ 264,872 | $ 243,727 | $ 268,008 |

Note 6. Deferred Income-Royalties

Prepaid book costs of $12,914 at June 30, 2001 represent expenditures to date for several publications. These costs will be expensed as these books are published and sold.

Note 7. Operating Lease Payable-Xerox

The organization leased a new copier with a 5 year lease payable to Xerox beginning on June 1, 1999. The lease is $528.20 per month and includes supplies and maintenance up to 8,000 copies per month.

Because this lease includes supplies and maintenance as a major part of the monthly payments, it is considered an operating lease, even though there is an option to purchase the copier at the end of the lease. The following is a schedule by years of future minimum lease payments under this lease:

Year Ended:

| | |
| --- | --- |
| June 30, 2003 | $ 6,338 |
| June 30, 2004 (11 months) | 5,810 |
| | $12,148 |

Note 8. Restricted Reserve Account

The Board has designated $55,412 as a Restricted Reserve Account to be set aside for future purposes. The income of this Restricted Reserve Account, formerly the Quasi-Endowment Fund, is to be used for operations.

Note 9. Publications Sales

The Board of Governors has also voted to use the net income from sales of publications and books to fund Special Projects.

The changes in Board Designated For Special Projects are as follows:

|  | 6/30/02 | 6/30/01 |
|---|---|---|
| Balance, beginning of year | $ 75,082 | $78,757 |
| Add: Publication income | 178,917 | 138,832 |
| Royalty income | 16,142 | 39,618 |
| Other income | 3,026 | 2,074 |
| Less: Publication expenses | (175,562) | (177,046) |
| Projects expenses | (9,014) | (7,153) |
| Balance, end of year | $88,591 | $ 75,082 |

Note 10. Annual Meeting Site Reservation Agreements

The organization has reserved hotel space for future annual meetings. The terms of these reservation agreements provide that a fee will be assessed to CLSA if the reservation is canceled due to a site change, within a specified period prior to the meeting dates.

Note 11. Operating Lease - Mail Machine

The organization is leasing a shipping system from Pitney Bowes under an operating lease. This lease is for a period of 63 months beginning on December 5, 1996 and its terms call for annual lease payments of $4,056. The organization does not have an option to purchase this system at the end of this lease, therefore, this lease is considered an operating lease and the lease payments are expensed as paid. This lease was bought out in July 2001 for $3,068.

Note 12. Retirement Benefits

The organization contributed $1,290 toward the retirement of the Executive

Coordinator and $2,358 toward the retirement of the administrative assistant during the fiscal year ended June 30, 2002 and $1,229 and $3,000 during the fiscal year ended June 30, 2001.

Note 13.  Convention Coordination Company

Beginning in October of 2001, CLSA hired an outside company to coordinate its annual convention.

Note 14. Investment Income

The elements of investment income are as follows:

|  | 6/30/02 | 6/30/01 |
|---|---|---|
| Interest and dividend income |  |  |
| Interest earned on checking accounts | $ 19 | $ 1,444 |
| Dividends and interest on investments held |  |  |
| by Schwab Institutional | 5,742 | 6,512 |
|  | $ 5,761 | $ 7,956 |
|  |  |  |
| Net realized gains/(loss) on investments |  |  |
| Realized loss on investments sold |  |  |
| by Schwab Institutional | $ (3,642) | $(26,694) |
|  |  |  |
| Net unrealized gains/(loss) on investments |  |  |
| Unrealized gains/(loss) on investments |  |  |
| held by Schwab Institutional | $(16,204) | $(10,601) |

Dividends and gains/(loss) on long-term investment-Temporarily Restricted Scholarship Fund

| Interest and dividend income |  |  |
|---|---|---|
| Interest and dividends earned on |  |  |
| investments held by Schwab Institutional | $ 8,156 | $ 8,168 |
|  |  |  |
| Net realized gains/(loss) on investments |  |  |
| Realized loss-investments held by Schwab |  |  |
| Institutional | $( 6,099) | $(30,824) |
|  |  |  |
| Net unrealized gains/(loss) on investments |  |  |
| Unrealized gains on investments held |  |  |
| by Schwab Institutional | $(16,862) | $(11,108) |

# PART II

# BUDGET SUMMARY
## Canon Law Society of America
## FY JULY 1, 2002 – JUNE 30, 2003

I.   GENERAL OPERATIONS

|            |              |
|------------|--------------|
| Income     | $182,250.00  |
| Expenses   | $186,218.00  |
| Difference | $(3,968.00)  |

II.  PUBLICATIONS

|            |              |
|------------|--------------|
| Income     | $220,945.00  |
| Expenses   | $203,799.00  |
| Difference | $17,146.00   |

III. CONVENTION

|            |              |
|------------|--------------|
| Income     | $123,664.00  |
| Expenses   | $122,473.00  |
| Difference | $1,191.00    |

IV.  CLSA SCHOLARSHIP

|            |              |
|------------|--------------|
| Income     | $19,500.00   |
| Expenses   | $19,400.00   |
| Difference | $100.00      |

# BUDGET SUMMARY
## Canon Law Society of America
### FY JULY 1, 2002 – JUNE 30, 2003

## INCOME

|  | Budget<br>FY 01.02 | Actual<br>FY 01.02 | Budget<br>FY 02.03 |
|---|---|---|---|
| **I. GENERAL OPERATIONS** | | | |
| Dues Income | $169,575.00 | $158,195.01 | $175,700.00 |
| Investment Income/Charles Schwab | $6,000.00 | $5,742.31 | $6,000.00 |
| Interest Income/CD | $550.00 | $0.00 | $550.00 |
| **TOTAL** | **$176,125.00** | **$163,937.32** | **$182,250.00** |
| Transfer from Publications | $20,000.00 | | |
| | **$196,125.00** | | |
| **II. PUBLICATIONS** | | | |
| Publication Sales | $230,000.00 | $161,457.44 | $195,000.00 |
| Interest Income/Checking | $100.00 | $18.91 | $200.00 |
| Xerox Sales | $1,620.00 | $2,407.28 | $1,620.00 |
| Reprint Permissions | $0.00 | $600.00 | $1,000.00 |
| Royalty Income | $13,925.00 | $16,142.13 | $5,125.00 |
| Shipping & Handling @ PMDS | $0.00 | $17,459.26 | $18,000.00 |
| **TOTAL** | **$245,645.00** | **$198,085.02** | **$220,945.00** |
| **III. CONVENTION** | | | |
| Convention Fees | $74,250.00 | $89,652.00 | $96,250.00 |
| Pre-Convention Fees | $14,400.00 | $7,325.00 | $20,900.00 |
| Interest Income/CD | $415.00 | $0.00 | $414.00 |
| Exhibitors | $0.00 | $0.00 | $2,100.00 |
| Sponsors | $0.00 | $0.00 | $4,000.00 |
| **TOTAL** | **$89,065.00** | **$96,977.00** | **$123,664.00** |
| **IV. CLSA SCHOLARSHIP** | | | |
| Investment Income | $8,120.00 | $8,156.35 | $9,000.00 |
| CLSA Publication Contribution | $2,500.00 | $0.00 | $2,500.00 |
| Member Contributions | $4,000.00 | $9,737.30 | $8,000.00 |
| Festschrift | $0.00 | $15,930.00 | $0.00 |
| **TOTAL** | **$14,620.00** | **$33,823.65** | **$19,500.00** |

# BUDGET SUMMARY
## GENERAL OPERATIONS
### Canon Law Society of America
### FY JULY 1, 2002 – JUNE 30, 2003

## EXPENSES

**Office of the Executive Coordinator**

|  | Budget FY 01.02 | Actual FY 01.02 | Budget FY 02.03 |
|---|---|---|---|
| Staff Salaries (3 items) | $57,750.00 | $54,736.70 | $59,041.00 |
| Staff Benefits (2 items) | $7,913.00 | $8,834.45 | $10,550.00 |
| Bank Service Charges | $900.00 | $336.84 | $700.00 |
| Schwab Management Fees | $0.00 | $1312.98 | $1,076.00 |
| Credit Card: Terminal & Fees | $1,500.00 | $1,107.78 | $1,728.00 |
| Books & Subscriptions | $650.00 | $515.10 | $675.00 |
| Insurance | $1,465.00 | $1,580.75 | $1,873.00 |
| Hospitality | $750.00 | $406.93 | $750.00 |
| Postage | $600.00 | $567.82 | $600.00 |
| Office Supplies | $1,230.00 | $1,853.27 | $962.00 |
| Telephone | $695.00 | $630.78 | $761.00 |
| Executive Coordinator Travel | $2,000.00 | $1,098.54 | $2,500.00 |
| Executive Coordinator Continuing Education | $1,000.00 | $625.00 | $1,000.00 |
| Accountant | $4,750.00 | $4,250.00 | $4,750.00 |
| Computer Consultants | $2,200.00 | $2,868.75 | $1,275.00 |
| Temporary Secretarial Help | $6,000.00 | $791.25 | $0.00 |
| Xerox Copier Lease & Copy Charges | $3,240.00 | $3,247.90 | $3,240.00 |
| Membership Services (7 items) | $34,749.00 | $28,565.88 | $46,012.00 |
| CUA Parking Fees | $900.00 | $578.00 | $600.00 |
| Capital Expense | $2,150.00 | $0.00 | $0.00 |
| SUB-TOTAL | $130,442.00 | $113,908.72 | $138,093.00 |

## BUDGET SUMMARY
## GENERAL OPERATIONS
## Canon Law Society of America
## FY JULY 1, 2002 – JUNE 30, 2003

### EXPENSES

| | Budget FY 01.02 | Actual FY 01.02 | Budget FY 02.03 |
|---|---|---|---|
| **Board of Governors** | | | |
| Food | $8,240.00 | $5,881.58 | $6,240.00 |
| Housing | $13,400.00 | $13,149.36 | $10,400.00 |
| Postage | $300.00 | $270.64 | $500.00 |
| Supplies | $555.00 | $321.61 | $555.00 |
| Telephone | $0.00 | $36.92 | $100.00 |
| Travel | $11,330.00 | $11,806.88 | $11,330.00 |
| Printing | $0.00 | $0.00 | $0.00 |
| SUB-TOTAL | $33,825.00 | $31,466.99 | $29,125.00 |
| | | | |
| President | $9,000.00 | $11,359.17 | $9,000.00 |
| Vice President | $1,200.00 | $1,055.91 | $1,200.00 |
| Treasurer | $2,250.00 | $284.01 | $2,000.00 |
| Secretary | $0.00 | $0.00 | $200.00 |
| Transition Meeting | $0.00 | $320.75 | $1,000.00 |
| SUB-TOTAL | $12,450.00 | $13,019.84 | $13,400.00 |
| | | | |
| **Committees** | | | |
| Resolutions | $170.00 | $0.00 | $150.00 |
| Roman Replies | $150.00 | $0.00 | $175.00 |
| *Ex Corde Ecclesiae* | $250.00 | $0.00 | $100.00 |
| Advisory Opinions | $150.00 | $93.02 | $175.00 |
| Marriage Research | $500.00 | $2,030.92 | $175.00 |
| Civil and Canon Law | $250.00 | $0.00 | $175.00 |
| Canonical Advocacy Study | $150.00 | $640.00 | $175.00 |
| Parish Viability | $500.00 | $397.20 | $175.00 |
| Selection of Bishops | $250.00 | $417.28 | $175.00 |
| Electronic Media | $500.00 | $0.00 | $175.00 |
| Nominations | $2,500.00 | $3,022.45 | $2,500.00 |
| BOG Designated Committees | $1,500.00 | $60.00 | $500.00 |
| Consecrated Life | $0.00 | $0.00 | $150.00 |
| Contingency | $0.00 | $5,000.00 | $500.00 |
| SUB-TOTAL | $6,870.00 | $11,660.87 | $5,300.00 |

## BUDGET SUMMARY
## GENERAL OPERATIONS
### Canon Law Society of America
### FY JULY 1, 2002 – JUNE 30, 2003

### EXPENSES

|  | Budget<br>FY 01.02 | Actual<br>FY 01.02 | Budget<br>FY 02.03 |
|---|---|---|---|
| **Asset Expenditures** |  |  |  |
| Computer Hardware | $0.00 | $485.93 | $300.00 |
| **TOTAL OPERATIONS** | **$183,587.00** | **$170,542.35** | **$186,218.00** |

# BUDGET SUMMARY
## PUBLICATIONS
### Canon Law Society of America
### FY JULY 1, 2002 – JUNE 30, 2003

## EXPENSES

|  | Budget FY 01.02 | Actual FY 01.02 | Budget FY 02.03 |
|---|---|---|---|
| Royalties/CCEO | $4,420.00 | $3,504.54 | $2,000.00 |
| Royalties/CIC | $4,200.00 | $3,324.92 | $3,200.00 |
| Royalties/Selected Issues | $750.00 | $413.64 | $500.00 |
| Royalties/*The Jurist* | $0.00 | $0.00 | $60.00 |
| Staff Salaries (3 items) | $37,933.00 | $35,162.51 | $38,794.00 |
| Staff Benefits (2 items) | $3,359.00 | $4,598.38 | $4,351.00 |
| Student Assistants | $1,750.00 | $0.00 | $500.00 |
| Accountant | $4,750.00 | $4,250.00 | $4,750.00 |
| Publication Advertising Postage | $5,690.00 | $1,888.24 | $19,190.00 |
| Publication Advertising Printing | $9,540.00 | $6,926.50 | $11,810.00 |
| Electronic Media | $1,415.00 | $570.95 | $1,472.00 |
| Computer Tech Support | $2,500.00 | $1,253.75 | $1,000.00 |
| Bank Service Charges | $360.00 | $127.15 | $360.00 |
| Credit Card Terminal — Novus | $1,180.00 | $1,810.87 | $1,410.00 |
| General Office Supplies | $535.00 | $511.60 | $264.00 |
| Publication Correspondence Postage | $2,180.00 | $1,764.91 | $635.00 |
| Scholarship Fund Contribution | $2,500.00 | $0.00 | $2,500.00 |
| Copy Right Permissions | $0.00 | $210.00 | $210.00 |
| Xerox Copier Lease | $3,240.00 | $3,286.35 | $3,240.00 |
| PMDS – Outsourcing | $51,550.00 | $53,390.98 | $57,700.00 |
| Pitney Bowes | $3,820.00 | $2,168.61 | $322.00 |
| Telephone | $695.00 | $785.74 | $761.00 |
| Publication Travel | $2,870.00 | $2,297.30 | $3,170.00 |
| SUB-TOTAL | $145,237.00 | $128,246.94 | $158,199.00 |

## BUDGET SUMMARY
## PUBLICATIONS
### Canon Law Society of America
### FY JULY 1, 2002 – JUNE 30, 2003

## EXPENSES

| | Budget<br>FY 01.02 | Actual<br>FY 01.02 | Budget<br>FY 02.03 |
|---|---|---|---|
| **Projects** | | | |
| CLSA Bibliography | $250.00 | $0.00 | $175.00 |
| Committee on Canon Law Digest | $750.00 | $104.47 | $750.00 |
| Publications Committee | $500.00 | $0.00 | $500.00 |
| *Festschrift* | $500.00 | $0.00 | $175.00 |
| Handbook on Parish Life | $0.00 | $0.00 | $0.00 |
| New Projects | $3,000.00 | $0.00 | $0.00 |
| Sacramental Law Handbook | $0.00 | $0.00 | $0.00 |
| Contingency | $0.00 | $8,840.40 | $500.00 |
| SUB-TOTAL | $5,000.00 | $8,944.87 | $2,100.00 |
| | | | |
| **Asset Expenditures** | | | |
| Printers Cost | $69,550.00 | $0.00 | $43,500.00 |
| | | | |
| **TOTAL PUBLICATIONS** | **$219,787.00** | **$137,191.81** | **$203,799.00** |

# BUDGET SUMMARY
## CONVENTION
**Canon Law Society of America**
**FY JULY 1, 2002 – JUNE 30, 2003**

### EXPENSES

| | Budget FY 01.02 | Actual FY 01.02 | Budget FY 02.03 |
|---|---|---|---|
| **Planning Services** | | | |
| Convention Chairperson | $3,000.00 | $424.70 | $2,000.00 |
| Assistant Convention Chair | $1,500.00 | $0.00 | $0.00 |
| Convention Planning Committee | $3,500.00 | $2,299.36 | $1,500.00 |
| SUB-TOTAL | $8,000.00 | $2,724.06 | $3,500.00 |
| | | | |
| **Pre-Conventions** | | | |
| Food | $5,200.00 | $4,648.71 | $5,000.00 |
| Honoraria | $3,000.00 | $3,000.00 | $3,000.00 |
| Lodging | $1,760.00 | $1,691.89 | $1,790.00 |
| Postage | $50.00 | $59.50 | $50.00 |
| Printing | $1,525.00 | $1,384.96 | $1,524.00 |
| Freight | $200.00 | $598.23 | $250.00 |
| Travel | $400.00 | $400.68 | $1,250.00 |
| Supplies | $55.00 | $40.00 | $92.00 |
| Telephone | $100.00 | $0.00 | $100.00 |
| Liturgy | $200.00 | $200.00 | $200.00 |
| Audio Visuals | $1,780.00 | $1,116.88 | $1,300.00 |
| SUB-TOTAL | $14,270.00 | $13,140.85 | $14,556.00 |
| | | | |
| **Convention** | | | |
| Food | $36,000.00 | $27,250.72 | $36,000.00 |
| Honoraria | $3,900.00 | $3,800.00 | $4,700.00 |
| Lodging | $1,550.00 | $2,763.51 | $4,142.00 |
| Postage | $2,650.00 | $2,731.48 | $2,648.00 |
| Printing | $9,200.00 | $9,000.24 | $10,635.00 |
| Freight | $600.00 | $1,794.72 | $500.00 |
| Travel | $1,500.00 | $1,479.50 | $1,000.00 |
| Supplies | $5,095.00 | $5,150.36 | $5,592.00 |
| Telephone | $350.00 | $100.00 | $350.00 |
| Liturgy | $2,550.00 | $2,078.86 | $2,500.00 |
| Audio Visuals | $7,000.00 | $2,237.12 | $3,250.00 |
| Hotel Taxes | $0.00 | $387.22 | $400.00 |
| SUB-TOTAL | $70,395.00 | $58,773.73 | $71,717.00 |

## BUDGET SUMMARY
## CONVENTION
## Canon Law Society of America
## FY JULY 1, 2002 – JUNE 30, 2003

### EXPENSES

|  | Budget FY 01.02 | Actual FY 01.02 | Budget FY 02.03 |
|---|---|---|---|
| **Professional Services** |  |  |  |
| Nix & Associates | $0.00 | $28,180.90 | $28,150.00 |
| Bank Service Charges | $250.00 | $5.11 | $250.00 |
| Credit Card Charges | $800.00 | $800.00 | $800.00 |
| Rome 2005 | $500.00 | $175.50 | $3,000.00 |
| Miscellaneous Expenses | $0.00 | $0.00 | $500.00 |
| SUB-TOTAL | $1,550.00 | $29,161.51 | $32,700.00 |
| **TOTAL CONVENTION** | **$94,215.00** | **$103,800.15** | **$122,473.00** |

# BUDGET SUMMARY
## CLSA SCHOLARSHIP
### Canon Law Society of America
### FY JULY 1, 2002 – JUNE 30, 2003

## EXPENSES

|  | Budget FY 01.02 | Actual FY 01.02 | Budget FY 02.03 |
|---|---|---|---|
| Bank/Investment Fees (3 items) | $600.00 | $1,352.83 | $1,250.00 |
| Postage | $1,200.00 | $2,142.61 | $2,200.00 |
| Printing | $130.00 | $3,008.74 | $3,650.00 |
| Committee Expenses (3 items) | $300.00 | $131.32 | $300.00 |
| Award | $12,000.00 | $6,500.00 | $12,000.00 |
| **TOTAL SCHOLARSHIP** | **$14,230.00** | **$13,135.50** | **$19,400.00** |

# REPORT OF THE EXECUTIVE COORDINATOR

Rev. Arthur J. Espelage, O.F.M.

Introduction:

It is with a sense of deep gratitude that I make this annual report to the members of the Society as I begin my second term as your Executive Coordinator. It is also with a deep sense of pleasure that I make this report in my hometown of Cincinnati, Ohio. Never in a million years would I have imagined that a "skinny kid" from the South Fairmount section of Cincinnati would be here in the Hilton Netherland Plaza Hotel on Fountain Square to report to the assembled members of this great society.

The events of 9-11 profoundly touched the hearts and minds of all Americans as well as our friends and even our foes. Life has changed in so many ways since that fateful day, but one lesson is that we are to be courageous in the face of our fears and our hurts. Other events in our Church during this fateful year have embarrassed many of us an challenged at times our identity. Upholding and defending the rule of law in our Church and our society remains the gift we can bring as canonists to help all people vindicate their rights and avoid surrendering our hearts and minds to baser thoughts.

The members of the Canon Law Society of America are in a unique position to continue advocacy for the rule of law. Our numbers remain strong; since my last report, seventy-two (72) of new members entered the CLSA. Our membership roles show one thousand eight hundred twelve (1812) active, associate, and student members. We also commend to God those of our members who passed from this world: Sister Louise E. Tessier, PM; Reverend Nathaniel Reeves, OSB; Reverend Benedict A. DeSocio; Brother Leonard Voegtle, FMS; Reverend Monsignor William J. Boone; Reverend Gerald Scholl; Reverend Monsignor Louis Naughton; Reverend Gary R. Steibel; Reverend Monsignor Sylvester F. Gass; Reverend Monsignor A. James Amos; Reverend James G. Karaffa, CSC.

In support of your activities, I offer the following report on the activities of the Office of the Executive Coordinator.

General Operations

From August 2001 to January 2002 of office was somewhat shorthanded with Mrs. Jennifer Miller being away on maternity leave after the birth of her and Chris' daughter Erin Marie. During that time Mrs. Joy Harrell came in to the office to help with the production of the 2001 *CLSA Proceedings* and to help with the December CLSA Scholarship Mailing. Also during this time, Mrs. Kay Winner joined our office as part-time bookkeeper. Both ladies were a wonderful addition to the office and helped to keep things running smoothly.

As a growth item arising out of 9-11, we also began this year an Operations Manual for the Executive's Office should the need arise. Work on this rather ambitious task continues to progress very nicely, and many of the thousand and one little details that go on throughout the year are being organized onto paper. We also have organized tape backups of the computer and off site storage to maintain up to date working records of the society's activities.

During this year, our office has relied heavily upon the names submitted by members to create a CLSA Referral List of approximately seventy-five names to provide inquirers with possible advocates. While we have not maintained an actual count nor any data on requests, there has been almost daily a very great interest in this area. It is our policy to provide contacts with the names of three possible canonists for the inquiring party to contact. To all of those who have been contacted by individuals seeking advocates, I thank you for your willingness to serve the People of God in this manner. For those who wish to add their names to the referral list as possible advocates, please contact me after the Convention.

One of our largest challenges this past year has been to keep the office fiscally responsible as costs of paper, supplies, postage, and membership services continue to rise. Due to a variety of reasons there was less income from sources other than membership dues into the society's account. I am deeply grateful to our new bookkeeper, Mrs. Kay Winner, for her attention to details and generating the checks and monthly reports to the Treasurer of the Society, Monsignor Alexander J. Palmieri. There skills in these economically challenged times are remarkable and deeply appreciated.

CLSA PUBLICATIONS

In general, CLSA Publications and its out sourcing agency, PMDS, remain viable. The events of 9-11 and the general downturn in the economy perhaps created a climate where people were not buying as many books as we may wish. Nonetheless, you can look at the budget figures in the reports booklet for more information.

This year the Society continued to be an exhibitor with three ventures. The first was the Religious Formation Convocation in Chicago, Illinois, November 1 – 4, 2001. The convocation was an opportunity for the CLSA to introduce itself to the many religious in attendance and offer them the services of the CLSA. The second exhibiting venture took place at the National Federation of Priests Councils meeting April 15 – 18, 2002 in Toronto, Ontario, Canada. This venue also was a wonderful opportunity to introduce the society and its work to others. The third venture as an exhibitor took place at our own CLSA Convention in Cincinnati. Becoming an exhibitor at these meetings is an important way in which the CLSA is able to be visible and to network with other professional societies. The Executive's Office plans to continue with one to three exhibiting ventures in the next year.

A major portion of time and energy this year was devoted to the production of materials for CLSA Publications. We continue to out source our distribution of books through PMDS, a direct mail service system, located in Annapolis Junction, Maryland. Their staff has worked well with us, and we continue to processes orders as efficiently and economically as possible. Unfortunately, increases in postage and shipping in the general public require that we "mind the shop" as closely as possible.

Production costs for books have soared over this past year. Costs of paper, ink, and services rose. I am most grateful to those members and others who have participated in our pre-publication offers for CLSA books. We have been able to meet our production and initial distribution costs and not have to take money out of the Society's coffers to print our books. We have kept the ledger sheets in the black on these projects which is an item due in part to diligence and in part to the good advice from members of the Board of Governors and advisors to the Society.

I am pleased to report that a number of printing projects were completed during this year of the society's activities.

- *CLSA Proceedings 2001* of the Albuquerque convention was produced and distributed by February of 2002. The office remains committed to the timely production and distribution of this resource of the Society.
- *CLSA Advisory Opinions (1994 – 2000)* continues the fine work of members who contribute time and talent to make canonical information available. This volume has a cumulative index with the earlier volume for both topics and canons to make it a "user friendly" resource.
- *Canonical Standards for Parishes: A Self-Evaluation Instrument* became available for sale at CLSA Publications in August of 2002. The Board of Governors decided in their April meeting that this valuable item was a most useful resource for parishes and pastoral planning.
- *Jurisprudence: A Collection of U.S. Tribunal Decisions* reached CLSA Publications after its initial distribution for pre-publication sales in early

September 2002. This particular item is unique in our book production as it contains a CD along with the printed text. We hope in the future to consider similar production for other CLSA books.

- *Roman Replies and CLSA Advisory Opinions 2002* arrived at our office in early July for formatting and production. Printing was completed the first week of September and sent to CLSA Publications
- *Judging Invalidity* by Lawrence G. Wrenn is the last of this year's printing project to go to the printers before the convention. Pre-publication brochures went out on this particular volume in September with a hopeful distribution date before Thanksgiving 2002.

At the present time, work continues on two major printing projects.

- *Canon Law Digest XII* materials were deposited at the Executive's Office for formatting and indexing. Work progressed on this project in July and the last part of September was the target date to send the materials to and indexer.
- *Compendium of Law Sections for Marriage Nullity Cases: Sources* from the Marriage Research Committee is the latest book under preparation at the Office of the Executive Coordinator. The Committee deposited the text and disks and a final reading is under way prior to preparation.

CLSA CONVENTIONS

I would like to begin by extending my gratitude to Mrs. Rita Joyce, our General Convention Chair, who has worked throughout this year to prepare for the Cincinnati convention. Since the last convention, she has worked with our office to refine the protocols to meet our growing needs. The thousand and one items which need to be addressed before each convention all fell into place with her skilled leadership. Her collaboration with Nix & Associates as well as the Executive Coordinator's Office on items with the hotel continues the high degree of professionalism needed to put on a convention.

I also wish to thank the Convention Planning Committee, chaired this past year by the Reverend James Conn, S.J. The committee oversaw the final preparation for speakers at this year's convention and began work on Portland 2003. The committee with the Reverend David Berberian as chair will meet during November 2002 in Washington to continue planning. Members who wish to submit possible seminar topics should do so in the next few weeks. A reminder about the call for papers will go out in the November 2002 *CLSA Newsletter*.

There are a number of innovations this year at the Cincinnati Convention. In this reports booklet, you will find a list of participants at the Cincinnati convention.

In doing this, we are providing a more permanent record of attendees. The Board of Governors decided on a new look for the Candidates Brochure which you will find in your convention bags. I appreciate the time and energy which the candidates expended to provide us with the curriculum vitae and vision statement on the Society. Also this year, we have a number of exhibitors present at the convention. The Board of Governors has received requests over the past few years to make this feature a part of our annual convention. This year we approached a number of firms and individuals who decided to join us at the convention. I certainly hope that you will take a few moments to visit the exhibiting area of the convention and meet these people. A third innovation this year was to seek out possible sponsors to offer convention attendees a few amenities. CLSA Publications will host the Monday night reception as a part of the *festschrift* festivities honoring the Reverend Lawrence G. Wrenn. I am grateful to both Key Printing of Laurel, Maryland, and Canon Law Professionals of Feura Bush, New York, for providing convention supplies. Finally, I would like to thank my Franciscan brothers of the St. John the Baptist Province, Cincinnati Ohio, for their cash donation to help defray the costs of the conventions receptions.

Finally, I would like to take a moment to note my own appreciation of the Rome 2005 Convention Committee under the chair of the Very Reverend Lawrence A. DiNardo, of Pittsburgh. Father Larry has worked quietly and efficiently over the past months to explore possibilities and work to make a Rome convention a reality.

CLSA SCHOLARSHIP

It remained a pleasure to work with the CLSA Scholarship Committee this past year. The Advent appeal letter was created, assembled, and sent out to the members on time. A great deal of credit on this year's appeal must go to Ms. Barbara A. Bettwy who worked tirelessly as committee chair to make this year's appeal a success. You will find her report in the committees section a fuller accounting of this most needed item. Work will begin after the Cincinnati convention to create a new Scholarship brochure for next year's appeal.

Also I wish to acknowledge the work of Monsignor Frederick C. Easton and his associate, the Reverend Patrick Cogan, OSA as well as the contributors to *The Art of the Good and Equitable*. The project would not have reached completion over this summer without their great skills and generous donation of time. I also wish to thank Mrs. Jennifer Miller and Mrs. Kay Winner for their typing and proof reading of the text.

CONCLUSION

The time since Albuquerque 2001 has swiftly sped by here at the Executive's office. Visitors who climbed the four flights of stairs in Caldwell Hall or ventured onto the building's elevator were and remain most welcome. Likewise, your telephone calls are never a burden but a great delight. It is one of the ways that the society keeps information flowing, and we are happy that we have been able to aid you in requests or simply have the pleasure of speaking with you.

We have goals for the upcoming year. A couple of them are carry overs from last year. We will continue to create and revise the Operations Manual for the Office. Secondly, we are hard at work on the production of *Canon Law Digest XII*. Pre-publication brochures for this item went out in the September 2002 *CLSA Newsletter*. Our office is also working closely with the editors of the next three volumes of *CLD*. The office will also continue to work with members of the Society and other professionals in the upcoming months with items associated with the charter and the essential norms. Your membership in the CLSA does make an important contribution for our future as a Church and a nation.

Finally, I would like to express my appreciation to all of the members of the Canon Law Society of America for your membership and contributions of time and talent to the needs of the society. We are enriched by the skills of our newest members and sustained by those of our long time members. At times there are so many voices speaking and it is not always clear where the messages are going. It is steadying and comforting to know that the Society has so many capable and competent members to study, implement, and bring into action the rule of law. From my perspective here in Washington, you are a great asset to our Church and our civil society.

Committee:    **Budget**

Constituted:  CLSA Constitution, Article X

Charge:       To prepare the annual budget of the CLSA

Membership:   Rev. Msgr. Alexander J. Palmieri, Chairperson (*ex officio*)
              Rev. Lawrence J. O'Keefe (*ex officio*)
              Rev. Msgr. F. Stephen Pedone (*ex officio*)

### Annual Report

The Budget Committee, assisted by Rev. Arthur J. Espelage, O.F.M. and Mrs. Jennifer Miller, met on February 27 & 28, 2002 at Catholic University of America, Washington, DC. The committee reviewed the preliminary budget for Fiscal Year 2002-2003, with its supporting information, which was well-prepared by the Executive Coordinator and his staff.

After detailed discussion and subsequent adjustments, the committee presented the proposed budget to the Board of Governors, which approved it, with minor revisions, at the April meeting. The approved budget for Fiscal Year 2002-2003 is published in the "Report of the Treasurer," as found in "Reports 2002."

Committee:    **Convention Planning**

Constituted:  CLSA Constitution, Article X

Charge:       1. Above all to work of the attainment of the purpose of the Society set forth in Article II of the Constitution;
              2. To submit to the Board of Governors for approval the names of speakers and topics for discussion at the annual general meeting;
              3. To initiate or cooperate in all research projects of the Society such as seminars, symposia and special studies relative to research and discussion, and to recommend to the Board of Governors honoraria for participants in these studies as well as for speakers at the annual general meeting;

4. To cooperation with the Executive Coordinator in arranging for all publications of the Society.

Membership: Rev. James Conn, S.J., Chairperson
Rev. David V. Berberian
Rev. Msgr. Michael Souckar
Rev. Arthur J. Espelage, O.F.M., *ex officio*
Rev. Msgr. Robert P. Deeley, *ex officio*

Annual Report

The theme of the 2003 Convention in Portland, Oregon, is to be "Levels of Church Authority: Conflict or Complementarity?

The following speakers were, with the approval of the Board of Governors, invited to address the Convention and have agreed to do so:

Keynote Address: Cardinal Avery Dulles, S.J.
*The Universal and the Particular Church: Theological and Historical Foundations*

Major Addresses: Sister Sharon A. Euart, R.S.M.
*General Decrees of Episcopal Conferences*

Rev. Gregory T. Bittner
*Tensions in Observing Subsidiarity*

Seminars: Dr. Barbara Ann Cusack
*Bishops and Catholic Schools*

Rev. Gregory Ingels
*CDF Rules on Certain Delicts*

Very Rev. William J. King
*The Corporation Sole and Subsidiarity*

Sister Patricia Smith, O.S.F.
*Religious Law: The* Ius Vigens

Rev. Msgr. Michael A. Souckar
*Subsidiarity and the CCEO*

Rev. William H. Woestman, O,M.I.
*Simulation and Marital Consent*

There will be one or two BOG-determined seminars and one seminar chosen from the call for papers.

The following seminar topics were identified by the Committee and approved by the BOG, but invited speakers either declined the invitation or accepted and later withdrew: *Canonical and Pastoral Problems in the RCIA, Ethical and Religious Directives, Problems between First- and Second-instance Tribunals, Self-evaluation of Tribunals.* The Committee and the BOG will have to determine whether to seek alternate presenters or alternate seminar topics.

Committee:    **Nominations**

Constituted:   CLSA Constitution, Article X

Charge:         The functions of the Committee on Membership and Nominations are:

    1. To submit to the active members, at least one month prior to the date of election, the names of nominees as provided for in Article IX of the Constitution;

    2. To propose for approval of the Board of Governors applicants for active membership under Article III, no. 2 of the Constitution, and to propose to the Board of Governors for honorary membership in the Society those who, in its opinion, qualify according to Article III;

    3. To formulate and recommend to the Board of Governors plans for maintaining and increasing the membership of the Society.

Membership:  Rev. Msgr. Nevin Klinger, Chairperson
Sr. Francine Quillin, P.B.V.M.
Rev. Paul Counce
Rev. Msgr. Robert P. Deeley, *ex officio*

Annual Report

The Nominations Committee met in Miami, Florida, from February 24 – 27, 2002. Our first order of business was to discuss the elections themselves. We decided to propose to the Board of Governors that the Nominations Committee prepare a survey regarding the nominations process and the elections. If the BOG approves) this survey will be given to the membership at this annual convention. It is our hope that the results of the survey will further enhance the work of this Committee.

Our second order of business was to suggest to the BOG that in the next 3 years an additional member be placed on each of the standing committees. This will broaden the list of potential candidates that can be considered for election. (The Committee unanimously agreed that the number on the Nominations Committee should not be expanded due to the increased difficulty of coming to a consensus.)

Third, we propose that the our Committee conduct a "Candidates Forum" to be held during the annual convention at 11:15 on Tuesday. The Forum would run approximately 45 minutes and the entire membership would be invited to attend. The Candidates could speak briefly about themselves and give the members an opportunity to ask questions. We propose that this be held in lieu of the candidates' appearance at the caucuses. We propose this because we believe that everyone in the society should have the same opportunity (which we believe is very beneficial) as the small groups meeting in caucus have had in the past. If the BOG approves, we would be pleased to prepare something for the next Newsletter informing the membership about this great opportunity.

Fourth, we propose that the Nominations Committee, together with the Vice President/ President-elect, host a luncheon for approximately 15 candidates from past elections who were unsuccessful in their run for office. We believe that this would give those former candidates the opportunity to point out any deficiencies they believe exist in the process/election. In addition members of the Committee would have the opportunity to discuss with them: (1) if unsuccessful candidates might consider accepting a nomination in the future; (2) if there were any ways they would propose that might make the election process less disappointing for candidates who do not win; (3) propose alternative ways of conducting the election, etc. We are convinced that the more input the process has, the better and more charitable it will be.

Finally: Lists of potential candidates were complied from: (1) recommendations submitted to the Committee from the membership at large; (2) possible candidates identified by the work of prior Nominations Committee; (3) suggestions offered by the Board of Governors; and (4) names surfaced in discussion of the members of the Nominations Committee.

In identifying prospective nominees, attention was given first and foremost to selecting those who would offer sound leadership of the Society. At the same time, the Committee was conscious that the mission of the CLSA is enhanced when its officers bring a diversity of gifts, backgrounds, and expertise to their service. Thus, the Committee strove to develop a slate of candidates that reflects the rich diversity of the membership, i.e., the vital participation of men and women, both religious and lay.

The following slate of candidates was forwarded to the Board of Governors for presentation to the members at the 2002 Convention of the Society in Cincinnati, Ohio.

*Office of Vice- President/President Elect:*

Reverend Monsignor Mark L. Bartchak (Diocese of Erie)
Sister Ann F. Rehrauer (Order of St. Francis)

*Office of Secretary:*

Deacon Gerald R. Jorgensen (Archdiocese of Dubuque)
Reverend Monsignor Michael J. Cariglio (Diocese of Youngstown)

*Office of Consultor:*

Reverend Patrick Cogan (Atonement Friars)
Reverend Monsignor Frank G. Del Prete (Archdiocese of Newark)
Reverend Paul Hartman (Archdiocese of Milwaukee)
Sister Ann Keevan (Congregation of Saint Joseph)
Reverend Monsignor Tam N. Nguyen (Archdiocese of Oklahoma)
Sister Mary Walsh (School Sister of Notre Dame)

Committee: **Professional Responsibility**

Constituted: *Code of Professional Responsibility*, canon 9c(i), d(i)

Charge: The three senior consultors of the Canon Law Society of America's Board of Governors constitute a standing Committee on Professional Responsibility. The committee shall receive complaints of any party aggrieved with respect to provisions of the *Code of Professional Responsibility*, to make an initial finding that the complaint is not frivolous; and in the event that a majority of the committee considers the complaint to be serious in character, to refer the matter to the hearing officers.

Membership:  Rev. Gregory Bittner, Chairperson
             Sr. Melanie Di Pietro, S.C.
             Rev. Msgr. F. Stephen Pedone

## Annual Report

This report covers the period from October 5, 2001 to September 5, 2002. The member of the Professional Responsibility Committee are Reverends Greg Bitter, Steve Pedone, and Sister Melanie DiPietro. The members are the senior consultors of the Board of Governors of the CLSA. The committee reports no activity as of this date. There have been no referrals requesting inquiry into any unethical conduct.

Committee:    **Resolutions**

Constituted:  CLSA Constitution, Article X

Charge:       The functions of the Committee on Resolutions are:

1. To solicit, develop and draft proposed resolutions which will express the concerns of the Canon Law Society of America;
2. To consult with the membership at large and, in particular with the Board of Governors, the standing and ad hoc committees of the Society, and the organizers of the convention;
3. To formulate resolutions on given points in response to requests of the members of the Society;
4. To compose differences in the formulation of similar proposals and to revise all proposals so that the meaning of each is clear;
5. To encourage resolutions which authentically express in a positive way the activities and concerns of the Society.

Membership:  Barbara Anne Cusack, Chairperson
             Rev. Kelly M. Vandehey
             Rev. Edward F. McGrath

## Annual Report

The three members of the Resolutions Committee consulted by means of conference call and e-mail several times throughout the past year. The activity of the Resolutions Committee at the 2001 Albuquerque Convention was reviewed and discussed, which led to discussing possible ways to improve the procedure for discussing proposed resolutions at the Annual Business Meeting. The Committee asked the BOG to consider the use of computer projection as a standard procedure during the Hearing Session and the Business Meeting and to consider the expense involved in hotel costs for equipment and set up as an ordinary Convention expense. The BOG concurred with this plan and, therefore, computer projection will be used at the 2002 Convention.

The June 2002 edition of the *CLSA Newsletter* put forth the call to membership for resolutions for the Cincinnati 2002 Convention. At the time this annual report was submitted to the Executive Coordinator's office, no resolutions had been proposed to or received by the Committee. The Committee Chair has been informed that two resolutions from the Lay Canonist LISTSERV are in preparation.

## ON-GOING COMMITTEES

Committee:     **Advisory Opinions**

Constituted:   44th Annual Meeting, 1982

Charge:        To issue advisory opinions on the meaning of the canons of the revised code after its promulgation. Such opinions are to provide non-official interpretations in response to requests for them.

Membership: Rev. James I. Donlon, Editor
            Sr. Ann Keevan, C.S.J., Associate Editor
            Sr. Mary Ann Hayes, C.S.J.

### Annual Report

The Committee on Advisory Opinions continued to facilitate the work of soliciting opinions from the membership of the Canon Law Society of America in response to any inquiries which were received. Additionally, the Committee sought from the members of the Society opinions which they may have already rendered to various diocesan officials or religious institutes and superiors. Each inquiry received was sent to one or more canonist(s) for opinions. This procedure was generally successful despite the busy schedules of the various canonists contacted by the Committee. Once the opinions were received by the Committee, they were edited and prepared for publication in the CLSA annual volume entitled *Roman Replies and CLSA Advisory Opinions*.

The Committee has also continued its endeavor at expanding the pool of canonists participating in this annual project of the Society. As it has for the past several years, the Committee has reached out to members of other canon law societies. Thus included in the 2002 edition of *Roman Replies and CLSA Advisory Opinions* will be seen contributions from members of the Canon Law Society of Australia and New Zealand, the Canadian Canon Law Society and the Canon Law Society of Great Britain and Ireland. This involvement of these canonists from other societies and nations broadens the scope and depth of opinions being presented to the membership. Further, the Committee continues in its efforts to recruit new contributors, especially the newer members of the Canon Law Society of America. This endeavor also continues to meet with success. Hopefully these efforts will continue to enhance the annual publication, reflecting the broad spectrum of the CLSA membership on the various canonical issues and thinking, and the types of questions and concerns being addressed within the various dioceses and religious communities. Thus, the Committee believes this will continue to make *Roman Replies and CLSA Advisory Opinions* a valuable tool for all canonists.

The Committee has also continued it efforts in inviting more members of the CLSA (and other canon law societies) to become involved in this annual endeavor, by submitting either responses to queries received by the Committee or responses and opinions already prepared for and submitted to diocesan officials and/or religious superiors. Often these responses already prepared for diocesan officials and/or religious superiors are particularly valuable in that the subject matter being treated concerns issues being presently confronted by other people. When the Committee receives such opinions that had been prepared for diocesan officials and/or religious superiors, the material is carefully editing so as to maintain confidentiality. All references to particular people or places are removed.

The 2002 edition of *CLSA Advisory Opinions* presents approximately fifty opinions, covering a broad spectrum of issue and canons. Thus, in the estimation of the Committee, this year's project has been a successful one. Hopefully the membership will agree!

In conclusion, the Committee on Advisory Opinions expresses its continuing gratitude to the members of the Canon Law Society of America and those others individuals who submitted inquiries and opinions during this past year. It is only as a result of this ongoing contributions and assistance of these canonists, generously sharing time and talent, that *CLSA Advisory Opinions* continues to meet with success and continues to be that valuable tool that so many people find it to be.

Work has already begun on the 2003 edition of *CLSA Advisory Opinions*.

Several questions and opinions have already been received. As ever, the Committee welcomes and invites the participation of all members of the Society. Members may assist in any of several ways.

1) Members may volunteer to be a part of the Committee's tool of canonists to whom queries would be forwarded for response. If any member wishes to be a part of such a pool, please contact the Committee, indicating one's area of particular interests and expertise. This greatly facilitates the Committee's work in submitting questions received.
2) Members are invited and encouraged to forward to the Committee opinions or advisory opinions already prepared for diocesan officials and/or religious superiors. As noted above, the Committee carefully edits these opinions so as to insure confidentiality.
3) Members are invited to forward to the Committee questions that would in turn be forwarded to other canonists for opinions to be published in next year's edition of *Roman Replies and CLSA Advisory Opinions*.
4) The Committee welcomes any other suggestions or the recommendations members may have.

Contributions and suggestions may be forwarded to the Committee on Advisory Opinions at the following address:

Rev. James I. Donlon
Diocese of Albany
40 North Main Avenue
Albany, New York 12203
(518) 453-6620
james.donlon@rcda.org

Committee:   **Editorial Board for the Collection of American Jurisprudence**

Constituted:   By the Board of Governors pursuant to Resolution seven at the 56th Annual Convention of the CLSA (Atlanta, Georgia, 1994)

Charge:   To publish regularly (no less than tri-annually) a collection of selected marriage nullity decisions issued by various tribunals throughout the United States.

Membership:  Msgr. John A. Alesandro, J.C.D., Chair
Msgr. J. James Cuneo, J.C.D.
Msgr. William A. Varvaro, J.C.D.
Sr. Victoria Vondenberger, RSM, J.C.L.

311

While many *In iure* sections of Rotal decisions and diocesan tribunals have been published, not many studies have explored the way that such canonical and theological explanations are concretely applied to the specific set of facts brought before the judges. Pursuant to a resolution passed at the CLSA's 1994 National Convention in Atlanta, the CLSA Board of Governors charged the editors of this Project with the task of producing a sampling of complete decisions from tribunals in the United States. The goal was to show not only the legal principles but the way that such principles were applied in particular cases through judicial reasoning.

Initially, a cautious response to the editorial board's call for decisions led to considerable delay. Eventually, however, over a two-year period, approximately sixty decisions were solicited. After a review of each by at least two committee members, about half were accepted for publication, representing in the opinion of the editors a reasonable cross-section of approaches and reasoning. The editors selected decisions in which the argument seemed particularly cogent, or the issues were unusual, or the canonical and theological principles of a ground of nullity were uniquely applied to the facts.

After a second review, the decisions were put into a uniform format. This proved to be more time-consuming than anticipated since, in order to protect anonymity, the editors decided to standardize certain details and replace references to specific tribunals, places or persons with fictional names. The final manuscript was readied during the spring of 2002. As with other CLSA publications, a special pre-Convention workshop, using the text, was arranged for Cincinnati, with two of the editors as presenters and facilitators.

The final task of sanitizing the sentences would not have been possible without the dedicated service of Tom Rich, a permanent deacon of the Diocese of Rockville Centre and student of canon law at CUA, who completed this tedious work. The editors also owe a debt of gratitude to all the tribunal personnel who took the time to research their decisions and submit samples for the committee's consideration. As this project is at long last brought to completion, the editors are hopeful that the goals of the CLSA's original resolution have been adequately met and that, if the publication proves valuable, it will pave the way for additional studies of jurisprudence among the tribunals in the United States.

Committee:     *Canon Law Digest* – Vol. 12 +

Constituted:   Board of Governors, 1998

Charge:        To prepare volumes 12 and beyond of the *Canon Law Digest*.

Membership:    Sr. Dominica Brennan, O.P., Chairperson

Annual Report

The committee completed its work with the compilation of the selections for *Canon Law Digest* XII and forwarded these to the Office of the Executive Co-ordinator after the April 2002 Board of Governors' Meeting. Preparation of the materials go forward with formatting and indexing of text. Pre-publication sale brochures were sent out in the September *CLSA Newsletter*.

Committee:     **Civil and Canon Law**

Constituted:   47th Annual Meeting, 1985

Charge:        1. Identify those norms of the code which require the Church to defer to secular law;
               2. Clarify the effects of secular law on canon law in various states and local jurisdictions;
               3. Identify those issues, organizations, resources, publications, and personnel to facilitate communications between canon and secular law;
               4. Identify possible areas of cooperation between canon and secular law.

Membership:    Dr. Diane L. Barr, Chairperson
               Rev. Joseph L. Tagg, III
               Rev. Thomas Paprocki

Annual Report

*(No report available at time of printing.)*

Committee:    **Eastern Canon Law**

Constituted:  46th Annual Meeting, 1984

Charge:       To serve CLSA as a resource body in the area of Eastern canon law and interritual matters, and to aid the CLSA membership in understanding the Eastern Catholic Churches.

Membership:   Rev. Richard Whetstone, Chairperson
              Rev. George D. Gallaro
              Rev. Frank Marini

Annual Report

*(No report available at time of printing.)*


Committee:    **Electronic Media**

Constituted:  Board of Governors, 1995

Charge:       To explore and develop ways that the CLSA can make use of electronic media.

Membership:   Rev. Paul Hartmann, Chairperson
              Rev. Lucian Martinez, SJ
              Mr. Pete Vere
              Rev. Arthur Espelage, OFM (*ex officio*)

Annual Report

OLD BUSINESS:

Since the April, 2002 report, the Committee has continued to focus primarily on the future of the CLSA website (www.clsa.org) and a series of questions that were raised by the BOG relative to the recommended Mission Statement. Consideration of these questions and recommendations are part of an ongoing process to improve the usefulness of the Society's on-line presence.

It is still be the goal of this committee to retain a webmaster and web-site hosting service where both maintain a close and consistent working relationship with the Office of the Executive Coordinator; given the costs and training involved with such a move, it was decided to take an interim step that will continue the improvements needed at the CLSA website (www.clsa.org). The decision has been made to move web-site hosting to Catholic Online. The URL (www.clsa.org) will remain the same. Transition steps were taken in August and September, 2002. A more complete report of this interim hosting step and the transition has been provided to the Board of Governors.

The Committee will shortly be requesting of the President the appointment of a new member who presently is a webmaster to a number of Catholic websites (all of which are presently hosted by Catholic Online). This is a move that entails no new costs and will bring new perspectives, and new blood to our website design. The committee is deeply thankful for all the work on the website put in by Fr. Paul Counce since its inception.

NEW BUSINESS:

The committee continues exploring the concept of electronic publishing, in order to forward a recommendation to the BOG and the general membership concerning the feasibility of making certain CLSA works available on-line for a fee. We also hope to do more research into Print-On-Demand (POD) technology, which makes it feasible to print one copy of a book at a time, thus reducing the cost of overhead for books with limited marketing potential as well as warehousing and storage [...] etc. A more complete report detailing each of these publishing opportunities has been provided to the Board of Governors.

| | |
|---|---|
| Committee: | **Institutes of Consecrated Life and Societies of Apostolic Life Committee** |
| Constituted: | On-going Committee |
| Charge: | 1. To identify and research topics with significant ramification for institutes of consecrated life and societies of apostolic life;<br>2. To propose at least one topic and speaker for a pre-convention seminar;<br>3. To identify those issues, organizations, resources, publications and personnel to facilitate a better understanding of developments in canon law regarding consecrated life. |
| Membership: | Sr. Rosemary Smith, SC, Chairperson<br>Sr. Nancy Reynolds, SP<br>Rev. Warren Brown, OMI |

Annual Report

The committee was constituted in February 2002 and the members met twice by conference call in order to develop a preliminary report for the April BOG meeting, as requested. The committee submitted recommendations for topics and presenters for upcoming conventions but, given the time frame, was unable to develop an overall plan or recommendations for research. Subsequent constraints placed on the Committee prevented further work on the mandate given to it. The committee anticipants meetings in conjunction with the convention.


Committee:   **Investment Review**

Membership: Rev. Msgr. Alexander J. Palmieri, Chairperson (*ex officio*)
Rev. John P. McDonagh
Sr. Nancy Reynolds, S.P.
Sr. Margaret Stallmeyer, C.D.P.


Annual Report

The Investment Review Committee met three times by conference call, on March 13, May 3, and August 12, 2002, with the purpose of reviewing the reports from Congress Asset Management Company (CAMC) regarding the general "CLSA Account" and the "Scholarship Fund." The reviews focused on the conformity of the asset allocations of our portfolios to the "Investment Guidelines" for policy targets and ranges, as approved by BOG. Attention was also directed to a review of the social and ethical responsibility of the various companies in which CAMC has invested our funds. After questions raised by the committee members were clarified by CAMC, no major concerns were raised in these areas.

The cumulative performance of the portfolios and the funds management costs were also reviewed, resulting in no major concerns in these areas. The committee realistically admits that the size of the CLSA portfolios does not provide for the degree of diversification possible with larger portfolios. As with nearly all other investors, the volatility of the markets at this time had a negative impact upon CLSA investments as well. However, despite the present environment, the committee strongly believes that management of our funds by CAMC has been responsible for keeping us ahead of the benchmarks.

It was necessary to withdraw $30,000 from the "CLSA Account" during FY 2001-2002, in order to pay bills resulting from the shortfall of anticipated income due to the fact that several publications, which had been previously budgeted for income, never went to press in time.

The committee extends its appreciation to our fund managers for their performance.

Committee:     **Marriage Research**

Constituted:   1978

Charge:        From 1984 Convention:

1. To identify specific areas of marriage research;
2. To identify scholars who have done or will do research in those particular areas and who will produce manuscripts for publication;
3. To facilitate the publication of this research either in the CLSA-sponsored publication *Marriage Studies* or in other scholarly or professional journals.

Membership: Rev. Mr. Gerald T. Jorgensen, Chairperson
            Ms. M. Margaret Gillett
            Rev. John P. Donovan
            Rev. Msgr. Ronald W. Gainer

Annual Report

Throughout this past year the Marriage Research Committee's major endeavor has been the completion of a resource document currently entitled *Composition of Law Sections for Marriage Nullity Cases: Sources*. As noted in last year's report, the project has evolved in multiple directions since the charge was first given to the Committee, ultimately resulting in two related but different publication endeavors. At present the Committee has completed work on the second publication endeavor to come out of the initial charge to the Committee following the 1994 Atlanta Convention. A draft document that consists of a specific resource section on 18 different grounds that might be joined as the *caput nullitatis* or *dubium* in a marriage case has been compiled. Fifteen different canonists have been involved in the development of the various grounds, with some canonists working conjointly and others working individually. An update on the entire project was held for those canonist contributors attending the 2001 Convention in Albuquerque. Then, in early January 2002, the Committee met at the offices of the Tribunal for the Diocese of Dallas to begin the final editing process in the document's development.

After meeting in Dallas, committee members worked diligently to finalize a document for final review by the Publications Committee and the Board of Governors. The Committee continues to be most grateful to all the contributors and the obvious work that they have put into this ambitious endeavor. This year marked substantial secretarial contributions by the Tribunal staff from the Diocese of Dallas, for which the Committee is most appreciative and grateful. Finally, the Committee endorsed the concept that hard copy be published accompanied by a copy in an electronic or digital format. The Committee intends to have the document in actual publication by the end of 2002. Without a doubt, this Committee has amassed innumerable hours working on this project.

In addition, the Committee continued to endorse the concept that the annual convention program include at least one program specific to marriage issues, addressing either jurisprudence or other related matters, and that, at least biannually, a pre-convention workshop address marriage issues. The 2002 Convention included both a pre-convention workshop and two convention programs involving marriage matters. As future pre-convention workshops, the Committee suggested the following topics: "Hot-Spots" in Tribunal Practice: Theory and Practice; Substantial Flaws in the Decisions of US Tribunals as Explicated in Rotal Decisions since 1993. For future convention programs, the following topics were suggested: an update on the proposed Vatican instruction on marriage nullity cases; the relationship between the *CIC* and the *CCEO* for marriage nullity cases. The Committee continues to solicit from the CLSA membership other ideas for pre-convention workshops and for convention programs. Not only topic suggestions but also possible presenters are also welcomed. Suggestions should be communicated directly to any committee member.

Committee:   **Publications**

Constituted:   Board of Governors, 2000

Charge:   1. To assist editors and authors of publications and other materials being developed on behalf of the Society;
2. To have immediate oversight of the works during the course of the preparation, seeing to it that they conform to language use, editorial and other publications guidelines established by the Society;
3. To make appropriate recommendations to the Board of Governors concerning the projects under its supervision.

318

Membership: Rev. Modesto Perez, Chairperson
Rev. Randolph Calvo
Sr. Joyce Hoben, S.N.D.
Rev. Arthur J. Espelage, O.F.M., *ex officio*

Annual Report

*(No report available at time of printing.)*

Committee: **Roman Replies**

Constituted: Board of Governors, October 1980

Charge: To collect and publish recent responses from various Roman
dicasteries which would be of wide interest to CLSA members.

Membership: Rev. Msgr. F. Stephen Pedone, Editor
Sr. Rose McDermott, S.S.J., Associate Editor

Annual Report

While the actual report to the membership is the volume itself, the Preliminary
report is presented for the Board of Governors and *Proceedings*. The Committee
is most grateful to all who responded, especially those who provided material for
publication. Several letters were again received from diocesan officials indicating
they had nothing to present for publication. Some noted how important this
publication is in their ministry and they look forward to its publication every year.
The Committee encourages the membership to continue to provide these replies
from the Holy See because of the benefit and assistance they provide.

There are twelve entries slated for publication this year. As before, the entries
will be arranged according to the canons of the *Code of Canon Law*. Hierarchical
recourse against a decree of a bishop claiming violation of rights (c. 221); Merger
of an Institute of Diocesan Right with an Institute of Pontifical Right (c. 582);
Dispensation from the Impediment of the Bond of Marriage (c. 643, §1, 2°);
Complementary Legislation Concerning Lay Preaching (c. 766); Complementary
Legislation Regarding Lay Teaching on Radio and Television (c. 772, §2);
Participation of Clerics and Members of Religious Institutes in Radio and
Television Programs (c. 831, §2); Use of Low Gluten Hosts (c. 924, §2); Use of
Mustum (c. 925); Dispensation from the Irregularity Regarding the Reception of
Orders Incurred in Procuring an Abortion (c. 1041, 4°); Appellate Tribunal

Admitting Case to an Ordinary Examination and Adding New Grounds of Nullity (c. 1682); Request for Transfer Between Churches Denied (*CIC* c. 35).

The Committee extends its gratitude to the National Conference of Catholic Bishops, the Congregation for Bishops, the Congregation for Clergy, the Congregation for Divine Worship and Discipline of the Sacraments, the Congregation for Institutes of Consecrated Life and Societies of Apostolic Life, the Congregation for Oriental Churches, and the Roman Rota for their support and assistance.

Committee:    **Scholarship Fund**

Constituted:  Board of Governors, 1987

Charge:       1. To conserve, invest, and disburse the monies of the Scholarship Fund according to the criteria established by the CLSA;
              2. To establish for approval by the Board of Governors the process for selecting recipients of the scholarship.

Membership: Rev. Langes Silva
              Rev. Lou Sirianni
              Rev. Msgr. Alex Palmieri *(ex officio)*
              Barbara A. Bettwy, Chair

Annual Report

The annual Scholarship Appeal was conducted by a letter to the membership of the CLSA in Advent of 2001. From that appeal, $ 6,348.00 was raised.

On April 23, 2002, Reverend Arthur Espelage, Executive Coordinator of the CLSA, mailed to all the committee members a packet of information on the scholarship applicants for this year's award. There were two applicants for the committee's consideration.

On May 20, 2002, the Scholarship Committee met via a conference call that was previously established and agreed upon. Reverend Langes Silva from Salt Lake City, Reverend Louis Sirianni from Rochester, Reverend Monsignor Alex Palmieri from Philadelphia, and myself from Erie, were all present on the call. Following discussion by the Committee members, an award recipient was chosen by unanimous vote. The recipient is Reverend Kenneth Laverone, OFM, a priest of the Order Friar Minor from Monterey, California who will be studying for the

JCL at the *Angelicum* in Rome.

According to policy, the Chair notified the President of the CLSA, Reverend Kevin McKenna, of the Committee's recommendation, with copies of that letter being sent to the Executive Coordinator, Reverend Arthur Espelage, and to the CLSA Vice-President, Reverend Lawrence O'Keefe. The President of the CLSA has the task of writing to inform Father Laverone that he was the recipient of the 2002 Scholarship award which this years totals $13,000.00. The Chair also wrote to thank the other applicant for this year's award and informed him that another recipient had been chosen.

The Committee then turned its attention to the continuing situation of so few qualified applicants each year for the Scholarship award. The Committee discussed the advisability of eliminating the requirement that an applicant must be a citizen of the United States. If this requirement were dropped, more persons would be eligible to apply for the scholarship. The Committee is aware that the original intent of the scholarship was to aid in the education of decreed canonists to serve in the dioceses of the United States. It discussed the possibility that the requirement that the recipient work for three years in canonical service in the United States might be sufficient to meet the original objective. The Committee is interested in encouraging more people to apply for the scholarship while at the same time does not want to undermine the original purpose for establishing the award. The Committee decided to recommend this matter to the Board of Governors for its deliberation.

Committee: **Translation of Legislative Texts**

Constituted: 2000

Charge: To translate the new norms of the Roman Rota and to undertake the translation of other legislative texts at the direction of the Board of Governors, with appropriate authorization and permission of the Apostolic See.

Membership: Very Rev. John A. Renken

Annual Report

The task of translating the *Norms of the Tribunal of the Roman Rota* will be completed and ready to present to the BOG in October 2002. Also to be completed is *Rules to be Observed to Declare the Nullity of Ordination*.

Also completed and submitted to the Office of the Executive Coordinator was the document entitled, *The Exercise of the Function of Legal Representative and Advocate Before the Dicasteries of the Roman Curia*, which will be inserted into *CLD* XII.

PROJECTS/TASK FORCES

Committee:    *Annotated Bibliography 1981 – 1995*

Constituted:   Board of Governors, 1996

Charge:       To make a bibliography of the writings of the CLSA members from 1981-1995.

Membership: Rev. Mark Mealey, O.S.F.S.

Annual Report

In the Fall of 2001, the project was granted permission from the Canon Law Society of Great Britain and Ireland (CLSGB&I) to use the annotation provided in the *Abstracts* for articles by CLSA members, who have died or are unable to compose a annotation of their articles or addresses, provided the CLSGB&I receives credit. At the present time, the committee is working on the integration of the Abstracts into the project format. In addition. the committee is reviewing the works cited in the project to compose a detailed index of works

Committee:    **Canonical Advocacy Study Committee**

Constituted:   Board of Governors, 1996

Charge:       To initiate and carry on a study to develop recommendations for the facilitation of informal canonical advocacy throughout the United States as a means of accomplishing the equitable resolution of disputes outside the formal processes.

Membership: Rev. Gregory Ingels, Chair
                Rev. Msgr. Craig A. Cox
                Sr. Sandra Makowski, SSMN
                Rev. Kenneth Schwanger

322

The committee has conducted a survey for the purpose of completing its study for the purpose of facilitating advocacy within the Society. This survey was distributed to the membership of the Society in the February, 2002, issue of the *CLSA Newsletter*. Thus far, 111 responses have been received; and they are currently being compiled.

When completed, this survey will provide information concerning a participant's involvement in the following areas:

- the number of cases in which canonical advice has been offered by a member and whether the matter was resolved outside of a formal process or necessitated formal advocacy;
- an identification of the nature of clients, that is, individuals who are either cleric, religious, or lay; religious institutes and societies; dioceses or other ecclesiastical authorities;
- the nature of the disputes which have given rise to need for canonical advice or advocacy;
- the nature of the assistance given, whether through mediation, the preparation of correspondence, or involvement in a formal process;
- the manner in which the matter was resolved;
- whether fees are charged for canonical advice and advocacy and the nature of the fee structure;
- whether, in the case of clerics or religious, the Ordinary or Superior has supported, endorsed or permitted an individual's involvement in providing canonical advice or advocacy and whether there any limitations have been placed on this service;
- whether the participant would be interested or want his or her name placed in a CLSA sponsored Registry of canonists who provide advice or advocacy.

Upon completion of the compilation of the survey a written report will be provided to the Board of Governors.

Committee:    *Ex Corde Ecclesiae* **Application**

Constituted:  Board of Governors, 1999

Charge:       To formulate and suggest to the appropriate office or committee of the NCCB measures toward the resolution of remaining issues and the completion of remaining portions of the Application norms. [The task force will report to the membership of the Society at an appropriate time.]

Membership: Rev. James Conn, S.J., Chairperson
Rev. David M. O'Connell, C.M.
Rev. Msgr. Robert P. Deeley

Annual Report

At its April 2002 meeting in Chicago, the BOG acknowledged that the 1999 mandate of this Committee has been accomplished, namely, to offer assistance to the USCCB in implementing the *Ex corde Ecclesiae* application and drafting guidelines for the academic *mandatum* of canon 812. At the same time, the BOG has asked the Committee to continue its service in the foreseeable future as a monitoring vehicle on the actual implementation of the Application and Guidelines.

The Committee accepts this extended mandate and will report to the BOG from time to time on any major situations or problems with the implementation of the Application and Guidelines as they may arise.

Committee: **General Editor of a *Festschrift* in Honor of Reverend Lawrence Wrenn**

Constituted: By the Board of Governors pursuant to Resolution Two at the 61st Annual Convention of the CLSA (Minneapolis, MN, 1999)

Charge: To oversee the publication of a *festschrift* in honor of Reverend Lawrence Wrenn

Membership: Rev. Msgr. Frederick C. Easton, General Editor

Annual Report

At its 61st Annual Convention, the members of the Canon Law Society of America approved the following resolution:

Be it resolved that the Canon Law Society of America, as an expression of its appreciation, gratitude, and esteem for his contribution to its publications, shall commission a *festschrift* in honor of Lawrence G. Wrenn.

At the meeting of the Board of Governors following this convention, the Board appointed Fred C. Easton as the General Editor to see to the completion of this resolution.

Since the last report, Patrick Cogan, S.A. volunteered as an assistant editor. Both he and the General Editor have read and edited each manuscript. All of the materials necessary for the *festschrift* have been sent and received at the Office of the Executive Coordinator. The next steps will include the task of formatting and preparing a camera-ready copy. After the editors have reviewed this text then the printers will prepare their proof copy known as the "blue lines." As this General Editor submits his report, he expects that we shall have joy of presenting a copy of the book, *The Art of the Good and Equitable,* to our honoree, Lawrence G. Wrenn, after the first session of the 2002 Convention in Cincinnati, Ohio.

As we go to press, there were 269 people who wanted to place their name in the book and who generously contributed at least $50.00. Among these contributors were cardinals, bishops, archbishops and some institutions as well as canonists and canonical practitioners. The names of some of Father Wrenn's family and friends are also in this list.

Thus, with the completion of the 2002 general convention, the work of this General Editor should be complete and this report should be his last regarding this marvelous and inspiring project.

Committee:  **Lay Ministry Handbook**

Constituted:  2001

Charge:       Mandate is to produce for publications a lay ministry handbook.

Membership:  Mr. Stephen Osborn
             Ms. Zabrina Decker
             Rev. Msgr. Ronald Gainer
             Ms. Linda Weigel, Chairperson

Annual Report

The mandate given to the Lay Ministry Handbook Committee is to produce for publication a lay ministry handbook. The book is to be a practical application of the law, for use by canonists and non-canonists. The initial contacts with the committee took place through e-mail in the late Spring of 2002. In June, the chair contacted Rev. Modesto Perez, Chairperson of the CLSA Publications Committee. The committee Chair set up a conference call to take place on August 5, 2002. An agenda was sent beforehand so the members could prepare for the conference call.

The following **topics** were discussed as possible chapters for inclusion in the handbook:

- Basic concepts of lay ministry, including those founds in General norms, and documents of Vatican II. The difference between baptismal ministry and official lay ministry, or "ecclesial lay ministry".
- Lay Ministry in the Code.
- Lay Ministry as a distinct vocation.
- How to discern the call of lay ministry.
- Models of lay ministry.
- Qualifications of lay ministers.
- Training and certification of lay ministers. Models for preparation.
- Hiring lay ministers with sample job descriptions.
- Contracts/work agreements/finances/insurance/liability for lay ministers.
- Rights and obligations of lay ministers/lay ministers in irregular marriages.
- Women in lay ministry.
- Terminology for lay ministers.
- Lay Ministry in the eastern code and churches.
- Lay ministers in the Chancery.
- Relationship between lay ministers and ordained ministers.
- Multicultural issues for lay ministers.
- Future Directions in Lay Ministry.

We surfaced numerous names of possible **authors**, both lay and ordained canonists. We also discussed possible non- canonist authors.

We discussed a tentative **timeline**:
- October 2002 convention – meet to finalize topics for the handbook and to further discuss authors. Each member will be assigned certain topics and authors. Detail work of the committee, and decide on format for author contributions and ways to follow up with authors and materials.
- November 2002 – complete contact of authors.
- June 2003 – authors to submit first draft of article and materials.
- August 2003 – editorial comments on first draft.
- August 2003 – send work to authors for review and critique.
- October 2003 convention – meet with committee and all authors for comments and critique.
- January 2004 – authors submit any redrafts to committee. Send to outside

reviewer, expert in the field to review entire work and offer editorial comments.

- March 2003 – outside expert in the field to review the entire work and offer editorial comments.
- April 2004 – send comments to authors. They may choose to make last additions or refinements. Authors also to submit a glossary for canonical terms.
- June 2004 – Committee meet with final text for final editing and submission of handbook.
- August 2004 – final text to CLSA publications office.

The committee also decided to look through recent issues of *Jurist, Studia Canonica* and *Origins* for suggested topics and authors, as well as through recent doctoral dissertations.

The committee will meet at the 2002 convention in Cincinnati.

Committee: **Marriage Procedures Handbook**

Constituted: 2001

Charge: Mandate is to prepare a practical marriage procedures handbook.

Membership: Rev. Daniel Smilanic, Chairperson
Sr. Victoria Vondenberger, R.S.M.
Mr. Larry Price

Annual Report

The *Marriage Procedures Handbook* Committee met in Chicago from Wednesday, August 21st to Thursday, August 22nd.

The work involved three tasks: refining the table of contents into developed sections that could be committed to various authors, drafting a focus instruction for the authors, and surfacing the names of authors. A concern that informed the entire effort was a reasonable suspicion that a new *Instruction* on the formal marriage nullity process is forth-coming from Rome. There appeared to be some reason to believe that the new *Instruction* might introduce some significant changes and that it might be published this Fall (2002). The committee realizes that the Table of Contents may have to be adjusted if a new *Instruction* is published. The committee will meet next at 2 pm on Monday, October 7th, during registration for the CLSA Convention.

The committee understands that this Handbook is destined to assist the average diocesan Tribunal practitioner. It is intended to compliment the *Code of Canon Law* and to have a very strong task-oriented flavor. We understand that while some of the users may not have a formal degree in Canon Law, it is designed for those with formal training in Canon Law who need a guide to conduct formal marriage nullity trials in a diocesan Tribunal.

With regard to the refinement of the table of contents, a copy has been included with this report. With the exception of Chapter V, every other chapter has been subdivided into two sections. The points made under each section will guide the authors. As the work of this committee progresses and reactions to the Table of Contents are received, the points for each section will develop more. Every chapter will be concluded with examples of documents to illustrate how the points made in the chapter could be implemented. If a willing contributor is found for each section, the work would require 11 authors. Each author would be asked to write about 15 to 20 pages. The form and layout of the Handbook has to be very accessible so that it can be quickly usable for the practitioner with a specific question. The index has to be thoroughly done.

The authors will be asked to write in a very practical, but not pedestrian fashion. In other words, while the Handbook will not be a scholarly, technical work, it also will not be for general public consumption. Insofar as is possible, each author will be asked to note whatever adaptations would have to be made for: more Catholic or less Catholic areas, more urban or more rural areas. Also each author will be asked to present practices that are ideal, and practices that are acceptable, and practices that may be problematic. For example, there is a divergence of practices concerning hearing a case as the forum of the Petitioner when the whereabouts of the Respondent are unknown. The authors will not repeat the Code; they will presume that the reader has a copy of the Code with which he/she is familiar. As recommended in the Chicago Style Manual, a grid will be constructed to guide the authors' use of capitalization; this was done for the recent book on Jurisprudence.

It was thought that the selection of authors should be delayed until the October meeting for two reasons. First of all, by the October meeting a new *Instruction* may be published. Secondly, it will be easier to identify and contact possible authors at the CLSA convention. Between now and the October meeting, the committee gave itself the task of surfacing names of authors and refining the table of contents.

# MARRIAGE PROCEDURES HANDBOOK

(developing Table of Contents)

I.  Assessing the Situation

   a) local assistance & support
   initial contact
   discussion of possible Tribunals
   cost of the process & timeline

   b) determining ecclesial status of the marriage and the parties
   'formal act'
   type of process and options

II.  Commencing the Formal Case

   petition & *libellus*
   competence
   Promoter of Justice
   citation of the Respondent

   joinder of issues
   changing grounds & adding grounds
   re-starting discontinued cases
   transferring cases

III.  Gathering of Proofs

   Parties
   Witnesses

   professional reports
   public records
   documents
   expert evaluations

IV.  Publication & Discussion

   Decree of Conclusion
   Publication of the Acts: citation of the parties and their response
   new proofs

Advocate's Briefs
Defender of the Bond

V. Resolution of Case

Abatement, Renunciation
Decision: Judges, Assessors

Sentence
standard of proof
Publication of the Sentence
handling negatives

Consequences of the Sentence

Appeals
Prohibitions/Restrictions (*vetitum*) & Recommendations/Cautions (*monitum*)
interactions with Rome

VII.  Tribunal Personnel

role & job definitions
organizational options
training programs & continuing education

outreach
speaker's bureau
relations with the wider diocese

Committee:     **Parish Viability**

Constituted:   Board of Governors, 1999

Charge:        To develop criteria for the viability of parishes.  To draft or assemble a set of standards, i.e., both canonical requirements and pastoral expectations, for parish communities and the ministries within them.  The criteria or standards are to be suitable to assess the health and effectiveness of parishes. The task force is to complete its work in two years time, and present its report, both in published forma and in a convention seminar, to the membership of the Society.

Membership:  Most Rev. R. Daniel Conlon, Chairperson
             Rev. Msgr. Ricardo E. Bass
             Mrs. Siobhan M. Verbeek

Annual Report

In the spring of 2002 the Parish Viability Committee submitted to the Board of Governors a revised version of the Parish Self-Evaluation Instrument. This version took into consideration the ideas which had been expressed by CLSA members at the hearing at the 2001 convention. At its spring meeting, the Board of Governors accepted this version and asked the Executive Coordinator to publish it in the way he deemed best for the good of the Society. Thus, the committee has completed its mandate.

Committee:     **Rome 2005 Convention**

Constituted:   Board of Governors, 1999

Charge:        To coordinate and oversee all aspects of the CLSA annual convention in Rome in 2005.

Membership:  Very Rev. Lawrence A. DiNardo, Chairperson
             Rev. Msgr. Frederick C. Easton
             Rev. Msgr. Nevin Klinger
             Rev. Modesto Perez
             Sr. Francine Quillin, P.B.V.M.
             Very Rev. John A. Renken
             Sr. Nancy Reynolds, S.P.

Rev. Lawrence O'Keefe
Rev. Arthur J. Espelage, O.F.M., *ex officio*
Mrs. Rita F. Joyce, *ex officio*

## Annual Report

Since the last report to the membership, the Committee, with the assistance of the General Convention Chair and Nix & Associates, has prepared and RFP (Request for Proposal) to various travel agencies for costs and packages to Rome for the Convention. This matter will be discussed at the Committee meeting in Cincinnati. The committee intends on presenting a full report with recommendations to the Board of Governors at its meeting in January of 2003.

The Committee will meet at the Cincinnati Convention to develop the program for the Rome Convention. The results of the survey will be used as the basis for discussing and planning the Convention program.

Committee: **Selection of Bishops**

Constituted: Board of Governors, 1987

Charge: To study the actual process for the appointment of bishops and make recommendations for its possible betterment.

Membership: Mr. J. Michael Ritty
Rev. James A. Coriden

## Annual Report

1. A final report is being prepared for submission to the BOG by the October, 2002 meeting. The assistance of CARA and Tom Green have contributed to the information that will be presented. The data gathered will show the current (as of June 1, 2002) demographic background of bishops. The current selection process is presented in as much detail as is available. The recommendations will provide elements of the current process as well as areas which might be enhanced.

2. Based upon the Mandate provided to the committee, the current work is considered completed.

3. Some additional suggestions for future work of the committee would include

a review of the recommendations and their implementation, the continued monitoring of the demographic data available on bishops, and the continued review of the selection process.

# REPORT TO THE CLSA MEMBERSHIP ON THE
# SELECTION OF BISHOPS

Committee:
J. Michael Ritty, chair
James A. Coriden

with additional assistance from:
Rev. Msgr. Thomas J. Green
Mary Gautier, Ph.D.
Sr. Mary Ann Hayes, CSJ
Sr. Marilyn Vassalo, CSJ

PREFACE

The Selection of Bishops Committee submits this report to the Board of Governors of the Canon Law Society of America. This report is a result of many hours of work by many people.

This committee was originally established by a resolution passed by the CLSA in 1996.[1]

The resolution stated:

Be It Resolved That:

1. The CLSA Board of Governors appoint a task force to study the actual process for the appointment of bishops and make recommendations for its possible betterment.

2. The task force shall report its findings and recommendations to the membership no later than the 1998 convention.

The charge to the present committee was " To study the  actual process for the appointment of bishops and make recommendations for its possible betterment."

The present committee was constituted in June, 2001 to build on the work of

---

[1] We note that a previous committee of the same name existed during the 1970s and 1980s. There was much work produced by that committee and its chair throughout most of those years, Fr. James Provost. This committee is thankful for that previous work.

previous committees. Since that time, work has ensued on the present study. The committee has interpreted its mandate in the following manner:

- to review the manner in which bishops have been selected historically;
- to present the current process of selecting bishops;
- to examine the demographic data available on current US bishops; and
- to present suggestions for the betterment of the selection process.

Special thanks are given to the Center for Applied Research in the Apostolate (CARA) at Georgetown University for sharing their database of information on bishops with Sr. Mary Anne Hayes, C.S.J. who prepared the initial database of information regarding the current bishops for this study. Special thanks, also, to Mary Gautier, Ph.D. of CARA for her work in evaluating the data base and in preparing much of the information presented below.[2] Very special thanks to Rev. Msgr. Thomas J. Green who stepped in almost as a committee member and assisted with the bibliography offered at the end of this report and for his assistance and wise counsel throughout this process.

The data gathered will show the current (as of June 1, 2002) demographic background of bishops. The current selection process is presented in as much detail as is available. The recommendations provide elements of the current process which are seen as useful and areas which might be enhanced.

While this report is respectfully submitted to the CLSA Board of Governors, it is suggested that the dialogue begun here be opened to the entire membership through a presentation or hearing at the annual convention. This will allow a wider forum for concerns to be raised as well as allow the opportunity to hear a wider range of suggestions for the betterment of the process.

---

[2] We note here that CARA will be continuing to update this database so that it will be available for future use and analysis.

The clergy sex abuse scandal of 2002 spotlighted two problematic factors related to the selection of bishops. One was the fact that five auxiliary bishops of Boston who were implicated in decisions there[3] are now all diocesan ordinaries elsewhere in the nation. The other was the transfer of Bishop Anthony O'Connell to the diocese of Palm Beach in 1999 after the diocese of Jefferson City had settled a suit against him for sexual abuse in 1996. In Palm Beach he replaced Bishop J. Keith Symons, the first U.S. bishop to resign (in 1998) because of sexual involvement with boys.[4]

The first of these factors says nothing about any fault or wrongdoing of the former Boston auxiliaries, but it speaks clearly about one of the major phenomena regarding the bishop selection process: three-fourths of bishops in the United States were first ordained as auxiliary bishops, usually in one of the larger archdioceses.[5] They remained auxiliaries for about of six years before becoming diocesan ordinaries.[6],[7] They were chosen for their loyalty and service to the bishop or archbishop, who was their own diocesan ordinary in the overwhelming number of cases, and then they were sent on to distant places, usually in other provinces, to become diocesan ordinaries.

The second event reveals a failure in the consultation involved in the selection process. It goes without saying that Bishop O'Connell would never have been moved to Palm Beach to replace Bishop Symons if anyone in the information-gathering process had known of the out-of-court settlement in Jefferson City. If the papal nuncio or the archbishops of St. Louis or Louisville had known of the settlement, it is inconceivable that the appointment would have gone forward. The president of the USCCB called the failure of the Jefferson City diocese to notify church officials of past sexual abuse by Bishop O'Connell before his promotion "a travesty." "In my humble opinion there is a serious obligation on the part of

---

[3] *The New York Times*, April 18, 2002.

[4] Associated Press report by Ken Thomas, March 8, 2002. O'Connell resigned his see on March 8, 2002, when it was revealed and he admitted that he had sexually abused a teen-aged student from 1977 to 1980 in the seminary which he headed in Hannibal, Missouri. Diocesan officials in Jefferson City, Missouri, settled out of court (for $125,000) a civil suit brought by the student, yet O'Connell was transferred to Palm Beach from Knoxville, Tennessee (where he had served as ordinary since 1988) in 1999.

[5] Thomas Reese, *A Flock of Shepherds: The National Conference of Catholic Bishops* (Kansas City, MO: Sheed & Ward, 1992) 7. In the twenty years from 1980 to 2000 the Archdiocese of Boston was served by sixteen auxiliary bishops. Eight of them have gone on to become ordinaries in eleven dioceses and archdioceses. Source: *The Official Catholic Directory.*

[6] Thomas Reese, *Archbishop: Inside the Power Structure of the American Catholic Church* (San Francisco: Harper & Row, 1989) 28.

[7] The above averages are confirmed in this current study cf. pages 9 and 10.

anyone, in conscience, to make such matters known," said Bishop Wilton Gregory. The Jefferson City diocesan attorney admitted that in hindsight he should have contacted the apostolic nuncio, but that "the problem was that there was no definite procedure."[8]

CURRENT BISHOPS OF THE UNITED STATES

In Fall 2001 the Canon Law Society of America (CLSA) engaged the Center for Applied Research in the Apostolate (CARA) at Georgetown University to conduct an analysis of the 294 active bishops that currently comprise the United States Conference of Catholic Bishops (USCCB). CARA and CLSA jointly compiled a database of demographic information on these bishops, primarily from information provided in the *Membership Photo Directory* published by the USCCB and from information published on the USCCB web site and on several official diocesan web sites. This database includes active bishops of both Latin Rite and of the Eastern Churches that belong to the USCCB, but excludes retired bishops and bishops that are assigned to the Vatican.

This brief analysis describes some characteristics of these bishops, including their age, age at ordination, where they attended seminary, the types of academic degrees they have, the age when they were elevated to the episcopacy, and some aspects of their career path since then.

| Important Life Events | | |
|---|---|---|
| | **Average** | **Median** |
| Age in 2002 | 65 | 66 |
| Age at ordination | 26 | 26 |
| Years as a priest | 25 | 25 |
| Age at elevation to bishop | 52 | 51 |
| Years as a bishop | 14 | 14 |

---

[8] *St. Louis Post-Dispatch*, March 17, 2002.

Overall, active bishops of the USCCB average 65 years of age. Their median age is 66, but they range in age from 45 to 80. At present, bishops have a mandatory retirement age of 75 (c. 401).

| Age Range of Bishops | | |
|---|---|---|
| 40-49 | 1% | 4 |
| 50-59 | 26% | 74 |
| 60-69 | 36% | 106 |
| 70-80 | 37% | 105 |

Bishops, on average, were ordained at age 26, spent a quarter century as a priest, and were elevated to the rank of bishop at age 52. They have served as bishop an average of 14 years.

For purposes of analysis, CARA typically categorizes respondents into generations based on their year of birth.[9] These generations span approximately 20 years and capture significant life events that influenced those coming of age during that period. Generation researchers have refined these categories to be descriptive of the major events that helped shape each generation. While there may be other possible categorizations, these provide a view that is consistent with other sociological and demographic studies. Where they are significant, such differences are noted in the report, using the following categories frequently used in generational research:

- The *World War II Generation* includes those who were born before 1925 and thus are age 78 or older in 2002. The world view and attitudes of members of this generation were affected primarily by World War II and the Great Depression. This generation is sometimes labeled the "builders" since they played a crucial role in building many of the institutions of twentieth century social and religious life. Some 3 percent of the bishops of the USCCB are of this generation.

---

[9] Building on the work of Strauss and Howe (*Generations: The History of America's Future, 1584 to 2069*, [Wm. Morrow and Co.: 1992]) and other generational researchers (as well as the work of James Davidson, et al. in *The Search for Common Ground*, [Our Sunday Visitor Press, 1997]), CARA employs generations that reflect realities of Church culture as well as secular culture that have influenced these generations.

- Members of the *"Silent Generation"* were born between 1925 and 1942 and are between the ages of 60 and 77 in 2002. This generation came of age in the 1950s. Like the generation before them, they were formed before the Second Vatican Council. Generational research refers to them as the "silent" generation because they largely conformed to the world built for them by the World War II Generation. Compared to the generations that followed, they can be termed "loyalists" since they tend to exhibit high levels of institutional loyalty, including to the institutional Church. Members of the Silent Generation make up 70 percent of the bishops.

- Members of the *Vatican II Generation* were born between 1943 and 1960 and are between the ages of 42 and 59 in 2002. Members of this generation came of age during the time of the Second Vatican Council and their formative years spanned a period of profound changes in the Church. To a large extent, this generation overlaps with the "Baby Boomers." In general, members of this generation are more likely than those before them to emphasize concerns of individual self-actualization over institutional commitment. Just over a quarter of the active bishops, 27 percent, are of the Vatican II Generation.

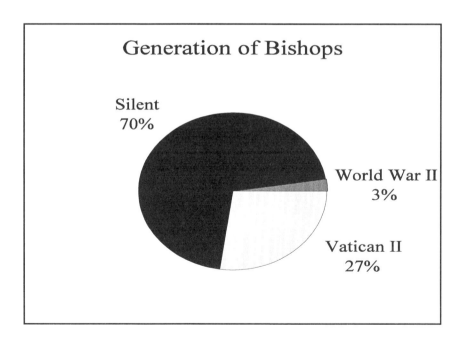

John Paul II was elected pope in 1978. Only one in six active bishops have been in that position prior to 1978. John Paul II has consecrated 85 percent of active bishops of the USCCB.

## RACE AND ETHNICITY

The bishops are far less diverse than the overall Catholic population in the United States today. They most closely resemble other Catholics of the World War II and Silent Generations, which is 88 percent white, 9 percent Hispanic/Latino, and 2 percent black.

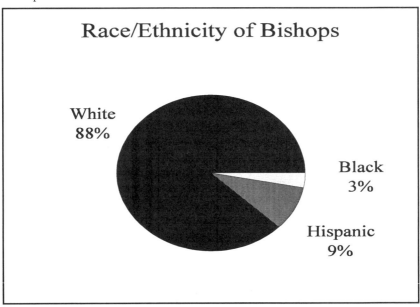

The race/ethnic composition of active bishops of the USCCB is 88 percent white, 9 percent Hispanic/Latino, 3 percent black/African American, nearly identical to the race and ethnic composition of other U.S. Catholics of their same age range.

## RANK WITHIN THE HIERARCHY

By rank, 11 percent are archbishops, just over half (55 percent) are bishops, and just over a third (34 percent) are auxiliary bishops. The distribution is as follows:

- 32 are archbishops (eight of whom are cardinals).

- 162 are bishops or equivalent rank (including one apostolic exarch, 16 bishop-eparchs, 143 bishops, and two coadjutor bishops).

- 100 are auxiliary bishops or equivalent rank (including 97 auxiliary bishops, two bishops-elect, and one administrator).

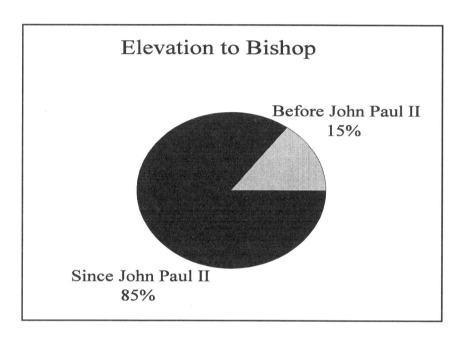

## Elevation to Bishop

Before John Paul II
15%

Since John Paul II
85%

PRIESTLY FORMATION

Bishops listed 76 different seminaries from which they received their priestly formation. Most of these seminaries, 71 percent, are located in the United States or Canada. One in five, 21 percent, placed their seminary formation in Rome. Another 5 percent identified a seminary in Europe, but outside of Rome. Only 2 percent received their seminary education in another country outside of North America or Europe.

Although bishops overall, regardless of rank, are most likely to have received their seminary education in North America, archbishops are more likely than bishops or auxiliaries to have received their seminary education in Rome.

Most bishops, regardless of current rank, received their seminary education in North America, typically at a seminary in the United States. Other findings relating to education and rank include:

- Thirty-eight percent of archbishops, compared to 19 percent of bishops, and 11 percent of auxiliaries, received their seminary education at the North American College in Rome.

- Ten percent of archbishops, compared to 9 percent of bishops, and 5 percent of auxiliaries, received their seminary education at one of the seminaries located in Washington, D.C.

- St. John's Seminary in Camarillo, St. Joseph's Seminary in Yonkers, and St. Mary's Seminary in Baltimore are the three seminaries in the United States that can count more than one currently active archbishop as an alumnus.

- Among bishops, 7 percent received their priestly formation at St. John's Seminary in Camarillo, 6 percent at Theological College of Catholic University in Washington, D.C., and 4 percent each at St. Charles Borromeo in Overbrook and St. Mary's Seminary in Baltimore.

- Auxiliary bishops are more likely to have received their priestly formation from St. John's Seminary in Camarillo (14 percent). Another 8 percent were seminarians at St. Mary of the Lake in Mundelein, and 7 percent attended Immaculate Conception Seminary in Huntington.

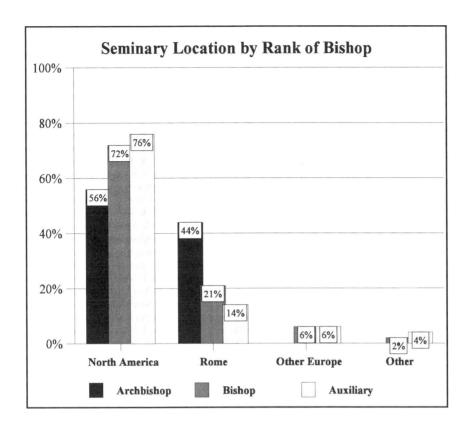

**Seminary Location by Rank of Bishop**

Thirty-six bishops (12% of all active bishops) are religious order priests. The most frequent orders are O.S.B., S.J., and S.V.D. (4 each) and O.F.M., Cap. and O.M.I. (3 each).

*Generational Differences*

Seminary education outside the United States was not a realistic option for bishops of the World War II Generation – all but two of them attended seminary in the United States. The two generations that followed them did have the opportunity to study abroad, however.

- More than one in five active bishops of the Silent Generation attended seminary in Rome. Another 5 percent completed their priestly formation in another seminary in Europe. Some 71 percent of that generation were educated in seminaries in the United States or Canada.

- Vatican II Generation bishops are even more likely to have attended seminary in Rome. Twenty-four percent were educated in Rome, 5 percent in another European seminary, and 69 percent in a seminary in North America.

PROMOTION

Only nine active bishops have had more than three appointments as bishop. Eight of those involved promotion from coadjutor bishop to bishop or archbishop as their fourth move. Cardinal McCarrick of Washington is the only bishop to have four distinct bishopric appointments (Auxiliary Bishop of New York, Bishop of Metuchen, Archbishop of Newark, and Archbishop of Washington).

Most bishops are appointed as auxiliary bishop upon being elevated to the rank of bishop. Two archbishops were elevated to the rank of archbishop upon their first appointment as bishop.

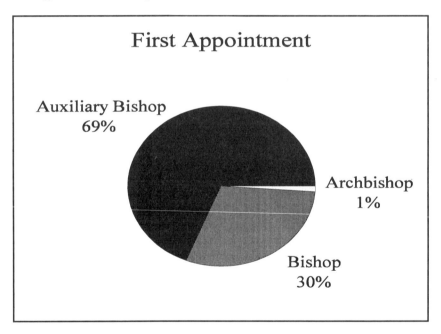

First Appointment

Auxiliary Bishop 69%

Archbishop 1%

Bishop 30%

Some 203 first appointments were made as auxiliary bishop. Another 89 (30 percent) were appointed bishop at their first appointment. In only two cases, the bishops of St. Louis and Mobile, was the first appointment made at the rank of archbishop.

Among the 203 bishops whose first appointment was as auxiliary bishop:

344

- 47 percent are still auxiliary bishops (two auxiliary bishops have been in their same position as auxiliary since 1968).

- 45 percent have since become diocesan ordinary (including one diocesan administrator who was elevated to bishop).

- 3 percent have been elevated from auxiliary bishop directly to archbishop.

- Another 3 percent of auxiliary bishops were next appointed coadjutor bishop and then assumed the episcopacy upon the retirement of the bishop.

- Two percent were elevated in some other manner. Two became apostolic administrators, then bishop. Three became diocesan administrators, then bishop.

The 89 priests that were first appointed as bishop, bishop-elect, or coadjutor bishop have had the following career path:

- 57 percent are still bishop in the same diocese to which they were first appointed. Two of them have been in the same appointment for many years – Paterson since 1977 and Grand Island since 1978.

- 11 percent were elevated to archbishop in their second assignment.

- Another three were elevated to coadjutor archbishop, and then archbishop, in their second and third assignments.

There were three dioceses where an auxiliary bishop from within the diocese was elevated to diocesan bishop or archbishop. These were Cincinnati, Newark and Richmond.

Ten percent of all active bishops were first appointed as an auxiliary bishop in one of five dioceses. The dioceses from which most auxiliaries have been chosen to head other dioceses are:

- Boston        14
- Chicago       12
- New York      12
- Detroit       10
- Los Angeles   10

*An Historical Overview of the Various Ways Bishops Have Been Selected*

The papal appointment of most bishops in the Latin church is a relatively recent development. It will help to mention very briefly some of the more common procedures used in the past:[10],[11]

- Apostolic Church to the Fourth Century – participation by the whole local church;
- Fourth to the Sixth Centuries – growing importance of the bishops of the province;
- Sixth to Eleventh Centuries – growing interference of secular powers;
- Mid-Eleventh to Early Twelfth Centuries – election by representatives of the clergy of the diocese, secular and religious;
- Twelfth to Sixteenth Centuries – election by the canons of the cathedral chapters or papal appointment;
- Sixteenth to Nineteenth Centuries – appointment by pope or ruler;
- Twentieth Century – free appointment of bishops by the pope.

The language of *CIC* canon 377, §1 frames the radical alternatives: "The Supreme Pontiff freely appoints bishops or confirms those legitimately elected." In other words the present rule provides for free appointment by the pope from a list of candidates compiled by the nuncio or some form of election within the diocese or province followed by a papal confirmation.

The free appointment process is quite recent and sacrifices many traditional and theological values. "Election by clergy and people" is an ancient slogan which reflects honored modes of selection which, in some form, deserve reconsideration.

CIC *Canon 377 on the Selection of Bishops in Operation*[12]

The 1983 *Code of Canon Law* provides for the selection of bishops in a single complex canon which includes four distinct procedures:

---

[10] These are the headings used by John Huels and Richard Gaillardetz, "The Selection of Bishops: Recovering the Traditions," *The Jurist* 59 (1999) 349-356.

[11] We also point the readers to a series of articles by Richard McBrien in *National Catholic Reporter*: "Bishops" – 7/29/02; "The selection of Bishops in History" – 8/5/02; "The Selection of Bishops in History II" – 8/12/02; "The Selection of Bishops in History III" – 8/19/02.

[12] The "operational" information which follows was obtained from personal interviews with knowledgeable people under the condition of non-attribution.

1) the regular compilation of lists of suitable candidates for the episcopacy;

2) the right of individual bishops to propose worthy candidates;

3) the *ternus* of candidates to be proposed to the Holy See by the nuncio when the appointment of a diocesan ordinary is to be made; and

4) the proposal of a list of candidates to the Holy See by a diocesan bishop when he requests an auxiliary.

In addition, a fifth process was authorized by the 1972 Norms and remains in effect:

5) the investigation of a candidate after he has been selected and before he is appointed.[13]

*1.* A list of suitable candidates, either diocesan or religious presbyters, is to be composed at least every three years by the bishops of the province, secretly and in common counsel, and sent to the Apostolic See.

The meetings of the bishops of each ecclesiastical province, including auxiliaries, are held, and they follow the detailed informational and secret balloting procedures in the 1972 Norms.[14] The lists of candidates are forwarded to the Congregation for Bishops through the good offices of the papal nuncio. The provincial lists are retained and consulted when an appointment is to be made. If a candidate is later proposed, on a *ternus* for a diocese or on a list for an auxiliary, whose name did not appear on the provincial list, the Congregation inquires about the omission.

It should be noted that sometimes diocesan bishops consult the priests of the diocese prior to making their recommendations at the provincial meetings.

2. Each bishop retains the right to make worthy and suitable candidates known to the Apostolic See individually.

The canon imposes no time frame, so the individual bishop can forward a name after failing to convince his provincial colleagues that his candidate was acceptable,

---

[13] Sacred Council for Public Affairs of the Church, "Norms for the Promotion of Candidates to the Episcopal Ministry in the Latin Church," (*Episcoporum delectum*,[ March 25, 1972]; *AAS* 64 [1972] 386-391) art. XII.

[14] However, apparently not all provinces are in complete compliance. On August 21, 2001, Archbishop Montalvo, the nuncio, sent a circular letter (N. 11.500) to the American bishops of the Latin Rite reminding them: 1) to hold the meetings at least every three years, 2) that retired bishops can't vote in them, 3) that the record of the meeting should contain the main points of the discussion on each candidate, the vote taken on each, the reasons why any candidate is judged ineligible, and the reasons why anyone on a previous list has been removed, 4) an updated curriculum vitae should be supplied for each candidate, and 5) that the names and signatures of all of the bishops in attendance should be appended as well as the name of the bishop secretary who is submitting the record of the meeting.

or in advance of an anticipated appointment, or simply in response to the prompting of the Holy Spirit. There is no doubt that bishops exercise this prerogative, but how often and for what reasons, could not be ascertained.

3. When a diocesan bishop (or a coadjutor) is to be appointed, the nuncio forwards a *ternus* to the Apostolic See, together with his own opinion, after individually seeking the suggestions of the metropolitan and the suffragans, as well as those of the president of the bishops' conference. The nuncio is to hear some members of the college of consultors, and, if he judges it expedient, he is also to seek (individually and secretly) the opinions of others, clergy (diocesan and religious) and wise lay persons.

The central and controlling role of the apostolic nuncio in this process is obvious. In fact, this is one of his principal responsibilities,[15] and occupies a large measure of the time and energy of the nuncio and his staff. Since the entire process is carried on under strict secrecy, it is very difficult to judge how well the nuncio performs this vital function. Only the results show.

The papal nuncio not only conducts the consultation process, he also makes the ultimate decision about what names are included on the *ternus* submitted to the Congregation for Bishops, and in what order they are listed. His recommendations carry great weight.

The extent and quality of the nuncio's consultation in reference to individual appointments is perhaps the most crucial in the "instructional phase" of the selection process. He and his staff assemble the *ternus*, but who does he talk to in the process? The 1972 Norms included among those to be consulted, in addition to those persons mentioned in canon 377, §3, the members of the priests' council (at least when the see was not vacant), but they are no longer included among those to be asked for suggestions.

In recent years, even the modicum of consultation recommended in this document (the 1972 Norms) has largely disappeared. Sometimes there has been no consultation whatever with the local clergy. Bishops of the region are usually consulted. But it is not uncommon that only selected bishops are consulted, not all the bishops of the province or region. It has been the custom for the papal representative to invite the comment of all the American cardinals when a diocese becomes vacant.[16]

There is no mention of cardinals in the present canon on the selection of bishops, nor was there in the 1972 Norms. Such a consultative role is not even hinted at in the canonical description of the cardinalatial office.

Canon 377, §3 does call for consultation with the president of the bishops'

---

[15] Canon 364, 4° specifies this task among his other responsibilities.

[16] John Quinn, *The Reform of the Papacy: The Costly Call to Christian Unity* (New York: Crossroad, 1999) 129.

conference. In the early 1970s the conference established a committee on the selection of bishops, with representatives from each of the conference regions, but the committee never really worked, and it does not function at all in the selection process, though it continues in existence.

The conference president (and vice president) has been consulted in various ways. When notified that an appointment is to be made, he is asked for an opinion on the state of the diocese and the kind of leadership that seems called for. Then when a list of candidates has been compiled, the nuncio sends it to the president for his reactions or suggestions. At one time the president received the final *ternus* before the nuncio sent it to the Congregation of Bishops, but that no longer occurs. And at one time the general secretary of the conference received the list of candidates as well as the president and vice president, but that no longer happens.

Given the geographic extent and ethnic complexity of the United States as well as the large number of dioceses, the consultation of the conference president in its present mode seems to be mainly a formality. The president does not know the candidates on the list, for the most part, unless they are already bishops and he has gained knowledge of them from their conference activities.[17]

The nuncio is charged to hear at least some members of the diocesan college of consultors. This consultation is individual and by mail, never as a college gathered as they are when electing a diocesan administrator for a vacant see.[18]

The nuncio may, "if he judges it expedient," consult other presbyters, both secular and religious, as well as lay persons outstanding for their wisdom. The actual extent of this optional consultation is difficult to discern. The names of those who are consulted "individually and in secret" are drawn from the officials listed in *The Official Catholic Directory*, from diocesan organizations or advisory committees, or from those suggested by the outgoing bishop or the diocesan administrator.

*4.* When a diocesan bishop judges that his diocese should be given an auxiliary bishop, the diocesan bishop proposes a list of at least three presbyters to the Apostolic See.

At this critical juncture, when three-fourths of bishops are initially chosen, the diocesan bishop operates without restraint. He is free to nominate diocesan or religious presbyters from his own diocese or from other dioceses. He may do so without consultation with his metropolitan or fellow suffragans. In fact, diocesan bishops often do consult both the priests serving in the diocese and with neighboring bishops, especially when seeking an auxiliary with special language skills or a particular ethnic background. The nominations receive scrutiny within the Congregation of Bishops, e.g., the list is compared with the lists previously

---

[17] Reese, *Archbishop,* pp. 8, 23-25.
[18] *CIC*, c. 421, §1.

submitted from the province, but the consistent quality of that review is difficult to verify.

5. The nuncio conducts a careful and wide-ranging inquiry into the candidate before his appointment. He consults those who know the candidate well, can provide information about him, and can make a prudent judgment about him. Bishops, priests, religious, and reliable lay persons are questioned (1972 Norms, art. XII).

This is a time-consuming process, and it accounts for some of the long delay in making appointments. Its thoroughness and accuracy is hard to judge because it is conducted in secret and is never reported. One evident weakness is that many of those who are questioned by the nuncio's office are suggested by the candidate himself, the bishop who nominated him, or those closely associated with one or the other.

*The* Code of Canons of the Eastern Churches *on the Selection of Bishops*

For eparchies within the territorial boundaries of patriarchal churches, the *CCEO* provides a system of nominations by the bishops who belong to the patriarchal synod, the prior or subsequent assent of the Roman Pontiff to the candidates, and election of the bishop within the synod.[19] The members of the synod, as part of the nomination process, may consult, individually and secretly, with presbyters and wise lay persons.

Bishops for eparchies outside the territorial boundaries of a patriarchal church are also chosen by the patriarchal synod. At least three candidates are chosen and proposed through the patriarch to the Roman Pontiff for appointment.[20]

VALUES IMBEDDED IN PREVIOUS PROCESSES THAT NEED TO BE PRESERVED

The following, in briefest synopsis, are some of the principal values which Huels and Gaillardetz raised up in their recent study:[21]

- The theological and ecclesial integrity of the local church – the reality of the church as *koinonia*, a communion, expressed sacramentally in the celebration of the Eucharist, a community that is the Body of Christ in this place;

---

[19] *CCEO*, cc. 181-186; 168.
[20] *CCEO*, c. 149.
[21] Ibid., 357-368.

350

- The bishop's fundamental relationship to the local church – a ministry within the local church, a mystical union, often compared to the marital union, between the one leader and the community, not transferable, no auxiliary bishops;

- Participation by representatives of the whole local church in the selection of the bishop – the two foregoing values led to the conviction that all of the clergy and people should have some part in choosing their bishop;

- The application of the principle of subsidiarity in preserving a diversity of methods of episcopal selection – churches should choose from among suitable ways of selecting their leaders, as long as the communion of the churches is not jeopardized;

- The elimination of the control or undue influence of powerful rulers over the process of the selection of bishops – civil authorities must not be permitted to manipulate the choice of bishops;

- The selection of suitable candidates for the episcopacy – qualifications for the office of bishop are specified, and the integrity of the selection process must insure that worthy candidates are found and installed;

- Participation by the bishops of the province and the bishop of Rome in the selection of bishops – the communion of the churches calls for the involvement of the metropolitan, comprovincial bishops, and Roman patriarch in choice and consecration of the bishop;

- Expeditious provision of a vacant episcopal office – in the past disputes and conflicts among electors led to harmful delays and the devolution of the selection to a higher authority, and similar provisions to avoid delays need to be in place today.

### IMPROVEMENTS IN THE PRESENT PROCESS

The following issues require serious reflection and evaluation with an eye toward improving the procedure for the selection of bishops in the U.S. Latin church:[22]

- auxiliary bishops, their proliferation and the process by which they are

---

[22] See ibid., 368-376, for a set of proposed canons that Huels and Gaillardetz suggest to embody the values they enunciated.

named and then transferred to become diocesan ordinaries; this pattern is the foremost problem with the present system, it has both theological and ecumenical implications;

- consultation on both the condition and needs of the diocese and on the quality of the candidates should be thorough and open; consultation is integral to ecclesial participation, and it deserves to be collegial as well as individual; laity must be included;

- secrecy shrouds abuses and favoritism at the same time that it protects reputations and personal feelings; greater transparency is needed and would breed confidence and enhance trust;

- role and influence of the nuncio is too great; the provincial bishops or a committee of the conference should determine the *ternus* rather than the papal legate; his should be a voice in the process, but not the dominant one;

- episcopal "problems" must be reported faithfully and effectively; credible accusations, personal failings, criminal activity, serious illness, etc., must not remain concealed, but revealed at some suitably confidential point in the process;

- transfers from one diocese to another, especially after short periods of time, are harmful to the church; they imply an unseemly desire for advancement rather than genuine service to the church; they reduce local churches to stepping stones.

## CONCLUSIONS

The clergy sex abuse scandal of 2002 has spotlighted a number of the shortcomings related to the selection of bishops in the United States. It has also put a great strain on the bishops and on the relationship between the bishops and the priests and people of their diocese. It has caused a rift to develop between priests and the bishops that may raise questions or concerns in those priests who are considered for future elevation to the rank of bishop. It has shown the great need for cooperation and collaboration in all levels of the church.

This scandal has also shown the great need for competent, caring and strong leadership at the episcopal level. It has shown a need for openness and transparency not only in the selection of bishops, but in many areas of the church. The scandal has also shown that stability within the local church is paramount. Bishops who move from one diocese to another or use smaller dioceses as stepping stones to larger sees may not always understand the needs of the local church and the local presbyterate. This is not to say that bishops should be chosen only from their local diocese, nor is it meant to say that they should never move from see to see. However, it does point to the need for local involvement in the selection process.

The movement of bishops can give rise to problems being passed from one administration to the next without ever being fully resolved. Hard decisions may be avoided or they may be made without the pastoral care needed for a particular diocese. Decisions made as auxiliary bishop may follow the diocesan ordinary and cause unnecessary concerns or challenges for a new diocese.

More important to this report, the limited involvement of a wide range of persons and a limited knowledge of the particular needs of a local church prohibit growth of the church. There is concern about a turn toward clericalism, secrecy and autocratic leadership.

The bishops of the Church in the United States spent much of the twentieth century developing and educating its clergy, religious and laity. The presbyterate and episcopacy grew to one of the most highly educated groups of men in the entire church world. At the same time, this reach for excellence pervaded the laity and helped to develop a highly educated, competent and involved group of laity for the church.

The challenge for the future is to use these highly competent and involved persons to assist in the future selection of bishops. The challenge is to develop a process that is both transparent and protects the secrecy necessary to examine and evaluate the background and abilities of prospective candidates. The challenge is to choose bishops willing and able to handle the growing challenges of the modern Church while continuing to lead Christ's faithful, or as the case may be, accompanying them, along the path to salvation.

Aimone Braga, P.V. "Partecipazione del potere civile nella nomina dei vescovi in accordi conclusi dalla Santa sede con i governi civili tra il 1965 e il 1976." *Apollinaris* 50 (1977) 572-586.

_____. "Partecipazione del potere civile nella nomina dei vescovi (1976-1981)." *Apollinaris* 54 (1981) 206-212.

Alberigo, G. & Weiller, A. "Election and Consensus in the Church." *Concilium* 77 (1972). New York: Herder & Herder, 1972.

Andrés Gutiérrez, Domingo. ed. *Il processo di designazione dei vescovi: storia, legislazione, prassi*: Atti del X Symposium Canonistico-Romanistico, 24-28 Aprile, 1995, in onore del Rev. mo P. Umberto Betti, OFM, già rettore della Pont. Univ. Laterano. Vatican City: Libreria Editrice Vaticana, 1996. Pp. 671. [The five articles in this collection that were written by Giorgio Corbellini, Agostino Montan, Pasquale Colella, Raphael Letayf, and Natale Loda are particularly pertinent to the contemporary episcopal selection problematic. The volume also contains a valuable alphabetical index of sources and authors, pp. 641-668.]

Barbarena, T. "Nuevas normas sobre nombramiento de obispos [...] commentario." *Revista Española de Derecho Canonico* 28 (1972) 661-682.

Bassett, W. ed., *The Choosing of Bishops*. Canon Law Society of America, 1971.

Bauer, J. "Die Bischofswahl, Gestern, Heute, Morgen." *Theologische-praktische Quartalschrift* 129 (1981) 248-254.

Benson, R. *The Bishop-Elect: A Study in Medieval Ecclesiastical Office* (Princeton, N. J.: Princeton University Press, 1968).

Bernhard, J. "The Election of Bishops at the Council of Trent." *Concilium* 137 (1980) 24-30.

Biemer, Günter. "Die Bischofswahl als neues Desiderat kirchlicher Praxis." *Theologische Quartalschrift* 149 (1969) 171-184.

Bolduc, N. "Report of CLSA Committee on Selection of Bishops." *CLSA Proceedings* (1988) 299-304.

Bonnet, P. & Gullo, C. ed. (A report on the role of civil governments in the nomination of bishops). *La Curia Romana nella Const. Ap. Pastor Bonus* (Cittá del Vaticano, 1990), Pp. 293-307.

Canon Law Society of America. *Procedure for the Selection of Bishops in the United States: A Suggested Implementation of Present Papal Norms.* CLSA, 1973.

Canon Law Society of America. "Report of a CLSA Survey on Auxiliary Bishops," *The Jurist* 53:2 (1993) 354-361.

Carcel Orti. V. "Los nombramientos de obispos durante el regimen de Franco." *Revista Española de Derecho Canonico* 51 (1994) 503-566.

Caron, P.G. "Les élections épiscopales dans la doctrine et la practique de l'Église." *Cahiers de Civilisation Médiévale* 11 (1968) 579-585.

Cereti, G. "The Ecumenical Importance of the Laity's Collaboration in the Choice of Bishops." *Concilium* 137 (1980) 48-53

Corral, C. "La libertad de la Iglesia e intervención de los Estados en los nombramientos episcopales." *Revista Española de Derecho Canonico* 21 (1966) 63-92.

Costalunga, M. "La Congregazione per i Vescovi. Procedure con i governi e privilegi in materia di nomine vescovili," in *La Curia Romana nella Cost. Ap. "Pastor bonus."* ed. P. A. Bonnet and C. Gullo. (Studi Giuridici, 21) [Vatican City: Libreria Editrice Vaticana, 1990] pp. 281-292.

D'Onorio, J. *La nomination des eveques. Procedures canoniques et conventions diplomatiques* (Paris: Tardy, 1986).

Ellis, John Tracy. "On Selecting American Bishops." *Commonweal* 85 (March 10, 1967) 643-649.

_____. "On Selecting Catholic Bishops for the United States." *The Critic* 26 (June-July, 1969) 42-48.

_____. "The Selection of Bishops." *American Benedictine Review* 35 (June, 1984) 111-127.

Eugui Hermoso de Mendoza, J. *La participación de la communidad cristiana en la elección de los obispos: siglos IV-V*. (Pamplona: EUNSA, 1977).

Feliciani, G. "Les nominations episcopales entre liberté de l'Eglise et intervention de l'état: la prénotification officieuse." *Revue de Droit Canonique* 46 (1996) 345-358.

Ganzer, K. *Papsttum und Bistumsbestezungen in der Zeit von Gregor IX. bis Bonifaz VIII* (Cologne/Graz: Böhlau, 1968).

Gaudemet, J. "La participation de la communauté au choix du pasteurs dans l'Eglise latine. Esquisse historique," *Ius Canonicum* 14 (1974) 308-326.

_____, et al. *Les élections dans l'Église latine des origines au XVI siècle* (Paris: Lanoré, 1979).

_____. "The Choice of Bishops: a Tortuous History" in *From Life to Law Concilium* 5 (Maryknoll, NY: Orbis, 1996) 59-65.

_____. *Eglise et cité: Histoire du droit canonique* (Paris: Cerf/Montchrestien, 1994).

Gerosa, L. "Die Bischofsbestellung in ökumenischer und kirchenrechtlicher Sicht" *Catholica* 46 (1992) 70-86.

Glasser, A. "Das Kirchenrecht als konsecutives Recht und die Bestellung der Bischofe," *Theologische-praktische Quartalschrift* 130 (1982) 4-19.

Goedert, R. "Selection of Bishops: A Canonical and Pastoral Critique of the New Norms," *CLSA Proceedings* (1972) 54-61.

Granfield, P. *Ecclesial Cybernetics*, 247-252; 257-267 (New York: Macmillan, 1973).

_____. "Episcopal Elections in Cyprian: Clerical and Lay Participation," *Theological Studies* 37 (1976) 41-52.

_____. "The Sensus Fidelium in Episcopal Selection," *Concilium* 137 (1980) 33-37.

Greshake, G. *Zur Frage der Bischofsernennungen in der römisch-katholischen Kirche* (Munich/Zurich: Verlag Schnell & Steiner, 1991).

Gryson, Roger. "Les élections ecclésiatiques au IIIe siècle," *Revue d'histoire ecclésiastique* 68 (1973) 353-404.

_____. "Les élections épiscopales en Orient au IVe siècle," *Revue d'histoire ecclésiastique* 74 (1979) 301-345.

_____. "Les élections épiscopales en Occident au IVe siècle," *Revue d'histoire ecclésiastique* 75 (1980) 257-283.

Harouel, J. *Les designations épiscopales dans le droit contemporaine*, (Paris: Presses Universitaires de France, 1977).

Helmholz, R.H. "Governance of the Church: The Law of Episcopal Elections," *The Spirit of Classical Canon Law* (Athens, GA: University of Georgia Press, 1996), pp. 33-60.

Hennesey, James. "'To Chose a Bishop': An American Way." *America* 127 (Sept. 2, 1972) 115-118.

Huels, J. and R. Gaillardetz. "The Selection of Bishops: Recovering the Traditions," *The Jurist* 59 (1999) 348-376.

Hughes, J. "Selecting Your Bishop," *America* 126:112 (1971) 310-312.

Huizing, P. and K. Walf, eds. *Electing Our Bishops,* Vol. 137 of English edition of *Concilium* (New York: Seabury, 1980).

Kaiser, Matthaeus. "Besetzung der Bischofsstuehle, Erfahrungen und Optionen," *Archiv für katholisches Kirchenrecht* 158 (1989) 69-90.

Khoury, J. "La scelta dei vescovi nel Codice dei Canoni delle Chiese Orientali," *Apollinaris* 65/1-2 (1992) 77-91.

_____. "The Election of Bishops in the Eastern Churches," *Concilium* 147 (1981) 20-27.

Kilmartin, E. "Episcopal Election: The Right of the Laity," *Concilium* 137 (1980) 39-43.

Kottje, R. "The Selection of Church Officials: Some Historical Facts and Experiences," *Concilium* 63 (New York: Herder & Herder, 1971) 117-126.

Lafont, Ghislain, *Imagining The Catholic Church: Structured Community in the Spirit* (Collegeville, MN: Liturgical Press, 2000) pp. 172-177.

Landau, P. "Der Papst und die Besetzung der Bischofsstuhle," *Zeitschrift für Evangelische Kirchenrecht* 37 (1992) 241-254.

Lorusso, L. "La designazione dei vescovi nel *Codex Canonum Ecclesiarum Orientalium.*" *Quaderni di Diritto Ecclesiale* 12 (1999) 46-57.

Lynch, J. "Co-responsibility in the First Five Centuries: Presbyteral Colleges and the Election of Bishops," in *Who Decides for the Church?* ed. J. Coriden, 14-53. Canon Law Society of America, 1971. Cf. *The Jurist* 31 (1971).

Maier, E. "Bischofsernennungen-Prufstein kirchenrechtlicher Legitimität," *Stimmen der Zeit* 113 (1988) 447-460.

Maritz, H. *Das Bischofswahl in der Schweiz unter besonderer Berücksichtigungder Entwicklung im Bistum Basel nach der Reorganisation* (St. Ottilien: EOS, 1977).

Mejía, Jorge, "El servicio de la Santa Sede a las iglesias particulares a traves de la Congregacíon para los Obisbos," *Anuario Argentino de Derecho Canonico* 3 (1996) 107-127.

Metz, R. "Innovation et anachronismes au sujet de la nomination des évèques dans des recentes conventions passées entre le Saint Siege et divers Etats (1973-1984)," *Studia Canonica* 20 (1986) 197-218.

_____. "L'independence de l'Eglise dans la choix des evèques. à Vatican II et dans le Code de 1983, aboutissment d'un demi-siècle d'effort diplomatique." *Revue de Droit Canonique* 37/3-4 (1987) 143-170.

_____. "La désignation des évèques dans le droit actuel: étude comparative entre le Code latin de 1983 et le Code oriental de 1990," *Studia Canonica* 27 (1993) 321-334.

_____. "Papal Legates and the Appointment of Bishops," *The Jurist* 52 (1992) 259-284.

Müller, H. *Der Anteil der Laien an der Bischofswahl: Ein Beitrag zur Geschichte der Kanonistik von Gratian bis Gregor IX* (Amsterdam: Verlag B. R. Gruner, 1977).

_____. "De episcoporum electione iuxta Concilium Vaticanum Secundum," *Investigationes Theologico-Canonicae* (Rome: Università Gregoriana Editrice, 1978) Pp. 317-332.

National Federation of Priests' Councils. *Selection of Bishops Process* [Chicago, 1974] (collection of various materials on selection process including CLSA's work).

Örsy, L., et al. "Selection of Bishops, A Symposium," *America* 127:5 (Sept. 2, 1972) 111-121.

Paarhammer, Hans. "Bischofsbestellung im CCEO. Patriarchen- und Bischofswahl und andere Formen des Bischofsbestellung." *Archiv für katholisches Kirchenrecht* 160 (1991) 390-407.

Primetshofer, B. "Die Ernennung von Bischöfen im Oesterreich, Deutschland und der Schweiz," *Theologische Quartalschrift* 118 (1996) 169-186.

Provost, J. "Selection of Bishops – Does Anybody Care?" *Chicago Studies* 18 (1979) 211-222.

_____ and Knut Walf, ed. *From Life to Law, Concilium* (Maryknoll, NY: Orbis, 1996/5).

Quinn, John. *The Reform of the Papacy: The Costly Call to Christian Unity* (New York: Crossroad, 1999) Pp. 117-139.

Reese, Thomas. "A Survey of the American Bishops," *America* 149:15 (Nov. 12, 1983) 285-290.

_____. "The Selection of Bishops," *America* 151:4 (Aug. 25, 1984) 65-72.

_____. *Archbishop: Inside the Power Structure of the American Catholic Church* (San Francisco: Harper & Row, 1989) pp. 1-52.

_____. "The Laghi Legacy," *America* 162:23 (June 23, 1990) 605-608.

_____. *A Flock of Shepherds: The National Conference of Catholic Bishops* (Kansas City: Sheed & Ward, 1992) pp. 1-17.

_____. *Inside the Vatican: The Politics and Organization of the Catholic Church* (Cambridge, MA: Harvard University Press, 1996) pp. 230-248.

Rivella, M. "Modalità speciali di designazione di alcuni vescovi," *Quaderni di Diritto Ecclesiale* 12 (1999) 35-45.

Sagmüller, J. *Die Bischofswahl bei Gratian* (Cologne: J.P.Bachen, 1908)

Sarrazin, L. "La nomination des évèques dans l'Eglise latine," *Studia Canonica* 20 (1986) 367-408.

Sarzi Sartori, G. "La designazione del vescovo diocesano nel diritto ecclesiale." *Quaderni di Diritto Ecclesiale* 12 (1999) 7-34.

Schmitz, Heribert. "Pläydoyer für Bischofs- und Pfarrerwahl," *Trier Theologische Zeitschrift* 79 (1970) 230-249.

Schotz, K. "Bischofswahlen.," *Stimmen der Zeit* 114 (1989) 291-307.

Stockmeier, P. "The Election of Bishops by Clergy and People in the Early Church," *Concilium* 137; *Electing Our Own Bishops* (New York: Seabury, 1980).

Swidler, L. ed. *Bishops and People* (Westminster, 1970).

Talamanca, A. "I procedimenti concordatari di nomina." *Ministero episcopale e dinamica instituzionali* (Bologna, 1981) pp. 63-125.

Thils, G. *Choisir les Évèques? Élire le Pape?* (Gembloux: Duculot, 1970).

Trevisan, G. "Le buone qualità del candidato all'episcopato," *Quaderni di Diritto Ecclesiale* 12 (1999) 58-69.

Trisco, Robert. "Democratic Influence on the Election of Bishops and Pastors and on the Administration of Dioceses and Parishes in the U.S.A.," *Concilium* 77 (1972) 132-138.

_____. "The Debate on the Election of Bishops in the Council of Trent," *The Jurist* 34 (1974) 257-291.

Tucci, R. "La scelta dei candidati all'episcopato nella Chiesa Latina.," *La Civiltà Cattolica* 123/2 (1972) 422-439.

| Committee: | **Special Task Force to Prepare for the 2002 Presidential Hearing on Clerical Sexual Misconduct** |
|---|---|
| Constituted: | By the Board of Governors at their meeting in April 2002 |
| Charge: | To assist the President in preparing for the 2002 President's Hearing on the canonical concerns revolving around clerical sexual abuse and the response of the U.S. Conference of Catholic Bishops during their Dallas meeting. |
| Membership: | Rev. Msgr. Frederick C. Easton, (chairperson)<br>Sr. Sharon Euart, R.S.M.<br>Rev. Gregory Ingels |

## Annual Report

At their meeting in April 2002, the Board of Governors established a special task force whose charge was to prepare the structure of the Presidential Hearing on Clerical Sexual Misconduct as it is entitled in the program for the 2002 CLSA Convention at Cincinnati. After this meeting the President, Kevin McKenna, appointed the members and designated the chairperson.

At the time of this report the task force has held two telephone conference calls and has also frequently communicated by e-mail. The chairman has been in regular communication with the President by e-mail.

In their initial meeting, the members of the Task Force agreed that the CLSA should place itself in the position of offering assistance in the proper implementation of the Dallas "Charter," since we noted that many bishops had indicated they were planning individually to incorporate the Charter in their own diocesan policies. Some bishops have decides to await the action of the Holy See before implementing the companion document, entitled "Essential Norms."

We also identified four different constituencies in the Church whom we believed needed the assistance of our Society:

> The diocesan bishops
> The victims
> The accused priests
> The canonists who may be called upon to assist any of the above

Pursuant to the first matter, it was our opinion that some action by the Society before the convention was urgently needed since the Charter was being immediately implemented. Therefore, we urged the President to authorize, if possible, a small committee to prepare a "guide" for implementation which would focus on implementation of the Charter in accord with the *Code of Canon Law* and any subsequent general legislation. We noted that several canonists had begun to prepare materials responding to this need. President McKenna authorized a committee to proceed with the proviso that the forthcoming document would have only the attribution of the Canon Law Society of America.

The special task force also agreed that there is a need for a comprehensive workshop to prepare canonists to be advocates for cases of clerical sexual abuse. We believe that such a workshop would benefit members who may be called upon to help, including serving in the role of promoter of justice or judge. We also agreed that the Department/School of Canon Law at The Catholic University of America should be asked to design and present such a workshop. If the Department/School of Canon Law is not in a position to do so, we recommend that the CLSA be asked to take on this task. We do not think we it is necessary to wait for *recognitio* for the "Essential Norms" before proceeding with such a workshop; the presentations would be based on the law in force at the time of the workshop.

Finally, our Task Force was asked to present an outline and process for the 2002 President's Hearing.

We recommend that President McKenna serve as chair and facilitator of the meeting.

The following presentations would be given: Fred Easton as Chair of the Task force on the Task Force's report with its recommendations; Greg Ingels on the *State of the Question* in the US.

These presentations would be followed by a brief response from members on their experience and perspectives following the Dallas meeting.

This would be followed by a discussion of the recommendations of the Task Force with an opportunity for members present to suggest other recommendations.

The Task Force recommends that the results of the Hearing be brought to the floor of the business meeting and presented in the form of a resolution which would support any action taken by the Society.

Further, the Task Force recommends that the President considering beginning

362

the hearing 30 minutes earlier at 2:00 PM thereby allowing 2 hours for the session.

The members of this Task Force believe they have responded appropriately to the request of the Board of Governors and the President and respectfully submit this report to the membership.

Committee:    **Task Force on Issues Related to Marriage and Undocumented Persons**

Constituted:  2001

Charge:        1. Identify and examine basic human rights, such as the right to marry;
2. Identify and examine legal and pastoral issues;
3. Prepare a legal and canonical analysis;
4. Prepare a legal and pastoral guide;
5. Propose actions to be taken by the CLSA.

Membership: Rev. Thomas Paprocki, Chairperson
Rev. Msgr. Mark Bartchak
Rev. Vicente DeLa Cruz

## Annual Report

The task Force on issues Related to marriage and Undocumented Persons has met by telephone conference call and has set forth the initial tasks to be undertaken by its members. Father Vincente De La Cruz will research areas of basic human rights, such as the right to marry; Father Thomas Paprocki will research pertinent civil law issues, such as the immigration laws pertaining to marriage and state laws and practices concerning the issues of marriage licenses; Monsignor Mark Bartchak will research the pertinent areas of canon law, especially concerning the suitability and applicability of the canons pertaining to secret marriages in the case of undocumented person. Out of this research we plan to fulfill the mandate of the Task Force by preparing a legal and canonical analysis and guide. We will also look at what actions, if any, should be proposed to be taken by the CLSA.

Our time line is for the members of the Task Force to confer at the 2002 Convention in cincinnati regarding the progress of our research. We will then plan on having a written draft of our work prepared by the end of December 2002. We will then work on the final text of our report and recommendations by the 2003 Convention in Portland, Oregon, in keeping with the convention Resolution establishing this Task Force.

Committee: **Convention Chairperson**

Membership: Mrs. Rita F. Joyce

Annual Report

The Convention is well under way. There are lots of last minute details that Nix & Associates, Father Art Espelage and I are working on. We are investigating the possibility of an overflow hotel at this time.

Our registration looks strong and we should have a wonderful convention in Cincinnati. The Hilton Netherland Plaza is a beautiful old hotel that will present plentiful meeting space and the Hall of Mirrors is delightful for the banquet.

This year for the first time we will host Exhibitors. We have reservations for 11 companies that will exhibit in the Hall of Mirrors from Monday until Wednesday at noon.

We have arranged bus transportation from the hotel site to St. Peter in Chains where the Convention liturgy will take place on Wednesday afternoon. Sister Vicki Vondenberger and Father Joe Binzer have been very helpful in Cincinnati detail. Staff from the Tribunal will be onsite to provide assistance during the convention.

Details for future conventions are Portland Oregon – Doubletree Hotel October 13-16, 2003 and Pittsburgh, Pennsylvania – Hilton October 11-14, 2004. Plans are still forming form Rome 2005 and for Dallas/Ft. Worth for 2006.


Committee: **Convention Liturgies**

Constituted: Board of Governors, 1990

Charge: Plan the convention liturgies and prayer services

Membership: Rev. James R. Bonke, Chairperson
Rev. Joseph Binzer
Rev. Ron Krisman

## Annual Report

The Convention Liturgy Committee, appointed following the 2001 Canon Law Society Convention, is composed of Rev. Joseph Binzer of the Archdiocese of Cincinnati, Rev. Ron Krisman of the Diocese of Orlando, and myself. I have met with Father Binzer and Father Larry Tensi, director of the Office of Worship of the Archdiocese of Cincinnati, twice in recent months to discuss plans for the various liturgies of the 2002 annual convention. I cannot stress how helpful both Father Binzer and Father Tensi have been in this process. Another meeting is planned in Cincinnati for early September to complete details for this year's convention liturgies. I am confident that the liturgies will be planned and executed with care and precision.

The close proximity of the Indianapolis and Cincinnati has facilitated the process of liturgy planning. The possibility of on-site visits and being able to sit down in personal settings has been extremely helpful in arranging for the convention liturgies. I recognize this will not always be possible, but I do feel that it has been an asset in completing the work for the liturgies at this year's Canon Law Society's annual convention.

TRIBUNAL STATISTICS FOR THE 2001 CALENDER YEAR

In January of each year, the Executive Coordinator's Office requests first and second instance statistics from tribunals throughout the United States of America. This material first appearing in *CLSA Proceedings* 1969 offers readers a variety of data for consideration. Participation in the compilation of statistics is purely voluntary. Likewise, tribunals submitting information may not offer data on all categories.

*How one uses this material:* The data is arranged in two parts: first instance statistics and second instance statistics. First instance statistics are divided into sections "a" through "h" which provide information on cases, finances, and personnel. The sections follow in alphabetical order the archdioceses, dioceses and eparchies of the United States. For example, all information offered by the Diocese of Wheeling, W.V. will be found in section "h" while the Archdiocese of Cincinnati, OH appears in section "a." Second instance statistics repeats the same format for the appeal courts in the United States.

# FIRST INSTANCE TRIBUNAL STATISTICS 2001

| Section A Arch/Diocese | Cases Previous Year | Cases New Year | Cases Accepted | Cases Decided | Mixed | Non-Cath. | Petitioner Renun. | Abated |
|---|---|---|---|---|---|---|---|---|
| Albany | | | | | | | | |
| Alexandria | 266 | 54 | 54 | 55 | 12 | 14 | 7 | 2 |
| Allentown | 196 | 299 | 288 | 263 | 56 | 69 | 1 | 84 |
| Altoona-Johnstown | 81 | 163 | 151 | 83 | 27 | 18 | | 9 |
| Amarillo | | | | | | | | |
| Anchorage | 24 | 28 | 28 | 34 | 9 | 13 | | |
| Arlington | 193 | 434 | 422 | 259 | 77 | 50 | 7 | 24 |
| Atlanta | 440 | 445 | 301 | 157 | 52 | 52 | 15 | 28 |
| Baton Rouge | 248 | 182 | 179 | 205 | 46 | 34 | 4 | 12 |
| Beaumont | 148 | 120 | 111 | 106 | 35 | 24 | 7 | 12 |
| Belleville | 184 | 122 | 122 | 189 | 44 | 67 | 1 | 13 |
| Biloxi | 186 | 83 | 104 | 68 | 14 | 26 | 4 | 6 |
| Birmingham | 132 | 93 | 109 | 94 | 22 | 53 | 4 | 2 |
| Bismarck | 87 | 71 | 71 | 85 | 28 | 16 | 5 | 2 |
| Boise | | | | | | | | |
| Boston | | | | | | | | |
| Bridgeport | 51 | 144 | 105 | 113 | 16 | 9 | 1 | 3 |
| Brooklyn | 80 | 202 | 291 | 291 | 46 | 8 | | |
| Brownsville | 127 | 102 | 102 | 60 | 5 | 3 | 2 | 22 |
| Buffalo | 70 | 213 | 213 | 191 | 42 | 17 | | 1 |
| Burlington | 58 | 96 | 91 | 100 | | | 1 | 2 |
| Camden | 233 | 157 | 113 | 133 | 40 | 8 | 5 | 28 |

**FIRST INSTANCE TRIBUNAL STATISTICS 2001**

| Section A Arch/Diocese | Ligamen | Other Decision | Lack of Form | *Rattum* non-con. | Priv. Of Faith | Pauline Priv. | 2nd Inst. Rec. | 2nd Inst. Dec. |
|---|---|---|---|---|---|---|---|---|
| Albany | | | | | | | | |
| Alexandria | 4 | | | | | | | |
| Allentown | | 1 | 140 | | | 2 | | |
| Altoona-Johnstown | 5 | | 27 | | 1 | 2 | | |
| Amarillo | | | | | | | | |
| Anchorage | 10 | | 43 | | | | | |
| Arlington | 22 | 2 | 318 | | 26 | 1 | | |
| Atlanta | 26 | | 277 | | 1 | | | |
| Baton Rouge | 8 | 6 | 177 | | 3 | 5 | | |
| Beaumont | 19 | | 68 | | | 5 | | |
| Belleville | 15 | | 72 | | | 11 | | |
| Biloxi | 10 | 3 | 80 | | | | | |
| Birmingham | 15 | 2 | 56 | | | 2 | | |
| Bismarck | 2 | 2 | 36 | | | 2 | | |
| Boise | | | | | | | | |
| Boston | | | | | | | | |
| Bridgeport | 3 | | 307 | | | | | |
| Brooklyn | | | 344 | | | | | |
| Brownsville | 2 | | 163 | | | | | |
| Buffalo | 4 | | 196 | | 1 | | | |
| Burlington | 2 | | | | | 1 | | |
| Camden | | 5 | | | 5 | | | |

# FIRST INSTANCE TRIBUNAL STATISTICS 2001

| Section A Arch/Diocese | Totally Subsidized | Partially Subsidized | Fee Schedule | Formal Case | Documentary Case | Lack of Form Case | Other | Total Expenditures |
|---|---|---|---|---|---|---|---|---|
| Albany | | | | | | | | |
| Alexandria | | x | x | x | x | | | $ 8,100.00 |
| Allentown | | x | x | $400 | $50 | $50 | | $ 108,320.00 |
| Altoona-Johnstown | x | | | | | | | $ 54,750.00 |
| Amarillo | | | | | | | | |
| Anchorage | x | | | $50 | $25 | $10 | | $ 2,175.00 |
| Arlington | | x | x | $500 | $150 | $25 | | $ 157,478.00 |
| Atlanta | | x | x | $0-$850 | $100 | $40 | | $ 52,975.00 |
| Baton Rouge | | x | x | $450 | $100 | $50 | $100 | $ 42,862.00 |
| Beaumont | | x | x | $350 | $100 | $25 | | $ 41,625.00 |
| Belleville | | x | x | $250 | $25 | | $475 | $ 4,200.00 |
| Biloxi | x | | | $250 | $50 | $15.00 | $15 | $ 134,016.00 |
| Birmingham | | x | x | $300 | $150 | $25 | $500 | $ 11,356.00 |
| Bismarck | | | x | $250 | $25 | $25 | $25 | |
| Boise | | | | | | | | |
| Boston | | | | | | | | |
| Bridgeport | | x | x | $400 | $200 | | | $ 321,870.00 |
| Brooklyn | | x | x | $1,100 | $600 | $50 | | $ 674,000.00 |
| Brownsville | | | x | $300 | $50 | $25 | | $ 151,297.00 |
| Buffalo | | x | x | $350 | $150 | $50 | | $ 71,990.00 |
| Burlington | | x | x | $450 | $75 | | | $ 25,901.00 |
| Camden | | x | x | $500 | $100 | $100 | | $ 77,900.00 |

# FIRST INSTANCE TRIBUNAL STATISTICS 2001

| Section A Arch/Diocese | Amount of Fees | Amount of Deficit/Subsidy | Canonists Full | Canonists Part | Indulted Full | Indulted Part | Advocates Full | Advocates Part | Staff Full | Staff Part |
|---|---|---|---|---|---|---|---|---|---|---|
| Albany | | | | | | | | | | |
| Alexandria | $ 108,874.00 | $ 100,774.00 | | 2 | | | 2 | 2 | 1 | |
| Allentown | $ 340,919.00 | $ 232,599.00 | 2 | 4 | 1 | 1 | 1 | 3 | 4 | |
| Altoona-Johnstown | $ 52,850.00 | $ 52,850.00 | | 2 | | 7 | | 8 | | 1 |
| Amarillo | | | | | | | | | | |
| Anchorage | $ 84,304.00 | $ 82,129.00 | 1 | 1 | 1 | | | | 1 | |
| Arlington | $ 621,263.00 | $ 463,785.00 | 2 | 5 | | 17 | | 7 | 3 | 2 |
| Atlanta | $ 275,887.12 | $ 222,917.12 | 2 | 2 | | 1 | 9 | 8 | 1 | 1 |
| Baton Rouge | $ 122,256.00 | $ 79,394.00 | 1 | 3 | | 7 | | 5 | 2 | 1 |
| Beaumont | $ 205,597.48 | $ 163,972.48 | | 8 | | 4 | | 1 | 2 | |
| Belleville | $ 110,594.19 | $ 106,394.19 | 3 | | | 5 | 1 | | 2 | |
| Biloxi | $ 31,542.00 | $ 102,474.00 | 2 | 3 | | 3 | | 2 | 2 | |
| Birmingham | $ 103,842.00 | $ 92,486.00 | 1 | 2 | | 6 | | 44 | 1 | 1 |
| Bismarck | | | | 4 | | 7 | 2 | 7 | 1 | |
| Boise | | | | | | | | | | |
| Boston | | | | | | | | | | |
| Bridgeport | $ 277,565.00 | | 4 | 5 | 2 | 5 | | 13 | 3 | 1 |
| Brooklyn | $ 812,244.67 | $ 138,244.67 | 5 | 3 | | | 3 | 2 | 5 | 2 |
| Brownsville | $ 26,070.00 | $ 125,227.00 | 1 | 2 | | 6 | 1 | 4 | 3 | |
| Buffalo | $ 266,814.00 | $ 194,824.00 | 3 | 4 | 1 | 11 | | 5 | 3 | 1 |
| Burlington | $ 105,089.83 | $ 79,188.93 | | 1 | 1 | | | 3 | 1 | 1 |
| Camden | $ 253,160.82 | $ (175,260.82) | 2 | 2 | | | | 1 | 4 | 1 |

| Section B Arch/Diocese | Cases Previous Year | Cases New Year | Cases Accepted | Cases Decided | Mixed | Non-Cath. | Petitioner Renun. | Abated |
|---|---|---|---|---|---|---|---|---|
| Charleston | 95 | 148 | 142 | 95 | 25 | 33 | 1 | 11 |
| Charlotte | | | | | | | | |
| Cheyenne | | | | | | | | |
| Chicago | 376 | 734 | 734 | 860 | 163 | 129 | 8 | 44 |
| Cincinnati | 292 | 579 | 579 | 535 | 149 | 167 | 20 | 10 |
| Cleveland | | | | | | | | |
| Colorado Springs | 124 | 83 | 79 | 71 | 16 | 17 | 4 | |
| Columbus | 270 | 309 | | 268 | 96 | 93 | | 6 |
| Corpus Christi | 396 | 108 | 108 | 140 | 23 | 25 | | 69 |
| Crookston | 22 | 50 | 50 | 30 | 7 | 8 | | 1 |
| Dallas | 234 | 379 | 375 | 223 | 64 | 71 | 3 | 36 |
| Davenport | 248 | 141 | 141 | 170 | 56 | 38 | 17 | 49 |
| Des Moines | 108 | 117 | 16 | 122 | 35 | 33 | 1 | 13 |
| Detroit | 221 | 907 | 895 | 850 | | | 1 | 53 |
| Dodge City | 47 | 38 | 33 | 52 | 18 | 14 | | 7 |
| Dubuque | 197 | 334 | 320 | 276 | 75 | 80 | 11 | 22 |
| Duluth | 46 | 50 | 50 | 35 | 43 | 17 | 4 | |
| El Paso | 66 | 85 | 85 | 67 | 9 | 7 | 4 | 9 |
| Erie | 11 | 222 | 213 | 213 | 51 | 41 | 2 | 4 |
| Evansville | 16 | 116 | 114 | 102 | 33 | 32 | 18 | |
| Fairbanks | 22 | 12 | 7 | 16 | 2 | 7 | | 2 |
| Fall River | 29 | 98 | 98 | 81 | 15 | 2 | 6 | 11 |

## FIRST INSTANCE TRIBUNAL STATISTICS 2001

| Section B Arch/Diocese | Ligamen | Other Decision | Lack of Form | Ratum non-con. | Priv. Of Faith | Pauline Priv. | 2nd Inst. Rec. | 2nd Inst. Dec. |
|---|---|---|---|---|---|---|---|---|
| Charleston | 12 | 1 | 82 | | 1 | 4 | | |
| Charlotte | | | | | | | | |
| Cheyenne | | | | | | | | |
| Chicago | 35 | | 187 | 2 | 25 | 2 | | |
| Cincinnati | 40 | | 299 | | 6 | 17 | 320 | 300 |
| Cleveland | | | | | | | | |
| Colorado Springs | 4 | | 101 | | | 8 | | |
| Columbus | 34 | 2 | 159 | | 5 | 12 | 147 | 121 |
| Corpus Christi | 6 | | 232 | | 1 | 1 | | |
| Crookston | 3 | | 26 | | | | | |
| Dallas | 37 | 2 | 54 | | 8 | 1 | | |
| Davenport | 17 | | 63 | | 1 | 1 | | |
| Des Moines | 9 | 13 | 45 | | 1 | | 110 | 110 |
| Detroit | 8 | | 569 | | 2 | 6 | 928 | 964 |
| Dodge City | 3 | | 41 | | | | | |
| Dubuque | 9 | 2 | 119 | | | 6 | | |
| Duluth | 1 | | 51 | | 1 | | | |
| El Paso | 4 | | 143 | | | | | |
| Erie | 9 | 3 | 105 | | 3 | 1 | | |
| Evansville | 7 | | 87 | | 9 | 2 | | |
| Fairbanks | | | 4 | | | | | |
| Fall River | | | 109 | 1 | 2 | | | |

# FIRST INSTANCE TRIBUNAL STATISTICS 2001

| Section B Arch/Diocese | Totally Subsidized | Partially Subsidized | Fee Schedule | Formal Case | Documentary Case | Lack of Form Case | Other | Total Expenditures |
|---|---|---|---|---|---|---|---|---|
| Charleston | | x | x | | | $50 | | $ 40,000.00 |
| Charlotte | | | | | | | | |
| Cheyenne | | | | | | | | |
| Chicago | | ' | x | 850 | 200 | | | $ 401,000.00 |
| Cincinnati | | x | x | $300 | $175 | $35 | | $ 448,384.00 |
| Cleveland | | | | | | | | |
| Colorado Springs | x | | | | | | | $ 15,717.00 |
| Columbus | x | | | | | | | |
| Corpus Christi | | x | x | $350 | | | | $ 96,813.00 |
| Crookston | | x | x | | $50 | $50 | | $ 58,626.69 |
| Dallas | x | | | | | | | $ 281,650.00 |
| Davenport | | x | | $275 | $50 | $30 | $375/$100 | $ 35,150.00 |
| Des Moines | | x | x | $300 | $60 | $30 | | $ 32,940.00 |
| Detroit | x | | | | | | | |
| Dodge City | | | x | $250 | $50 | $25 | | $ 5,300.00 |
| Dubuque | | x | x | $400 | $125 | $25 | | $ 80,465.00 |
| Duluth | | x | | $200 | | | | $ 4,405.00 |
| El Paso | | x | x | $325 | | $25 | $100 | $ 50,533.00 |
| Erie | | x | x | $400 | $50 | $25 | $50 | $ 50,487.00 |
| Evansville | | x | x | $350 | $50 | $25 | $100 | $ 27,880.00 |
| Fairbanks | x | | x | $250 | $50 | $25 | $325 | $ 1,725.00 |
| Fall River | | x | | $275 | $100 | $25 | | |

## FIRST INSTANCE TRIBUNAL STATISTICS 2001

| Section B Arch/Diocese | Amount of Fees | Amount of Deficit/Subsidy | Canonists Full | Part | Indulted Full | Part | Advocates Full | Part | Staff Full | Part |
|---|---|---|---|---|---|---|---|---|---|---|
| Charleston | $ 195,500.00 | $ 155,571.00 | 1 | 3 | | 5 | | | 2 | |
| Charlotte | | | | | | | | | | |
| Cheyenne | | | | | | | | | | |
| Chicago | $ 910,000.00 | $ 509,000.00 | 7 | 4 | 2 | | | 6 | 7 | |
| Cincinnati | $ 446,461.79 | | 3 | 1 | | 1 | 4 | | 1 | |
| Cleveland | | | | | | | | | | |
| Colorado Springs | $ 113,628.00 | $ 97,911.00 | | 1 | | | | 4 | 1 | |
| Columbus | | | 4 | 8 | 1 | 21 | 6 | 3 | | 1 |
| Corpus Christi | $ 131,274.89 | $ 34,461.89 | | 3 | 2 | 1 | 14 | | 2 | |
| Crookston | $ 58,626.69 | $ 45,656.69 | | 3 | | 1 | 1 | | | 1 |
| Dallas | $ 287,059.00 | $ 5,409.00 | 2 | 5 | | | | 48 | 4 | 1 |
| Davenport | $ 139,388.55 | $ 104,238.55 | 1 | 1 | | 1 | 1 | | 1 | |
| Des Moines | $ 86,589.00 | $ 53,649.00 | | 7 | | 6 | 1 | 10 | 1 | 1 |
| Detroit | | | 7 | 10 | 1 | 1 | 5 | 1 | 9 | |
| Dodge City | $ 42,307.06 | $ 37,007.06 | 1 | 2 | | | | 6 | 1 | |
| Dubuque | $ 244,227.00 | $ 163,762.00 | 2 | 4 | | | | | 2 | |
| Duluth | $ 45,201.00 | | 1 | 1 | | | 1 | | | |
| El Paso | $ 109,058.00 | $ (58,525.00) | | 2 | 1 | 7 | 2 | 5 | 2 | |
| Erie | $ 327,177.00 | $ 276,690.00 | 3 | 4 | | | 2 | 1 | 2 | |
| Evansville | $ 229,473.00 | $ 201,593.00 | 3 | 1 | | 4 | 2 | | 2 | |
| Fairbanks | | | | 2 | | 1 | | 17 | | 1 |
| Fall River | | | 1 | 7 | | 1 | | 12 | 2 | 1 |

# FIRST INSTANCE TRIBUNAL STATISTICS 2001

| Section C Arch/Diocese | Cases Previous Year | Cases New Year | Cases Accepted | Cases Decided | Mixed | Non-Cath. | Petitioner Renun. | Abated |
|---|---|---|---|---|---|---|---|---|
| Fargo | 134 | 63 | 63 | 80 | 24 | 23 | 8 | 27 |
| Fort Wayne-South Bend | | | | | | | | |
| Fort Worth | 303 | 249 | 249 | 192 | 120 | 35 | 7 | 10 |
| Fresno | | 201 | 200 | 183 | 23 | 33 | 3 | 21 |
| Gallup | 26 | 31 | 20 | 21 | 9 | 5 | 1 | 3 |
| Galveston-Houston | 300 | | 472 | 375 | 97 | 79 | 12 | 23 |
| Gary | 255 | 186 | 108 | 127 | 23 | 28 | 6 | 19 |
| Gaylord | 88 | 99 | 96 | 89 | 23 | 21 | 2 | |
| Grand Island | 87 | 59 | 59 | 65 | 27 | 25 | 6 | 5 |
| Grand Rapids | 90 | 256 | 256 | 170 | 20 | | 1 | 3 |
| Great Falls-Billings | 29 | 32 | 32 | 25 | 5 | 8 | 3 | 8 |
| Green Bay | 82 | 248 | 246 | 244 | | | | 6 |
| Greensburg | 88 | 163 | 163 | 181 | 55 | 40 | 1 | |
| Harrisburg | 320 | 265 | 265 | 324 | 108 | 110 | 3 | 9 |
| Hartford | 171 | 264 | 256 | 160 | | | 64 | 24 |
| Honolulu | 106 | 72 | 72 | 73 | 22 | 8 | | 4 |
| Houma-Thibodaux | 50 | 27 | 27 | 30 | 7 | 4 | | |
| Indianapolis | 254 | 181 | 162 | 129 | 41 | 27 | 8 | 54 |
| Jackson | 68 | 105 | 105 | 59 | 17 | 25 | | 5 |
| Jefferson City | 225 | 180 | 163 | 161 | 44 | 52 | 4 | 8 |
| Joliet | 352 | 559 | 332 | 423 | | | | |
| Juneau | 8 | 5 | 5 | 7 | | | | 1 |

# FIRST INSTANCE TRIBUNAL STATISTICS 2001

| Section C Arch/Diocese | *Ligamen* | Other Decision | Lack of Form | *Ratum non-con.* | Priv. Of Faith | Pauline Priv. | 2nd Inst. Rec. | 2nd Inst. Dec. |
|---|---|---|---|---|---|---|---|---|
| Fargo | 5 | | 45 | | 1 | 1 | | |
| Fort Wayne-South Bend | | | | | | | | |
| Fort Worth | 34 | | 251 | | | 4 | | |
| Fresno | 12 | 12 | 278 | | | | 121 | 121 |
| Gallup | 3 | | 46 | | 6 | | | |
| Galveston-Houston | 31 | 2 | 83 | | | 2 | | |
| Gary | 5 | | 91 | | 2 | 9 | | |
| Gaylord | 4 | | 72 | | | 3 | | |
| Grand Island | 5 | | 51 | | | | | |
| Grand Rapids | 7 | 2 | 133 | | | 4 | | |
| Great Falls-Billings | 3 | | 38 | | 2 | | | |
| Green Bay | 6 | | 123 | | | | 460 | 460 |
| Greensburg | 4 | 1 | 84 | | | 1 | | |
| Harrisburg | 15 | 129 | | | | 4 | | |
| Hartford | 2 | | 217 | | 2 | 1 | | |
| Honolulu | 10 | 2 | 100 | | | 8 | | |
| Houma-Thibodaux | 1 | | 39 | | | | | |
| Indianapolis | 19 | 1 | | 1 | 33 | 11 | | |
| Jackson | 14 | | 51 | | | | | |
| Jefferson City | 11 | | 77 | | 3 | 7 | | |
| Joliet | 24 | 2 | 262 | | | 4 | | |
| Juneau | 1 | | 10 | | | | | |

# FIRST INSTANCE TRIBUNAL STATISTICS 2001

| Section C Arch/Diocese | Totally Subsidized | Partially Subsidized | Fee Schedule | Formal Case | Documentary Case | Lack of Form Case | Other | Total Expenditures |
|---|---|---|---|---|---|---|---|---|
| Fargo | | x | | $650 | | $25 | | $ 26,690.00 |
| Fort Wayne-South Bend | | | | | | | | |
| Fort Worth | | | | | | | | $ 68,443.29 |
| Fresno | | | | | | | | |
| Gallup | | | x | $300 | | | $25 | $ 4,675.00 |
| Galveston-Houston | | x | x | $400 | $100 | $35 | | $ 147,836.00 |
| Gary | | x | x | $500 | $75 | $10 | $500 | $ 57,577.00 |
| Gaylord | x | | | | | | | $ 100,569.00 |
| Grand Island | | x | x | $150 | $50 | $25 | | $ 5,205.00 |
| Grand Rapids | x | | | | | | | $ 147,350.00 |
| Great Falls-Billings | | x | | $200 | $50 | $50 | $375 | $ 6,335.50 |
| Green Bay | | x | x | $350 | $50 | $50 | | $ 95,872.00 |
| Greensburg | | x | x | $275 | $15 | $10 | | $ 35,570.00 |
| Harrisburg | | x | | | | | | |
| Hartford | | x | x | $350 | | | $375 | $ 43,658.00 |
| Honolulu | | x | x | $450 | $35 | $35 | | $ 40,880.00 |
| Houma-Thibodaux | | x | x | $400 | $50 | | | $ 14,000.00 |
| Indianapolis | | x | x | | | | | $ 430,000.00 |
| Jackson | x | | | | | | | |
| Jefferson City | x | | | | | | | |
| Joliet | | x | x | $175 | $30 | | | |
| Juneau | | | | | | | | |
| | | | | | | | | $ 547,804.00 |

# FIRST INSTANCE TRIBUNAL STATISTICS 2001

| Section C Arch/Diocese | Amount of Fees | Amount of Deficit/Subsidy | Canonists Full | Canonists Part | Indulted Full | Indulted Part | Advocates Full | Advocates Part | Staff Full | Staff Part |
|---|---|---|---|---|---|---|---|---|---|---|
| Fargo | $ 109,048.00 | $ 82,358.00 | | 2 | | 9 | 1 | | 1 | 2 |
| Fort Wayne-South Bend | | | | | | | | | | |
| Fort Worth | $ 275,912.30 | $ 207,469.01 | | 1 | | 12 | 3 | 3 | 1 | 2 |
| Fresno | | | 3 | 3 | | 3 | | 3 | 1 | 2 |
| Gallup | | | 1 | 2 | | | | 1 | | |
| Galveston-Houston | $ 331,823.00 | $ 183,987.00 | 2 | 6 | | 4 | | 11 | 4 | 1 |
| Gary | $ 201,336.00 | $ 143,759.00 | 1 | 3 | | | 2 | 2 | 2 | |
| Gaylord | $ 88,200.00 | | 3 | | 2 | | 1 | 1 | | |
| Grand Island | $ 144,734.00 | $ 139,529.00 | | 4 | | 1 | 2 | 1 | 1 | |
| Grand Rapids | $ 147,350.00 | | 1 | 2 | | 3 | | 3 | 2 | |
| Great Falls-Billings | $ 78,357.44 | $ (72,091.94) | | 2 | | | 1 | | 1 | |
| Green Bay | $ 280,475.00 | $ 184,602.00 | | 7 | | 5 | | 8 | 2 | 1 |
| Greensburg | $ 134,229.00 | $ 96,669.00 | 1 | 3 | | | | 3 | | 3 |
| Harrisburg | | | 3 | 1 | | 2 | | 4 | 1 | 3 |
| Hartford | $ 335,378.00 | $ 311,720.00 | 3 | 3 | | | | | 3 | |
| Honolulu | $ 206,739.66 | $ 165,859.66 | 2 | 1 | | 3 | | | 2 | |
| Houma-Thibodaux | $ 83,000.00 | $ (69,000.00) | 1 | | | 6 | | | 1 | |
| Indianapolis | $ 430,000.00 | $ 348,000.00 | 2 | 5 | 1 | 7 | 4 | | 2 | 4 |
| Jackson | $ 106,240.00 | | 1 | 5 | | 4 | | 4 | 1 | 1 |
| Jefferson City | $ 137,415.32 | | | 1 | 1 | 7 | | | 1 | |
| Joliet | $ 506,470.00 | $ 41,334.00 | 4 | | | | 2 | | 5 | 2 |
| Juneau | | | | 1 | | | | | | 1 |

# FIRST INSTANCE TRIBUNAL STATISTICS 2001

| Section D Arch/Diocese | Cases Previous Year | Cases New Year | Cases Accepted | Cases Decided | Mixed | Non-Cath. | Petitioner Renun. | Abated |
|---|---|---|---|---|---|---|---|---|
| Kalamazoo | 193 | 217 | 117 | 105 | 37 | 35 | 1 | 8 |
| Kansas City, KS | 185 | 404 | 369 | 358 | 62 | 84 | 8 | 105 |
| Kansas City-St. Joseph | 222 | 221 | 216 | 259 | 58 | 105 | 3 | 17 |
| Knoxville and Nashville | 158 | 209 | 209 | 220 | 69 | 36 | 6 | 26 |
| La Crosse | 174 | 304 | 270 | 236 |  |  | 9 | 9 |
| Las Cruces | 186 | 77 | 77 | 57 | 7 | 10 | 13 | 2 |
| Las Vegas | 78 | 115 | 106 | 72 | 31 | 12 |  | 6 |
| Lafayette | 632 | 217 | 3 | 96 |  |  |  | 16 |
| Lafayette - in -IN | 91 | 231 | 161 | 114 |  |  | 4 | 3 |
| Lansing | 142 | 276 | 275 | 287 | 94 | 54 | 2 | 12 |
| Lexington | 127 | 91 | 72 | 67 | 19 | 29 | 6 | 5 |
| Lincoln | 57 | 63 | 48 | 39 |  |  |  | 4 |
| Little Rock | 121 | 131 | 124 | 71 | 19 | 34 | 1 | 19 |
| Los Angeles | 944 | 698 | 697 | 520 |  |  | 7 | 63 |
| Louisville | 76 | 208 | 208 | 251 | 70 | 62 | 52 |  |
| Lubbock | 46 | 61 | 56 | 25 | 5 | 4 |  | 20 |
| Madison | 114 | 137 | 185 | 96 | 35 | 18 | 5 | 5 |
| Manchester | 423 | 233 | 233 | 288 |  |  | 3 | 2 |
| Marquette | 100 | 83 | 78 | 99 | 33 | 14 | 2 |  |
| Memphis | 219 | 122 | 122 | 134 | 49 | 57 | 2 | 4 |
| Metuchen | 23 | 213 | 212 | 145 | 40 | 8 |  | 3 |
| Military Services | 338 | 340 | 228 | 231 | 57 | 62 | 4 | 14 |

# FIRST INSTANCE TRIBUNAL STATISTICS 2001

| Section D Arch/Diocese | Ligamen | Other Decision | Lack of Form | Ratum non-con. | Priv. Of Faith | Pauline Priv. | 2nd Inst. Rec. | 2nd Inst. Dec. |
|---|---|---|---|---|---|---|---|---|
| Kalamazoo | 9 | 3 | 77 | | | 1 | | |
| Kansas City, KS | 27 | 1 | 152 | | | 1 | | |
| Kansas City-St. Joseph | 35 | | 142 | | | 7 | | |
| Knoxville/Nashville | 24 | | 28 | | 3 | 7 | | |
| La Crosse | 7 | | 90 | | | 2 | | |
| Las Cruces | | | 79 | | | | | |
| Las Vegas | 5 | | 164 | | | 13 | | |
| Lafayette | 3 | | 191 | | | | | |
| Lafayette - in - IN | 19 | | 88 | | 29 | 1 | 126 | 125 |
| Lansing | 21 | 1 | 203 | | | 14 | | |
| Lexington | 8 | | 38 | | 1 | 5 | | |
| Lincoln | 1 | 1 | 48 | | 3 | 1 | | |
| Little Rock | 30 | 1 | 97 | | 8 | 3 | | |
| Los Angeles | 16 | 13 | 926 | | 47 | 20 | | |
| Louisville | 25 | 1 | 2 | | 22 | 10 | 129 | 134 |
| Lubbock | 1 | | 34 | | | 1 | | |
| Madison | 1 | | 69 | | | 1 | | |
| Manchester | 3 | 1 | 171 | | | 1 | | |
| Marquette | 1 | | 77 | | | 1 | | |
| Memphis | 18 | 2 | 57 | | | | 198 | 198 |
| Metuchen | | 1 | 154 | | | 4 | 132 | 132 |
| Military Services | 10 | | 213 | | 1 | 8 | | |

## FIRST INSTANCE TRIBUNAL STATISTICS 2001

| Section D Arch/Diocese | Totally Subsidized | Partially Subsidized | Fee Schedule | Formal Case | Documentary Case | Lack of Form Case | Other | Total Expenditures |
|---|---|---|---|---|---|---|---|---|
| Kalamazoo | | x | x | $200 | $50 | $25 | | $ 22,875.00 |
| Kansas City, KS | | x | x | $150-$550 | $75 | $75 | | $ 88,454.00 |
| Kansas City-St. Joseph | | x | x | $400 | $75 | $75 | $75 | |
| Knoxville/Nashville | x | | | | | | | |
| La Crosse | | x | x | $400 | $25 | | | $ 240,665.00 |
| Las Cruces | | x | x | x | | | | $ 26,740.00 |
| Las Vegas | x | | | | | | | $ 67,045.00 |
| Lafayette | | | x | $350 | | | | |
| Lafayette - in - IN | x | | | | | | | $ 254,825.00 |
| Lansing | | x | x | $200 | $50 | $25 | $85 | |
| Lexington | x | | | | | | | |
| Lincoln | | x | x | $200 | $50 | $25 | | |
| Little Rock | | x | x | $150 | $25 | $25 | $375 | |
| Los Angeles | | x | x | $450 | $90 | $40 | | $ 96,085.00 |
| Louisville | | x | x | $300 | $100 | | $100 | $ 45,779.00 |
| Lubbock | | | x | $350 | $65 | $35 | $35 | |
| Madison | | x | | $350 | $25 | $50 | | $ 173,700.00 |
| Manchester | | | x | $400 | | | | |
| Marquette | | x | x | $200 | | | | $ 70,232.00 |
| Memphis | x | | | | | | | $ 83,570.00 |
| Metuchen | | x | x | $475 | $150 | $50 | | $ 92,297.00 |
| Military Services | | x | x | $450 | $150 | $50 | | $ 79,929.00 |

# FIRST INSTANCE TRIBUNAL STATISTICS 2001

| Section D Arch/Diocese | Amount of Fees | Amount of Deficit/Subsidy | Canonists Full | Canonists Part | Indulted Full | Indulted Part | Advocates Full | Advocates Part | Staff Full | Staff Part |
|---|---|---|---|---|---|---|---|---|---|---|
| Kalamazoo | $ 61,694.00 | $ 38,819.00 | | 5 | | | | 3 | 1 | 1 |
| Kansas City, KS | $ 131,112.00 | $ 42,658.00 | | 2 | | 3 | 3 | 15 | 1 | 2 |
| Kansas City-St. Joseph | | | 2 | 4 | | | | | | 1 |
| Knoxville/Nashville | $ 207,962.40 | $ 207,962.40 | 1 | 3 | | 2 | 3 | | 1 | |
| La Crosse | $ 240,665.00 | | 2 | 1 | | | 1 | 2 | 3 | 1 |
| Las Cruces | $ 75,062.00 | | | 3 | | | 1 | 1 | 1 | |
| Las Vegas | | | | 4 | | | | 2 | 1 | 1 |
| Lafayette | $ 191,088.25 | | 1 | 2 | | 1 | | 1 | 1 | |
| Lafayette - in - IN | | | 1 | 2 | | 1 | 2 | | 1 | |
| Lansing | $ 254,825.00 | $ 184,825.00 | 2 | 3 | 1 | 2 | | 7 | 1 | 1 |
| Lexington | $ 92,426.64 | $ 92,426.64 | 2 | 5 | 1 | 7 | | 9 | 2 | |
| Lincoln | | | 1 | 5 | | | | 19 | | |
| Little Rock | | | | 2 | | 4 | | 15 | 2 | |
| Los Angeles | $ 985,585.00 | $ 889,500.00 | 12 | 5 | | 3 | 8 | 3 | 9 | 1 |
| Louisville | $ 298,055.00 | $ 252,276.00 | 2 | 2 | | 11 | 2 | 67 | 3 | |
| Lubbock | | | 1 | | | | 6 | | 1 | |
| Madison | $ 41,600.00 | $ 132,100.00 | | 3 | | | 2 | | 1 | |
| Manchester | | | 1 | 3 | | | 2 | 15 | 3 | |
| Marquette | $ 10,225.00 | $ 60,007.00 | | 3 | | 1 | | 2 | 1 | 1 |
| Memphis | $ 87,619.00 | $ 4,049.00 | 1 | 2 | | 4 | | | 2 | 1 |
| Metuchen | $ 301,757.00 | $ 209,460.00 | 3 | 3 | | | 3 | | 2 | |
| Military Services | $ 192,032.00 | $ 112,103.00 | 2 | 9 | | | | 2 | 2 | |

## FIRST INSTANCE TRIBUNAL STATISTICS 2001

| Section E Arch/Diocese | Cases Previous Year | Cases New Year | Cases Accepted | Cases Decided | Mixed | Non-Cath. | Petitioner Renun. | Abated |
|---|---|---|---|---|---|---|---|---|
| Milwaukee | 376 | 570 | 557 | 403 | 140 | 102 | 19 | 70 |
| Mobile | 105 | 79 | 93 | 101 | 35 | 38 | 2 | 32 |
| Monterey | 87 | 67 | 63 | 52 | 16 | 7 | 3 | 6 |
| Nashville | | | | | | | | |
| New Orleans | 326 | 231 | 231 | 183 | 28 | 11 | 1 | 3 |
| New Ulm | 54 | 61 | 61 | 66 | 89 | 25 | 1 | 4 |
| New York | 641 | 468 | 468 | 572 | | | | |
| Newark | 296 | 346 | 259 | 259 | | | 7 | 49 |
| Norwich | 43 | 91 | 134 | 112 | 24 | 13 | | |
| Oakland | 249 | 189 | 189 | 155 | 26 | 22 | 4 | 5 |
| Ogdensburg | 144 | 18 | 118 | 161 | 21 | 12 | 18 | 7 |
| Oklahoma City | 292 | | 235 | 204 | 32 | 124 | 5 | 24 |
| Orlando | 1085 | 453 | 453 | 431 | 120 | 120 | 31 | 26 |
| Our Lady of Lebanon | 13 | 28 | 28 | 15 | 6 | 4 | 1 | 1 |
| Owensboro | 127 | 66 | 62 | 61 | 17 | 15 | 4 | |
| Palm Beach | | 208 | 200 | 211 | 70 | 128 | 11 | 13 |
| Parma | | 13 | 13 | 11 | 2 | 4 | | |
| Paterson | 154 | 117 | 117 | 117 | 28 | 6 | 10 | 14 |
| Pensacola-Tallahassee | | | | | | | | |
| Philadelphia, Ukrainians | | 13 | 12 | 11 | 3 | | | |
| Phoenix | 581 | 318 | 317 | 410 | 83 | 39 | | |
| Pittsburgh | 506 | 372 | 372 | 461 | | | | 12 |

## FIRST INSTANCE TRIBUNAL STATISTICS 2001

| Section E Arch/Diocese | *Ligamen* | Other Decision | Lack of Form | *Ratum non-con.* | Priv. Of Faith | Pauline Priv. | 2nd Inst. Rec. | 2nd Inst. Dec. |
|---|---|---|---|---|---|---|---|---|
| Milwaukee | 2 | | 295 | | | 2 | 703 | 674 |
| Mobile | 3 | | 63 | | 1 | | | |
| Monterey | | 2 | 78 | | | 1 | | |
| Nashville | | | | | | | | |
| New Orleans | 13 | 2 | 268 | | 8 | 2 | | |
| New Ulm | 2 | | 26 | | | | | |
| New York | 12 | 2 | 501 | | 10 | 13 | | |
| Newark | 1 | 2 | 406 | | 1 | 2 | | |
| Norwich | 3 | | 93 | | 1 | 8 | | |
| Oakland | 12 | 6 | 224 | | 1 | 1 | | |
| Ogdensburg | 1 | 59 | | | 4 | 1 | | |
| Oklahoma City | 2 | | 159 | | | 2 | | |
| Orlando | 35 | | 401 | | 1 | 3 | | |
| Our Lady of Lebanon | | 2 | 12 | | | | | |
| Owensboro | 11 | | | | 14 | 6 | | |
| Palm Beach | 19 | 22 | 132 | | 4 | 8 | | |
| Parma | | | 1 | | | | | |
| Paterson | | 6 | 146 | | 1 | | | |
| Pensacola-Tallahassee | | | | | | | | |
| Philadelphia, Ukrainians | | 2 | 3 | | | | | |
| Phoenix | 27 | 3 | 256 | | 6 | 8 | 6 | 6 |
| Pittsburgh | 4 | 8 | 298 | | | 2 | 300 | 279 |

## FIRST INSTANCE TRIBUNAL STATISTICS 2001

| Section E Arch/Diocese | Totally Subsidized | Partially Subsidized | Fee Schedule | Formal Case | Documentary Case | Lack of Form Case | Other | Total Expenditures |
|---|---|---|---|---|---|---|---|---|
| Milwaukee | | x | x | $425 | $75 | $ | $425 | $ 177,925.00 |
| Mobile | | x | x | | | | | $ 44,500.00 |
| Monterey | | x | x | $500 | $150 | | | $ 27,400.00 |
| Nashville | | | | | | | | |
| New Orleans | | x | x | $400 | $75 | $15 | $450/$100 | $ 114,409.68 |
| New Ulm | | x | | | | | | $ 4,250.00 |
| New York | | x | x | $1,000 | $300 | $50 | | $ 58,626.00 |
| Newark | | | x | $400 | $50 | $25 | | $ 388,537.00 |
| Norwich | | x | x | $350 | $125 | $50 | | $ 30,115.00 |
| Oakland | | x | | $500 | $150 | $60 | | $ 115,557.00 |
| Ogdensburg | | x | x | $325 | $200 | $50 | $425 | $ 36,000.75 |
| Oklahoma City | x | | | | | | | |
| Orlando | | x | | $250 | $50 | $15 | $100 | $ 293,737.00 |
| Our Lady of Lebanon | | | x | $450 | | $25 | | $ 12,050.00 |
| Owensboro | | x | x | $200 | $25 | | | $ 7,545.00 |
| Palm Beach | | | x | | | | | |
| Parma | | | x | | | | | |
| Paterson | | x | x | $600 | $200 | $100 | | $ 87,340.00 |
| Pensacola-Tallahassee | | | | | | | | |
| Philadelphia, Ukrainians | | x | x | $250 | $50 | $25 | $50 | |
| Phoenix | | x | x | $450 | $100 | $25 | $500 | $ 332,040.00 |
| Pittsburgh | | x | x | $500 | $100 | $35 | | |

# FIRST INSTANCE TRIBUNAL STATISTICS 2001

| Section E Arch/Diocese | Amount of Fees | Amount of Deficit/Subsidy | Canonists Full | Canonists Part | Indulted Full | Indulted Part | Advocates Full | Advocates Part | Staff Full | Staff Part |
|---|---|---|---|---|---|---|---|---|---|---|
| Milwaukee | $ 695,364.00 | $ 517,439.00 | 4 | 1 | 1 | 1 | 4 | 2 | 4 | |
| Mobile | $ 44,500.00 | | 2 | 1 | 1 | 1 | | 1 | 2 | |
| Monterey | $ 110,200.00 | $ 82,800.00 | | 4 | | 4 | 1 | 2 | | 1 |
| Nashville | | | | | | | | | | |
| New Orleans | $ 307,577.27 | $ (193,167.59) | 2 | 4 | | 5 | 1 | 3 | 3 | |
| New Ulm | $ 116,667.00 | $ 112,417.00 | 1 | 3 | | 2 | | 12 | 1 | |
| New York | $ 820,679.00 | $ 562,053.00 | 5 | 5 | | 1 | 4 | 10 | 14 | 5 |
| Newark | $ 277,392.00 | | 1 | 13 | 2 | 6 | | 12 | 3 | |
| Norwich | | | 1 | 4 | | 8 | 2 | 8 | 1 | |
| Oakland | $ 406,617.00 | $ 291,060.00 | 3 | 2 | | 1 | | 5 | 3 | 1 |
| Ogdensburg | $ 89,850.88 | $ 53,850.13 | 1 | 3 | | 1 | | 10 | 2 | 1 |
| Oklahoma City | | | 1 | 3 | | 2 | | 3 | 1 | |
| Orlando | $ 290,599.35 | $ 215,777.00 | 2 | 4 | 1 | | 1 | | 4 | |
| Our Lady of Lebanon | $ 11,000.00 | | | 2 | 1 | | | 2 | | 1 |
| Owensboro | $ 92,914.00 | $ 85,369.00 | 2 | 2 | | 1 | 2 | 20 | 2 | |
| Palm Beach | | | 2 | 5 | | | | 45 | 3 | 1 |
| Parma | | | 3 | | 1 | | | 2 | 1 | |
| Paterson | $ 165,276.27 | $ 77,936.27 | 3 | 3 | | 2 | | 4 | 2 | |
| Pensacola-Tallahassee | | | | | | | | | | |
| Philadelphia, Ukrainians | | | | | | | | 3 | | |
| Phoenix | $ 339,503.00 | $ 7,463.00 | 4 | 1 | 1 | 2 | 3 | 3 | 4 | |
| Pittsburgh | | | 5 | 3 | 4 | 14 | 1 | 6 | 4 | 1 |

| Section F Arch/Diocese | Cases Previous Year | Cases New Year | Cases Accepted | Cases Decided | Mixed | Non-Cath. | Petitioner Renun. | Abated |
|---|---|---|---|---|---|---|---|---|
| Portland in Oregon | 472 | 248 | 229 | 238 | 78 | 86 | 3 | 1 |
| Providence | 447 | 226 | 111 | 128 | 11 | 8 | 1 | 5 |
| Pueblo | 76 | 53 | 41 | 52 | | 8 | 1 | 23 |
| Raleigh | 336 | 162 | 164 | 1487 | 50 | 71 | 6 | 1 |
| Rapid City | 27 | 28 | 27 | 28 | 9 | 1 | 2 | 3 |
| Reno | 43 | 45 | 45 | 39 | 13 | 9 | | 3 |
| Richmond | 196 | 346 | 315 | 315 | 85 | 133 | 3 | 8 |
| Rochester | 161 | 346 | 342 | 318 | 96 | 59 | 3 | 14 |
| Rockford | 297 | 288 | 288 | 332 | 128 | 102 | 6 | 12 |
| Rockville Centre | 462 | 574 | 574 | 422 | | | 24 | 101 |
| Sacramento | 218 | 190 | 190 | 174 | 60 | 49 | 25 | 60 |
| Saginaw | 127 | 301 | 301 | 242 | 65 | 32 | | 3 |
| St. Augustine | 158 | 170 | 170 | 183 | 42 | 77 | 6 | |
| St. Cloud | 72 | 155 | 154 | 120 | 22 | 14 | 6 | 6 |
| St. Josaphat | 14 | 8 | 6 | 8 | | 2 | 1 | 2 |
| St. Louis | 316 | 567 | 554 | 496 | | | 1 | 53 |
| St. Paul and Minneapolis | | | | | | | | |
| St. Petersburg | 92 | 382 | 382 | 351 | 17 | | 15 | 27 |
| Salina | 83 | 95 | 97 | 103 | 30 | 49 | 10 | 5 |
| Salt Lake City | 42 | 76 | 118 | 73 | 17 | 18 | | |
| San Angelo | 36 | 64 | 64 | 68 | | 22 | 2 | |
| San Antonio | 29 | 465 | 342 | 277 | 73 | 50 | 11 | 5 |

# FIRST INSTANCE TRIBUNAL STATISTICS 2001

| Section F Arch/Diocese | Ligamen | Other Decision | Lack of Form | Ratum non-con. | Priv. Of Faith | Pauline Priv. | 2nd Inst. Rec. | 2nd Inst. Dec. |
|---|---|---|---|---|---|---|---|---|
| Portland in Oregon | 21 | 1 | 167 | | | 19 | 424 | 407 |
| Providence | 3 | | 205 | | 2 | 1 | | |
| Pueblo | 1 | | 63 | 1 | 7 | 1 | | |
| Raleigh | 20 | | 169 | | | 6 | | |
| Rapid City | 2 | | 29 | | | | | |
| Reno | 20 | 2 | 80 | | | 9 | | |
| Richmond | 33 | | 248 | | | 8 | | |
| Rochester | 2 | | 161 | | 2 | 1 | | |
| Rockford | 9 | 1 | 227 | | | | | |
| Rockville Centre | 2 | 8 | | | | | | |
| Sacramento | 24 | 1 | 221 | | 16 | 7 | | |
| Saginaw | 14 | 3 | 119 | | | 3 | 239 | 239 |
| St. Augustine | 51 | | 160 | | | | | |
| St. Cloud | 7 | | 65 | | | | 67 | 60 |
| St. Josaphat | | | 6 | | | | | |
| St. Louis | 32 | 1 | 337 | | 7 | 8 | | |
| St. Paul/Minneapolis | | | | | | | | |
| St. Petersburg | 61 | | 355 | | | 7 | | |
| Salina | 2 | | 48 | | | | | |
| Salt Lake City | 11 | | 78 | | 7 | 25 | | |
| San Angelo | 10 | 1 | 116 | | | 1 | | |
| San Antonio | 24 | 2 | 6 | | | 3 | | |

## FIRST INSTANCE TRIBUNAL STATISTICS 2001

| Section F Arch/Diocese | Totally Subsidized | Partially Subsidized | Fee Schedule | Formal Case | Documentary Case | Lack of Form Case | Other | Total Expenditures |
|---|---|---|---|---|---|---|---|---|
| Portland in Oregon | | x | | $275 | $50 | $25 | | $ 60,767.00 |
| Providence | | x | x | $750 | $50 | $50 | | $ 101,049.00 |
| Pueblo | | x | x | $75 | $10 | $10 | $25 | $ 5,883.00 |
| Raleigh | | x | x | x | | x | x | $ 187,003.20 |
| Rapid City | | x | x | $305 | $20 | $20 | | $ 10,905.74 |
| Reno | | x | x | x | | | | $ 15,975.00 |
| Richmond | x | | x | $400 | | | | $ 397,717.90 |
| Rochester | | x | x | $350 | $100 | $50 | $100 | $ 191,942.75 |
| Rockford | | x | | $400 | $150 | $50 | | $ 411,603.03 |
| Rockville Centre | | x | x | $1,000 | | | | |
| Sacramento | | x | x | $450 | $150 | $40 | | $ 87,731.00 |
| Saginaw | x | | | | | | | $ 103,356.08 |
| St. Augustine | | | | | | | | $ 151,042.00 |
| St. Cloud | | x | x | $500 | $100 | $100 | | $ 108,592.00 |
| St. Josaphat | | | x | $250 | $100 | $50 | | $ 1,200.00 |
| St. Louis | | x | x | $500 | $100 | $50 | $500 | $ 218,216.00 |
| St. Paul/Minneapolis | | | | | | | | |
| St. Petersburg | | x | x | $200 | $50 | $25 | | $ 15,740.00 |
| Salina | | x | x | $250 | | $15 | | |
| Salt Lake City | | x | x | $225 | $50 | $25 | $50 | $ 80,373.78 |
| San Angelo | | x | x | $160 | | | | $ 72,406.00 |
| San Antonio | | x | x | $375 | $60 | | $5 | $ 257,376.00 |

## FIRST INSTANCE TRIBUNAL STATISTICS 2001

| Section F Arch/Diocese | Amount of Fees | Amount of Deficit/Subsidy | Canonists Full | Canonists Part | Indulted Full | Indulted Part | Advocates Full | Advocates Part | Staff Full | Staff Part |
|---|---|---|---|---|---|---|---|---|---|---|
| Portland in Oregon | $ 233,216.00 | $ 172,449.00 | 1 | 2 | | 1 | | 1 | 2 | 1 |
| Providence | $ 381,220.00 | $ 280,171.00 | 1 | 6 | | | | 3 | 4 | |
| Pueblo | $ 83,792.91 | $ 77,909.91 | | 2 | | 1 | | 9 | | 1 |
| Raleigh | $ 189,836.23 | $ (2,833.03) | | 2 | 1 | | | 60 | 2 | 1 |
| Rapid City | $ 46,297.79 | $ (35,392.05) | | 1 | | 1 | | 5 | 1 | |
| Reno | $ 72,009.86 | $ 56,034.86 | 1 | 3 | | 2 | | 2 | 1 | 1 |
| Richmond | $ 397,717.90 | | 1 | 5 | | 2 | | 1 | 4 | |
| Rochester | $ 353,720.06 | $ 161,777.31 | 3 | 7 | 1 | 5 | | 11 | 2 | 1 |
| Rockford | $ 411,603.03 | | 4 | 1 | | | 2 | | 3 | |
| Rockville Centre | | | 6 | | | | | 82 | 5 | 1 |
| Sacramento | $ 371,374.00 | $ 281,829.00 | 1 | 4 | | 2 | 4 | 1 | 2 | |
| Saginaw | $ 103,356.08 | | 1 | 5 | | 1 | | | 1 | |
| St. Augustine | $ 73,256.00 | $ 151,042.00 | 1 | 2 | | 1 | | 3 | 2 | |
| St. Cloud | $ 166,337.00 | $ 57,745.00 | 1 | 6 | | 8 | | 3 | 2 | |
| St. Josaphat | $ 1,649.00 | $ (449.00) | | 3 | | | | | | |
| St. Louis | $ 367,186.00 | $ 148,870.00 | 5 | 1 | | | | 1 | 2 | 1 |
| St. Paul/Minneapolis | | | | | | | | | | |
| St. Petersburg | | | 6 | 1 | | | | | 3 | 1 |
| Salina | $ 74,471.94 | $ 58,731.94 | | 3 | | | | 1 | 1 | |
| Salt Lake City | $ 79,513.78 | | 1 | 2 | | 3 | | 1 | 1 | |
| San Angelo | $ 72,406.00 | | | 4 | | 4 | | 54 | 1 | |
| San Antonio | $ 250,082.00 | $ 7,293.00 | 1 | 1 | | 8 | 2 | 1 | 5 | |

# FIRST INSTANCE TRIBUNAL STATISTICS 2001

| Section G Arch/Diocese | Cases Previous Year | Cases New Year | Cases Accepted | Cases Decided | Mixed | Non-Cath. | Petitioner Renun. | Abated |
|---|---|---|---|---|---|---|---|---|
| San Bernardino | 205 | 180 | 154 | 127 | 16 | 31 | 12 | 23 |
| San Diego | 290 | 357 | 357 | 242 | 60 | 62 | 6 | 25 |
| San Francisco | 181 | 189 | 165 | 127 |  | 20 | 3 | 5 |
| San Jose | 10 | 219 | 201 | 145 | 33 | 7 | 3 | 3 |
| Santa Rosa | 58 | 56 | 56 | 46 | 11 |  | 1 | 3 |
| Savannah | 80 | 178 | 161 | 134 | 48 | 48 | 8 | 23 |
| Scranton | 176 | 353 | 353 | 323 | 71 | 46 | 4 | 27 |
| Seattle |  |  |  |  |  |  |  |  |
| Shreveport | 75 | 119 | 119 | 61 | 18 | 24 |  | 5 |
| Sioux City | 109 | 143 | 131 | 117 | 23 | 33 | 5 | 12 |
| Sioux Falls | 76 | 126 | 126 | 92 | 29 | 25 | 5 | 9 |
| Spokane | 50 | 85 | 85 | 82 | 18 | 33 |  | 8 |
| Springfield, IL | 119 | 236 | 235 | 241 | 82 | 69 | 7 | 13 |
| Springfield, MA | 127 | 254 | 254 | 225 | 42 | 32 | 2 | 27 |
| Springfield-Cape Girardeau | 201 | 212 | 208 | 147 | 31 | 77 | 7 | 24 |
| Stamford |  |  |  |  |  |  |  |  |
| Steubenville | 59 | 104 | 90 | 94 | 39 | 32 |  | 2 |
| Stockton |  |  |  |  |  |  |  |  |
| Superior | 62 | 107 | 107 | 110 | 76 | 34 |  |  |
| Syracuse | 98 | 299 | 299 | 282 |  |  | 6 | 32 |
| Trenton | 188 | 185 | 185 | 188 | 73 | 20 | 7 | 23 |
| Tucson | 141 | 120 | 101 | 69 | 1 | 1 | 11 | 30 |

## FIRST INSTANCE TRIBUNAL STATISTICS 2001

| Section G Arch/Diocese | Ligamen | Other Decision | Lack of Form | Ratum non-con. | Priv. Of Faith | Pauline Priv. | 2nd Inst. Rec. | 2nd Inst. Dec. |
|---|---|---|---|---|---|---|---|---|
| San Bernardino | 6 | | 282 | | 1 | 2 | | |
| San Diego | 17 | | 396 | | 16 | 7 | 282 | 265 |
| San Francisco | 9 | 5 | 161 | | 8 | 2 | | |
| San Jose | 5 | 6 | 176 | | | 12 | 233 | 225 |
| Santa Rosa | 11 | | 55 | | | 3 | | |
| Savannah | 14 | 1 | 81 | | | 2 | | |
| Scranton | | | 146 | | | | | |
| Seattle | | | | | | | | |
| Shreveport | 25 | 1 | 70 | | | | | |
| Sioux City | 7 | | 50 | | 2 | | | |
| Sioux Falls | 9 | | 59 | | | 3 | | |
| Spokane | 11 | 1 | 71 | | | 6 | | |
| Springfield, IL | 21 | 1 | 128 | | 18 | 4 | | |
| Springfield, MA | 8 | 169 | 2 | | | | 550 | 548 |
| Springfield-Cape Girardeau | 11 | 1 | 76 | | | | | |
| Stamford | | | | | | | | |
| Steubenville | 9 | | 2 | | | | | |
| Stockton | | | | | | | | |
| Superior | 2 | | 64 | | | | | |
| Syracuse | 1 | | 138 | | | 1 | | |
| Trenton | 2 | 3 | 243 | | | | 130 | 130 |
| Tucson | 2 | | 152 | | | | | |

## FIRST INSTANCE TRIBUNAL STATISTICS 2001

| Section G Arch/Diocese | Totally Subsidized | Partially Subsidized | Fee Schedule | Formal Case | Documentary Case | Lack of Form Case | Other | Total Expenditures |
|---|---|---|---|---|---|---|---|---|
| San Bernardino | | x | x | $350 | $50 | $25 | $50 | $ 28,700.00 |
| San Diego | | | x | $300 | $100 | $25 | | $ 81,545.00 |
| San Francisco | | x | | $400 | $50 | $25 | | |
| San Jose | | x | x | $400 | | | | $ 71,011.81 |
| Santa Rosa | | x | x | $400 | $100 | $25 | | $ 22,585.00 |
| Savannah | | x | x | $300 | $50 | $25 | $50 | $ 42,090.00 |
| Scranton | | x | x | $400 | $100 | $30 | | $ 137,034.50 |
| Seattle | | | | | | | | |
| Shreveport | x | | | | | | | $ 120,710.00 |
| Sioux City | | x | | $250 | $50 | $25 | $425/$75 | $ 61,989.00 |
| Sioux Falls | | x | x | $25 | $25 | $25 | | $ 122,105.00 |
| Spokane | | | | | | | | $ 94,491.00 |
| Springfield, IL | | x | x | $450 | | $10 | | $ 87,131.75 |
| Springfield, MA | | x | x | $300 | $50 | $10 | | $ 60,715.00 |
| Springfield-Cape Girardeau | | | | | | | | $ 23,410.00 |
| Stamford | | | | | | | | |
| Steubenville | | x | x | $250 | $50 | | | $ 70,136.00 |
| Stockton | | | | | | | | |
| Superior | | x | x | $200 | | $50 | | $ 22,075.00 |
| Syracuse | | x | x | $450 | $150 | $50 | | $ 144,404.00 |
| Trenton | | x | x | $400 | $250 | $50 | $600 | $ 140,000.00 |
| Tucson | | x | x | $450 | $100 | $50 | $100/$450 | $ 44,776.00 |

# FIRST INSTANCE TRIBUNAL STATISTICS 2001

| Section G Arch/Diocese | Amount of Fees | Amount of Deficit/Subsidy | Canonists Full | Canonists Part | Indulted Full | Indulted Part | Advocates Full | Advocates Part | Staff Full | Staff Part |
|---|---|---|---|---|---|---|---|---|---|---|
| San Bernardino | $ 274,000.00 | $ 30,000.00 | 2 | 3 | | 4 | 1 | 7 | 3 | |
| San Diego | $ 266,405.00 | $ 184,860.00 | 5 | 3 | | | 3 | | 2 | |
| San Francisco | | | 4 | 5 | | | 2 | | 3 | |
| San Jose | $ 398,870.26 | $ 327,858.45 | 4 | 3 | | 1 | 2 | | 1 | |
| Santa Rosa | $ 84,245.00 | $ 61,660.00 | 1 | 2 | | 4 | 1 | 5 | | |
| Savannah | $ 189,844.00 | $ 147,754.00 | 1 | 2 | | 1 | 1 | 2 | 1 | 1 |
| Scranton | $ 247,868.32 | $ 110,833.82 | 2 | 6 | | 1 | 1 | 4 | 3 | 1 |
| Seattle | | | | | | | | | | 1 |
| Shreveport | $ 119,932.00 | | 1 | 2 | 4 | | 5 | | 2 | |
| Sioux City | $ 61,349.00 | | 4 | 2 | | 5 | | 19 | 1 | |
| Sioux Falls | $ 115,305.00 | | 1 | 5 | 1 | 6 | | 6 | 1 | |
| Spokane | $ 58,542.00 | $ 49,051.00 | 1 | | | 2 | | | 1 | |
| Springfield, IL | $ 168,247.90 | $ 81,116.15 | 1 | 3 | | 1 | | 5 | 2 | |
| Springfield, MA | $ 219,047.94 | $ 158,332.94 | 4 | 6 | | | 4 | 2 | 2 | |
| Springfield-Cape Girardeau | $ 136,698.00 | $ 113,288.00 | 2 | 1 | 1 | 3 | 1 | 2 | 1 | 1 |
| Stamford | | | | | | | | | | |
| Steubenville | $ 19,240.00 | $ 50,896.00 | 1 | | | 6 | | 4 | 1 | |
| Stockton | | | | | | | | | | |
| Superior | $ 115,565.00 | $ 93,490.00 | | 3 | | 1 | 1 | | 1 | |
| Syracuse | $ 156,396.00 | $ 11,992.00 | | 6 | | | 2 | | 1 | |
| Trenton | $ 295,000.00 | $ 155,000.00 | 2 | 4 | 3 | | | | 3 | |
| Tucson | $ 100,090.00 | $ 55,314.00 | 1 | 1 | | 7 | | 16 | 2 | |

# FIRST INSTANCE TRIBUNAL STATISTICS 2001

| Section H<br>Arch/Diocese | Cases<br>Previous Year | Cases<br>New Year | Cases<br>Accepted | Cases<br>Decided | Mixed | Non-Cath. | Petitioner<br>Renun. | Abated |
|---|---|---|---|---|---|---|---|---|
| Tulsa | 58 | 144 | 143 | 130 | 72 | 58 | 2 | 11 |
| Tyler | 126 | 84 | 70 | 100 | 22 | 44 | 3 | 6 |
| Van Nuys | | | | | | | | |
| Victoria | 22 | 74 | 74 | 75 | 15 | 16 | | |
| Wheeling-Charleston | 89 | 148 | 148 | 113 | 38 | 48 | 1 | 9 |
| Wichita | 159 | 285 | 285 | 280 | 93 | 89 | 2 | 4 |
| Wilmington | 308 | 118 | 118 | 109 | 17 | 52 | 6 | 6 |
| Winona | 253 | 81 | 81 | 119 | | | | 65 |
| Worcester | 55 | 163 | 148 | 154 | | | | |
| Yakima | | | | | | | | |
| Youngstown | 180 | 214 | 199 | 164 | 32 | 36 | 5 | 20 |

## FIRST INSTANCE TRIBUNAL STATISTICS 2001

| Section H Arch/Diocese | Ligamen | Other Decision | Lack of Form | Ratum non-con. | Priv. Of Faith | Pauline Priv. | 2nd Inst. Rec. | 2nd Inst. Dec. |
|---|---|---|---|---|---|---|---|---|
| Tulsa | 25 | | 72 | | 1 | 3 | | |
| Tyler | 14 | | | | | 2 | | |
| Van Nuys | | | | | | | | |
| Victoria | 3 | | 74 | | | | | |
| Wheeling-Charleston | 26 | | 80 | | | 6 | | |
| Wichita | 26 | | 131 | | | 3 | 451 | 451 |
| Wilmington | 12 | | 77 | | | 4 | | |
| Winona | 1 | | 44 | | | 2 | 74 | 58 |
| Worcester | 4 | | 120 | | | | | |
| Yakima | | | | | | | | |
| Youngstown | 16 | 5 | 159 | | 5 | 7 | | |

# FIRST INSTANCE TRIBUNAL STATISTICS 2001

| Section H Arch/Diocese | Totally Subsidized | Partially Subsidized | Fee Schedule | Formal Case | Documentary Case | Lack of Form Case | Other | Total Expenditures |
|---|---|---|---|---|---|---|---|---|
| Tulsa | x | | | | | | | $ 17,762.50 |
| Tyler | | x | x | $375 | $60 | | | |
| Van Nuys | | | | | | | | |
| Victoria | | | | | | | | $ 18,228.25 |
| Wheeling-Charleston | | | | | | | | |
| Wichita | | x | | $275 | $100 | $40 | | $ 85,000.00 |
| Wilmington | | x | x | $550 | $125 | $25 | $275/$375 | $ 64,093.00 |
| Winona | x | | | | | | | |
| Worcester | | | | $350 | $125 | $40 | | $ 53,919.00 |
| Yakima | | | | | | | | |
| Youngstown | | x | x | $250 | $100 | $25 | | $ 37,152.00 |

# FIRST INSTANCE TRIBUNAL STATISTICS 2001

| Section H Arch/Diocese | Amount of Fees | Amount of Deficit/Subsidy | Canonists Full | Canonists Part | Indulted Full | Indulted Part | Advocates Full | Advocates Part | Staff Full | Staff Part |
|---|---|---|---|---|---|---|---|---|---|---|
| Tulsa | $ 67,682.48 | $ 67,682.48 | | 4 | | 3 | | 3 | 1 | |
| Tyler | $ 41,647.19 | $ 23,884.69 | | 3 | | 1 | | 2 | 1 | 1 |
| Van Nuys | | | | | | | | | | |
| Victoria | $ 71,567.58 | $ 53,339.33 | | 2 | | 11 | | 4 | | 1 |
| Wheeling-Charleston | | | 2 | 1 | | | 5 | | 1 | |
| Wichita | $ 90,000.00 | $ 5,000.00 | 1 | 5 | | | 1 | | | 1 |
| Wilmington | $ 263,416.44 | $ 199,323.44 | 2 | 2 | 2 | | 38 | | 2 | 2 |
| Winona | | | 1 | 5 | | 3 | | 3 | 3 | |
| Worcester | $ 267,378.00 | $ 213,460.00 | 2 | 2 | | 1 | | 9 | 3 | 1 |
| Yakima | | | | | | | | | | |
| Youngstown | $ 237,099.00 | $ 199,927.00 | 1 | 6 | | 2 | 1 | 3 | 2 | 2 |

# SECOND INSTANCE TRIBUNAL STATISTICS 2001

| Section A<br>Appeal Court | Cases Pending Previous Year | Cases Received Review | Cases Ratified by Decree | Admitted Full Hearing | Decided Full Hearing | Decision Concordant 1st Instance | Decisions Reversing 1st Instance |
|---|---|---|---|---|---|---|---|
| Atlanta | 35 | 636 | 641 | 9 | 6 | 5 | 1 |
| Bridgeport | 5 | 71 | 67 | 5 | 4 | 2 | 2 |
| Camden | 18 | 116 | 111 | 9 | 7 | 1 | 6 |
| Chicago | 11 | 1994 | 1980 | 8 | 21 | 12 | 9 |
| Davenport | | 127 | 127 | | | | |
| Des Moines | | 110 | 110 | | | | |
| Detroit | 1 | 552 | 552 | | 1 | 1 | 1 |
| Detroit | | 239 | 239 | 1 | 1 | | |
| Detroit | 111 | 928 | 964 | 6 | | | 5 |
| Dubuque | 16 | 351 | 367 | 1 | 1 | 1 | |
| Evansville | 14 | 112 | 110 | 8 | 3 | 2 | 1 |
| Gary | | 100 | 100 | | | | |
| Hartford | 11 | 232 | 224 | 5 | 2 | 2 | |
| Indianapolis | 41 | 84 | 83 | 14 | 9 | 7 | 2 |
| Lincoln | 1 | 177 | 165 | | | | |
| Los Angeles | 36 | 203 | 200 | 2 | 16 | 11 | 5 |
| Louisville | 2 | 88 | 85 | 3 | 2 | | |
| Louisville | 28 | 129 | 134 | 5 | 5 | 5 | |
| Metropolitan Appeal | | 331 | 331 | 2 | | | |
| Milwaukee | 25 | 706 | 674 | | | | |
| Mobile | 36 | 134 | 121 | 14 | 14 | | 12 |

# SECOND INSTANCE TRIBUNAL STATISTICS 2001

## Section A

| Appeal Court | Cases 1st Instance Reversed | Petitioners Renunciation | Closed by Abatement | Cases Appealed 3rd Instance | Appealed Roman Rota | Appealed Special 3rd Instance |
|---|---|---|---|---|---|---|
| Atlanta | | 2 | | | | |
| Bridgeport | | | 1 | | | |
| Camden | | | | | | |
| Chicago | | 3 | | | | |
| Davenport | | | | | | |
| Des Moines | | | | | | |
| Detroit | | 1 | | | | |
| Detroit | | | | | | |
| Detroit | | | | | | |
| Dubuque | | | | | | |
| Evansville | | | 1 | 1 | 1 | |
| Gary | | | | | | |
| Hartford | | 3 | | | | |
| Indianapolis | | | 1 | | | |
| Lincoln | | | | | | |
| Los Angeles | | | 2 | | | |
| Louisville | | | | | | |
| Louisville | 2 | | | | | |
| Metropolitan Appeal | | | | | | |
| Milwaukee | | | 1 | | | |
| Mobile | | 1 | | | | |

## SECOND INSTANCE TRIBUNAL STATISTICS 2001

### Section A

| Appeal Court | Court of Third Instance Cases Received | Cases Decided | Totally Subsidized | Partially Subsidized | Fee Schedule | Fees Schedule for Petitioner/Respondent Mandatory 1st Affirmative | 2nd Instance Formal Trial |
|---|---|---|---|---|---|---|---|
| Atlanta | | | | | | | |
| Bridgeport | | | | | | | |
| Camden | | | x | | | | |
| Chicago | | | x | | | | $ 100.00 |
| Davenport | | | | | | | |
| Des Moines | | | | | | | |
| Detroit | | | | | x | $ 25.00 | |
| Detroit | | | | | | | $ 25.00 |
| Detroit | | | x | | | | |
| Dubuque | | | | | x | | $ 200.00 |
| Evansville | | | | | | | |
| Gary | | | | x | | | |
| Hartford | | | x | | | | |
| Indianapolis | | | x | | | | |
| Lincoln | | | | x | | | |
| Los Angeles | | | x | | | | |
| Louisville | | | x | | | | |
| Louisville | | | x | | | | |
| Metropolitan Appeal | | | | | x | $ 25.00 | |
| Milwaukee | | | | | | | |
| Mobile | 1 | | x | | | | |

## SECOND INSTANCE TRIBUNAL STATISTICS 2001

**Section A**

| Appeal Court | Total Income | Total Expenditures | Total Deficit/Subsidy | Degreed Canonists Full Time | Part Time | Indulted Officials Full Time | Part Time |
|---|---|---|---|---|---|---|---|
| Atlanta | | | | 2 | 2 | | 12 |
| Bridgeport | | | | | | | |
| Camden | $ 153,474.00 | $ 11,600.00 | $ 11,600.00 | 1 | | | |
| Chicago | | $ 153,474.00 | | 3 | 28 | | 5 |
| Davenport | | | | | 5 | | 5 |
| Des Moines | | | | | | | |
| Detroit | $ 13,800.00 | $ 2,275.00 | | 1 | 4 | | 15 |
| Detroit | $ 5,950.00 | $ 5,950.00 | | 1 | 5 | | 1 |
| Detroit | | | | 7 | 10 | 1 | 1 |
| Dubuque | | | | | 10 | | 1 |
| Evansville | | | | | | | |
| Gary | $ 2,940.00 | 5597.5 | 2657.5 | | 4 | | 2 |
| Hartford | | | | 3 | 4 | | |
| Indianapolis | | | | 2 | 5 | 1 | |
| Lincoln | | | | 1 | 7 | | 7 |
| Los Angeles | | | | | 5 | | |
| Louisville | | | | | | | |
| Louisville | $ 8,950.00 | | | 2 | 2 | | 11 |
| Metropolitan Appeal | | $ 8,100.00 | | 2 | 5 | 3 | |
| Milwaukee | | | | 2 | 2 | 1 | |
| Mobile | $ 50,000.00 | $ 50,000.00 | | 2 | 2 | | 1 |

# SECOND INSTANCE TRIBUNAL STATISTICS 2001

## Section A

| Appeal Court | Auditors/Advocates | | Secretarial Staff | |
|---|---|---|---|---|
| | Full Time | Part Time | Full Time | Part Time |
| Atlanta | | 5 | | 1 |
| Bridgeport | | | | |
| Camden | | | | 1 |
| Chicago | | 17 | 1 | |
| Davenport | | | | |
| Des Moines | | | | |
| Detroit | | | 2 | |
| Detroit | | | 1 | |
| Detroit | | | 1 | |
| Dubuque | | | | 1 |
| Evansville | | | | |
| Gary | 2 | | 1 | |
| Hartford | | | 3 | |
| Indianapolis | | 2 | | 2 |
| Lincoln | | 3 | 1 | |
| Los Angeles | | | | 1 |
| Louisville | | | | |
| Louisville | | | 3 | |
| Metropolitan Appeal | 3 | 10 | 2 | 3 |
| Milwaukee | | 2 | 1 | |
| Mobile | | | | |

## SECOND INSTANCE TRIBUNAL STATISTICS 2001

| Section B Appeal Court | Cases Pending Previous Year | Cases Received Review | Cases Ratified by Decree | Admitted Full Hearing | Decided Full Hearing | Decision Concordant 1st Instance | Decisions Reversing 1st Instance |
|---|---|---|---|---|---|---|---|
| Nashville | 6 | 140 | 141 | | | | |
| New Orleans | 47 | 540 | 475 | | | | |
| New York | 270 | 2587 | 2622 | 4 | | 4 | |
| Newark | 26 | 332 | 343 | | | | |
| Orange | 31 | 531 | 535 | 38 | 23 | 23 | |
| Owensboro | 16 | 74 | 76 | | | | |
| Paterson | 17 | 123 | 125 | 135 | 135 | 131 | 4 |
| Pittsburgh | 12 | 329 | 313 | 4 | 4 | 3 | 1 |
| Providence | 15 | 159 | 171 | 1 | | | |
| Providence | | 62 | 60 | 2 | | 1 | 1 |
| San Bernardino | 3 | 105 | 107 | 1 | 1 | | |
| San Diego | 6 | 282 | 265 | 2 | 1 | 1 | 1 |
| Sioux City | 5 | 41 | 34 | | | | |
| Steubenville | 18 | 111 | 121 | | | | |
| Texas | 478 | 1922 | 1910 | 17 | 16 | 15 | 1 |
| Youngstown | 32 | 228 | 230 | | | | |

# SECOND INSTANCE TRIBUNAL STATISTICS 2001

| Section B Appeal Court | Cases 1st Instance Reversed | Petitioners Renunciation | Closed by Abatement | Cases Appealed 3rd Instance | Appealed Roman Rota | Appealed Special 3rd Instance |
|---|---|---|---|---|---|---|
| Nashville | | | | | | |
| New Orleans | | | | | | |
| New York | | | 2 | | | |
| Newark | | | | | | |
| Orange | | | 2 | | | |
| Owensboro | | | | | | |
| Paterson | | | | | | |
| Pittsburgh | | | | | | |
| Providence | | | | | | |
| Providence | | | | | | |
| San Bernardino | | | | | | |
| San Diego | | | | | | |
| Sioux City | | 1 | | | | |
| Steubenville | | | | | | |
| Texas | | 1 | | | | |
| Youngstown | | | | | | |

## SECOND INSTANCE TRIBUNAL STATISTICS 2001

| Section B | Court of Third Instance | | | | | Fees Schedule for Petitioner/Respondent | |
| | Cases | Cases | Totally | Partially | Fee | Mandatory | 2nd Instance |
| Appeal Court | Received | Decided | Subsidized | Subsidized | Schedule | 1st Affirmative | Formal Trial |
| --- | --- | --- | --- | --- | --- | --- | --- |
| Nashville | | | x | | | | |
| New Orleans | | | | x | | | |
| New York | | | | x | | | |
| Newark | | | x | | | | |
| Orange | | | x | | | | |
| Owensboro | | | x | | | | |
| Paterson | | | | | | | |
| Pittsburgh | | | | x | | $ 85.00 | $ 250.00 |
| Providence | | | x | | | | |
| Providence | | | | | | | |
| San Bernardino | | | | | | | |
| San Diego | | | x | | | | |
| Sioux City | | | | | | | |
| Steubenville | | | x | | | | |
| Texas | | | | | x | $ 60.00 | |
| Youngstown | | | | | | | $ 60.00 |

## SECOND INSTANCE TRIBUNAL STATISTICS 2001

### Section B

| Appeal Court | Total Income | Total Expenditures | Total Deficit/Subsidy | Degreed Canonists | | Indulted Officials | |
|---|---|---|---|---|---|---|---|
| | | | | Full Time | Part Time | Full Time | Part Time |
| Nashville | | | | | 1 | | 3 |
| New Orleans | $ 20,400.00 | | | | 2 | | 3 |
| New York | $ 120,140.00 | $ 124,740.00 | $ (4,600.00) | | 38 | | 21 |
| Newark | | | | 1 | 13 | 2 | 6 |
| Orange | | | | 5 | | 1 | |
| Owensboro | | | | | 2 | | 2 |
| Paterson | | | | 3 | 5 | | 2 |
| Pittsburgh | | | | 5 | 3 | 4 | 14 |
| Providence | | | | 1 | | | 1 |
| Providence | | | | 2 | 3 | | 4 |
| San Bernardino | | | | 5 | 3 | | |
| San Diego | | | | 4 | 3 | | 5 |
| Sioux City | | | | 1 | 2 | | 3 |
| Steubenville | | | | | | | |
| Texas | $ 112,800.00 | $ 109,415.00 | | 1 | 11 | | 14 |
| Youngstown | | | | | 3 | | |

## SECOND INSTANCE TRIBUNAL STATISTICS 2001

**Section B**

| Appeal Court | Auditors/Advocates | | Secretarial Staff | |
|---|---|---|---|---|
| | Full Time | Part Time | Full Time | Part Time |
| Nashville | | | | |
| New Orleans | 1 | | | 1 |
| New York | | | 2 | 8 |
| Newark | | 12 | 3 | |
| Orange | | | 1 | |
| Owensboro | | | | 1 |
| Paterson | | | 2 | |
| Pittsburgh | 1 | 6 | 4 | |
| Providence | | | 1 | |
| Providence | | | | |
| San Bernardino | 1 | 7 | 3 | |
| San Diego | 3 | | 2 | |
| Sioux City | | | 1 | |
| Steubenville | | 3 | 1 | |
| Texas | | 3 | 2 | |
| Youngstown | | | | 1 |

·

**CANON LAW SOCIETY OF AMERICA**
**SIXTY-FOURTH ANNUAL CONVENTION**
Hilton Cincinnati Netherland Plaza
Cincinnati, Ohio
7-10 October, 2002

THEME:  COLLEAGUES IN SERVICE: CLERGY AND LAITY IN THE CHURCH

*Monday, 7 October, 2002*

CALL TO ORDER AND OPENING PRAYER:

President Kevin E. McKenna called the Sixty Fourth Annual Convention of the Canon Law Society to order at 4:00 P.M. on Monday, 7 October, 2002 at the Hilton Cincinnati Netherland Plaza Hotel.  Evening prayer was then prayed by all participants.

OPENING OF THE GENERAL SESSION:

President McKenna then welcomed all participants to the "Queen City," and acknowledged a number of special guests at the convention: the presidents of the faculties of canon law in North America and the presidents of canon law societies in Canada, Great Britain and Ireland, Australia and New Zealand.

President McKenna then introduced Nevin Klinger, Chair of the Nominations Committee, who submitted the names that have been placed in nomination for the Board of Governors of the CLSA.  For the office of Vice-President/President Elect, the nominees were Mark Bartchak and Ann Rehrauer.  For the office of Secretary, the nominees were Michael Cariglio and Gerald Jorgensen.  For the office of consultor, the nominees were Patrick Cogan, Frank Del Prete, Paul Hartmann, Ann Keevan, Tam N. Nguyen, and Mary Lou Walsh.

President McKenna then introduced Arthur Espelage, the Executive Coordinator of the Canon Law Society of America who introduced Patrick Lagges as press officer for the convention, directing any and all representatives of the media present at the convention to contact him.  He then invited the General Convention Chair, Rita Joyce, to address the assembly.  She offered points of practical assistance for the participants in the convention.

President McKenna then formally presented the theme of the convention, and introduced the keynote speaker, The Most Reverend Daniel Pilarczyk who presented his address on "Theological and Vatican II Foundations of Roles and Complementarity."

After the keynote speaker, President McKenna made a presentation of the *Festschrift* to Rev. Lawrence G. Wrenn.

A reception followed.

*Tuesday, 8 October, 2002*

7:30 AM – 8:00 AM      MASS

                              SPECIAL EVENTS:
8:00 AM – 8:45 AM      New Members' Breakfast
                              Black and Hispanic Concerns Caucus

9:00 AM – 10:30 AM     SEMINARS:

A. Subsidiarity: State of the Question
   *Rev. Msgr. Roch Pagé*

The presentation examined how the principle of subsidiarity is presently understood and then focused on possible abuses in referring to it, especially in light of certain recent documents from the Holy See.

B. Privilege of the Faith Cases
   *Rev. Msgr. Frederick C. Easton*

On April 30, 2001, the Congregation for the Doctrine of the Faith issued new norms with its instruction, *Potestas Ecclesiae.* Early in 2002, the congregation issued "notes Regarding the Documentary and Procedural Aspects of Favor of the Faith Cases." This seminar explained how the new norms and explanatory notes function. The seminar offered practical assistance to practitioners, explaining the differences in application from the 1973 Norms.

C. Sources of Liturgical Law and Liturgical Documents
   *Sr. Ann Rehrauer, O.S.F., J.C.L.*

This presentation was a basic introduction to liturgical documents and sources for both clergy and laity. Participants examined documents and various forms of interpretation of those documents.

D. From Words to Deeds: The Inclusivity of Ministry
   *Sr. Lynn M. Jarrell, O.S.U., J.C.D.*
   *Rev. Daniel J. Ward, O.S.B., J.C.L.*

When and how are all members of the Church called to ministry? What specific official ministries and offices do not have ordination or gender limitations? What is the future of inclusive ministry in the Church?

11:00 AM – 12:30 PM    SEMINARS:

A. The Parish and Its Employees:  Until Something Better Comes Along?
*Mrs. Linda A. Budney, J.C.L.*

With declining numbers of clergy and increasing demands for pastoral care, the Church turns to salaried lay persons to meet many of its needs. The employer/employee relationship establishes rights and obligations for both parties which arise not only from universal, particular, and civil law, but also from the Church's moral teachings on the nature and dignity of labor. This presentation examined the issues in light of church and civil laws and Church statements.

B.  Parishes Entrusted to the Care of Religious
*Rev. Msgr. Alexander J. Palmieri, J.C.L.*

This seminar examined canon 520 regarding the entrustment of a parish to a clerical religious institute or a clerical society of apostolic life along with canons 673-738. The presentation will focus on the process of entrustment, the written agreement, and the appointment of the pastor. Sample agreements were reviewed.

C.  The McGrath Thesis and Issues Related to Sponsorship
*Rev. Daniel C. Conlin, J.C.D.*

The McGrath thesis was an influential legal theory in Catholic educational and health care circles in the late 1960s and early 1970s in regard to ownership of Catholic institutions. This presentation examined the origins and canonical implications of McGrath's understanding of incorporation and ownership.

D. Hostility in the Tribunal Context
*Rev. Peter G. Gori, O.S.A., J.C.D.*

In marriage cases, Respondents come in many and varied ways. To be cooperative, opposed, or ambivalent, to be hostile, afraid or contentious, to be offensive or defensive is but to name some of the ways. This session examined the various positions of a Respondent and described both the canonical and pastoral resources available.

1:00 PM – 1:45 PM        Women's Concerns Caucus


2:30 PM – 4:00 PM        SEMINARS:

A. Presidential Hearing on Clerical Sexual Misconduct
   *Rev. Kevin E. McKenna, J.C.D.*
   *Rev. Lawrence J. O'Keefe, J.C.D.*

Statements in the press of the civil society as well as the Church concerning sexual misconduct by some clergy occasioned the Presidential Press release of March 20, 2002. This time slot offered members an opportunity to place their ideas and observations before the leadership of the Board of Governors.

B. The Relationship of Public and Private Worship
   *Rev. John J. M. Foster, J.C.L.*

The *munus sanctificandi* encompasses the public worship of the Church in her liturgy as well as the private worship of the faithful in pious and sacred exercises. This presentation: (1) examined the rights and duties of the clergy and laity as they collaborate in worship; and (2) facilitated discussion of approaches dioceses have taken in ordering the public and private worship of the faithful.

C. From Words to Deeds: The Inclusivity of Ministry (repeat)
   *Sr. Lynn Jarrell, O.S.U., J.C.D.*
   *Rev. Daniel J. Ward, O.S.B., J.C.L.*

D. Sources of Liturgical Law and Liturgical Documents (repeat)
   *Sr. Ann Rehrauer, O.S.F., J.C.L.*

4:00 PM – 6:00 PM    BUDGET REPORT AND OPEN HEARING ON RESOLUTIONS

6:00 PM – 7:00 PM    ALUMNI RECEPTIONS: The Catholic University of America
                                        Saint Paul University
                                        Rome, Italy Universities
                                        Louvain University

*Wednesday, October 9, 2001*

7:30 AM – 8:30 AM     SPECIAL EVENTS:
Past Presidents' Breakfast
Eastern Canonists Caucus
Lay Canonists Caucus

9:15 AM – 10:45 AM     MAJOR ADDRESS:

Lay Ministry and Complementarity
*John J. Grogan, Esq.*
*Dr. Myriam Mijlens, J.C.D.*

The presentation began with the identification of the specific canonical position of clergy, laity who hold an office in the Church, and laity who volunteer in the Church. The speakers examined some concrete examples of complementarity of professional laity and other members of the People of God.

11:00 AM – 12:15 PM     SIXTY-FOURTH ANNUAL BUSINESS MEETING

1. *Call to Order and Prayer*

The meeting was called to order at 11:07 by President Kevin McKenna, who then called upon Louis Siriani to offer the opening prayer. He then called on James Bonke to discuss arrangements for the liturgy later in the day, and invited Rita Joyce to come forward to discuss the arrangements for the banquet and for the afternoon sessions.

2. *Appointments and Rules*

Lawrence DiNardo was appointed parliamentarian and the rules for participation in the business meeting were reviewed. In particular, President McKenna highlighted Article 5.3, which allows associate members to address the assembly if so moved. It was so moved and so passed. President McKenna then called upon CLSA Secretary Patrick Lagges to read the minutes of the last business meeting, unless there was a proposal to accept the minutes as published in *Reports*. It was so moved and so passed.

3. *Election of New Officers*

Nevin Klinger, Chair of Nominations Committee, came forward to place the names into nomination for the various offices of the Canon Law Society of America.

The nominees were presented as:

OFFICE OF VICE PRESIDENT/PRESIDENT ELECT
    Mark L. Bartchak
    Ann Frances Rehrauer

*The floor was opened for further nominations, and, with no other nominations forthcoming, the nominations were considered closed.*

OFFICE OF SECRETARY
    Michael J. Cariglio
    Gerald T. Jorgensen

*The floor was opened for further nominations, and, with no other nominations forthcoming, the nominations were considered closed*

OFFICE OF CONSULTOR
    Patrick J. Cogan
    Frank G. Del Prete
    Paul B.R. Hartman
    Ann Keevan
    Tam N. Nguyen
    Mary Lou Walsh

*The floor was opened for further nominations, and, with no other nominations forthcoming, the nominations were considered closed*

The Chair then reviewed the rules for voting, and asked the voting members of the Society to mark their ballots. The ballots were then collected and the scrutineers attended to their task.

4. *Reports*

President McKenna pointed to the fact that his President's Report could be found in the *Reports* booklet that all participants received with their convention packet. However, he entertained questions about the Report. William Varvaro referred to pp. 5-6 regarding studies of Islamic legal tradition, recommending that the Resolution continue to be implemented by the BOG. The President indicated he would pass this on to the next BOG.

President McKenna also called attention to the fact that reports of the activities of CLSA committees could also be found in the *Reports* in the booklet, and entertained questions about these reports. There were no comments, questions, or discussion.

## 5. *Treasurer's Report*

Treasurer Alexander Palmieri was absent due to illness. In his place, President McKenna invited Executive Coordinator Arthur Espelage to entertain questions about the Treasurer's Report. Art pointed out that in the report, beginning on p. 19 in the Reports booklet, pp. 22-23 are to be considered together. He reported out that the notes in the Report are the more important part of the Treasurer's Report. It became necessary to withdraw $30,000 from investments because of lower anticipated income. Income was lower because of lower rate of return on investments and fewer sales, as well as the $5000 contribution that Resolution #1 from last year directed us to contribute to the James Provost lecture. Although the bottom line figures seem to indicate we did quite well, that includes the $30,000 taken out of investments. Rosemary Smith spoke on p. 42 (the budget summary for the current year), indicating that the Committee expenses are very small and inadequate to carry on the mandated activities of the Committees. Nancy Reynolds supported Rosemary's remarks. Lynn Jarrell asked whether there was a possibility for more money for an individual committee if they demonstrate the need. Harmon Skillen remarked on the same issue. Lawrence O'Keefe said that this is a concern of the Budget Committee and invited Committees to determine where they need to go with the Committee and develop a cost study of that, so that the BOG can review this.

## 6. *Resolutions*

President McKenna indicated the rules for entertaining resolutions from the floor. There were no resolutions from the floor. He then invited the Resolutions Committee to come forward to present the resolutions.

Resolution Proposal #1
Title: Authentication of "Catholic" Internet Sites
Proposed by: James A. Coriden

*Be it resolved* that the Board of Governors appoint a special committee to study the possibility and advisability of such a system of approval or verification of "Catholic" Internet sites to provide pastoral guidance to the Catholic faithful. The committee will report its findings and recommendations to the Board and the membership no later than the 2004 convention.

417

*Implementation by means of* a committee, possibly a convention hearing, and a written report (duly posted on the Net).

*Anticipated cost:* $3,000
*Cost supplied by* the CLSA treasury

*Discussion:* The Resolutions Committee did not recommend the adoption of this resolution. James Coriden moved that it be adopted and his motion was seconded. James then spoke to his resolution: This was a request to do a feasibility study of the two above-stated requests, and had asked the Proposal to be sent to the Electronic Media Committee for such a study. Carl Flach remarked that this was a large undertaking and that a book has already been produced in this regard. He also pointed out that this would have to be an ongoing project. Joseph Matt opposed the resolution from a technical standpoint since Web Sites can change from one hour to the next, so there would be no possibility of monitoring such a site. He did not see any possibility of the proposal having any ability to be implemented. Michael Nolan mentioned that it might be possible to license a site for a year to three year period through Verisign. Thomas Anslow said that this also involves a canonical opinion as well as technical consideration. Thomas Lesneski said that the point of the Resolution is to ask the Electronic Media Committee to look into the feasibility of this. Paul Hartman from Electronic Media Committee said that there were probably ways of doing this, and that his committee has the ability to look into the feasibility.

A vote was taken, and in the opinion of the Chair, it was not adopted.

Resolution Proposal #2
Title: CLSA Response to Sexual abuse in the Church
Proposed by: James Coriden and Charles Guarino

*Be it resolved* that the Board of Governors appoint a task force to undertake an immediate study of canonical issues involved in this crisis, and to make recommendations for the Society's future actions regarding sexual abuse, including possible amendments and additions to church law as needed and,

*Be it further resolved* that the CLSA publish and circulate to all the Arch/bishops of the United States of America, the canons and commentary pertinent to due process and the right to recourse for accused and accusers, a succinct explanation of how to implement these processes, and to make available, through the Executive Coordinator's office, a list of canon lawyers available to function as advocates for all those whose rights need to be vindicated, and

*Be it further resolved* that the Society endorse and accept the Guide to Implementation commissioned by the Board of Governors and discussed at the Presidential Hearing.

*Implementation By Means Of:* The formation of a task force who would study the issue, produce a written report of its findings, offer a seminar at the 2003 convention, and with the prior approval of the Board of Governors to publish, in brochure or handbook format, a summary of due process and recourse canons.

*Anticipated Cost:* $3,000

*Cost supplied by* the CLSA treasury

*Discussion:* The Resolutions Committee moved that this resolution be adopted. Some discussion followed.

John Skvorak spoke about the priests who are suffering because of their removal and said that the new resolution does not require quick enough action. He asked that the BOG circulate the Guide immediately. Philip Brown spoke in favor of proposal but indicated that in the first "be it resolved" clause, any study should be conducted in conjunction with moral theology, since the right to be made whole is something that transcends the law. He *proposed an amendment* that the first "be it resolved clause" also include "undertake an immediate study including their bases in canonical tradition and moral theology." The motion was seconded. *Discussion on amendment:* None. There was a call to question and the amendment *passed* on a voice vote. Michael Hoeppner *proposed an amendment* after the 2nd "be it resolved" clause, that the CLSA endorse and accept the Guide commissioned by BOG "and publish and circulate this to all archbishops and bishops of the United States. USA, and that the CLSA publish and circulate a list of canons on the right to recourse. The amendment was seconded. *Discussion on amendment:* William Varvaro spoke against amendment because in the previous discussion on the Guide there were many issues brought up which indicate a need for a revision. With no further discussion, there was a call to question. The amendment *did not pass* in a voice vote. However, Arthur Espelage called attention to the fact that the Executive Coordinator's office already has a list of advocates and that he regularly gives accused and accusers a list of three names, usually on a regional basis. *Discussion on the resolution resumed.* Michael Ritty spoke in favor of Resolution, stating that we needed something immediate. He also *proposed an amendment* to the 3rd "be it resolved" clause: "that the Society endorse and accept the Current Guide and any revision that would be commissioned and approved by the BOG. His motion was seconded. *Discussion on the amendment*: Thomas Paprocki spoke in favor of proposed amendment since Guide as it now exists is helpful only to a

419

certain extent since it reads like a defense brief and needs more balance. William Varvaro spoke against amendment since at the Presidential hearing there were things that need to be changed in the Guide even as it is currently written. He asked if the BOG had plans to revise the Guide immediately or after we hear from Rome. Lawrence O'Keefe said that he did not understand that the body wants to approve anything that will be done in the future, and that there needs to be some broadening of the Guide so that we do not appear to be ignorant of the plight of victims. With no further discussion, there was a call to question. The amendment **did not pass** on a voice vote. *Discussion on the resolution resumed.* Michael Sullivan said that if the Norms are approved by Rome in the next couple of weeks, most of the Resolution will become moot. He saw the Guide as a list of concerns that canonists have with regard to the Charter and Norms and *proposed an amendment*: To add a further "be it resolved" clause: That the Guide and a copy of this Resolution be forwarded to the appropriate dicasteries in Rome as some concerns of the Canon Law Society of America with regard to the "Dallas Charter." The motion was seconded. *Discussion on the amendment*: Lawrence O'Keefe clarified that it is the Norms that were forwarded to Rome, not the Charter. The author accepted this correction as a friendly amendment to the amendment. Joseph Fox spoke in favor of amendment, indicating that it is important for the CLSA to speak on this, even though the dicasteries have not asked for such a commentary. Lawrence Jurcak spoke against since it calls into question the relationship between CLSA and USCCB. With no further discussion, there was a call to question. A voice vote was inconclusive, so a vote count was taken. Results: In favor: 178. Against: 76. *The amendment was adopted.*

*The results of the election were then announced:*

*Vice President     Total votes casted  310, 156 absolute majority*
*        174 Mark Batchak*
*        135 Ann Rehrauer*
*          1 abstention*
*Mark Bartchak was declared elected.*

*Secretary Total votes casted 307, with 154 absolute majority*
*        146 Michael Cariglio*
*        156 Gerald Jorgensen*
*          5 abstentions*
*Gerald Jorgensen was declared elected*

*Consultor Total votes casted 306, with 154 absolute majority*
*        186 Patrick Cogan*
*        137 Frank Del Prete*

*195 Paul Hartmann*
*112 Ann Keevan*
*104 Tan Nguyen*
*131 Mary Lou Walsh*
  *2 abstentions*
  *Patrick Cogan and Paul Hartman were declared elected, and a runoff election held between Frank Del Prete and Mary Lou Walsh*

*Further discussion on resolution as amended.* John Skvorak offered a friendly *amendment* that the CLSA do their study within one month. There being no discussion on the amendment, a voice vote was taken. The ***amendment passed***. *Further discussion on resolution as amended.* William Varvaro offered an amendment, asking that "as discussed at Presidential hearing" be stricken from the resolution, and that "as an initial fulfillment of this goal" and that "a revised Guide to Implementation" be included. The motion was seconded, and with no further discussion, a voice vote was taken. The ***amendment passed*** on voice vote. *Further discussion on resolution as amended.* A motion was made that everywhere we use "sexual misconduct" we use "sexual abuse of minors by priests, deacons or other personnel," since this is the wording of the Norms. The motion was seconded. *Discussion on amendment.* James Coriden said that this unnecessarily narrows it. John Porter said that Dallas used priests, deacons, and other personnel to exclude bishops. With no further discussion, there was a call to question. By voice vote, the ***amendment failed***. Paul Golden moved that the Task Force complete its work by the next CLSA Convention. The motion was seconded. With no discussion, there was a call to question. By voice vote, the ***amendment passed***. *Further discussion on the proposal as amended.* Diane Barr expressed her concern that the resolution does not accurately the discussion at the Presidential Hearing. She indicated she had grave concerns about accepting and endorsing the proposed Guide, since it appeared so limited in scope. Therefore, she *proposed an amendment* "Be it further resolved that the CLSA develop, publish, and distribute comprehensive guide with consideration of the "Guide to Implementation," within one month to all archbishops and bishops." The motion was seconded. *Discussion on the amendment.* When Patrick Cogan pointed out we had already approved an amendment that indicated a deadline of one month, Diane amended her amendment to be "ninety days." It was clarified that this meant ninety days from the close of the convention. With no further discussion, there was a call to question. When the voice vote was inconclusive, an actual vote was taken. The *amendment passed,* 123-102.

*Nevin Klinger returned with the following runoff ballot with 297 votes:*
  *123 Frank Del Prete*
  *174 Mary Lou Walsh*

*1 invalid vote*
*Mary Lou Walsh was declared elected.*

*Return to discussion on resolution as amended.* William Varvaro proposed an *amendment* that "Guide" be changed to "Revised Guide." The motion was seconded. *Discussion on the amendment.* Michael Souckar asked that *every time* the term "Guide" is used we actually use "Revised Guide." William Varvaro said that this was already understood in the amendment. With no further discussion, there was a call to question. On a voice vote, the **amendment passed.** *Further discussion on the resolution:* Diane Barr moved that we drop the third "be it resolved" clause since the Guide is so limited. The motion was seconded. *Discussion on the amendment:* Thomas Paprocki spoke in favor of it. With no further discussion, there was a call to question. On a voice vote, the **amendment passed.** *Further discussion on the resolution:* Gerald Jorgensen proposed substituting "sexual misconduct" for "sexual abuse." The motion was seconded. *Discussion on the amendment:* Dennis Burns said that the BOG has a sense of the immediacy and the necessity of the issue and proposed a call to question. James Coriden said that the proposers accepted this as friendly amendment. A voice vote was taken, and the **resolution as amended passed.**

Therefore, the approved resolution reads:

*Be it resolved*
*that the Board of Governors appoint a task force to undertake an immediate study of canonical issues including their bases in canonical tradition and moral theology involved in this crisis, and to make recommendations for the Society's future actions regarding sexual abuse, including possible amendments and additions to church law as needed and, the task force will complete its work by the next convention, and*

*Be it further resolved*
*that the CLSA develop, publish and distribute a comprehensive guide, with consideration of the "Guide to Implementation," within ninety days from the end of this convention publish and circulate to all the Arch/bishops of the United States of America, the canons and commentary pertinent to due process and the right to recourse for bishops, the accusers and the accused, a succinct explanation of how to implement these processes, and to make available, through the Executive Coordinator's office, a list of canon lawyers available to function as advocates for all those whose rights need to be vindicated, and*

*Be it Further resolved*
*this Guide to Implementation and a copy of this resolution be forwarded as some*

*concerns of the CLSA to the appropriate dicasteries in Rome.*

*Implementation By Means Of: The formation of a task force who would study the issue, produce a written report of its findings, offer a seminar at the 2003 convention, and with the prior approval of the Board of Governors to publish, in brochure or handbook format, a summary of due process and recourse canons.*
*Anticipated Cost: $3,000*
*Cost supplied by the CLSA treasury*

So endeth the chronicle.

Resolution Proposal #3
Proposed by: Patricia Dugan, Michael Ritty
Title: Lay Canonists Committee

Be it resolved
that the CLSA establish a Committee on Lay Canon Lawyers to address issues concerning Lay Canon Lawyers and their ministry in the Church and issues concerning the laity and their ministry in the salvific role of our Church.

Implementation By Means Of: Action of the BOG
Anticipated Cost: Usual committee expenses
Cost supplied by the CLSA annual budget

*Discussion:* The Resolutions Committee moved the adoption of this resolution, and the authors spoke briefly to it. Michael Maginot offered friendly ***amendment*** to change "our Church" to "the Church." ***Discussion on the amendment:*** The authors accepted it as a friendly amendment. With no further discussion, there was a call to question. By voice vote, the ***resolution as amended passed.***

Therefore, the approved resolution reads:

Be it resolved
that the CLSA establish a Committee on Lay Canon Lawyers to address issues concerning Lay Canon Lawyers and their ministry in the Church and issues concerning the laity and their ministry in the salvific role of the Church.

Implementation By Means Of: Action of the BOG
Anticipated Cost: Usual committee expenses
Cost supplied by the CLSA annual budget

7. *Old Business*
There was no old business.

8. *New Business*
There was no new business.

Rita Joyce made announcements about the *Festschrift,* regional conventions, changed room numbers for the afternoon sessions, the liturgy and the banquet.

9. *Closing*

There was a motion to adjourn, which was heartily approved by the membership. Final announcements were made as Vice-President Lawrence O'Keefe asked to meet with the newly elected officers and consultors after the meeting. The meeting was declared adjourned at 1:00 p.m. with a prayer by Lynn Jarrell.

*The convention seminars continued.*

2:30 pm – 4:00 pm      SEMINARS:

A. Islamic Legal Tradition:  An Overview
   *Dr. Jane Damen McAuliffe*

The Islamic legal traditions rest upon an understanding and affirmation of divine revelation that expresses itself in the *Qur'ān* and the exemplary life of the prophet Muhammad.  Its elaboration into various "schools" respects both developmental variation and the probative value of scholarly consensus.  While centuries of jurisprudential activity have generated countless legal decisions, they have also produces a vast corpus of theoretical and methodological reflection.

B. Subsidiarity:  State of the Question (repeat)
   *Rev. Msgr. Roch Pagé, J.C.D.*

C. Privilege of the Faith Cases (repeat)
   *Rev. Msgr. Frederick C. Easton, J.C.D.*

D. Hostility in the Tribunal Context (repeat)
   *Rev. Peter Gori, O.S.A., J.C.D.*

5:15 pm – 6:30 pm      CONVENTION MASS

6:45 pm – 7:30 pm      CONVENTION RECEPTION

424

| 7:30 pm – 9:00 pm | CONVENTION BANQUET AND PRESENTATION OF THE "ROLE OF LAW" AWARD |

After dinner, President Kevin E. McKenna presented the Role of Law Award to Sister Rose McDermott, to the great approval of those in attendance. Sister McDermott spoke of the role of law in light of the current crises in the Church.

*Thursday, 10 October, 2001*

| 7:30 am – 8:00 am | MASS |

| 8:30 am – 9:00 am | CONVENTION PRAYER SERVICE: INSTALLATION OF OFFICERS |

| 9:00 am – 10:30 am | MAJOR ADDRESS: |

Clergy and Complementarity
*Rev. Lawrence A. DiNardo, J.C.L.*

The Second Vatican Council and the *Code of Canon Law* offer great insights into the role of the Christian faithful in the service of the Church. Clergy and laity together are colleagues in ministry. The address focused on how the clergy view or should view the laity as being complementary to their work and ultimately in service to the People of God.

At the end of Lawrence DiNardo's address, newly installed President Lawrence O'Keefe thanked all presenters and participants, and entertained a motion for adjournment. It was so moved and so passed, by unanimous voice vote.


Respectfully submitted 5 November, 2002.

Patrick R. Lagges
Secretary

## CITATION FOR HONORING
## REVEREND LAWRENCE G. WRENN

Two years ago, the membership of the Canon Law Society in a resolution that was drafted with the goal of honoring one of our most illustrious and deserving members, voted overwhelmingly to commission a *Festschrift* that would in a small but hopefully significant way show the appreciation of our Society for his many contributions.

Lawrence Wrenn was born in New Haven, Connecticut on June 26, 1928. He attended St. Thomas Seminary in Bloomfield Connecticut and did theology at St. Bernard's Seminary In Rochester, New York. He was ordained a priest for the Archdiocese of Hartford on May 14, 1955. After serving as assistant pastor in two assignments, he received the assignment that was to begin a long-term ministry – he was appointed Notary for the Metropolitan Tribunal of the Archdiocese of Hartford. There followed canonical education at the Lateran University in Rome where he would receive his licentiate and doctoral degrees. He has exercised a variety of canonical ministries in his home diocese including Secretary, and Officialis. He has served as a Consultor for the Pontifical Commission for the Authentic Interpretation of the Code of Canon Law where he is presently serving his third term. We are particularly grateful for the many contributions he has made to our Society, most especially the many books that have guided and helped so many canonists in tribunal ministry. Father Wrenn received the Role of Law Award from our Society in 1976. We feel it incumbent upon us to once again thank him for his work on behalf of our society and proudly and thankfully this evening present him with this *Festschrift* in his honor. Father Lawrence Wrenn.


## RESPONSE OF REVEREND LAWRENCE WRENN
## TO *FESTSCHRIFT* PRESENTATION

Thank you so much, Kevin, and thank you everybody for this wonderful gift. Barbara Kingsolver, in a recent essay, described herself as "breathless with gratitude," and I want you to know that I'm pretty breathless myself tonight. My grateful heart goes out to each of you for your great kindness to me.

I am, of course, particularly grateful to those who have had a special connection to the *Festschrift*. To Jim Coriden, first of all, who submitted and promoted the original resolution. To Randy Calvo who came up with the idea of a *Festschrift*. To Fred Easton, of course, who, as editor, has, with much energy and skill, spent hours and hours and hours bringing the seed to fruition. To Art Espelage who has so enthusiastically served as publisher, to Bishop Dave Fellhauer for his gracious introduction, and to each of the authors. Two of them, Fred Easton and Jim Coriden, I've already mentioned. My gratitude goes as well to John Beal, Dick Cunningham, Luigi DeLuca, Tom Green, John John, Aidan McGrath, Kevin McKenna, Gus Mendonça, Elissa Rinere, and Myriam Wijlens.[*]

I have not yet seen a word of the *Festschrift* but I understand that each chapter is a gem, and I'm looking forward to it with pleasure.

I remember hearing once about a woman who lived over a store. One day she looked out the window and saw a rather shabbily dressed man standing below. As she watched she saw several people approach him, say a few words to him and hand him a little something. So she felt sorry for the man, put a couple of dollars in an envelope, wrote "Godspeed" on it, and threw it down to him.

A couple of days later she looked out the window again. The same man was there and soon he looked up and said "Oh, lady, I've been looking for, I have your $56.00. Godspeed came in first and paid 28 to 1."

Well tonight I kind of feel like that lady. Like I've made some modest little contribution and, by some fluke or very good luck, have been rewarded 28 to 1. Actually much more than that. More like a thousand to one with this great treasure you've given me.

So thank you everybody. And, as the Irish say, "as you slide down the bannister of life, may the splinters never point the wrong way." Thank you and God bless you.

---

[*] The reason I did not, on this occasion, express my gratitude to Adam Cardinal Maida for his warm and thoughtful *Preface* was that, at the time of my remarks, I was unaware of its existence. The editor and publisher wanted it to be a surprise for me, and it was – a delightful one.

# HOMILY

## PRESIDENT KEVIN E. McKENNA

October 9, 2002

KEVIN E. MCKENNA

It is by God's grace no doubt, as we gather for Eucharist this evening, that the Scriptures provided for our reflection contain an excerpt from Paul's letter to the Galatians. This is the famous epistle of Paul that invites us to reflect on Freedom and the Law.

Legal experts of civil law will tell us that one of the problems with laws is that there are too many of them. Legislative dockets are constantly bulging with bills and amendments, and amendments to the amendments straining to be enacted into law. To aggravate the problem, there are thousands upon thousands of old laws kept on the books, which have long since lost any semblance of meaning and purpose. For example, until recently the State of Maryland still had a law on the books making it illegal to hold one's nose longer than a second. North Carolina law made it illegal to plow a cotton field with an elephant. In Portland, Oregon, it has been against the law to roller skate in a public restroom. Inserting pennies in your ear was a violation of Hawaii law. A Kentucky law prohibited appearing on a highway unless you were carrying a club. A resolution could come some day from our society to review our own legislation, our canon law to identify those canons that may be outmoded and ripe for revision.

A society such as our own CLSA, devoted to a system of law must, like our secular counterparts, always guard against the dangers of excessive legalism, the propensity to approach every human problem, every human aberration, every human endeavor, legalistically. And for this, St. Paul becomes a wonderful help.

Paul's letter to the Galatians contains another account of his conversion. Paul did not seek to destroy Christianity because he viewed it as a competing religion. Rather, Paul believed firmly that his persecution of the Church was absolutely necessary in order to uphold the elevated status of the Mosaic Law within Judaism. By punishing those whom he considered Jewish apostates, in light of their presumed indifference towards the Torah, Paul undoubtedly wanted to reinforce the Jewish belief that the Mosaic Law was of vital importance in obtaining righteousness. As we know, although Paul had previously sought to put an end to Christianity, it was God who put an end to Paul's anti-Christian activity.

It is clear that a monumental transformation took place in Paul's life as a result of his incredible experience of Jesus Christ on the road to Damascus. "He who had set me apart before I was born, and had called me through his grace, was pleased to reveal his Son to me, in order that I might preach him among the Gentiles" (Gal 1:15-16). One of the recurring themes of Galatians is that the person of Christ has changed everything. Through grace, Paul had come to view himself, his religious tradition, and his society in an entirely new light. Paul goes so far as to say that whatever he had previously considered important, he now considers as "loss" for the sake of Christ (Phil 3:8). Like the great prophets Isaiah and Jeremiah, Paul considers himself to be have been chosen for divine service even before he was born. No longer an enemy of the Church, he is now an apostle of the risen Lord, who has been foreordained to preach the faith he once tried to destroy.

Perhaps the best way to describe the fundamental shift that took place in Paul's life is to say that he became "Christ-centered in all things." Like all those who have been called to active ministry in the Church, including canonical ministry, the apostle was involved in a variety of activities. Since he was often traveling, composing letters, settling disputes, answering theological problems, suffering all kinds of hardship. Paul's life, somewhat like or own, was varied and hectic. Nevertheless, his life was anything but "scattered." In the midst of his missionary activity and all that this involved, Paul's life remained forever centered on the risen Lord. He viewed all aspect s of his life in the light of his relationship with Christ Jesus, the one he describes in chapter 2, "who loved me and gave himself to me."

It was his Christ-centeredness that also permitted Paul to proclaim with little doubt or hesitation his message, even with opposition to his teaching. Paul goes to Jerusalem at the prompting of the Spirit, not because his proclamation of the Good News was under suspicion. Paul's confrontation with Peter and the other Christian leaders in Antioch acts as a grand finale to his argumentation that he is not inferior to those who were apostles before him. Paul lets it be known that he personally condemned Peter to his face because this highly esteemed apostle was obviously in the wrong. Before the other Christian leaders, Paul scolded him for separating himself at table from the Gentiles, although the fisherman from Galilee had not previously thought it necessary to do so. "If you, though a Jew, live like a Gentile and not like a Jew, how can you compel the Gentiles to live like Jews" (2:14)?

It was Paul's conversion to Christ, that enabled him to see the role of law in his life. It was the law that told humanity what sin was; and it was the law that would drive a person to the grace of God. The law shows us our own helpless, convinces us of our own insufficiency, and our need for God's grace.

Paul shared his life story with the Galatians in order to win them over to his point of view. Perhaps one of the great lessons of the apostle's autobiographical account is that God intervenes in most unexpected of ways. Two thousand years later we still marvel at the spectacular turn of events that took place in the life of this fascinating personality of the first century. The apostle has provided us a wonderful example of how Christians should gear their lives once they have detected the presence of the risen Lord in our midst.

We would never want to revisit the pain of this past year in the life of the Church. But as many have testified that even in the midst of this trauma and tragedy, God's grace has intervened in remarkable ways to lift many from despair to hope and from confusion to commitment.

As canonists and practitioners of the law, we have come to realize its importance perhaps as never before, as a safeguard against arbitrariness, one of the greatest threats to a legal system. And I am sure that in the midst of our own struggles to grapple with the complexity and myriad details of the crisis we have faced, it has been our faith that has anchored us. Paul's Christ-centered existence is of particular importance in this regard. He viewed all of life with the spectacles of his Christian faith. Literally everything that he had considered of value before his encounter with the glorified Christ took on secondary importance after his mystifying religious experience.

Although we may not have had the privilege of receiving a divine revelation of the risen Lord, we have nevertheless have our own story to tell of how God the Father has revealed His Son to us. Within our canonical ministry, we are challenged to imitate Paul in his missionary capacity, proclaiming our belief in the Good News, that each person is made in the image of God, with a personal dignity and respect owed him or her which no one can take away. May God give each one of us the grace of being faithful in word and in deed in our commitment to Jesus Christ each and every day of our life.

431

## CITATION
## ROLE OF LAW AWARD

### Rev. Kevin E. McKenna

The recipient of our 2002 Role of Law award exhibits in a most profound and worthy way the attributes and qualities that the award is intended to honor. Our recipient has been actively involved in the ministry of canon law in a variety of settings and ministries. Our recipient has contributed most especially in the field of education, beginning in high school and parochial schools in three archdioceses (Philadelphia, Newark and Washington, DC and two dioceses, Camden and Harrisburg). Our recipient received a Bachelor's degree in English and History at Chestnut Hill College in 1969 and an M.A, in Religious Studies from Providence College in Rhode Island in 1974. Our recipient received a doctorate in canon law from the Catholic University of America in 1979.

Since receiving that degree our recipient has been involved in a variety of teaching positions in the field of canon law, including classes in Canon Law for the Laity at Boston College and Trinity College in Washington; has also taught in seminary formation programs at Mary Immaculate Seminary (Vincentian Seminary) in Northampton, Pennsylvania, St. Charles Archdiocesan Seminary in Philadelphia, Pennsylvania, and seminarians from Theological College and Washington Theological Consortium at Catholic University.

In addition, our recipient has served as a canonist for several Institutes of Consecrated Life and Societies of Apostolic Life, has served as a consultant for many bishops, chancellors and Vicars in promoting Consecrated Life.

Our recipient presently serves as a Consultor for the Congregation for Institutes of Consecrated Life and Societies of Apostolic Life, an appointment renewed in 2000 for five more years.

Our recipient has published articles on consecrated life in *Review for Religious, The Jurist, Commentarium pro Religiosi, Studia Canonica, Bulletin de Saint-Sulpice,* and *Jeevadhara.* The award winner has contributed articles to the *New Catholic Encyclopedia* as well as to the commentaries on the canons on consecrated life in *The Code of Canon Law: A text and Commentary* (1985) and *New Commentary on the Code of Canon Law* (2000).

Most importantly – our recipient has been a member of the Canon Law Society of America since 1977, serving on the Board of Governors from 1980 – 1982. She has been Assistant Editor of *Roma Replies and CLSA Advisory Opinions* since 1991. She is presently Associate Professor of Canon Law at Catholic University of America, where in addition to the work she does with licentiate students, continues to be available to assist any and all who call her as a consultant on matters of Consecrated Life and other issues. And she says that her greatest claim to fame is that she is a Sister of St. Joseph. I am extremely proud to present this year's winner of the Role of Law Award, Sister Rose McDermott.

## RESPONSE

## ROLE OF LAW AWARD

### Sister Rose McDermott, SSJ

Good evening dear colleagues in Christ. When Kevin called and advised me he had just returned from the meeting of the Board of Governors, I conjured up in my mind a stack of mail on his desk with a complex case in consecrated life sitting squarely on top returning him to canonical normalcy! Rather, he shocked me with the board's decision that I was to receive the Role of Law Award. I recall stammering, "But Kevin, I don't deserve that;" to which he replied, "Well, Rose, obviously others think you do and that is our decision."

After our brief conversation, I stood a little disoriented in my office, slowly realizing that perhaps I did deserve the award; not because of any merit on my part, but like Mary, because of God's bountiful grace manifested through so many persons who have brought me to this moment. During my twenty-five years as a canonist, I am ever conscious that I stand on the shoulders of giants and walk among giants in our profession. I am deeply grateful to all of you and to many absent from this assembly – some who have gone before us – who encouraged, supported, and challenged me as a canonist.

Those who have gone before us – My former general superior, Sister Alice Anita Murphy, had the wisdom to assign sisters to theological and canonical studies at the crest of conciliar renewal. With her presentation, John Cardinal Krol appointed me to the Office of Vicar for Religious in the Archdiocese of Philadelphia and exemplified extraordinary administrative skill that validated all Father Robert Kennedy taught me in Church administration. Father John Ruef, a Redemptorist priest succeeded Msgr. (now Bishop) Galante as Vicar for Religious and coaxed me into the complexities of computer technology. Father James Provost invited me to the Department (now School) of Canon Law at The Catholic University, guiding me from my fledgling years to the tenure process.

Those remaining with us – I am deeply grateful to my present general superior, Sister Patricia Kelly for permitting me to continue teaching canon law and to Bishop Joseph Galante for introducing me to the practice of law for consecrated persons. How can I thank my sister in nature and grace, present with us this evening and representing our congregation. Peggy has been a constant support to this lone canonist in our religious institute. I am deeply grateful to the community of the School of Canon Law: Fathers Robert Kennedy, John Beal, Ronny Jenkins, Robert Kaslyn, S.J. and Sister Elissa Rinere, C.P. whose witness and friendship render the teaching ministry a joy. My students, past and present, have taught me so much, enabling me to be a better teacher. Finally, I could not end this expression of gratitude without singling out one who has been my teacher, my friend, and my colleague. It is no surprise to this assembly that Msgr. Thomas Green deserves my special gratitude. Without his careful mentoring, ceaseless challenging, and unfailing friendship, I would not be standing here this evening.

During twenty-five years as a canonist, I have focused my research and practice in consecrated life, an area little traversed by most of you. I delight in advising my students (and anyone else who listens) that this part of the law is to the code what the Psalter is to the Bible. A Scripture scholar once observed that if all of the books of the Bible were lost with the exception of the Psalter, the Bible could be reconstructed by studying the prayer of God's people in the psalms. This seems somewhat analogous to book II, part III of the code. In our class on consecrated life, we need to be familiar with public juridic persons, church governance, elections, postulations, and ecclesiastical offices in book 1; associations of the faithful, Roman curial offices, diocesan structure and the authority of bishops in book 2; catechetics, missionary activity, and Catholic education in book 3; the faculties of clerical religious for sacred ministry in book 4; temporal goods, their administration and alienation in book 5; sanctions dismissing or mandating the dismissal of a religious in book 6; and the process for recourse against administrative decrees with the removal of a religious pastor in book 7. So you see, we who serve the Church in this specialized area of canon law are not enjoying our little island divorced from the rest of you. However, it is not any topic of my specialty that I wish to address this evening. Rather, as I reflected on the past year and the tragic issue of sexual abuse of clergy that shocked our Christian sensitivities and tested our faith, I feel compelled to call all of us to a renewal of commitment to our canonical vocation and *Code of Professional Responsibility.*.

In his apostolic constitution, *Sacrae disciplinae leges,* Pope John Paul II reminds us that canon law addresses the saving mission entrusted to the Church. Our juridical-legislative tradition is rooted in Sacred Scripture and canon law is an indispensable instrument to ensure harmony in the lives of individuals, society, and the Church's activity. Canon law provides that the mutual relations of the Christian faithful are ordered in accord with justice and charity with the rights of individuals well-defined and guaranteed.

We have committed, indeed professed ourselves through our *Code of Professional Responsibility,* to the rule of law in the Church. I ask that we renew this profession in this most critical period for the Church. Our neglect of the non-negotiable rule of law in response to the admittedly heinous and objectively immoral crime of abusing children or minors can and will place us in a position antithetical to our canonical ministry.

If we, trained in the law, stand in silence while: allegations are treated as crimes, reputations are irretrievably lost before a formal trial, grave complaints are reviewed by unskilled persons, the rights of the accused to advocacy, defense, and recourse are denied; therapeutic evaluations are ordered prior to a penal process,

436

statutes of limitation and the non-retroactivity of law are forgotten, and the mitigating circumstances lessening imputability and tempering penalties are neglected, we have failed in our ministerial vocation.

There is no place in our Church for zero-tolerance. If there were, Christ would not have come, Mary would not be our "tainted nature's solitary boast," Peter would not be Rock, the Apostles would not be the pillars of the Church, and Mary Magdalene would claim no date in the Sanctoral Cycle. Indeed, we would not be convened this week to discuss a law prescribed for a people of God that are *simul justi et peccatrices.*

I acknowledged this evening that I am truly graced through the persons God has placed in my life. Let us recommit ourselves as canonists to the rule of law and our *Code of Professional Responsibility;* those we serve deserve no less. Then, we will surely be the persons we were destined to become through baptism and our canonical calling. The poet, Gerald Manly Hopkins describes our vocation beautifully:

> ...the just man (one)* justices; keeps grace:
> that keeps all his (the) goings graces;
> Act in God's eye what in God's eye he is (you are) –
> Christ – for Christ plays in ten thousand places,
> Lovely in limbs, and lovely in eyes not his
> To the Father through the features of men's (your) faces.

(As kingfishers catch fire, dragonflies draw flame)

* Recipient's use of inclusive language.

# CONTRIBUTORS

Linda A. Budney, J.C.L., works in parish in Potomac, Maryland.

Daniel C. Conlin, J.C.D., is a Judicial Vicar and priest for the Archdiocese of St. Paul and Minneapolis and Pastor of St. Columbia in St. Paul, Minnesota.

Lawrence A. DiNardo, J.C.L., is Vicar for Canonical Services in the Diocese of Pittsburgh, Pennsylvania.

Frederick C. Easton, J.C.L., is Judicial Vicar for the Archdiocese of Indianapolis, Indiana.

Arthur J. Espelage, O.F.M., J.C.D., is Executive Coordinator of the Canon Law Society of America in Washington, DC.

John J.M. Foster, J.C.L., is Judicial Vicar for the Diocese of Stockton, California.

Peter G. Gori, O.S.A., J.C.D., is Court Advocate for Respondents for the Archdiocese of Boston, Massachusetts.

John J. Grogan, Esquire, is Attorney for the Law Offices of Sandels & Langer in Philadelphia, Pennsylvania.

Lynn Jarrell, O.S.U., J.C.D., is a Teacher for the Jesuit School of Theology at Berkeley and Saint Patrick Seminary in Menlo Park, California.

Jane Dammen McAluffe, Ph.D., is Dean of the College at Georgetown University and Professor in the Department of History and the Department of Arabic at Georgetown University in Washington, DC.

Rose McDermott, S.S.J., J.C.D., is professor at the School of Canon Law at The Catholic University of America in Washington, DC.

Kevin E. McKenna, J.C.D., is President of the Canon Law Society of America and pastor of St. Cecilia's in Rochester, New York.

Roch Pagé, J.C.D., is Dean of the Faculty of Canon Law at St. Paul University in Ottawa, Canada

Alexander J. Palmieri, J.C.L., is Treasurer of the Canon Law Society of America and Vicar for Religious in the Archdiocese of Philadelphia in Pennsylvania.

Daniel E. Pilarczyk, S.T.D., Ph.D., is the Archbishop for the Archdiocese of Cincinnati, Ohio.

Ann F. Rehrauer, O.S.F., J.C.L., is President of Sisters of St. Francis of the Holy Cross in Green Bay, Wisconsin.

Daniel J. Ward, O.S.B., J.C.L., is the Executive Director for the Legal Resource Center for Religious in Silver Spring, Maryland.

Myriam Wijlens, J.C.D., is Assistant Professor of Canon Law at Tilburg in The Netherlands and Professor of Canon Law in Münster, Germany.

Lawrence G. Wrenn, J.C.D., is Judge in the Metropolitan Tribunal at the Archdiocese of Hartford, Connecticut.